Communicating

FIFTH EDITION

ANITA TAYLOR

GEORGE MASON UNIVERSITY

ARTHUR MEYER

ST. LOUIS COMMUNITY COLLEGE AT FLORISSANT VALLEY

TERESA ROSEGRANT

GEORGE WASHINGTON UNIVERSITY

B. THOMAS SAMPLES

ST. LOUIS COMMUNITY COLLEGE AT FLORISSANT VALLEY

PRENTICE HALL, Englewood Cliffs, New Jersey 07632

LIBRARY OF CONGRESS
Library of Congress Cataloging-in-Publication Data

Communicating / Anita Taylor ... [et al.]. -- 5th ed.
    p.   cm.
  Includes bibliographies and index.
  ISBN 0-13-154337-7
  1. Communication.
P90.C624 1989
001.51--dc19

88-25260
CIP

Editorial/production supervision: Serena Hoffman
Manufacturing buyer: Ed O'Dougherty
Cover and interior design: Sue Behnke
Cover art: "October" by Alexej Jawlensky
  Courtesy of Leonard Hutton Galleries, New York

 © 1989, 1986, 1983, 1980, 1977 by Prentice-Hall, Inc.
A Division of Simon & Schuster
Englewood Cliffs, New Jersey 07632

Printed in the United States of America
10 9 8 7 6 5 4 3 2 1

ISBN 0-13-154337-7

Prentice-Hall International (UK) Limited, *London*
Prentice-Hall of Australia Pty. Limited, *Sydney*
Prentice-Hall Canada Inc., *Toronto*
Prentice-Hall Hispanoamericana, S.A., *Mexico*
Prentice-Hall of India Private Limited, *New Delhi*
Prentice-Hall of Japan, Inc., *Tokyo*
Simon & Schuster Asia Pte. Ltd., *Singapore*
Editora Prentice-Hall do Brasil, Ltda., *Rio de Janeiro*

Contents

10 Communicating in the Family   264

11 Preparing Speeches: Organizing Thoughts   291

12 Preparing Speeches: Developing Ideas   316

13 Public Speaking: Using Voice and Body   334

14 Persuasion: Theory and Practice   355

Exercises

Preface

To both students and teachers who will use this book: Be assured that in this new edition we have done our best to preserve the best quality of the earlier book—its practicality. Our aim in rewriting has been to take out what wasn't useful, to expand what was too brief to be helpful, and to update. The basic elements of this text remain. It has one basic purpose—to help people communicate more effectively *in their daily lives*. To accomplish that purpose, we include explanations of certain basic communication principles and suggestions for applying those principles to the situations people commonly experience.

In more than 75 years of teaching, the combined experience of those of us who wrote this book have taught us important lessons. To use Carl Rogers's term, perhaps the most significant learning we have gained from our students is that knowledge without application seems useless, while application without knowledge too often results in shallow, ineffective, or even destructive communication. Thus we have tried to provide knowledge in introducing the principles of communication and to show how the principles can be applied in everyday living. We have tried always to keep in mind the question: *How can this information be used?*

In response to suggestions from those who used earlier editions, we have retained our expanded treatment of public speaking and the simplified treatment of intrapersonal communication. This most recent edition involves four significant changes: (1) we have added a concrete formula for incorporating active listening and appropriate feedback into a process for coping with conflict; (2) we have incorporated throughout what has recently been learned about the effects of gender and culture in communication; (3) we have updated the material in our chapter on communicating at work for better fit with the modern work environment; and (4) we have added the latest findings on the effects of mass communication in modern life to the final chapter.

Because the book is still intended primarily to be useful in students' daily lives, we've retained our unique treatment of work and family communication, while amplifying aspects of group communication, listening, conflict management, and persuasion.

Throughout this book are many learning aids, based on beliefs we have about teaching. Two of these are especially important. First, we believe people learn best from experience. Only with experience do people really internalize their understandings. Thus, for many important concepts, we've included exercises or suggested experiences. Some of these exercises are for students to do by themselves; others are to be shared with classmates; some guided by the instructor; some completely independent. All are intended to help students experience the ideas discussed, and thus to understand how to use the concepts more effectively.

More experiences are suggested than any one person or class could use. The choices will enable students and instructors to concentrate on their own interests and needs. Part of these exercises are included in the *Instructor's Manual*. Also available are forms and directions that allow the option of self-paced learning and individualized study of speech communication. Students and teachers may combine these materials with the text, allowing students to design their own course and set their own goals and timetables. If these activities are combined with a contract approach, instructors and students have great flexibility within a well-structured sequence of studies. Some students who followed these guides have finished the course in three weeks; others took two full semesters to get done. Such an approach allows great independence to those who choose to use it. Anyone interested in self-pacing should contact Anita Taylor.

A second belief upon which the book is based is that people learn best when they know what they're trying to learn. Thus, for each chapter we've identified a goal and listed the objectives students should be able to accomplish by reading the material and doing the exercises. These objectives are also guides to testing. If students think they cannot do the stated objectives after reading the text, they can use the objectives to decide what else they need to study. Similarly, each exercise has an objective so students can know why they are doing each exercise.

We wish we could share with you the names of those to whom we owe credit for this book. Persons quoted directly are cited at the appropriate places, but otherwise all the names cannot be listed. Too many people helped us. We owe much to our sensitive, perceptive editors, and to a good production and design team. We are also indebted to critical and thoughtful reviewers for this and previous editions (including Rudolf Busby, San Francisco, California; Marjorie Esco, Broward Community College; Beth McRae, Valdosta State College; Lois Self, Northern Illinois University; Betty Jo Welch, University of North Carolina; and Joan Aitken, University of Missouri at Kansas City). To friends and colleagues, to several proofreaders, to tireless and devoted secretaries, to teachers we've had and authors we've read, our sincere thanks. We owe so very much to our best friends—our families—who shared with us the ordeals of writing, rewriting, editing, re-editing, and authors' disagreements with each other. But perhaps we owe the most of all to people really too numerous to mention, those thousands of students who taught us how to teach—for never have we left a classroom without learning from those we met there. To all of our students we are in debt. To all of them, this book is dedicated.

1 Relating to Your World: Communication

Man has developed only two methods for settling differences—to shoot it out, or talk it out. Both require skill. Both require discipline. Both require training. If a society wants to become free, or to remain free, it must develop leaders who have skill, discipline, and training in how to talk it out.

WILLIAM NORWOOD BRIGANCE

If all my talents and powers were to be taken from me by some inscrutable Providence, and I had my choice of keeping but one, I would unhesitatingly ask to be allowed to keep the Power of Speaking, for through it, I would quickly recover all the rest.

DANIEL WEBSTER

All epoch-making revolutionary events have been produced not by the written but by the spoken word.

ADOLPH HITLER

GOAL

To understand why it is useful to see communication as process

OBJECTIVES

The material in this chapter should help you to:
1. Explain the significance of referring to communication as a process rather than an act.
2. Distinguish among intended messages, perceived messages, and message carriers.
3. Distinguish between responses and feedback.
4. Explain why participants in communication are both source and receiver at the same time.
5. Create a model that illustrates the impact of the various elements and processes of communication. The model should include:

Source	Messages	Sending
Receiver	Responses	Receiving
Sensory receptors	Feedback	Perceiving
Message carriers	Situation	Interpreting

6. Be able to explain your personal communication model so that listeners will understand how it represents the process view of communication.
7. Cite personal experiences that illustrate each of the factors that cause perception to vary.
8. Define:

| Intrapersonal communication | Public communication |
| Interpersonal communication | Mass communication |

Communication is the primary activity that determines the quality of our lives. Most of the time, most of us communicate well enough. Usually when we order a hamburger, that's what we get. But too often we don't communicate as well as we want to or could. Consider the following situations:

Scene: Two office workers on coffee break.

Chris: Boy, this city is certainly going to the dogs!
Pat: Then why don't you move somewhere else?
Chris: Why should I?
Pat: Didn't you just say you were fed up with this place?
Chris: No, I said that it was going to the dogs!
Pat: As far as I'm concerned, it means that you don't like it here. It sure doesn't mean that you're happy here, does it?
Chris: Listen, you, why don't you mind your own damn business!
Pat: Now hold on there, I didn't start this conversation—you did. If you didn't want my opinion, you should have just kept your mouth shut.

Scene: A parent and a teenager at dinner.

Teen: Hey, may I use the car tonight?
Parent: Well, I don't know; it's a school night.
Teen: Aw, come on. It's early. The whole gang is going to the drive-in tonight.
Parent: I don't know. Don't you have homework?
Teen: Naw, got it all done.
Parent: Are you sure? Your grades haven't been too good lately. I don't think you're concentrating enough on school these days. That crowd you've been hanging around with isn't a very good influence on you.
Teen: You're always bitching, running me down. Why don't you get off my back? My grades are *my* business. Anyway, I can't remember the last time I saw *you* read a book!

What happened in these situations? What do they have in common? In each, the listeners received messages different from those the senders intended. As a result, both were angry and upset. All of us could give examples like this from our own experiences. Yet few of us want such things to happen. And that's why we wrote this book—because so many people want to communicate better than they do now. The ideas presented here can help you avoid the kinds of outcomes—anger and frustration—that the examples show. By applying these principles in your daily life, you can learn to communicate more effectively.

Please understand, though, this isn't a "cookbook." It has no simple recipes, no formulas that will suddenly make you a superstar communicator. No one avoids occasional misunderstandings. But principles exist that if you learn to apply, you can improve your skills at communicating.

These principles are like tools. With practice using them, you become more skillful. So read the information in this book; discuss the suggested questions with others; do the exercises.[1] You can learn how communication works, and how you can make it work better for you.

---

[1] You may feel at first that you're getting nothing but a list of new terms. But remember, learning most new information starts with the vocabulary. Once you have names for ideas, you can talk about them, see how they apply to you. To help, we've developed a list of key words at the end of the book. The words and phrases included appear in bold type the first time they are used in text or when they are defined.

COMMUNICATION: A PROCESS VIEW

In communicating, we stay in touch with the world. Through communication we know the world outside our own skins. As we receive stimuli and interpret them, we communicate with the source of the stimuli and with ourselves. As Ray Birdwhistle points out, "Individuals do not communicate; they engage in or become part of communication."[2] Indeed, each of us receives and interprets stimuli all the time. Hence our talk with other people is part of a larger, ongoing stream of communication activity described as a process. Viewing communication in this way influences all the ideas in this book. So, let's examine what it means to say that communication is a process.

Each communicator is part of an endless stream of messages.

[2] *Schizophrenia: An Integrated Approach*, Alfred Auerbach, ed. (New York: The Ronald Press Co., 1959), p. 104.

Process Defined

The word **process** refers to *an ongoing series of interactions among elements that results in something different from the original elements.* For example, film is processed into pictures, wheat into flour; applications are processed; new cars are made in an assembly-line process. In each case, elements interact, creating a new product (result) from the raw materials. In each case, the raw materials (elements) are changed, but nothing is eliminated. As pictures are developed, film is not destroyed. As flour is made, wheat is changed, not eliminated. Information on applications may be transferred to a computer tape and the application form burned, but the information isn't lost, and the paper becomes carbon and gases in the burning. In manufacturing cars, ore is changed from rock to iron to steel to car frames and bodies. Many by-products are created in the process, but nothing is eliminated. The significance of applying this description to communicators is immense.

Effects of Process

Within any individual communication event, many different elements, human and otherwise, exist and interact. Each element affects the others as part of a series of interactions that began before the specific event and continues long after the event is over. Some of the interactions within communication are repeated regularly and might themselves be thought of as communication processes—or subprocesses. The precise label is less important, however, than remembering that all the parts of communication, whether thought of as elements or subprocesses, are *dynamic* and *interactive.* Each facet of the communication process affects every other facet. No part stands by itself, nor does the end of a communicative interaction between two people mean the communication is over.

Moreover, the events (interactions) in a process do not just happen and then end. Each element or event interacts with and affects other events. In the examples given, a product is created, but the process doesn't end. Products are sold, used, worn out, discarded, recycled, etc. Each interaction in turn creates something new that will also affect other elements—and so on, in a never-ending cycle. Processes are therefore dynamic; they create something new by changing raw materials. And because everything is interrelated, everything affects everything else. The significance of this for communicators is immense.

Recognizing communication as process can significantly affect our approach to talking with others. To think of what we say and do as part of an ongoing, endless *stream* of thought and talk puts it in quite a different light from thinking of it as an event that occurs and is done with. Such a viewpoint helps us remember that our actions (and talk is a form of action) do not occur in isolation. Thinking of communication as process helps us remember that no single word, or series of words, constitutes "a communication." Whatever we are saying right now is affected by what happened before; our current talk will affect what happens in the future. Keeping that in mind will influence not only what we say, but how we say it.

When we talk, all parts of the communication process happen almost simultaneously—and they interact as they occur. But to study communication, it helps to look at each part in isolation. It is as if we were watching a football game on television, and an instant replay stopped the action at a crucial point in a play. The single-frame picture shows only one part of the action; it does not show the entire play. But using the stop-action camera, which can isolate several parts of the play, helps us understand what happened.

That is what we will do here: We will isolate parts of the communication process. We do this to make the entire process more clear. By understanding the parts, we can better understand how they work together.

COMMUNICATION ELEMENTS AND PROCESSES

An examination of the parts of the communication process shows that it involves many interrelating subprocesses and elements. At least eight distinct elements are involved: source(s), receiver(s), sensory receptors, message carriers, messages, responses, feedback, and situation or context. Let's look more closely at each of them.

Source and Receiver

To illustrate the elements, let's look at an example of communication: your reading of this book. The book is the **source.** You are the **receiver.** Your eyes and hands receive sensations that you interpret as meaningful. You see the book, the words and pictures in it, and feel it in your hands. The nerves and muscles of your eyes and hands receive signals and transmit sensations of sight and touch to your brain. That is why you are described as a receiver (see Figure 1–1 on p. 6).

If the communication situation involved a conversation between two people, each person would be a source as well as a receiver. Each would see and hear the other. Each has **sensory receptors,** nerve endings that receive sensations and transmit them to the brain. Thus, *when talking about interpersonal communication, think of each person as both source and receiver.*

Throughout this book, we often describe the people in interpersonal communication as sources and receivers instead of as speakers and listeners. We do that to emphasize that all sensations, not just words, can lead to communication. In the most common types of interpersonal communication, we see people as well as hear them. We learn much from what they look like, how they dress and move, and so on. In addition, people may shake hands or hug one another when they meet, thus communicating through touch. They may wear perfume or cologne, after-shave and deodorants, all sources of information communicated through smell. The nonverbal sources of information in communication are so important that we devote all of Chapter 4 to discussing how people communicate nonverbally.

As you read further in this book, keep in mind that when we use the term *communicator* we usually want you to think of this source/receiver. Some of the suggestions in the book are intended to apply specifically to the communicator as

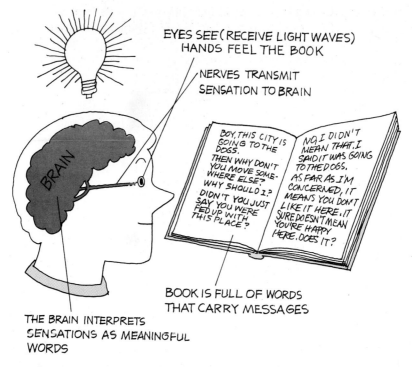

FIGURE 1–1. The communication process.

source or sender of messages; some are more important when the communicator is a receiver of messages. But since each communicator is both source and receiver most of the time, the principles apply in both roles. In short, effective communicators are not just effective message sources; they also receive messages accurately and efficiently.

Messages and Message Carriers

Important elements in communication are the messages. Let's look at two important types: the intended and the perceived. Then we'll look at the medium—message carriers.

Intended Messages In interpersonal communication, **intended messages** are *the ideas or feelings a source wants a receiver to understand or know.* Intended messages exist only "in" the source. To be spoken (or written), intended messages must be **coded.** This term describes how language, and perhaps nonverbal messages also, function in communication. To code intended messages, we choose words and sentence structures to express what we want to say. Note the distinction. What a source *wants* to communicate is the intended message; the words are not. *Words merely represent, or stand for, an intended message.*

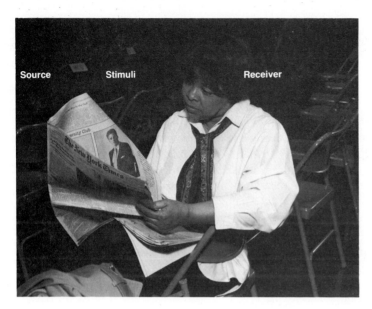

Source　　　Stimuli　　　　　　　　Receiver

The communication process.

Perceived Messages　**Perceived messages** are what receivers **decode** from sensations received. Thus, hearing, seeing, touching, smelling, or tasting alone do not create perceived messages. Decoding is needed as well. A person who hears words receives sensations, but without interpreting (decoding) that person doesn't perceive a message. Decoding is interpreting what is received, giving some meaning to the sensations. If you hear a sound in the next room, your brain must interpret it before you know whether you heard a meaningful sentence, a musical instrument, dishes breaking, or something you don't recognize.

Hearing the word *Pojo* would not lead to a meaningful perceived message unless you knew the code of the Russian language. Instead, your perceived message may be that you are hearing a foreign language, or that the speaker didn't pronounce a word correctly, or that something is wrong with the speaker. Several other interpretations are also possible. The point is that the perceived message is whatever you *interpret*, not the actual words someone has said.

We must make one final point about differences between intended and perceived messages. Often a receiver will perceive messages that a source had no intention of sending. Much information that we get (and respond to) is not intended by any source. Receivers draw conclusions from things that aren't said, from the way a person looks or sounds, or from something that is *not* done. These are perceived messages, even though a source may intend none of them. Unintentional message sending is most true of nonverbal communication but isn't limited to that. Many receivers interpret words differently from the way a source intended. Perceived messages are *whatever meaning a receiver attaches to sensations received*, whether sent intentionally or unintentionally.

If we all remembered and acted on these important distinctions between intended and perceived messages, we could communicate more effectively. We would remember that our words are not our meanings, that words will not always be received by others as sent nor will they always be perceived as intended.

Message Carriers *The things a person actually says and does while communicating are referred to as* **message carriers.**[3] Many things besides written or spoken words also carry messages: gestures, movements from one place to another, smiles, frowns, objects, use of time and space, and smells or other types of stimuli that a person might "give off" while talking or listening to another person.[4]

This part of the communication process is short-lived. Most message carriers exist at one moment and cannot be recaptured. A videotape can catch a lot of message carriers, but not all of them. Besides, how many of us have tapes to record everything we say and do when we're communicating with someone else? Keeping in mind that most message carriers don't last, we can improve our communication. We can be more alert to all possible message carriers and more careful to use feedback to check the accuracy of the messages we perceive.

Response and Feedback

During interpersonal communication, receivers usually respond to the words they hear and decode. The conversations at the beginning of this chapter illustrated the give-and-take nature of most interpersonal communication. After the first comment, each person's remark could be described as a **response.** *Any reaction to a perceived message is a response*, whether the reaction is internal or external, whether it is words or actions.

Feedback, in contrast, refers to a *receiver's response as interpreted by the source.* Although everything that one person does in reaction to another's words is a response (and therefore part of the communication process), not every response is feedback.

Let's use the example of your reading this book to illustrate the differences between response and feedback. As you read this book, you respond. The response may be just recognizing the words and understanding what we say. On the other hand, you may find a particular idea difficult to understand or to believe. You may think, or even say, "Wait a minute, that doesn't make sense." You may think, "What does that word mean?" and pull out your dictionary or turn to the glossary at the end of the book. If so, your responses to the words include specific behaviors— actions people can see or hear. But, unless you take out an envelope, stamp it, and mail your comments to us, your responses will not be feedback to us.

Another example may clarify the differences between responses and feedback. Suppose three people, Vincent, Jerry, and Maria, are talking. Maria speaks, and

---

[3] At this point it might be useful to refer to our earlier example. In describing the communication involved in your reading this text, some people would call us (the authors) the sources and the book a message carrier. Either description is accurate.

[4] To be accurate, we should point out that human beings actually have many more senses, but for our purposes here, the easily recognized senses are all we need to keep in mind.

Jerry interrupts to say, "Did you just say you *would* or would *not* go?" Jerry's question is feedback to Maria. And when Maria answers, "I said I would," it is feedback to Jerry. If, during the exchange between Maria and Jerry, Vincent sat back with a disgusted look on his face, that would be a response. But if neither Maria nor Jerry saw Vincent's action, it would be feedback to neither. If Maria saw it, she might conclude that Vincent was disgusted with her for agreeing to go. If Jerry noticed, he might conclude Vincent was disgusted with his question. Each interpretation would have been feedback, even though Vincent said nothing.

An absence of overt (observable) response can also be feedback. For example, suppose some friends are having coffee in the student union. Ben asks his friend Sara if she will share the theme she has just written for English class. Sara continues a conversation with another person at the table. Ben interprets her lack of response as an answer: "No, I won't." That would be feedback, whether Sara heard the question or not. She might not have heard, so her failure to respond may not have been a "no" answer. But her silence was still feedback, because that was how Ben interpreted it.

This distinction between feedback and response is important. If you think of response and feedback as the same thing, you can run into trouble. You'll forget that feedback is like all other messages in communication: The intended meaning may be close to or quite different from the perceived message. Feedback differs from other messages only in that it is an interpretation of a response (or nonresponse) to a message. Properly used, feedback can be a way to check on the accuracy or effectiveness of message sending. Improperly used, feedback can lead to ineffective or scrambled communication.

Situation

All communication takes place within a setting (a situation), and that situation influences the meanings—especially perceived messages—within the communication. The **situation** is *the total context in which the source and the receiver interact,* and we use the word interchangeably with the term **setting.** Although not every

aspect of a situation is relevant to every message, understanding the communication process requires understanding the influence of situation.

Physical Aspects   The obvious aspects of situation are those of the physical setting: location, room size, furniture, number of people present, if they're seated or standing, physical barriers between them, and so on. Physical setting also includes less obvious items, such as temperature and humidity, background noise, light, and color of walls and furniture. The physical aspects of a setting are external—outside the persons communicating.

Social-psychological Aspects   Probably even more important in influencing communication outcomes are the social and psychological aspects of the situation. These exist largely in the minds of the communicators, shaping strongly perceptions and interpretations of meanings. Among these factors are the purposes of the communicators, their cultures, roles, and relationships. Each of these affects what is said, what is received, how words and actions are interpreted, what responses are seen as appropriate, and so on. We discuss each of these factors in more detail in later chapters. Here we want you to remember that these factors are part of the situation, and as such, they influence the communication.

RELATIONSHIPS   Some scholars believe relationships so affect communication situations that they use relationships as one factor that distinguishes among types of communication.[5] Interpersonal communication, for instance, can be defined by whether the interactions between people rely on personal or role-related perceptions. Though we do not use this definition, we do find the idea useful in showing how relationships affect communication.

Whenever people intentionally engage in communication, they choose what they say and do using conscious and unconscious predictions about the outcome. How you greet people you meet, for example, is strongly influenced by how you expect them to respond. Social or role-related factors in the situation lead to some predictions. "I can't speak to her unless she speaks to me first. She is a bank president, and bank presidents pay no attention to student employees." At other times, personal knowledge of the individual(s) involved forms the base for predictions. "I can't speak to him without being spoken to first; he is very status-conscious and would be offended if I spoke first."

Clearly different relationships between communicators cause them to make different outcome predictions, and, hence, different communication behaviors. Indeed, the relationships themselves lead to particular predictions. The bank president, for instance, might think, "I must smile and nod when I arrive in the morning because the employees expect their boss to be pleasant upon arriving at work." In another situation, the boss thinks, "I can tell my subordinates that I'm angry about last month's profit-loss statement because it will emphasize to them how serious the problem is for the company, and they'll work harder." In short, the relationships

[5] Gerald R. Miller and Mark Steinberg, *Between People: A New Analysis of Interpersonal Communication* (Chicago: Science Research Associates, Inc., 1975).

among the communicators help *establish the predictability in the situation*, which affects what all the parties involved do and say.

Another important effect of relationships in communication occurs when predictions of the future can't accurately be based on the past. When we expect a certain kind of behavior from a person based on past experience and our perception of an unchanged relationship, we base what we do and say on that expectation (prediction). But if something changes the relationship; the outcomes will differ from what we expected (predicted). In short, changes in relationships require changes in how we communicate.

Communicator purpose, culture, role, and relationship affect communication outcomes. Later chapters of this text will include more discussion of them.

Effects of Situation   Sometimes the effects of setting in communication are called noise, but this description is only occasionally accurate. Certainly, when something in the situation causes intended and perceived messages to differ widely, it has the effect of **noise.** Such interference may be external, as when a jet flies overhead. Or the interference can be internal, as when shock at inappropriate use of profanity prevents a listener from paying attention to what a speaker says, or when a parent is incensed at a child who "talks back" and pays no attention to the child's words.

Many, if not most, elements of situation have a more positive effect. Using the situation to interpret messages may be the only way to understand them. Suppose a person is jumping up and down, yelling loudly, arms waving wildly. What that means is influenced by whether the person is at a football game or on a road beside a stopped car. Cues from situation add clarity and information. Understanding communication messages requires that we use information from both the physical and social or psychological aspects of the situation.

In many cases, aspects of situation must be known before the words or nonverbal cues make sense. Usually, we use what we know about the situation to infer meanings without consciously noting that we have done so. But cases in which communicators fail to take situational factors into account are common and often result in serious misunderstandings—or worse. One significant example is what therapists have learned about treating some people described as "mentally ill." They now know that identifying an "illness" without taking the situation into account can result in an inaccurate diagnosis, and that attempting treatment without considering the situation may be ineffective, and often will be dangerous. Some quite natural reactions to a situation seem to be psychotic behaviors when seen out of context. A work of popular literature described one such situation so appropriately that it resulted in widespread adoption of the term *Catch 22* to describe situations in which a double-bind can cause schizoid behavior in normal people.

Receiving and Sending

We have defined eight elements of the communication process. Several subprocesses connect these elements. Sending and receiving message carriers are two such subprocesses. To intentionally send messages, we talk, write, and perform other associated

Responses and feedback interact but aren't identical.

behaviors. These are parts of a process, as are the receiving behaviors of hearing and reading. Many interactions occur from the time our ear picks up sound waves to the time we decide the meaning of a sentence. In both talking and listening, nerves, brain, and muscles interact.

This all seems so obvious we too often take these parts of the communication process for granted. We forget that speaking is a complex set of learned physical coordinations. We forget that how an intended message is sent—meaning how the words are pronounced and how clearly they are articulated—influences how it is perceived. How people say words may be as important as what words they say. If you set a time to meet friends, it matters whether the time is 3:50 or 3:15. A perceived message may depend not on the words, but on how clearly they are articulated or on how well a receiver hears. It could be quite upsetting if you were going to a show that started at 3:15 and you appeared at 3:50!

Perceiving and Interpreting

The processes of perceiving and interpreting may involve the most complex and most important interactions during communication. For that reason, we devote much space to their explanation. To begin, however, it might be helpful to define what we mean by these two terms.

Perception *refers to the mental process of recognizing the stimuli we receive.* **Interpretation** *refers to the organizing of incoming stimuli into a meaningful whole.* We do not believe the exact differences between these two words have much importance to the beginning student of communication. Indeed we often use the two words interchangeably. What is important is the understanding that people must both recognize and interpret sensations received before they have a perceived message.

EXERCISE 1.1   **INTENDED AND PERCEIVED MEANINGS**

OBJECTIVE   **To become aware that intended meanings may not be the same as perceived meanings**

DIRECTIONS
1. Ask four people to help you in a class project (not all at the same time).
2. Give them a piece of paper and ask them to follow your instructions to draw the design in Figure 1–2. Give them any objects needed to draw the correct size—rulers, compass, etc.
3. Stand with your back to them as you give the instructions so that you can't see them as they draw. Give verbal instructions only. Answer no questions.
4. Collect the drawings and number them in the order they were made.
5. Compare the first drawings with the last. Were the last more accurate? Did your symbol choices become more precise?
6. How does this experience illustrate the differences between intended and perceived messages?
7. List the principles of communication this experience illustrates.

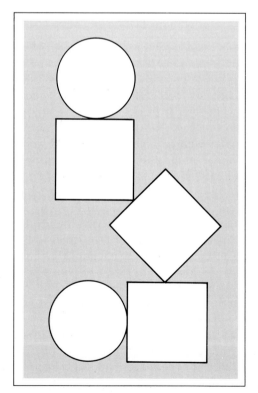

FIGURE 1–2.

Doing this (interpreting sensations received) requires memory, reconstruction, and recall; it uses both conscious and unconscious thinking processes and often involves evaluation. We discuss these processes in detail throughout the next three chapters, beginning with an examination of the role of perception in communication.

PERCEPTIONS ARE LEARNED

Perceived messages often differ widely, even among people within the same situation. As you know, it is common for two people who have seen the same event to report widely different versions of what happened. Just ask the fans of the two opposing teams in the Super Bowl to describe a referee's pass-interference call! What are the reasons different people perceive the same stimulus differently? Knowing the reasons can help you cope with communication problems caused when perceptions differ.

A Learned Process

Probably the most important reason perception varies is that it is a learned process. Infants are born with the ability to receive sensations and to respond to them, but they *learn* how to interpret those sensations. Babies do not inherit a store of meanings in their brains.

As infants, we first learned what sensations "meant" by responding directly to pain or pleasure, or by finding out whether the sensations satisfied our needs. The first time we sensed heat from a fire, we didn't know it would burn or how painful that burn could be. But once having touched something hot, we knew. The next time we felt heat, even if from an iron or a stove we had never seen before, we didn't have to touch it. We knew it would hurt. We had learned to perceive what hot "means"—it hurts. Only gradually did we learn to associate the sensation of hot with a number of other meanings. Learning that painful "hot" fires help cook, warm a house in winter, and heat our bath water was a gradual process.

We all have different experiences as we mature, so *what* people learn as they grow up explains much of *why* people perceive things differently. Obviously, people who grow up in different cultures learn to perceive differently. An Eskimo infant in the far north of Canada, for instance, not only grows up speaking a language different from English, but learns a relationship to nature radically different from that of most other North Americans. What this person will perceive as warm will likely feel cold to those accustomed to central heating and long, hot summers.

Less obviously, individuals can speak the same language and come from quite different cultures. These apparently similar people learn different ways of perceiving and interpreting events. And, perhaps least obvious, people who grow up in similar environments also have different experiences and learn different things. Even these actually similar people will perceive some things differently.

Experience as a broad category explains most perceptual differences, but not all of them. Moreover, because perception so strongly influences communication, we find it useful to be more specific about the reasons two different people may perceive the same event quite differently—and, therefore, communicate about it quite differently. We identify seven such factors, each of which relates to learning and to culture, but each of which is worth noting separately.

Influence of Expectations   *We tend to perceive what we expect.* Look at the nine dots in the box in Figure 1–3. Try the following exercise. With a pencil connect all nine dots using only four straight lines. Don't lift your pencil from the paper, and don't retrace any lines. Try several times before you give up.

Can you do it? If not, it is because of your expectations. You perceived the dots as a square and expected that the lines should follow the boundaries of the square. If you did that, you couldn't accomplish the task. You need different expectations. (The solution is on p. 36.)

Here is another illustration. The triangles in Figure 1–4 on p. 16 contain some common sayings. Read them aloud.

Now look carefully. If you didn't read two *the's* in the first two phrases and two *a's* in the third, you didn't perceive what is there. If this happened, it was because you expected these sayings to be as you have seen them before.

Influence of Emotions   *We tend to perceive sensations according to the feelings we have at the time.* If you're angry, you'll hear what a person says much differently from the way you'd hear it if you were happy. If you feel guilty or defensive about something you did, you may take a neutral or even a friendly comment about it as

FIGURE 1–3.   Nine Dots Puzzle.

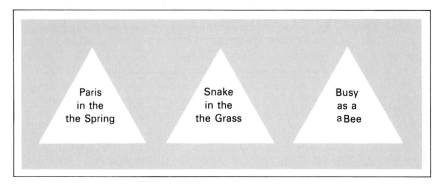

FIGURE 1–4. Perceptions Triangles.

criticism. This is also illustrated by the way fans at a baseball game respond to an umpire's calls. We see a pitch as a strike or a ball depending on whether the pitcher is on "our side" or not. Our emotions can influence whether we see a certain behavior as careful or cowardly, an ad as information or propaganda, a person as outgoing or loudmouthed, and so on.

Influence of Language   Related to the effects of emotions are those of language. The labels we give things have a powerful impact on how we perceive them. There are many examples of this, but a good one is the care with which manufacturers name their products. The success of Ford's Mustang was at least partly due to the ideas and feelings associated with the name. People associated wildness and freedom with the car. The success of Mustang spawned many imitations: Pinto, Colt, Cougar, Lynx. Another "class" of car owed its high prestige, at least in part, to such names as Imperial, Seville, Marquis, Riviera. Soap labeling shows the same principle. The smallest box of laundry soap you can buy in most places is the "giant" size, and the middle-sized box is the "jumbo."

Although it may be true that a rose by any other name would smell as sweet, only those who speak Russian will think of *Роза* as a lovely flower. Was it this influence of language on perception the lawyers had in mind when they placed the ad shown in Figure 1–5?

Influence of Attitudes and Values   Attitudes and values also influence perception, in part because they affect emotions, expectations, and language. *We tend to perceive things according to our attitudes and our values.* The results of one research study may illustrate. During President Franklin Roosevelt's administration, three groups were selected to hear a ten-minute speech that contained nearly equal amounts of pro- and anti-New Deal comments. One group consisted of people who favored the New Deal; another group was neutral; and the third opposed these policies. After the speech, listeners were given a test to see which of forty-six specific items they heard. The items included twenty-three comments that were favorable toward

DO YOU NEED A LAWYER?
LEGAL SERVICES AT REASONABLE RATES

Simple WILL	**$ 35.00**
(2 Wills—Husband & Wife)	**60.00**
DISSOLUTION OF MARRIAGE (Uncontested with Property Settlement)	**200.00** (Plus Court Costs)
INITIAL INTERVIEW on OTHER MATTERS	**15.00** (½ hr. Maximum)

Ask for fee quotation on other matters
CONVENIENT HOURS AVAILABLE UNTIL 8:00 P.M.
(Monday through Saturday) Call for Appointment

FIGURE 1–5. Language of Advertising.

the New Deal and an equal number that were unfavorable. These results show how much listeners' attitudes influenced what they perceived.[6]

	Items Recognized	
	Pro-New Deal	*Anti-New Deal*
Favorable listeners	16.1	9.9
Neutral listeners	12.8	11.8
Unfavorable listeners	10.9	13.0

Influence of Attention Another reason perception varies is how the receiving process itself works. We are constantly bombarded by millions of sensations. At any one time, we see more than we are aware of seeing; we hear more than we are aware of hearing; we feel more than we are aware of feeling, and so on. To put it simply, *we must select what we perceive.* We simply cannot perceive every possible stimulus around us.

Stop reading for a minute. Focus on everything you can see around you. Can you see everything at once? Don't you always view some surroundings in the "corner of your eye"? Is the radio or TV on? Were you consciously listening, or was the sound in the background until just now? What about the chair you're sitting on? Had you noticed it? Probably not, unless it is uncomfortable. But you would have noticed if it began to give way under you.

This discussion shows some of the ways attention affects perception. Attention allows us to focus on only *part* of the sensations it's possible to receive at any one time. Moreover, we are not consciously aware of all the sensations we do receive. We perceive what we focus on differently from what we receive marginally. And what we don't notice can affect how we perceive what we do notice. If you were watching a hockey game and saw a forward start swinging at a lineman, you might believe that only the forward should be penalized. You might need a television

[6] Study conducted by Allen L. Edwards, "Rationalization in Recognition as a Result of a Political Frame of Reference," *Journal of Abnormal and Social Psychology*, 36 (1941), 224–36. Copyright 1941 by the American Psychological Association. Reprinted by permission.

replay to show you that the defensive player had first tried to trip the forward. If you were at the game, of course, you'd never see the trip if you had missed it when it happened. What you didn't see, however, would strongly affect how you perceived what you did see.

Since attention is important to effective communication, we'll take a closer look at what it is. **Attention** is a complex physiological process. It can be defined as *an adjustment of the receiving senses.* For example, you pay attention when you look in the direction of someone you expect to speak or to whom you are listening. Focusing all senses on the speaker is described as **focal attention.** In contrast, we receive many sensations without focusing directly on their sources. This is referred to as peripheral or **marginal attention.** Much of the information we use to guide our lives is received marginally. Crossing a street while talking to a friend, we focus on the conversation, but we also give marginal attention to the street, watching for cars. Knowing when it is necessary to shift from marginal to focal attention is important to effective communication.

Perspective influences what we perceive.

Influence of Perspective   Perspective also influences perceptions. The photos on p. 18 illustrate one kind of perspective. What do they seem to be pictures of? They do not appear to be trees, but they are. From two inches away, a tree looks quite different from the way it looks from the usual perspective. Figure 1–6 on p. 20 notes how *physical perspective influences what we perceive*. Some movie stars are so convinced of this they permit photographs from only one side.

Another type of perspective is cultural or psychological; it might be called *mental set*. A standard of living that includes running water and indoor toilets but excludes restaurant meals or an automobile would be perceived as luxurious by a starving person in New Delhi or Arizona. But from the perspective of a person born into the Rockefeller or Kennedy family, that living standard would probably be regarded as poverty level. You can think of this perspective as attitudes or socialization. Whatever you call it, it strongly affects perception.

Influence of Physical Condition   Because the physical condition of our receiving senses varies, what we perceive varies too. To read, we perceive marks on the page that we interpret as words. People who can't see well have trouble reading. People with physical impairments perceive differently from others. Deaf people can dance to music by "feeling" the rhythm; blind people touch and hear much more sensitively than do those of us who can see. Fatigue affects how all of us see and hear. Illness also affects our senses. The quality of all our senses (hearing, taste, touch, smell, vision) affects our perceptions.

Differences in perception account for many communication problems. People "see" things differently; thus they respond to and talk about them differently. People do not see things alike because they attend to them differently, have different perspectives, have learned, expect, or want to see them differently. Because they perceive things differently, people attach different meanings to the same event, feel differently about that event, value it differently.

Perhaps equally important, one person can perceive the same thing differently at different times. Given changes in time, perspective, experience, emotion, or physical state, each of us experiences personal variation in our perceptions. Thus, to improve our communication with ourselves and with others, we should remember the reasons why perception varies and how it happens.

OVERVIEW

At this point let's establish a framework for the study of the communication process. First, note that talk about communicating can often confuse you because the tool for the study is the subject itself. Worse, however, are habits of, and attitudes about, communication formed long before you ever picked up this book. As you read, you will need to engage in constant examination of your own communication patterns and be willing to discard attitudes that include a number of popular misconceptions about communication.

FIGURE 1–6. (Reprinted with permission of Macmillan Publishing Company, from *Communication: The Transfer of Meaning*, by Don Fabun. Copyright © 1968, Kaiser Aluminum and Chemical Corporation.)

Popular Misconceptions

Communications As Transactions   People often talk about communications. You may not have noticed, but this plural term, *communications*, rarely occurs in this book. That is because we view communication as process. Many events take place as people talk and those events are plural, but the communication that results is not.

One useful way to study communication is to look at the events involved, thinking of them as *transactions*. But in so doing, keep in mind our very specialized use of that term. As used by communication scholars, a **transaction** is a statement and the response to it. This definition focuses on transaction as a concept used as a unit of analysis. Just as the study of individual cells can lead to a better understanding of anatomy, so the study of communication transactions can lead to a better understanding of communication. That applies, however, only as long as you remember the special definition, and keep in mind that no single transaction—or series of transactions (a conversation, interview, or speech)—is the communication in the situation.

The popular definition of the term, however, leads to misunderstanding the *transactional approach* to communication. Most people use the word in the commercial sense, in which something is exchanged—money is exchanged for goods or services, for example. The concept of exchange commonly carries over into talk about communication and leads to serious misunderstanding of the process.

Whenever we talk about communicating so that the "message gets across," we illustrate the misunderstanding. As if ideas could be wrapped up and sent as packages! We also hear people define communication as "transfer of meaning." The process view of communication helps us understand that meaning cannot be transferred. Ideas in one person's head don't reproduce and show up in another person's head. Instead, ideas must be coded—and the signals transmitted. The other person then receives and decodes the signals. If things work as we want, the decoding results in the receiver having ideas similar to those intended by the source. But meaning is not transferred; it cannot be—at least not without some form of extrasensory perception.

Communication Breakdowns   Another commonly misused concept is that of communication "breakdowns." People say, "I just can't communicate with him," or "I just can't get through to her." Well, we *know* communication never *really* breaks down. It may be hostile and lead to aggressive acts; we may be misunderstood; what we want may not happen. Our intended messages may not be understood as we wish. But communication never really breaks down unless the fact of our existence becomes irrelevant.

Even in arguments that end with parties vowing never to speak again, some messages were perceived; some responses occurred. Even when people actually never do speak again, the parties involved remember the interactions. Their memories keep the communication alive; this previous communication often affects later interactions with other people. Thus, communication may be unproductive, ineffective, unpleasant, or hostile; but to be any of those it must exist. Communication does not break down.

Types of Communication

We also think it useful if you understand the different types of communication. The process doesn't change from situation to situation. Communication occurs whenever stimuli are received and interpreted.[7] But the factors involved may change as situations change. If the received stimuli are internal, we describe that as **intrapersonal communication.** Sometimes this is described as information processing. When you hear yourself speak, feel yourself move, interpret the world around you, think about ideas or things you see and do, this is intrapersonal communication. Consciously or unconsciously, intrapersonal communication continues as long as you are alive. It occurs simultaneously with all other types of communication.

 Interpersonal communication occurs when you communicate directly with other people in a one-to-one situation or in small groups. The word parts *inter* and *personal* suggest that *interpersonal* means any communication between persons. But that includes all human communication. We think it's more useful to define interpersonal communication as interactions in which participants have a one-to-one relationship. Practically speaking, these situations usually involve two to eight persons, but the number of people is not what creates interpersonal communication. Direct interaction on a one-to-one basis is the essential feature.

 Public communication takes place in *situations where many people receive messages largely from one source.* A movie, television show, sermon, political speech, advertiser's message, professor's lecture, and committee report are all examples of public communication. Some are examples of mass communication as well. **Mass communication** involves *electronic or mechanical* transmission of message carriers. Television, radio, movies, newspapers, books, and magazines are all examples of mass communication.

 In public communication, most participants are receivers of verbal messages from only one or a few others. Speeches are the best-known examples of public communication. Participants in public communication do not interact in direct one-to-one relationships. There is interaction, but it is different from that in interpersonal situations. In public communication, the receiver's responses are mostly nonverbal. The professor who changes his lecture style because students fall asleep or look bored and the politician who becomes angry when her audience boos her proposal have both received and responded to feedback.

Models of Communication

Modeling is a common way to learn. At one time or another, all of us have built models. Yours may have been model airplanes, cars, doll houses, trains, or sand

---

[7] We define the term *communication* as the process of receiving stimuli and interpreting them, which is assigning meaning to stimuli received.

Examples of public communication: New York Governor Mario Cuomo and Presidential candidate Jesse Jackson.

castles on the beach. But modeling is not limited to play. Aircraft engineers make models and test them in wind tunnels; architects create scale models of buildings; auto manufacturers create prototype models of cars; children model their parents' behavior as they grow up. All these models serve a purpose. So, too, will your creating one. It will create a framework for you to understand how communication works.

In Figure 1–7 we present some models of the communication process. We intend that these examples help you understand the elements and interactions in-

FIGURE 1–7. Three Models of Communication.

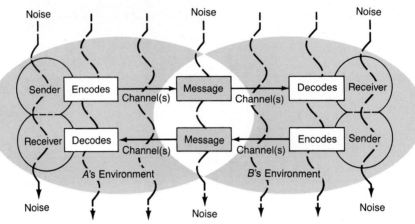

(Ronald Adler and George Rodman, *Understanding Human Communication*. Copyright © 1982 by Holt, Rinehart and Winston. Reproduced by permission of the publisher.

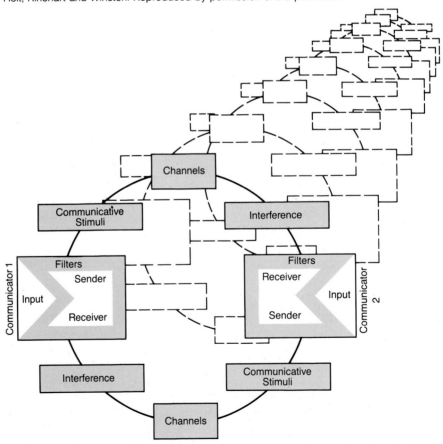

(Stewart Tubbs and Sylvia Moss, *Human Communication*, 3rd ed. New York: Random House, 1980, p. 23. Reprinted by permission.)

FIGURE 1–7.   (Continued)

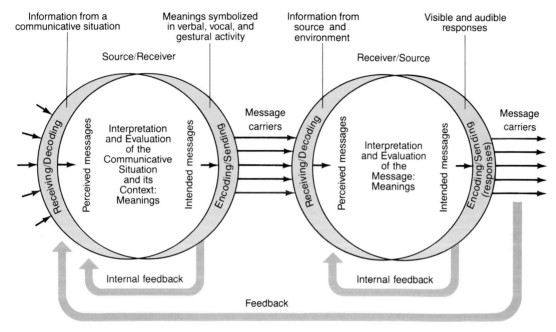

(Adapted from Donald Bryant and Karl Wallace, *Fundamentals of Public Speaking*, 4th ed., p. 29. © 1976. Adapted by permission of Prentice-Hall, Inc.)

volved in communication, and that you remember that no one of these can fully represent the reality.

Many different models of communication can be created. None is perfect; each has special qualities and some problems. Further reading on this topic of modeling the communication process is available in the starred items in the reading list on pp. 35–36. Most important, though, is that your model make sense to you, that it show how elements and processes of communication relate to each other. In that way, your model will do what it is supposed to do: establish a perspective for your study of communication.

EXERCISE 1.2   MAKING MODELS OF COMMUNICATION

OBJECTIVE   **To apply your understanding of the processes of communication by creating a model that represents them.**

DIRECTIONS   1. The task of this assignment is to create your own picture or three-dimensional representation of the communication process. The only limitation is that you should not use any model presented in the text unless it is adapted enough to be recognizably different. Be sure your model includes the elements and subprocesses involved in communication and shows how the parts interact.

2. Your instructor will indicate whether this is to be a group or individual project.
   a. *Group*: In groups assigned by the instructor, 4 to 6 persons will develop a group model, to be presented by all participants. Members of the group may represent elements of communication or verbally present parts of the model.
   b. *Individual*: In a 3- to 5-minute speech, explain your model so that classmates will understand how it represents the communication process.
3. The model must be shown (or demonstrated) as you explain it, or explained after it has been demonstrated.
4. List the principles of communication this experience illustrates.

REVIEW

Provide brief answers that may be a writing assignment or the basis for class discussion.
1. What should a model of communication illustrate?
2. Name all the elements and subprocesses that should be included in a model.
3. What was the most important communication principle illustrated or learned from this exercise?

Note: If your model was graphic, attach it to this worksheet.

An excellent example of the concept of process is provided by the following Ray Bradbury story, "A Sound of Thunder." Your instructor may assign a written or oral report or a class discussion using the questions at the end of the story.

A SOUND OF THUNDER*

Ray Bradbury

The sign on the wall seemed to quaver under a film of sliding warm water. Eckels felt his eyelids blink over his stare, and the sign burned in this momentary darkness:

TIME SAFARI, INC.
SAFARIS TO ANY YEAR IN THE PAST.
YOU NAME THE ANIMAL.
WE TAKE YOU THERE.
YOU SHOOT IT.

A warm phlegm gathered in Eckels' throat; he swallowed and pushed it down. The muscles around his mouth formed a smile as he put his hand slowly out upon the air, and in that hand waved a check for ten thousand dollars to the man behind the desk.

"Does this safari guarantee I come back alive?"

"We guarantee nothing," said the official, "except the dinosaurs." He turned. "This is Mr. Travis, your Safari Guide in the Past. He'll tell you what and where to shoot. If he says no shooting, no shooting. If you disobey instructions, there's a stiff penalty of another ten thousand dollars, plus possible government action, on your return."

Eckels glanced across the vast office at a mass and tangle, a snaking and humming of wires and steel boxes, at an aurora that flickered now orange, now silver, now blue. There was a sound like a gigantic bonfire burning all of Time, all the years and all the parchment calendars, all the hours piled high and set aflame.

A touch of the hand and this burning would, on the instant, beautifully reverse itself. Eckels remembered the wording in the advertisements to the letter. Out of chars and ashes, out of dust and coals, like golden salamanders, the old years, the green years, might leap; roses sweeten the air, white hair turn Irish-black, wrinkles vanish; all, everything fly back to seed, flee death, rush down to their beginnings, suns rise in western skies and set in glorious easts, moons eat themselves opposite to the custom, all and everything cupping one in another like Chinese boxes, rabbits into hats, all and everything returning to the fresh death, the seed death, the green death, to the time before the beginning. A touch of a hand might do it, the merest touch of a hand.

"Unbelievable." Eckels breathed, the light of the Machine on his thin face. "A real Time Machine." He shook his head. "Makes you think. If the election had gone badly yesterday, I might be here now running away from the results. Thank God Keith won. He'll make a fine president of the United States."

"Yes," said the man behind the desk. "We're lucky. If Deutscher had gotten in, we'd have the worst kind of dictatorship. There's an anti-everything man for you, a militarist, anti-Christ, anti-human, anti-intellectual. People called us up, you know, joking but not joking. Said if Deutscher became president they wanted to go live in 1492. Of course it's not our business to conduct Escapes, but to form Safaris. Anyway, Keith's president now. All you got to worry about is—"

"Shooting my dinosaur," Eckels finished it for him.

"A Tyrannosaurus rex. The Tyrant Lizard, the most incredible monster in history. Sign this release. Anything happens to you, we're not responsible. Those dinosaurs are hungry."

Eckels flushed angrily, "Trying to scare me!"

"Frankly, yes. We don't want anyone going who'll panic at the first shot. Six Safari leaders were killed last year, and a dozen hunters. We're here to give you the severest thrill a real hunter ever asked for. Traveling you back sixty million years to bag the biggest game in all of Time. Your personal check's still there. Tear it up."

Mr. Eckels looked at the check. His fingers twitched.

"Good luck," said the man behind the desk. "Mr. Travis, he's all yours."

They moved silently across the room, taking their guns with them, toward the Machine, toward the silver metal and the roaring light.

First a day and then a night and then a day and then a night, then it was day-night-day-night. A week, a month, a year, a decade! A.D. 2055. A.D. 2019. 1999! 1957! Gone! The Machine roared.

They put on their oxygen helmets and tested the intercoms.

Eckels swayed on the padded seat, his face pale, his jaw stiff. He felt the trembling in his arms and he looked down and found his hands tight on the new rifle. There were four other men in the Machine. Travis, the Safari Leader, his assistant, Lesperance, and two other hunters, Billings and Kramer. They sat looking at each other, and the years blazed around them.

"Can these guns get a dinosaur cold?" Eckels felt his mouth saying.

"If you hit them right," said Travis on the helmet radio. "Some dinosaurs have two brains, one in the head, another far down the spinal column. We stay away from those. That's stretching luck. Put your first two shots into the eyes, if you can, blind them, and go back into the brain."

The Machine howled. Time was a film run backward. Suns fled and ten million moons fled after them. "Think," said Eckels. "Every hunter that ever lived would envy us today. This makes Africa seem like Illinois.

The Machine slowed; its scream fell to a murmur. The Machine stopped.

The sun stopped in the sky.

The fog that had enveloped the Machine blew away and they were in an old time, a very old time indeed, three hunters and two Safari Heads with their blue metal guns across their knees.

"Christ isn't born yet," said Travis. "Moses has not gone to the mountains to talk with God. The Pyramids are still in the earth, waiting to be cut out and put up. Remember that. Alexander, Caesar, Napoleon, Hitler—none of them exists."

The man nodded.

"That"—Mr. Travis pointed—"is the jungle of sixty million two thousand and fifty-five years before President Keith."

He indicated a metal path that struck off into green wilderness, over streaming swamp, among giant ferns and palms.

"And that," he said, "is the Path, laid by Time Safari for your use. It floats six inches above the earth. Doesn't touch so much as one grass blade, flower, or tree. It's an anti-gravity metal. Its purpose is to keep you from touching this world of the past in any way. Stay on the Path. Don't go off it. I repeat. Don't go off. For any reason! If you fall off, there's a penalty. And don't shoot any animal we don't okay."

"Why?" asked Eckels.

They sat in the ancient wilderness. Far birds' cries blew on a wind, and the smell of tar and an old salt sea, moist grasses, and flowers the color of blood.

"We don't want to change the Future. We don't belong here in the Past. The government doesn't like us here. We have to pay big graft to keep our franchise. A Time Machine is finicky business. Not knowing it, we might kill an important animal, a small bird, a roach, a flower even, thus destroying an important link in a growing species."

"That's not clear," said Eckels.

"All right," Travis continued, "say we accidentally kill one mouse here. That means all the future families of this one particular mouse are destroyed, right?"

"Right."

"And all the families of the families of the families of that one mouse! With a stamp of your foot, you annihilate first one, then a dozen, then a thousand, a million, a billion possible mice!"

"So they're dead," said Eckels. "So what?"

"So what?" Travis snorted quietly. "Well, what about the foxes that'll need those mice to survive? For want of ten mice, a fox dies. For want of ten foxes a lion starves. For want of a lion, all manner of insects, vultures; infinite billions of life forms are thrown into chaos and destruction. Eventually it all boils down to this: fifty-nine million years later, a caveman, one of a dozen on the entire world, goes hunting wild boar or saber-toothed tiger for food. But you, friend, have stepped on all the tigers in that region. By stepping on one single mouse. So the caveman starves. And the caveman, please note, is not just any expendable man, no! He is an entire future nation. From his loins would have sprung ten sons. From their loins one hundred sons, and thus onward to a civilization. Destroy this one man, and you destroy a race, a people, an entire history of life. It is comparable to slaying some of Adam's grandchildren. The stomp of your foot, on one mouse, could start an earthquake, the effects of which could shake our earth and destinies down through Time, to their very foundations. With the death of that one caveman, a billion others yet unborn are throttled in the womb. Perhaps Rome never rises on its seven hills. Perhaps Europe is forever a dark forest, and only Asia waxes healthy and teeming. Step on a mouse and you crush the Pyramids. Step on a mouse and you leave your print, like a Grand Canyon, across Eternity. Queen Elizabeth might never be born, Washington might not cross the Delaware, there might never be a United States at all. So be careful. Stay on the Path. Never step off!"

"I see," said Eckels. "Then it wouldn't pay for us even to touch the grass?"

"Correct. Crushing certain plants could add up infinitesimally. A little error here would multiply in sixty million years, all out of proportion. Of course maybe our theory is wrong. Maybe Time can't be changed by us. Or maybe it can be changed only in little subtle ways. A dead mouse here makes an insect imbalance there, a population disproportion later, a bad harvest further on, a depression, mass starvation, and finally, a change in social temperament in far-flung countries. Something much more subtle, like that. Perhaps only a soft breath, a whisper, a hair, pollen on the air, such a slight, slight change that unless you looked close you wouldn't see it. Who knows? Who really can say he knows? We don't know. We're guessing. But until we do know for certain whether our messing around in Time can make a big roar or a little rustle in history, we're being careful. This Machine, this Path, your clothing and bodies, were sterilized, as you know, before the journey. We wear these oxygen helmets so we can't introduce our bacteria into an ancient atmosphere."

"How do we know which animals to shoot?"

"They're marked with red paint," said Travis. "Today, before our journey, we sent Lesperance here back with the Machine. He came to this particular era and followed certain animals."

"Studying them?"

"Right," said Lesperance. "I track them through their entire existence, noting which of them lives longest. Very few. How many times they mate. Not often. Life's short. When I find one that's going to die when a tree falls on him, or one that drowns in a tar pit, I note the exact hour, minute, and second. I shoot a paint bomb. It leaves a red patch on his side. We can't miss it. Then I correlate our arrival in the Past so that we meet the Monster not more than two minutes before he would have died anyway. This way, we kill only animals with no future, that are never going to mate again. You see how careful we are?"

"But if you came back this morning in Time," said Eckels eagerly, "you must've bumped into us, our Safari! How did it turn out? Was it successful? Did all of us get through—alive?"

Travis and Lesperance gave each other a look.

"That'd be a paradox," said the latter. "Time doesn't permit that sort of mess—a man meeting himself. When such occasions threaten, Time steps aside. Like an airplane hitting an air pocket. You felt the Machine jump just before we stopped? That was us passing ourselves on the way back to the Future. We saw nothing. There's no way of telling if this expedition was a success, if we got our monster, or whether all of us— meaning you, Mr. Eckels—got out alive."

Eckels smiled palely.

"Cut that," said Travis sharply. "Everyone on his feet!"

They were ready to leave the Machine.

The jungle was high and the jungle was broad and the jungle was the entire world forever and forever. Sounds like music and sounds like flying tents filled the sky, and those were pterodactyls soaring with cavernous gray wings, gigantic bats of delirium and night fever. Eckels, balanced on the narrow Path, aimed his rifle playfully.

"Stop that!" said Travis. "Don't even aim for fun, blast you! If your guns should go off—"

Eckels flushed. "Where's our Tyrannosaurus?"

Lesperance checked his wristwatch. "Up ahead. We'll bisect his trail in sixty seconds. Look for the red paint! Don't shoot till we give the word. Stay on the Path. Stay on the Path!"

They moved forward in the wind of morning.

"Strange," murmured Eckels, "Up ahead, sixty million years, Election Day over, Keith made president. Everyone celebrating. And here we are, a million years lost, and they don't exist. The things we worried about for months, a lifetime, not even born or thought of yet."

"Safety catches off, everyone!" ordered Travis. "You, first shot, Eckels. Second, Billings. Third, Kramer."

"I've hunted tiger, wild boar, buffalo, elephant, but now, this is it," said Eckels. "I'm shaking like a kid."

"Ah," said Travis.

Everyone stopped.

Travis raised his hand. "Ahead," he whispered. "In the mist. There he is. There's His Royal Majesty now."

The jungle was wide and full of twitterings, rustlings, murmurs, and sighs.

Suddenly it all ceased, as if someone had shut a door.

Silence.

A sound of thunder.

Out of the mist, one hundred yards away, came Tyrannosaurus rex.

"It," whispered Eckels. "It. . . ."

"Sh!"

It came on great oiled, resilient striding legs. It towered thirty feet above half of the trees, a great evil god, folding its delicate watchmaker's claws close to its oily reptilian chest. Each lower leg was a piston, a thousand pounds of white bone, sunk in thick ropes of muscle, sheathed over in a gleam of pebbled skin like the mail of a terrible warrior. Each thigh was a ton of meat, ivory, and steel mesh. And from the great breathing cage of the upper body those two delicate arms dangled out front, arms with hands which might pick up and examine men like toys, while the snake neck coiled. And the head itself, a ton of sculptured stone, lifted easily upon the sky. Its mouth gaped, exposing a fence of teeth like daggers. Its eyes rolled, ostrich eggs, empty of all expression save hunger. It closed its mouth in a death grin. It ran, its pelvic bones crushing aside trees and bushes, its taloned feet clawing damp earth, leaving prints six inches deep wherever it settled its weight. It ran with a gliding ballet step, far too poised and balanced for its ten tons. It moved into a sunlit area warily, its beautifully reptilian hands feeling the air.

"Why, why," Eckels twitched his mouth. "It could reach up and grab the moon."

"Sh!" Travis jerked angrily. "He hasn't seen us yet."

"It can't be killed," Eckels pronounced this verdict quietly, as if there could be no argument. He had weighed the evidence and this was his considered opinion. The rifle in his hands seemed a cap gun. "We were fools to come. This is impossible."

"Shut up!" hissed Travis. "Walk quietly to the Machine. We'll remit half your fee."

"I didn't realize it would be this big," said Eckels. "I miscalculated, that's all. And now I want out."

"It sees us!"

"There's the red paint on its chest!"

The Tyrant Lizard raised itself. Its armored flesh glittered like a thousand green coins. The coins, crusted with slime, steamed. In the slime, tiny insects wriggled, so that the entire body seemed to twitch and undulate, even while the monster itself did not move. It exhaled. The stink of raw flesh blew down the wilderness.

"Get me out of here," said Eckels. "It was never like this before. I was always sure I'd come through alive. I had good guides, good safaris, and safety. This time, I figured wrong. I've met my match and admit it. This is too much for me to get hold of."

"Don't run," said Lesperance. "Turn around. Hide in the Machine."

"Yes." Eckels seemed to be numb. He looked at his feet as if trying to make them move. He gave a grunt of helplessness.

"Eckels!"

He took a few steps, blinking, shuffling.

"Not that way!"

The Monster, at the first motion, lunged forward with a terrible scream. It covered one hundred yards in six seconds. The rifles jerked up and blazed fire. A windstorm from the beast's mouth engulfed them in the stench of slime and old blood. The Monster roared, teeth glittering with sun.

The rifles cracked again. Their sound was lost in shriek and lizard thunder. The great level of the reptile's tail swung up, lashed sideways. Trees exploded in clouds of leaf and branch. The Monster twitched its jeweler's hands down to fondle at the men, to twist them in half, to crush them like berries, to cram them into its teeth and its screaming throat. Its boulderstone eyes leveled with the men. They saw themselves mirrored. They fired at the metallic eyelids and the blazing black Iris.

Like a stone idol, like a mountain avalanche, Tyrannosaurus fell. Thundering, it clutched trees, pulled them with it. It wrenched and tore the metal Path. The men flung themselves back and away. The body hit, ten tons of cold flesh and stone. The guns fired. The Monster lashed its armored tail, twitched its snake jaws, and lay still. A fount of blood spurted from its throat. Somewhere inside, a sac of fluids burst. Sickening gushes drenched the hunters. They stood, red and glistening.

The thunder faded.

The jungle was silent. After the avalanche, a green peace. After the nightmare, morning.

Billings and Kramer sat on the pathway and threw up. Travis and Lesperance stood with smoking rifles, cursing steadily.

In the Time Machine, on his face, Eckels lay shivering. He had found his way back to the Path, climbed into the Machine.

Travis came walking, glanced at Eckels, took cotton gauze from a metal box, and returned to the others, who were sitting on the Path.

"Clean up."

They wiped the blood from their helmets. They began to curse too. The Monster lay, a hill of solid flesh. Within, you could hear the sighs and murmurs as the furthest chambers of it died, the organs malfunctioning, liquids running a final instant from pocket to sac to spleen, everything shutting off, closing up forever. It was like standing by a wrecked locomotive or a steam shovel at quitting time, all valves being released or levered tight. Bones cracked; the tonnage of its own flesh, off balance, dead weight, snapped the delicate forearms, caught underneath. The meat settled quivering.

Another cracking sound. Overhead, a gigantic tree branch broke from its heavy mooring, fell. It crashed upon the dead beast with finality.

"There." Lesperance checked his watch. "Right on time. That's the giant tree that was scheduled to fall and kill this animal originally. He glanced at the two hunters. "You want the trophy picture?"

"What?"

"We can't take a trophy back to the Future. The body has to stay right here where it would have died originally, so the insects, birds, and bacteria can get at it, as they were intended to. Everything in balance. The body stays. But we can take a picture of you standing near it."

The two men tried to think, but gave up, shaking their heads.

They let themselves be led along the metal Path. They sank wearily into the Machine cushions. They gazed back at the ruined Monster, the stagnating mound, where already strange reptilian birds and golden insects were busy at the steaming armor.

A sound on the floor of the Time Machine stiffened them. Eckels sat there, shivering.

"I'm sorry," he said at last.

"Get up!" cried Travis.

Eckels got up.

"Go out on that Path alone," said Travis. He had his rifle pointed. "You're not coming back in the Machine. We're leaving you here!"

Lesperance seized Travis's arm. "Wait—"

"Stay out of this!" Travis shook his hand away. "This fool nearly killed us. But it isn't that so much, no. It's his shoes! Look at them! He ran off the Path. That ruins us! We'll forfeit! Thousands of dollars of insurance! We guarantee no one leaves the Path. He left it. Oh, the fool! I'll have to report to the government. They might revoke our license to travel. Who knows what he's done to Time, to History!"

"Take it easy, all he did was kick up some dirt."

"How do we know?" cried Travis. "We don't know anything! It's all a mystery! Get out of here, Eckels!"

Eckels fumbled his shirt. "I'll pay anything. A hundred thousand dollars!"

Travis glared at Eckels' checkbook and spat. "Go out there. The Monster's next to the Path. Stick your arms up to your elbows in his mouth. Then you can come back with us."

"That's unreasonable!"

"The Monster's dead, you idiot. The bullets! The bullets can't be left behind. They don't belong in the Past; they might change anything. Here's my knife. Dig them out!"

The jungle was alive again, full of the old tremorings and bird cries. Eckels turned slowly to regard the primeval garbage dump, that hill of nightmares and terror. After a long time, like a sleepwalker he shuffled out along the Path.

He returned, shuddering, five minutes later, his arms soaked and red to the elbows. He held out his hands. Each held a number of steel bullets. Then he fell. He lay where he fell, not moving.

"You didn't have to make him do that," said Lesperance.

"Didn't I? It's too early to tell." Travis nudged the still body. "He'll live. Next time he won't go hunting game like this. Okay." He jerked his thumb wearily at Lesperance. "Switch on. Let's go home."

1492. 1776. 1812.

They cleaned their hands and faces. They changed their caking shirts and pants. Eckels was up and around again, not speaking. Travis glared at him for a full ten minutes.

"Don't look at me," cried Eckels. "I haven't done anything."

"Who can tell?"

"Just ran off the Path, that's all, a little mud on my shoes—what do you want me to do—get down and pray?"

"We might need it. I'm warning you, Eckels, I might kill you yet. I've got my gun ready."

"I'm innocent. I've done nothing!"

1999. 2000. 2055.

The Machine stopped.

"Get out," said Travis.

The room was there as they had left it. But not the same as they had left it. The same man sat behind the same desk. But the same man did not quite sit behind the same desk.

Travis looked around swiftly. "Everything okay here?" he snapped.

"Fine. Welcome home!"

Travis did not relax. He seemed to be looking through the one high window.

"Okay, Eckels, get out. Don't ever come back."

Eckels could not move.

"You heard me," said Travis. "What're you staring at?"

Eckels stood smelling of the air, and there was a thing to the air, a chemical taint so subtle, so slight, that only a faint cry of his subliminal senses warned him it was there. The colors, white, gray, blue, orange, in the wall, in the furniture, in the sky beyond the window, were . . . were. . . . And there was a feel. His flesh twitched. His hands twitched. He stood drinking the oddness with the pores of his body. Somewhere, someone must have been screaming one of those whistles that only a dog can hear. His body screamed silence in return. Beyond this room, beyond this wall, beyond this man who was not quite the same man seated at this desk that was not quite the same desk . . . lay an entire world of streets and people. What sort of world it was now, there was no telling. He could feel them moving there, beyond the walls, almost, like so many chess pieces blown in a dry wind.

But the immediate thing was the sign painted on the office wall, the same sign he had read earlier today on first entering.

Somehow, the sign had changed:

TIME SEFARI INC.
SEFARIS TU ANY YEER EN THE PAST.
YU NAIM THE ANIMALL.
WEE TAEKYUTHAIR.
YU SHOOT ITT.

Eckels felt himself fall into a chair. He fumbled crazily at the thick slime on his boots. He held up a clod of dirt, trembling. "No, it can't be. Not a little thing like that. No!"

Embedded in the mud, glistening green and gold and black, was a butterfly, very beautiful and very dead.

"Not a little thing like that! Not a butterfly!" cried Eckels.

It fell to the floor, an exquisite thing, a small thing that could upset balances and knock down a line of small dominoes and then big dominoes and then gigantic dominoes, all down the years across Time. Eckels' mind whirled. It couldn't change things. Killing one butterfly couldn't be that important! Could it?

His face was cold. His mouth trembled, asking: "Who—Who won the presidential election yesterday?"

The man behind the desk laughed. "You joking? You know very well. Deutscher, of course! Who else? Not that fool weakling Keith. We got an iron man now, a man with guts!" The official stopped. "What's wrong?"

Eckels moaned. He dropped to his knees. He scrabbled at the golden butterfly with shaking fingers. "Can't we," he pleaded to the world, to himself, to the officials, to the Machine, "can't we take it back, can't we make it live again? Can't we start over? Can't we—"

He did not move. Eyes shut, he waited, shivering. He heard Travis breathe loud in the room; he heard Travis shift his rifle, click the safety catch, and raise the weapon.

There was a sound of thunder.

QUESTIONS

1. How is the idea of process illustrated by "A Sound of Thunder"?
2. Does everything really affect everything else?
3. What small incidents in your life have had major and long-lasting effects?
4. What are the implications of referring to communication itself as a process?

SUMMARY

We all have reasons to study communication: to avoid or minimize poor communication; to understand better how we use communication to relate to the rest of the world; and to learn how we use communication to try to satisfy many of our human needs. This study can give us tools to help handle various communication situations, but it cannot give simple answers, because communication is not a simple process.

Communication is a process of processes. It involves sending, receiving, perceiving, and interpreting many stimuli. To describe communication as a process suggests two things: Communication is composed of interactions among many elements, and it is ongoing. Each part of the process interacts with and affects the other parts. Communication includes at least eight elements: (1) source(s), (2) receiver(s), (3) sensory receptors, (4) message carriers, (5) messages, (6) responses, (7) feedback, and (8) situation or context.

Four subprocesses—sending, receiving, perceiving, and interpreting—are involved in communication. Using perception and interpretation, we assign meaning to stimuli. Parts of the communication process are simultaneous and interactive; they occur almost all at the same time, and they work together and affect each other. Although all parts of the process affect each other, looking at each separately can help us understand the total process.

Perception, the process of recognizing and assigning meaning to the sensations received, is learned. Therefore it is infinitely variable (it can be different in as many ways as there are people). Perception is influenced by expectations, emotions, language, attitudes, and values. It is also influenced by the perceiver's attention, physical state, and perspective. Attention plays an important role in perception because it is selective. It chooses to focus on some things and not on others. Attention is defined as an adjustment of the receiving senses; receivers adjust their senses to pay attention. If they adjust their senses to concentrate on something, they are giving it focal attention. If they adjust their senses only a little ("listen with half an ear"), their attention is marginal.

We identify types of communication by situation: intrapersonal, interpersonal, and public. Intrapersonal communication takes place internally; it is communicating with self. Interpersonal communication is direct one-to-one interaction. This usually occurs when there are two persons or within a small group. Public communication occurs in a situation where a large number of people receive stimuli primarily from one source. Mass communication, sending messages mechanically or electronically to many widely separated receivers, is a special type of public communication.

QUESTIONS FOR DISCUSSION

1. Why study communication?
2. What does describing communication as a process mean?
3. What are the processes of communication?
4. When two people communicate, why should both be described as source and receiver?
5. What does distinguishing between intended and perceived messages suggest for improving communication?
6. What are the message carriers in communication?
7. What differences do you see among the types of communication?
8. What is the difference between response and feedback in communication?
9. Can you explain eight reasons perceptions vary?

SUGGESTIONS FOR FURTHER READING

Applebaum, Ronald L., Owen O. Jenson, and Richard Carroll, eds. *Speech Communication, A Basic Anthology*, 2nd ed. New York: Macmillan, 1979.

Barker, Larry. *Communication Vibrations*. Englewood Cliffs, N.J.: Prentice-Hall, 1974.

*Barker, Larry L., and Robert J. Kibler, eds. *Speech Communication Behavior: Perspectives and Principles*. Englewood Cliffs, N.J.: Prentice-Hall, 1971.

Bartley, S. Howard. *Introduction to Perception*. New York: Harper & Row, 1980.

Civikly, Jean M., ed. *Contexts of Communication*. New York: Holt, Rinehart and Winston, 1981.

Coren, Stanley et al. *Sensation and Perception*, 2nd ed. New York: Academic Press, 1984.

Dance, Frank, ed. *Human Communication Theory, Comparative Essays*. New York: Harper & Row, 1982.

Devito, Joseph. *The Psychology of Speech and Language*. New York: University Press of America, 1981.

* Starred items are those including examples of graphic models of communication.

————. *Communication Concepts and Processes*, 3rd ed. Englewood Cliffs, N.J.: Prentice-Hall, 1981.

————. *Communicology*: *An Introduction to the Study of Communication*, 3rd ed. New York: Harper & Row, 1981.

Gibson, James W., ed. *A Reader in Speech Communication*. New York: McGraw-Hill, 1971.

*Hanneman, Gerhard, and William J. McEwen. *Communication and Behavior*. Reading, Mass.: Addison-Wesley, 1975.

Mortensen, C. David., ed. *Basic Readings in Communication Theory*, 2nd ed. New York: Harper & Row, 1979.

*Steinfatt, Thomas., ed. *Readings in Human Communication*. Indianapolis. Bobbs-Merrill, 1977.

Stewart, Charles J. *On Speech Communication*. New York: Holt, Rinehart and Winston, 1972.

Stewart, John, ed. *Bridges Not Walls*. Reading, Mass.: Addison-Wesley; 1977.

Watzlawick, Paul. *How Real Is Real*? New York: Random House, 1977.

*Weinberg, Sanford, ed. *Messages*: *A Reader in Human Communication*, 3rd ed. New York: Random House, 1980.

*Wood, Julia. *Human Communication, A Symbolic Interactionist Perspective*. New York: Holt, Rinehart and Winston, 1982.

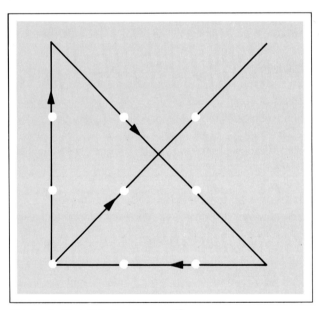

Solution to Nine Dots Puzzle on p. 15.

2 How We See Ourselves: Self-Concept, the Central Attitude

"True self-love and social are the same; . . .
And all our Knowledge is, ourselves to know."

ALEXANDER POPE

GOAL

To understand how self-concept influences communication

OBJECTIVES

The material in this chapter should help you to:
1. Define self-concept.
2. Define attitude, and explain what describing self-concept as "the central attitude" suggests.
3. Explain the process by which self-concept develops.
4. Describe the impact of gender role and culture in the development of self concept.
5. Identify one "significant other" in your life, and describe the ways that person has influenced your self-concept.
6. Cite personal experiences that illustrate five influences of self-concept in communication:
   Pygmalion effect
   Self-fulfilling prophecy
   Selective exposure, perception, and retention
   Openness
   Self-confidence
7. Define self-confidence.
8. Describe some ways to cope with communication anxiety.

Suppose two persons are chosen to interview for a job. Only one will be hired. Since their experience and education are equal, the interview will determine who gets the job. During the interview, one person is relaxed and poised, clearly at ease with herself, while the other is nervous and fidgety. Which would you hire?

Self-concept largely influenced how these two job applicants handled the interview, because it is the basis for how they feel about themselves. Since self-concept is at the heart of the communication processes, its influence strongly affects most behavior. What we see and hear, how we think and feel, and how we respond to others all depend on how we think and feel about ourselves. An understanding of self-concept can provide the basis for communicating more effectively in all types of situations.

THE NATURE OF SELF-CONCEPT

What actually is self-concept? It is a combination of many factors, much more than simply who we are. Self-concept has many facets, or aspects. Think for a minute about how you'd answer the question, Who are you? You could answer that question by giving your name and occupation. But that's not you, is it? Who are you, really? You could point to your physical self, but you are more than that, aren't you? An important part of you—we think the most important part—is the concept you have of your self. Yes, you are also ideas in your own head.

These ideas, or self-concept, include what you think you look like, your name, and your perceptions of the important things you do and have done. "I am Chris Smith." "I am a student." "I am a plumber, lawyer, police officer, doctor, father, mother, wife . . ." Yet self-concept also includes more than the things you do. It includes how you feel about yourself, your attitudes toward yourself. Think about these questions:

> What do you look like?
> How do others see you?
> How do you behave?
> How do others' perceptions affect you when you talk?
> When introduced to others, how do you identify yourself?
> What is important about you?
> How do you feel about your looks? your skills? your talents? your intelligence?

How you answer these questions reveals much about your self-concept. But it includes still more. These questions illustrate that no single statement can include the many dimensions of self-concept. **Self-concept** consists of all of one's physical, emotional, social, and intellectual perceptions of self. It is *the total complex of ideas, feelings, and attitudes people have about themselves*. Note that this definition involves dimensions of identity (who and what you are), of valuing (how you evaluate aspects of self), and that it directly relates to behavior (what you do and say).

Self-Concept and Attitudes

We subtitled this chapter "The Central Attitude." What does it mean to describe something as an attitude? "Attitude" is an important concept for students of communication. We use a common definition: **Attitude** *refers to a predisposition to respond to stimuli in a particular way*. An attitude reflects a learned set of evaluations about particular stimuli that influence how we respond to them. For example, if your attitude toward school is positive, you are likely to respond positively to attending school, doing homework, and so on. In short, you are predisposed to respond favorably whenever you are presented with stimuli related to school. In contrast, if your attitude is negative, you will tend to respond negatively. You won't like classes or doing homework; you'll find things wrong with teachers, books, rooms, assignments.

Attitudes and values relate. Our values are part of the way we form our attitudes. In Chapter 1, we noted how attitudes influence perception. Now let's look at some other aspects of attitudes that will help in understanding the effects of self-concept in communication.

Attitudes and Values Are Internal States   Attitudes and values function internally. They cannot be seen or touched. They are intangible, abstract concepts. But they are, nonetheless, important concepts for communicators. For example, your love for a mate or friend can't be seen, but it's important. Attitudes and values are like love; they are invisible realities that affect behavior.

ATTITUDES AND VALUES AFFECT BEHAVIOR   Attitudes and values are internal; they are not behavior. To open a bottle of champagne is behavior; the attitude that predisposes you to celebrate an event is not. Behavior is observable, something you can see. And though an attitude may predispose us to a behavior, the actual relationship between behavior and attitude varies from situation to situation. Similar attitudes affect behavior differently. Suppose you grew up and attended high school with a small group that became close friends. You are all of the same ethnic group— say Jewish, Polish, or Hispanic—and each of you has a positive attitude toward your ethnic group and toward each other. Now, suppose further that each of you goes away to college and meets new friends at a school TGIF party. Someone there makes a remark you consider insulting to your ethnic group. In that situation, you and each of your friends would probably be offended and develop a negative attitude toward this new "friend." In other words, you'd all be predisposed to respond negatively to this person now and in the future. But how the behavior of each of you will reflect the attitude will vary. You might tell that person off; another might get angry and leave, saying nothing; a third might respond violently; a fourth might sit still, steaming but silent. These and many other possible behaviors can result from similar attitudes.

None of these behaviors itself is an attitude. The attitude is the internal system of beliefs and feelings that leads to the behavior. The actual behavior will depend on the situation—on who did the insulting, where it happened, who was around, your culture, your self-confidence, and probably other factors.

Behavior, as we use the term, *is observable action.*[1] Thus, behavior includes talking. The coding process—choosing which words to say—is internal, but expressing words is an act. Values and attitudes are internal states, about which people can and do make statements. The statements may be opinions or descriptions of feelings. But the statements are not the attitudes. Stating an opinion is a behavior that reflects one or more elements of an attitude.

ATTITUDES AND VALUES INVOLVE BOTH FEELINGS AND IDEAS   Interacting ideas and feelings create a tendency toward behavior. Just as attitudes aren't opinions, they aren't emotions either. We define **emotion** as *an aroused physiological and psychological response to a stimulus.* In this sense, emotions, like opinions, are behavior—although they are not as easily observed as many behaviors. The emotion may come from the idea, as when you get angry because you believe someone insults you. The reverse may also be true. When we are feeling depressed or blue, we often try to find reasons to explain why. Of course, positive feelings also relate to ideas. We are joyful when we believe someone we love returns our love or wants to be with us.

ATTITUDES AND VALUES VARY IN STRENGTH AND SPECIFICITY   A person can be moderately or very favorable toward someone else. You can like someone a little or a lot. The stronger the intensity, the more likely behavior will result from an attitude. If you love your mother a lot, you'd react to an insult to her much more strongly than if you barely knew her. The strength of an attitude also influences how difficult it might be to change it.

Some attitudes are quite specific—the one that leads you to refuse liver when it's served, for example. Others are more general, such as liking to dance or loving music. The degree to which attitudes and values actually influence behavior depends on how intense and specific they are. It also depends on the situation. Since situations differ, one's behavior tendency and actual behavior will not always be the same. Take the case of musicians who are generally negative toward rock music. They wouldn't usually attend rock concerts. But they might go if a group of friends were having an afternoon beach party and heard about a festival nearby.

Attitudes and Values Organize Concepts   The attitude and value system is an internal mental structure. It could be compared to the steel framework of a high-rise building. It grows with experience. Once in place, it affects where and how all other materials and parts of experience fit into a meaningful whole.

As a steel framework holds a building together, the framework our attitudes and values provide helps humans make sense of the world. This attitude system influences how we perceive, interpret, and respond to messages. It can cause us

---

[1] You may know that sometimes the word *behavior* is used in other ways. Some people do not consider stating an opinion to be behavior. Others consider behavior more broadly to include physiological factors not overtly observable, such as heart rate, glandular secretions, etc. The latter, while technically accurate, doesn't provide for the external-internal distinction we find useful in analyzing communicative behavior.

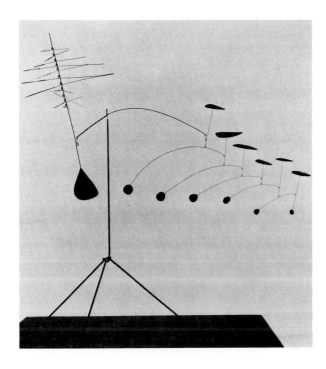

Attitude and value systems function in an interlocking and interactive manner.

to reject certain information, influence what we remember and how we recall what we have stored. This valuing and organizing aspect of attitudes is one of the strongest influences in communication.

Attitudes and values interact, interlock, and affect each other. Perhaps that's obvious. But remember, this internal evaluative system is not a consistent, rational system. The comparison of the attitude system to the structural framework of a building is based on functions not form. The form of the human attitude system is more like a large house that began as a one-room cabin. As the family grew in size and wealth, they added bedrooms to the cabin, then a garage and a family room. Still later, a formal dining and living room were added, then a den and more bedrooms. The house grew according to the family's experience. So it is with attitudes and values. They develop as we have experiences, and life doesn't occur in an organized, preplanned way. Thus, attitude systems are not rationally organized.

Life experiences are almost random, so our learned evaluative responses to those experiences will have a similar pattern. A mobile may usefully illustrate. Like the mobile, each part of the attitude system relates in some way to each other part, even though there is no consistency or similarity among the parts. Thus, each part that is moved or changed affects all other parts.

We include the discussion of attitudes and values in this chapter because of the effects of self-concept in communication. If you know that attitudes are internal states based on ideas and feelings that influence behavior more or less strongly, and that self-concept includes attitudes toward self, you can easily see how important self-concept is in understanding how to communicate more effectively. If you can see that you value different aspects of yourself with varying degrees of intensity, whether positively or negatively, you can see how your responses might be affected when those aspects of self are involved in the interactions.

You may have quite positive attitudes toward some specific ability—say being able to cook or catch a baseball—so you'll laugh at or ignore someone who comments negatively about that ability. In this case, your positive self-concept keeps a potentially negative communication situation from developing. But a person can be positive about something specific, such as athletic ability, while the general attitude toward self is negative. People who can say, "I like myself," and really mean it can probably communicate well with others in most situations. Those who cannot say they like themselves (and many cannot) usually have problems in communicating. Negative attitudes toward self strongly affect how we interact with others, a point we discuss more fully in later chapters. To see how this effect occurs, we now examine how self-concept develops, and later we discuss specific influences of self-concept upon communication.

DEVELOPMENT OF SELF-CONCEPT

As children grow, they develop attitudes toward the being they call "me." Throughout life, as they communicate with the people and environment around them, this concept of self grows and changes. Because the early years of childhood set the foundation for the lifelong development of self-concept, we should understand those early years.

Awareness of Self

In the early months of life, infants seem to have little understanding of their own bodies. Then they begin gripping, pulling, and tasting. Gradually they learn to reach for, grab, and hold objects and to put them into their mouths. Slowly they develop self-awareness. They learn to recognize the distinction between self and not-self, between their bodies and the rest of their environment.

Self-awareness occurs as children learn to distinguish between sensations and the conditions that produce them. Only gradually do children learn to recognize body parts, name, feelings, and behaviors as parts of a single self. Slowly, they begin to understand the meaning of "me."

As their experience broadens, children learn to include things aside from self in their sense of personhood. They learn to distinguish "mine" from "not-mine" much as they learned to distinguish self from not-self. During this time, they also acquire language, which in turn becomes an important factor in development of self-concept. Children learn that a name identifies the self. They also learn the pronouns *mine, me, I, you,* and learn to associate the words with the concepts. "My" comes to include such things as home, possessions, groups belonged to, values held, and people. Children who identify parents or brothers and sisters are extending their sense of self. Likewise, they identify pets, toys, and other possessions as theirs. This process of identification is the basis for expansion of the concept of self.

Awareness of Others and Roles

Imitating Models   When growing children mature enough to recognize differences among people, what do they do? At first, they simply imitate models. They see people around them do certain things and copy what they see. One of us, for instance, habitually leans forward from the waist when laughing. She was never aware of this habit until she noticed a two-year-old niece leaning over peculiarly several times during a family gathering. No one could determine what the child was doing until finally we realized she was imitating her aunt's laughing. She was **modeling**—*observing her environment and imitating the behaviors around her.*

Children learn that certain behaviors are associated with certain people. They see behaviors, and they play by repeating the behaviors. In this modeling, children don't really understand why or what they are doing. They just see that some kinds of behaviors are identified with some people, like Mommy and Daddy, and they copy those behaviors.

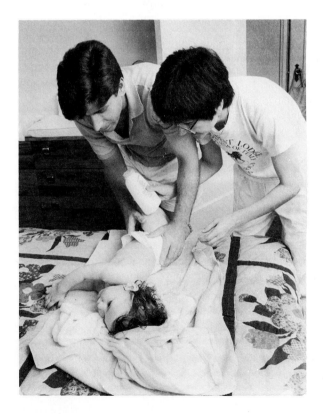

Self-awareness begins to develop early in infancy.

The experiences of early childhood are important in the development of self-concept.

Some things children learn from models become essential parts of self—for example, learning language. Children imitate the language patterns and sounds of people they are around during the years of language development. A child growing up in Alabama imitates a totally different dialect model from a child in Brooklyn. The accent is learned by copying. Yet later in life, the Southern or Brooklyn accent becomes an essential characteristic of the personality. Speech therapists often find that youngsters who stutter have a parent who stutters. The children have simply copied the parent's speech pattern.

Role Playing Gradually, children learn to associate the behaviors they've connected to Mommy with more than the person Mommy. They learn that the behaviors have a reason. They learn to interpret the behaviors as related to a role, that of mother.[2] Children meet other people called mothers and learn that other children have mothers different from their own. The concept of a mother role is learned. At this point, children can role play. At first, **role playing** involves only an understanding that the behaviors are associated with the role. It is *acting out the observed behavior related to the role*, but it doesn't require understanding of the role itself.

A child can role play a police officer simply by having observed a police officer. He or she only needs to have seen that person do certain things: direct traffic, drive a police car, arrest people, wear a special uniform, and so on. But this role playing doesn't include really understanding what the role involves. Maintaining

[2] The concept of *role* may be new to you. We use the term to refer to the set of behaviors expected of a person in specific social positions. Roles, therefore, vary from one social group to another and, of course, each person occupies many roles. You, for instance, are a son or daughter, student, friend, perhaps a brother or sister, employee or boss, and so on. In each social position, the role (behaviors expected) differs somewhat.

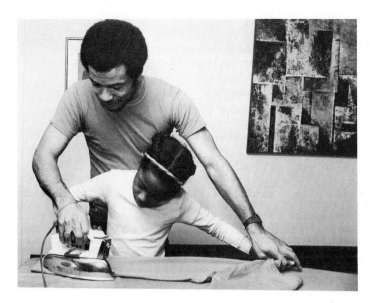

Children learn appropriate role behavior from significant people in their lives.

order or enforcing justice wouldn't be meaningful role behavior to the child. At this point, children don't anticipate events related to the role concepts or formulate responses different from the behaviors they've observed.

As children mature, role playing involves greater understanding. They learn concepts associated with behaviors; in other words, they learn reasons for behaviors associated with roles. When they "play" roles, they can anticipate events and behave according to their own understanding of how the concepts should affect the behavior. After a certain stage of maturity, for instance, children can role play a police officer without just copying behaviors. They can apply their own concept of justice to their play as officer.

Developing Self-Identification

Role Taking   Growing children soon begin to identify with roles. We describe this as **role taking**—*internalizing of role-related behaviors and motivations.*[3] It is more than just repeating or assuming a role interpretation. It involves self-identification with the behaviors. When children who have reached this stage of development say, "I am a Free Methodist," they do more than understand the behaviors that identify someone as a Free Methodist. A child who could explain why one religion differs from others in respect to drinking beer, taking communion, and being baptized, could role play the various religions. But youngsters who believe that they sin by

---

[3] Sometimes the term *role taking* is applied to the mature concept of role playing discussed in the preceding section. We do not use that definition. To us, the important distinction is that in role playing one *assumes* certain behaviors and motivations as explanations for behaviors. In role taking, these behaviors and motivations have become internalized; we identify them as important aspects of ourselves.

drinking liquor have taken a role. They have identified with the values, beliefs, and behaviors associated with the role.

Internalized roles become facets of self-concept, especially if the role is perceived as important. The importance of roles varies as people identify more or less strongly with them. Two youngsters might be raised to take both the role of Baptist and of football player. For one, the role of Baptist might be the most important influence in life, the role of football player only a way to a college education. The other person might think of the role of Baptist as incidental and identify self primarily by the role of football player. The first might work to become a missionary, the other a Dallas Cowboy, and the two would live very different lives.

GENDER Internalized roles as part of self-concept affect communication in significant ways. Among the roles most people identify as valued aspects of self are **gender roles**. These are the *expectations for the behavior of men and women (and boys and girls) based on the person's sex.* Gender expectations involve a complex of behaviors seen as feminine or masculine and thought to be differently appropriate for each sex. Girls, for example, are expected to behave in ways that are thought of as feminine (be soft-spoken, pretty, and intuitive, for example); boys are expected to be masculine (strong, athletic, rational).

Gender perceptions strongly affect how we see ourselves, how others see us, what communication behaviors others expect of us, and what we expect of ourselves. For many people, an important element of self-concept is whether they are masculine or feminine. Such people define maleness or femaleness by the behaviors identified as masculine or feminine. When a boy growing up in such an environment is not perceived as demonstrating appropriate masculine behaviors or, worse, is perceived as feminine, he will be subject to intense pressure to behave differently. A similar, though probably less strong, norm to behave in a feminine way will be applied to girls. These pressures result in gender roles becoming important facets of self-concept for many people.

CULTURE These factors and others that affect the development of self-concept are part of our culture, one of the most important influences on how we communicate. Regardless of their culture, all humans develop a sense of self, but what that self-concept includes—the values, attitudes, and beliefs that shape our sense of what behavior is appropriate—depends heavily on the culture in which we grow up.

As we noted earlier, a major part of self-concept is evaluative, giving us a sense of what is "right" or "wrong" in particular situations. We have discussed how that sense develops through the interaction of an individual with other individuals—parents, family members, friends, teachers, acquaintances. It's important to remember, however, that each individual interaction takes place within a social context and is part of a larger web of interlocking belief and behavior systems. Thus, each individual develops a sense of self within and influenced by that larger context. No individual or role is usefully considered separate from its cultural context.

In one sense the interaction between individual and culture is much like that between awareness of one's own behaviors and the generalized concept of how others see us (to be discussed shortly). Culture does not imprint a concept of

Adult role playing involves more than modelling.

self upon people; it does not *determine* our beliefs or values or behavior. It does strongly influence us, however, because each of us develops our own set of beliefs and values only through interaction with the broader cultural system. Indeed, one measure of the extent to which we "belong" to a culture is the degree to which we share the beliefs, values, and behaviors of the culture.

All of this may seem self-evident to you, but that is exactly our reason for pointing out the influence of culture. Our culture is so pervasive and so "obvious" to us that we rarely notice its influence. Because we have unconsciously learned how to perceive things and to value and to think about them as we do, the influence of our culture in that learning remains largely invisible. We internalize the value and belief system of our culture, unaware that we learned it. We develop a set of values, beliefs, and behaviors that seem so "natural" that we think them inherent to being human.

We noted the importance of culture in Chapter 1 when we discussed the impact of perceptual variability in communication. We'll revisit this concept—that an awareness of culture is important to improving communication—several times throughout the book.

Others Provide the Looking Glass Development of a sense of self doesn't happen to children simply by association. Other people are the major way children

Significant others help shape self-concept.

gain images of themselves. Interactions with others provide the "looking glass" by which they learn to interpret themselves. For example, parents who repeatedly reward their children for reading, and who often repeat how good they are at it, lead the youngsters to think of themselves as good readers. Growing children learn to "see" themselves through the responses of others.

SIGNIFICANT OTHERS   *Persons whose attitudes toward us strongly influence our own thoughts and feelings about ourselves* are described as **significant others**.[4] Early in life these persons are parents or people who play the parent role and others who live in the home. Later, friends, relatives, teachers, priests, ministers, or employers may become significant others.

Children actively seek rewards and acceptance from their significant others. You've surely heard children say repeatedly, "See what I did, Mommy," or "Daddy, watch! Watch me." Efforts to gain rewards from significant others do not stop with childhood. As we mature, we become less concerned about rejections or criticisms by those who are not important, but all of us seek reinforcement from those who are important to us.

THE GENERALIZED OTHER   As infants mature, they realize that parents, sisters, and brothers aren't the only people in their lives. Growing children also seek interpretations of self from persons other than family and close peers. In this process, they internalize attitudes from casual friends, teachers, and distant relatives as well as from the significant others. They develop general attitudes of what other people

[4] Original development of this concept was by George Herbert Mead in *Mind, Self, and Society* (Chicago: University of Chicago Press, 1934).

think about them. These attitudes create a composite evaluation derived from the **generalized other**. The generalized other is defined as *the composite view you have of others' views of you*.

Take, for example, a student named Lari. The following are others' typical views about Lari.

Mother: Lari, I'm really disappointed in your schoolwork. I know you can do better.
Boyfriend: Hey, you sure goofed up that English exam. I thought you studied for it!
Principal: Lari, you've got to pull your grades up. You've really done very badly this year, and I know you can do better.
Neighbor: Hey, Lari, what's this I hear about you maybe flunking out of school? Surely that's not true.
Buddy: You've got to do something about your grades! We can't afford to lose you from the basketball team.

Many sources—tests, teachers, friends, and parents—tell Lari she hasn't done as well as expected. All their interpretations are reflected in Lari's conclusion, "I'm not a very good student." This conclusion is not a simple description of self. It reflects Lari's perceptions of the attitudes of many others, both significant and not. It is a composite evaluation, the generalized other.

THE LOOKING GLASS   In some ways, the generalized other is like a looking glass. People cannot see themselves directly, so they use other people as mirrors. But self-concept is not merely a mirror reflection of others' views. Just as children pick and choose among possessions, they select among the images of self offered by others.

As people mature, they learn to evaluate their own behavior in terms of its consequences. Part of those consequences are rewards from other people, to be sure. But other consequences are measured by results. Each of us evaluates the effects of what we do or say, no matter what others say about it. This happens especially because others' reactions are seldom the same. In reaction to our behavior, it is common for one person to say, "That was a dumb thing to do!" while another remarks, "That was terrific!" In these cases, we decide which opinion to accept and which to reject. We do not always agree with or accept the evaluations of others.

As growing persons looking into the mirror presented by others, we do more than accept or reject images we see. We magnify or reduce parts of the images. We interpret them. Thus, our perceptions and attitudes are more than responses to what happens. They also result from how we interpret and feel about what happens.

Ability to reject or modify images in the mirror of others' views varies according to the stages of a person's development. The less mature a person is, the less stable is the concept of self and the more subject it is to influence. That's why the reactions of significant others at early stages of life have such long-lasting effects on self-concept. If those interactions result in positive reinforcement, children develop positive views of self. But if children are abused, neglected, or constantly criticized, or if they have negative experiences they interpret as their own fault, they can develop strong negative views of self. These attitudes may be so deep and strong that they affect communicative behavior throughout life.

Face Making Having reached a certain stage of development, we go beyond reacting to others' interpretations. We begin trying to affect others' interpretations. If, for example, you want to be thought of as a certain type of person, you'll behave as you believe that type of person does, even if the image is not an accurate reflection of how you see your "actual" self. This is behaving strategically to influence how others perceive you. *Constructing images presented to others* is described as **face making** or **masking**.[5]

A medical doctor, for instance, attempts to project an image of being considerate, concerned, knowledgeable and trustworthy. In some cases, a doctor may really not care about the individual patient or know what the diagnosis ought to be. But a doctor learns not to project an uncaring, unsure image. A doctor who isn't sure of a diagnosis knows that fear and anxiety could harm recovery if the patient perceives the doctor's uncertainty. The doctor will try to project a "face" or "mask" of competence and knowledge to reduce the anxiety.

Many daily interactions seem to require masking strategies. Salespersons must appear interested in the customer even if they aren't; parents try to behave supportively toward children even when they don't feel like it; you act respectfully toward your boss even if you don't feel respectful. Face making seems necessary in many roles of life, but we don't recommend it as a dominant strategy in interpersonal behavior.

Still, understanding the development of self-concept requires awareness of how strategic presentation of self influences the process. After repeated face making, people may come to believe the masks they've been putting on. After a particular image of self has been projected for a long time, it may no longer be just masking or role playing. The image becomes identified with self. Strategic presentation of self may become irretrievably mixed with other beliefs about self. When that happens, the mask is as much a part of self-concept as the physical self or any other facet of self.

Lifelong Development

Self-concept is not static. It changes with life experiences. Changes may seem to be fewer after adolescence, but they continue throughout life and are often quite dramatic in later years. Changes in education, occupation, life style, health, or social environment can set forces in motion that radically change our views of self. Reaching thirty, forty, or fifty; being forced into retirement; losing a job, a long-time mate, close friends, or relatives can cause us to see ourselves in new ways. As a result, events like these may change our entire view of life.

[5] This concept of face making is developed thoroughly in the work of Erving Goffman. See especially *Encounters* (New York: Bobbs Merrill, 1961) and *The Presentation of Self in Everyday Life* (Garden City, NY: Doubleday Anchor Books, 1959) for his discussion of masking.

We all know persons who illustrate this: a housewife who returns to school at thirty-five and blossoms by learning she can compete successfully with twenty-year-olds; a man who tackles a new career at forty; a widow who successfully takes over and manages the business her husband had run before his death; the couple who sell all their worldly possessions and move to a small farm in the mountains. Many changes, of course, are less obvious. But self-concept is a dynamic dimension that constantly changes. Lewis Carroll's tale of Alice in Wonderland captures this interaction between self-concept and experience:

> The Caterpillar and Alice looked at each other for some time in silence; at last the Caterpillar took the hookah out of its mouth, and addressed her in a languid, sleepy voice.
> "Who are you?" said the Caterpillar.
> This was not an encouraging opening for a conversation. Alice replied, rather shyly, "I—I hardly know, Sir, just at present—at least I know who I was when I got up this morning, but I think I must have been changed several times since then."[6]

Not long ago the book *Passages* became a best seller. Using a case-study approach, the book illustrated what other studies in human development have demonstrated: Significant changes in our view of self occur simply as a consequence of the stages of life through which we pass. Part of the continuing popularity of *Passages* derives from readers' sense of self-confirmation when they learn that others, too, must adjust their sense of self to the major physical and psychological events of life.[7] The list of readings at the end of this chapter includes studies in the lifelong development of self-concept that you may wish to examine.

[6] Lewis Carroll, "Advice from a Caterpillar," *Alice's Adventures in Wonderland* (New York: Grosset and Dunlap, 1972).

[7] Gail Sheehy, *Passages: Predictable Crises of Adult Life* (New York: Dutton, 1976).

EXERCISE 2.1   YOUR MANY SELVES (AN INTRAPERSONAL COMMUNICATION EXERCISE)

OBJECTIVE   To become aware of some aspects of your many selves

DIRECTIONS
1. Self concept can be compared to a many-faceted diamond. Each facet contributes to the brilliance of the stone, but each is separate. In this exercise, you will examine some of the facets of your self. Begin by completing, on a separate page, the statements below. Complete each statement as openly and honestly as you can. *Note that how you complete the items is quite personal. You will need to share these responses with no one unless you wish to do so.*
2. Retain these answers; you may use them in a later exercise.
3. Prepare for class discussion (or writing assignment) of this topic by answering the following questions:
    a. How can awareness of the many facets of self-concept help you improve your ability to communicate?

b. What was the most important communication principle illustrated by or learned from this exercise?

Thoughts and Attitudes

I believe that
1. Religion is . . .
2. Religion should be . . .
3. Politics is . . .
4. Politics should be . . .
5. Women are . . .
6. Women should be . . .
7. Men are . . .
8. Men should be . . .
9. I am . . .
10. I should be . . .
11. I want to be . . .
12. My wife/husband is . . .
13. My wife/husband should be . . .
14. My girl/boyfriend is . . .
15. My girl/boyfriend should be . . .

Feelings

1. I am happy when I . . .
2. I am sad when I . . .
3. Next Saturday night I want to . . .
4. Five years from now I want to . . .
5. I am happy when my wife/ husband . . .
6. I am happy when my parents/ children . . .
7. I am happy when my boy/ girlfriend . . .
8. I am sad when my wife/ husband . . .
9. I am sad when my parents/ children . . .
10. I am sad when my girl/ boyfriend . . .

Perceptions of Physical Aspects

1. I am attractive/handsome when . . .
2. My . . . is attractive/handsome.
3. My . . . is ugly.
4. My . . . is sexy.
5. I am ashamed of my . . .
6. I am proud of my . . .
7. I am unattractive when . . .
8. If I were a movie star, I could play the kind of roles that . . . does.
9. I look terrible in . . .
10. If I would change my looks, I would . . .
11. I wish my voice were . . .
12. The worst thing about my voice is . . .
13. The best thing about my voice is . . .
14. If I could change my voice it would sound like . . .
15. If I could change my walk I would walk like . . ..

Values

1. I am good at . . .
2. I have trouble with . . .
3. I love . . .
4. I like . . .
5. . . . should be destroyed.
6. . . . are the most important things in life.
7. I want . . .
8. People are . . .

COMMUNICATION AND SELF-CONCEPT

Self-concept is the most important variable in communication. It develops through communication experiences and in turn strongly influences how we talk and act. Self-concept is a major factor in determining our ability to develop and maintain long-term interpersonal relationships. Below we discuss five ways self-concept influences communication: the Pygmalion effect; the self-fulfilling prophecy; selectivity in attention, exposure, perception, and retention; the tendency toward open or closed communication; and the degree of self-confidence.

The Pygmalion Effect

As we have seen, self-concept develops, in part, through others' appraisals of us and the social positions we hold. When we behave or believe as significant people expect us to, we receive reinforcing feedback. Then the effect spirals. Reinforcement leads to repeated behavior, which is again reinforced, and so on. This is called the **Pygmalion effect**.[8] The term comes from the Greek myth in which Pygmalion fell in love with a statue of a beautiful woman and the statue came to life. Most people are familiar with the modern version of the myth—the musical "My Fair Lady." In this play, Professor Higgins sees that Eliza Doolittle can become more than a common flower girl; she responds to his expectations with behaviors that Higgins, his mother, and Colonel Pickering reinforce. In the process, she changes from a street urchin to a lady of social grace and charm.

We recall a student a few years ago who was elected to chair a group of students for a class project. This student appeared to be a shy, quiet person, but he did a remarkable job of leading the group. After the assignment was completed, the instructor complimented the young man. He responded, "You know, I was scared to death. I didn't think I could do it. But then I got to thinking about it and figured that if they thought I could be a leader, I'd *act* like a leader, even if I had to fake it. I took charge like I had all the confidence in the world, a real snow job. Then a strange thing happened. The others in the group began to treat me as if I really *was* [sic] confident. They seemed to expect me to have the answers. Pretty soon I didn't know which was the fake me and which was the real me."

Both Eliza Doolittle and this student illustrate an important point about self-concept: *Others' expectations* influence our behavior toward them, *and our behavior influences our self-concept.* These expectations exert a major influence on interpersonal communication. The strongest results of the Pygmalion effect may be from interactions with significant others, but it is not limited to these. The effect is so powerful that social scientists have learned it can affect results in experiments. What the experimenter expects to happen has been shown to influence the outcome of the experiment. Similarly, what teachers expect students to do influences the students' performances on tests. Indeed, the Pygmalion effect can be present in

---

[8] A clear discussion of the Pygmalion effect is presented in Robert Rosenthal, "The Pygmalion Effect Lives," *Psychology Today* (September 1973), pp. 56–63.

cathy®   by Cathy Guisewite

("Cathy" by Cathy Guisewite. Copyright 1986 Universal Press Syndicate. Reprinted by permission. All rights reserved.)

both trivial and important situations, in interactions among people with both significant and seemingly insignificant relationships. *We all tend to communicate and behave as we think others expect us to*—in other words, to display the Pygmalion effect.

The Self-Fulfilling Prophecy

Conscious awareness of self makes the Pygmalion effect more than a matter of simple reinforcement. Each of us interprets our own experiences, attaching personal meaning to them. These personal meanings create self-expectations, which in turn influence our behavior. *We all tend to behave as we expect ourselves to behave.* This effect of self-concept is described as the **self-fulfilling prophecy**.

Do you see yourself as a good student? Then you probably study diligently, attend class regularly, and participate actively. As a result, you fulfill your own prophecy: You get good grades. Do you think of yourself as a poor student? Then you may cut classes, not do the assignments on time or well, seldom speak up in class—and do poorly in school. Do you see yourself as attractive? Then you probably spend a lot of time getting dressed each day, styling your hair, choosing the right combinations of clothes. Do you see yourself as friendly, outgoing? Then you are probably quick to make new friends and often start conversations with others. All these cases illustrate that we tend to behave in ways that confirm our expectations. We create prophecies and then fulfill them.

The self-fulfilling prophecy may be what causes the Pygmalion effect. It may be that others' expectations of us affect how we talk and act largely because they influence our own expectations of ourselves. Most likely two separate but interacting effects exist. First, we behave in certain ways because we respond directly to rewards received when we fulfill others' expectations. Second, other people influence what we see ourselves as capable of doing and what we expect of ourselves.

A student of communication should understand that both effects influence how we communicate. We tend to talk with people as they expect us to *and* as we expect ourselves to. Either way, *expectations strongly affect what we say, when we say it, how we say it, and to whom we are willing to talk.*

Selectivity

Another way self-concept influences communication is that our view of self *influences what messages we expose ourselves to, how we perceive them, and what we remember.* Self-concept is the filter on the lens through which we see the world. How we interact with others depends on what passes through the filter of self-concept.

Selective Exposure, Attention, and Perception   Do you see yourself as friendly, easy to get along with, and fun in social situations? Then you will perceive a party as an event to be enjoyed and go to parties often. But if you believe yourself to be shy, not good at conversation, and socially awkward, you'll perceive that party as an event to be avoided if possible. You'll try not to go and perceive it as painful if you must go. Self-concept determines what situations you expose yourself to, and what communications you pay attention to.

If you think of yourself as athletic, you probably watch games, participate, and pay attention to sports news. You discuss players and games with like-minded friends, and you remember facts about players and teams. On the other hand, if you don't like sports, you may see games as endless, boring bits of nonsense. When people talk sports, you tune out; you skip the sports section of the paper and turn to something that interests you more. You screen out some messages and admit others based on self-concept. These are all effects that result from selective exposure, attention, and perception.

Selective Retention   We not only tend to expose ourselves to events and people we see as matching or appropriate to our self-image; we also remember most readily those things that fit. *We retain things according to how they affect us or relate to our self-concept.* We all know people who seem to remember everything about a particular sport. They can recall specific plays in specific games from years ago, along with statistics, players' first, last, and middle names, and many other details. In contrast, another person remembers nothing about sports events but idolizes Elvis Presley. This person will know all his songs, recall every movie Elvis ever made, the name of each character he played, and each gold and platinum album. Because self-concept affects our beliefs about what is important, it strongly affects what we remember and how we recall it.

Self-concept influences the people we choose to talk to, what we talk about, what we decide to listen to, and what we remember. It is probably the major cause of **selectivity in exposure, attention, perception, and retention** of communication.

Openness and Self-Confidence

Self-concept also affects how we relate to others. It may cause us to be open and honest with others or to be quite guarded in our interactions. This effect relates to the idea noted earlier, that self-concept includes both specific and general attitudes toward self. If we don't like something about ourselves, it will affect our willingness to talk about it.

If we have a generally negative attitude toward ourselves, it can have many different influences on our communication. We may be generally negative about almost everything because our self-concept filter causes us to perceive incoming messages negatively. A negative attitude will interfere with our ability to develop and maintain long-term interpersonal relationships. It could cause us to be especially critical—to always be down on ourselves. We might constantly compare ourselves to others, always finding the others better. This can make us too quick to accept the opinions of others and cause us to devalue our own ideas and feelings. We may hesitate to speak up when we disagree with others or be unsure and insecure about the validity of our own reactions. We may hesitate to talk about ourselves or our opinions.

Positive effects in communication usually result from generally positive attitudes toward self. We are most likely to be open and honest with others if we like ourselves. We will have less to hide from them. We will be less insecure and less threatened by others. Positive attitudes toward self contribute to improved interpersonal communication because they decrease defensiveness and thus improve our ability to interact effectively with others. Positive attitudes toward self are essential if we are to develop and maintain long-term interpersonal relationships. In Chapter 7 we return to this important subject: how to use openness to improve interpersonal communication. The ability to do that is closely related to self-concept.

Self-Esteem   The great American philosopher Ralph Waldo Emerson said, "Self-trust is the first secret of success." He was referring to one important effect of self-concept in our communication. How we see ourselves is a major factor in the confidence with which we approach communication situations. Most people with a positive self-concept will experience little communication anxiety; they will have little difficulty talking with people in most situations. Even in unfamiliar situations, they will be able to overcome the natural uneasiness.

People without positive attitudes toward self often have little self-esteem and lack self-confidence. They feel uncomfortable on many occasions. They are often unable to cope effectively with important or unfamiliar situations. Some find any communication situation a source of great anxiety. Depending on the degree of anxiety, they may have reactions that range from nervousness to nausea. Some choose to cope by avoiding situations. They never give speeches, ask favors, or willingly talk to the boss. They may even cross the street to avoid meeting someone with whom they'd feel obligated to talk.

Ability to Deal with Fear   Low self-esteem certainly isn't the only factor related to nervousness or speech anxiety. Many factors cause anxiety when communicators face unfamiliar or important situations, including aspects of the situation. To understand the relationships between communication anxiety and self-concept, it helps to understand that to have self-confidence does not mean to be totally without communication anxiety. We have all had times when we felt we couldn't handle a situation. Who hasn't experienced the sweaty palms and short breath that come when we have to stand up and talk at a meeting, or go to a job interview, or have a conference with the boss?

The term **self-confidence** refers to *the ability of individuals to predict with fair accuracy that they can do what needs to be done to eliminate any potential harmful results of a situation.* This doesn't mean people do not have fear. It means they believe they can cope with fear-producing situations.

FEAR EXPLAINED   Think about the following a minute.

1. Fear is bad and undesirable.
2. Fear is a sign of weakness or inferiority.
3. Brave people do not have fear; only cowards are afraid.
4. Self-confidence eliminates fear.

Do you agree with these statements? If so, you're not unusual. These are common *misconceptions* about fear, and these mistaken beliefs reduce the ability of many people to cope with communication anxiety. Too few people understand the nature of fear or how to deal with it.

Fear is *a biological process through which a person develops adequate energy to do important tasks.* Fear is a normal condition in many situations. And fear, it should be recognized, does not result only from threats to physical well-being; it also results from threats to psychological well-being.

Fear *energizes* an organism, whether it is a human being or another animal. If a deer, for instance, smells a mountain lion, fear prepares the animal for self-protection. Instinct says, "Move—move quickly." But running at full speed requires a great deal of energy. So fear calls on body nerves, muscles, and chemicals needed to move rapidly. Thus, fear is useful. You've heard of cases in which a person lifted an automobile to rescue someone trapped underneath or bent iron bars on a window to escape a burning building. Fear was what called up an extra supply of adrenalin and created the extra energy.

When people face a communication situation they fear, it energizes their body in the same manner. Their hearts beat faster; their hands get sweaty (often a cold sweat); they have trouble breathing; their mouths get dry; they get butterflies or cramps in the stomach. These all result from the same physical process that allows the deer to run away from the mountain lion or a human to lift an auto off an injured friend. It's a natural reaction.

COPING WITH FEAR   Knowing that fear is a natural physical and psychological reaction can help you learn to cope with it. Several other steps are possible, once you understand fear and its effects. The following case illustrates them.

A professor asked a student, Aaron, to see her after class. Immediately Aaron thought, "No one else has been asked to stay. What have I done?" His heart started pounding, and his face felt flushed. His hands got sweaty, and he had butterflies in his stomach. Nervously, he waited after the class. The professor asked if he would participate in a panel discussion before the local Junior Chamber of Commerce. She offered credit for doing it. Aaron's butterflies got worse. His heart pounded so loudly he was sure she would hear it instead of the strange, tense voice that stammered, "I-I can't. I-I have a part-time job, and I have to work every evening."

After leaving the classroom, Aaron felt terrible. What was the matter with him? The teacher must have thought he was really dumb not to accept the opportunity for extra credit. The worst thing was that he didn't even have a job! Aaron had let fear drive him away from receiving extra credit because he lacked the self-confidence to predict he could do well enough to avoid failure.

When Margo was faced with the identical situation, she behaved differently. True, her first reaction was also anxiety. However, when she thought about it, she decided she knew the subject well enough, and besides, there'd be that extra credit. She concluded, "I'm sure I can do it so I won't embarrass myself or anyone else. In fact, I'll bet I can do a pretty good job!"

As the time for the discussion got closer, she got butterflies again, especially when working on the assignment. But at the Jaycee meeting, Margo was "up" for the event. Her heart was pounding, she was anxious; her hands were sweaty. But she knew what was happening, so the fear didn't grow, feeding on itself. Margo had confidence that she would perform adequately. Before the discussion started, she moved around to use up some of the extra energy. At first her hands shook a little, but as soon as she got started that stopped. Her energy helped as she talked and listened to the others. It made her sound enthusiastic and interested, and improved her reaction time in responding to questions and ideas raised by others.

The differences are obvious. Both students had fear. Margo, however, had self-confidence, which helped her feel she could prepare and perform adequately. She predicted in advance that she could cope with the situation and get positive results. She knew that the physical effects of fear could be controlled. She recognized the fear as natural, and did what we all can learn to do: used that energy to prepare for the situation. She planned for the task, planned some physical activity right before speaking, and welcomed the extra energy to help her do the job well.

Margo's attitude itself helped reduce the harmful effects of excessive fear. By understanding the physical effects of fear, she didn't let them create more fear. She prevented the effects of fear from growing into a vicious spiral. In addition, by doing the job instead of running away, she confirmed her ability to predict accurately that the results would not be harmful. Thus, she increased her self-confidence for handling similar situations in the future.

Accepting and completing communication tasks that cause anxiety for you can improve your ability to cope with them. Each successful communication makes further successes more probable. Using your knowledge of self-concept and fear, you can accept fear for what it is: natural and useful. You can then channel it to your benefit, instead of using it to run away or letting it feed on itself and grow to unmanageable proportions. Repeated successes in dealing with speech anxiety can increase your positive attitudes toward yourself. As a result, you'll gain many other benefits of improved self-esteem.

Physiological Signs of Fear

Increased pulse rate
Increased perspiration
Dry mouth
Shaking hands and knees
Shortness of breath
Nervous stomach

Coping with Fear Symptoms

Analyze the situation.
  How serious are the consequences?
  Can I handle the job?
Recognize fear as natural.
  Don't let effects spiral.
Prepare adequately.
Visualize positive results.
Plan physical movement (such as walking or using visual aids) to use up excess energy.

EXERCISE 2.2   SELF-CONCEPT AND COMMUNICATION

OBJECTIVE   **To increase awareness of how your self-concept affects your communication.**

DIRECTIONS

1. Identify four beliefs you hold strongly, one in each of the following areas:
   a. Marriage
   b. Religion
   c. The "older generation"
   d. Your ability to succeed at work and in interpersonal relationships.
2. In brief statements, write your beliefs as stated in items 1a, 1b, 1c and 1d.
3. Review your responses to Exercise 2.1 and list the facets of self you believe to be related to the strong beliefs stated above.
4. Find a picture of yourself taken ten years ago. Think about answers to these same questions for the person in the picture.
5. Visualize yourself ten years from now. What likely differences in the answers will there be then?
6. This is the most difficult, and most useful, part of the exercise. Identify, as accurately as you can, the reasons you made each specific connection between the items in Exercise 2.1 and your statements. Your instructor may assign you to groups of 2 to 4 persons to discuss this item.
7. When you are talking about topics with friends or family, in the areas named in item 1, how does your self-concept affect your communication? How does it affect how well you listen? How well you understand? How you express yourself?
8. What aspects of your self-concept would you like to change? How would those changes affect your communication?
9. List the principles of communication this experience illustrates.
10. Write an answer to the following question. You will be asked to turn it in as a writing assignment or use it as the basis for class discussion.
    a. Using your responses to Exercises 2.1 and 2.2, examine how your concept of self contributes to strengthening your communication and identify those aspects of your self-concept that interfere with effective communication.

SUMMARY

Self-concept, one of the most important variables in the communication process, is the total complex of beliefs and attitudes you have about yourself. Attitude is defined as a predisposition to respond in a particular way to stimuli. Some aspects of attitudes are worth noting: They are interrelated internal states; and they involve both feelings and ideas, which vary in intensity and specificity. These feelings and ideas organize concepts and influence behavior. Attitudes toward self are important in how people perceive others, events, and themselves in relation to the outside world.

Self-concept develops through a person's communication experiences. Beginning in infancy, one first develops an awareness that self is distinguished from the rest of the world, and this awareness grows to an identification with objects and events in the environment. Feelings of self-worth, of what and who one is, develop as the child matures. A child acquires an ability to identify self with various roles in life, first through modeling those around, then through role playing, and finally, when he or she realizes what the role is supposed to be, a child becomes able to take roles. This process of role taking strongly identifies cultural and gender roles with one's sense of self. Children acquire much of their understanding of their selves and abilities through the reactions of significant others to them. Later they acquire a concept of the generalized other—a composite of others' views of them. Sometimes children (and adults) create faces or masks, projecting an image to the outside world that may not be consistent with what they perceive themselves to be. Such masking behavior sometimes becomes part of the concept of self, and the individual fulfills the prophecy of the image. After adolescence, most people's concept of self stabilizes, though it is constantly subject to change with new experiences, especially when major changes in life occur.

Self-concept influences communication in five ways that interact in a sometimes spiraling effect. The Pygmalion effect is the tendency for a person to become what signifcant others see her or him as. The self-fulfilling prophecy is a tendency to become what you expect yourself to be. Self-concept is one major cause of selective exposure, attention, perception, and retention. It determines to a large extent what people expose themselves to and what they perceive and remember of what they are exposed to. Self-concept affects the tendency to disclose important things about self. A person with acceptance and esteem of self will be more likely to be open and honest in communication with others than will a person with low self-esteem.

Finally, self-concept relates to the self-confidence with which people approach communication situations. Self-confidence, the ability to predict that you can do what needs to be done to eliminate any potentially harmful results of a situation, is improved by positive self-concept. Having self-confidence will not eliminate fear, but it will increase belief in ability to handle situations and avoid harmful results. Self-confidence and understanding of fear and its effects can help reduce the intensity of fear and improve the ability to cope with anxiety-producing communication situations.

QUESTIONS FOR DISCUSSION

1. What is self-concept?
2. What does describing self-concept as an attitude suggest?
3. Can you explain the processes in the development of self-concept?

4. How do gender role and culture relate to self-concept?

5. Name and cite examples of five ways in which self-concept influences communication.

6. What positive steps can you take to reduce the intensity of the effects of fear in communication situations?

SUGGESTIONS FOR FURTHER READING

Allen, Ronald. *Developing Communication Competence in Children.* Skokie, Ill.: National Textbook Co., 1976.

Allport, Gordon. *Becoming.* New Haven, Conn.: Yale University Press, 1955.

Blumer, Herbert. *Symbolic Interactionism, Perspective and Method.* Englewood Cliffs, N.J.: Prentice-Hall, 1969.

Canfield, Jack, and Harold Wells. *100 Ways to Enhance Self-Concept in the Classroom: A Handbook for Teachers and Parents.* Englewood Cliffs, N.J.: Prentice-Hall, 1976.

Erikson, Erik. *Identity and the Life Cycle.* New York: Norton, 1980.

Gergen, Kenneth J. *The Concept of Self.* New York: Irvington, 1984.

Gilligan, Carol. *In a Different Voice.* Cambridge, Mass.: Harvard University Press, 1982.

Goffman Erving. *Presentation of Self in Everyday Life.* Garden City, N.Y.: Doubleday, 1959.

Gordon, Chad, and Kenneth J. Gergen, eds. *The Self in Social Interaction*, Vol. 1. New York: Wiley, 1968.

Hammacheck, Don. *Encounters with the Self.* New York: Holt, Rinehart and Winston, 1971.

Jourard, Sidney. *The Transparent Self*, 2nd ed. Princeton, N.J.: Van Nostrand, 1971. (Reprinted by Krieger Pub. in 1979 as *Experimental Analysis of the Transparent Self.*)

Lair, Jess. *I Ain't Much Baby, But I'm All I've Got.* Greenwich, Conn.: Fawcett Publications, 1978.

Maas, Henry, and Joseph A. Kuypers. *From Thirty to Seventy.* San Francisco: Jossey-Bass, 1974.

Mead, George H. *Mind, Self, and Society*, ed. Charles W. Morris. Chicago: University of Chicago Press, 1962.

Mead, Margaret. *Male and Female.* New York: William Morrow, 1984 (reprint of 1949 ed.).

Miller, Jean B. *Toward a New Psychology of Women.* Boston: Beacon Press, 1977.

Missildine, W. Hugh. *Your Inner Child of the Past.* New York: Pocket Books, 1982.

Muuss, Rolf, ed. *Adolescent Behavior and Society*: A Book of Readings, 3rd ed. New York: Random House, 1980.

Rosenthal, Robert, and Lenore Jacobson. *Pgymalion in the Classroom: Teacher Expectations and Pupils' Intellectual Development.* New York: Irvington, 1968.

Rogers, Carl. *On Becoming a Person.* Boston: Houghton Mifflin, 1961.

Samovar, Larry A. and Richard Porter, eds. *Intercultural Communication*: A Reader 4th ed. (Belmont, Calif.: Wadsworth, 1985).

Shaver, Phillip, and Clyde Hendrick, eds. *Sex and Gender.* Newbury Park, Calif.: Sage, 1987.

Sheehy, Gail. *Passages: Predictable Crises of Adult Life.* New York: Dutton, 1976.

Still, Henry. *Surviving the Male Mid-Life Crisis.* New York: Crowell, 1977.

3 The Use of Language: Sharing Meanings

> . . . segmentation of nature is an aspect of grammar . . . We cut up and organize the spread and flow of events as we do, largely because, through our mother tongue, we are parties to an agreement to do so, not because nature itself is segmented in exactly that way for all to see.
>
> BENJAMIN WHORF

> Words are like glass—they obscure whatever they do not help us to see.
>
> JOSEPH JOUBERT

> Okie use 'ta mean you was from Oklahoma. Now it means you're scum. Don't mean nothing itself, it's the way they say it.
>
> JOHN STEINBECK

GOAL

To understand how symbols are used to communicate meaning

OBJECTIVES

The material in this chapter should help you to:
1. Describe a situation that illustrates the differences between symbols and meaning.
2. Explain the statement, "Words don't have meanings; people do."
3. Explain how a language categorization system influences the way we perceive realities.
4. Use language in ways that reduce ambiguity.
5. Explain why a larger vocabulary improves your ability to communicate.
6. Cite examples illustrating both connotative and denotative meanings.
7. Use an understanding of connotative and denotative meanings to achieve more effective use of language.
8. Describe the role of grammar in communication.
9. State the effects of dialect in communication.
10. Use various language styles appropriately for different situations.

What does it mean to say that humans use language to share meanings? For most of us, it means we talk (or write) to others, and when they hear (or read) our words, they understand what we mean. Yet far too many of us do not fully understand the nature of the words with which we communicate. We do not know how words fit together to become language; we assume things that are not true of language; and we behave in ways that contradict what we do know to be true of language. As a result, we often communicate less successfully than we want to or could.

To help you better understand how language functions and use it to avoid communication problems are the goals of this chapter. First, we'll discuss the nature of meaning and the relationships between words and meanings. We'll note how these relationships shape a person's view of reality and introduce some ways to use language more effectively.

THE MEANING OF MEANING

Have you ever thought what you mean by the word *meaning*? A word's meaning is not its definition. Though a definition is part of the meaning of a word, it is not all the meaning. You can define love, but that isn't its real meaning, is it?

We use the term **meaning** to refer to *the entire set of reactions that people assign to a symbol.* Your "meaning" for a word is the sum total of reactions you have when you hear, read, or think about that word.

Words Are Not Meanings

Too often we forget that our words are not our meanings. We talk as if our reactions to the world outside us were the same as that world. We say, "It sure is hot in here," or, "This room is cold," as if the words *hot* and *cold* were the same as the

(© King Features Syndicate, Inc., 1974; reprinted with special permission of King Features Syndicate, Inc.)

Many objects are both things and symbols.

air. We fail to remember that a word is not its **referent,** which is *the thing represented or referred to by the word.*

Of course, you have no trouble remembering that you are not your name. If the registrar's office has no record of your grades from last semester, your name may be lost, but you haven't been. That's easy to see. What we all tend to forget is that the relationship between us and our names is the same as the relationship between all words and the "things" they represent.

Words Are Symbols

A name is a symbol used to represent or refer to a person; it is not the person. Similarly, words are used to talk about things and about reactions to things. Words represent or refer to things. Thus, words are symbols, because **symbols** are *anything used to refer to or stand for something else.* Note carefully that the last part of that sentence, not the first, is the definition. We describe the function of words by calling them symbols.

Of course, not all symbols are words. Many other things are symbols too. For example, a wedding ring symbolizes a relationship between two people; a flag symbolizes a country or an organization; a trademark symbolizes a product. These symbols may confuse us. We think of them as things when they are both things and symbols. The clothes we wear are things in that they provide warmth and protection, but they may also function as symbols. Dozens of other examples could be cited.[1] People can and do assign meanings to objects, sounds, pictures, or actions.

The ability to symbolize has been called the process that distinguishes humans from the other animals. As more is learned about animal communication systems, this popular concept is being questioned.[2] But the questions do not ask whether the symbolic ability is important. They ask whether other animals use symbolic systems we haven't learned to understand. The importance of the symbolizing process is not in doubt.

Types of Symbols   Symbols can be classified in many ways. We use the term **verbal** to refer to *spoken or written words* and **nonverbal** to denote *all nonword symbols*. When talking, humans combine voice with words using both verbal and nonverbal symbols. Inflection and timing are major symbolic parts of spoken language. A rising vocal inflection can make a question from a sentence that without voice would appear to be a statement, such as, "You want to come?" The voice substitutes for the missing word, *do*. A pause at the end of a sentence or phrase can signal to other communicators that it is their turn to talk. Elements adding meaning to spoken language include voice quality, tempo of speaking, pitch, and volume. These and other elements of nonverbal communication are so important that we devote Chapter 4 and much of Chapter 13 to discussing them.

Connecting Symbols and Referents   The point to remember is that all symbols, including words, only *represent* meanings. Just as your name is not you, so words are not the ideas they stand for. Yet haven't you often heard, "My car is a mess," or "My car is a luxury car," as if the words were the car? We say, "Ross is beautiful," or "Ross is brilliant," or "Ross is a poor student," as if somehow the person Ross and the words referring to him were identical.

These examples reflect what may be the most common bad habit of communicators—acting as if words have meanings. Words, however, do not have meanings. People do. People associate meanings with words. An observer sees Ross as having a certain quality and applies the label: beautiful or brilliant, or poor student, or many other things. But only the user connects the labels to the ideas they stand for. Ogden and Richards used a triangle to illustrate the relationship between the labels and the ideas they stand for, which we show in Figure 3–1.[3] The dotted

[1] Many writers distinguish between functions of signs and symbols, and certainly such useful categories can be made. We do not, however, think such a distinction helps in improving your ability to use either to communicate. If the difference in function interests you, we recommend further reading from the sources cited at the end of this chapter.

[2] R. Allen and B. T. Gardner, "Teaching Sign Language to a Chimpanzee," *Science*, 165 (August 1969), 664–72, is one of the earliest reports of symbolic activity by chimpanzees. Later reports include "The Education of S*A*R*A*H," *Psychology Today*, September 1970, pp. 54–58; "Language in Chimpanzee?" *Science*, 178 (May 1971), 808–22; and "Teaching Language to an Ape," *Scientific American*, 227 (October 1972), 92–99; all by David Premack. Another study appeared in *Science*, "Reading and Sentence Completion by a Chimpanzee," by D. M. Rumbaugh et al., *Science*, 182 (November 1973), 731–33; the rejoinder by J. L. Mistler-Lachman and R. Lachman appeared in *Science*, 185 (September 1974), 871–73.

[3] C. K. Ogden and I. A. Richards, *The Meaning of Meanings: A Study of the Influences of Language upon Thought and of the Science of Symbolism* (New York: Harcourt, Brace & World, 1923) was one of the pioneer publications in the study of semantics (the study of meanings).

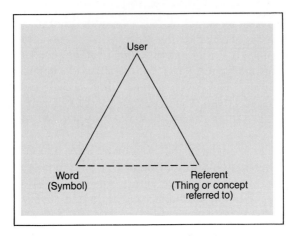

FIGURE 3–1. The Triangle of Meaning.

lines show that word and referent aren't really related. The solid lines show the real connection between the word and the thing or idea it stands for—the user. For example, if they were asked what is shown in Figure 3–2, some people reading this book would reply, "a cow," while others would say "a Longhorn." But the native speaker of Spanish might think "vaca," "buey," or "toro," or depending on the age or sex of the animal, "novilla" or "novillo." Each term would reflect different viewers' perceptions.

We all know that different people use different words to refer to the same things. Still, we all often behave as if there were some necessary connection between words and the ideas or objects they refer to. We act as if words instead of users have meanings. That happens, for example, when we act (as we often do) as if others should understand what we mean just because they heard what we said. Don't we all remember an argument or misunderstanding that happened because we followed someone's instructions (we thought) only later to find them very upset because we didn't do what they wanted? This kind of communication problem is common. Worse, it often evokes emotions that complicate the effort to clarify and fix what went wrong.

Shortly, we'll discuss dealing with problems of this sort, when misunderstandings are complicated by feelings and attitudes, but first we want to introduce another principle of language use.

FIGURE 3–2.

Words Represent Concepts

Most of the words in any language represent concepts or ideas. Words like *true*, *square*, *dogs*, *liquid*, and *love* represent concepts. They select common aspects of things that are in many respects quite different and bring them together into a single classification with one meaning. The things we regard as "true" are infinitely different, but the concept of truth allows people to select and connect similarities, so "That is true" is a meaningful statement.

Concepts Reflect Synthesis   People form concepts as they begin to understand or gain a general idea about an object. Concepts are the thoughts people use to see relationships among things. We have a concept for *round*, for instance, or for *rose*. The idea (concept) of round helps us see something similar in a ball, a roll of tape, the full moon, and a ring. The concept of rose helps us see many varieties of roses as the same kind of flower and yet know that petunias, orchids, and daisies are not roses.

Humans develop concepts through the process of **conceptualizing.** They synthesize or combine mental images about experiences into ideas (concepts). At first these images are hazy. But as understanding develops, the ideas take focus. As babies, we did not have different concepts for cats or dogs, especially small ones. All were greeted by the same term—perhaps *fuwi*. Later, we came to see these two types of animals as very different. We replaced the one vague concept of furry, four-legged creatures with ideas of cat-ness and dog-ness. As adults, each of us has a clear concept of cat and dog. Our ideas about cats and dogs have been synthesized into concepts that blend all we have experienced about cats and dogs.

Concepts: *Ideas Created by Experience*   Concepts are ideas we have learned. They are meanings we have. But take care not to confuse concepts with definitions. Think of your concepts of dog and cat. They're clear, aren't they? You have meanings for cat and for dog. Now, try to state what makes cats different from dogs. Difficult, isn't it? That's because your meanings for cat and dog are not definitions; they are ideas.

Some experience, internal or external, is required to form a concept. To know red as a color, we had to experience the visual impression of redness. A person born blind couldn't have the concept as others do. Think of describing red to a blind person. If you say, "Fire is red," the receiver might think of red as a sensation of heat. Can you imagine trying to describe the concept of snow to a person who has always lived in the tropics?

At this point you might be thinking, "So what? What difference does it make whether I know what concepts are?" The answer is that we use concepts (and the words that represent them) to explain our experiences. In other words, concepts are ideas people develop to explain internal and external realities. Concepts are not the realities, any more than words are the things they refer to. Yet because we have organized our experiences, using words, into concepts that are meaningful ideas, we tend to believe that our way of talking about the world is the way the world is. We confuse our ideas and our language with the realities. For most of us, this confusion causes many communication problems.

Many examples could be cited to illustrate this. Think about boarding a 747 bound for Denver. Imagine you have taken your seat, fastened your seatbelt, and the plane is taxiing toward the runway. Over the intercom you hear the pilot's voice reporting the weather, saying that the plane will soon be cleared for take-off, and telling the flight attendants to sit down. As you read this and imagine the situation, it all seems real so far. It fits with your concepts.

Now let us add some details. The pilot's voice is deep, resonant, confident. But imagine now that the pilot speaks English with a strong accent. You don't recognize it, but you think of a movie version of Russian. Makes you nervous, doesn't it? Doesn't fit your concept of an airline captain, does it? Or, instead of an accent, imagine the pilot's voice as soft, high-pitched, and hesitant. Are you now even more nervous? Most readers would be if they also hear that voice as female. Most people do not have a concept of reality that includes soft-voiced female airline pilots. So when they encounter such a reality, they are uneasy, partly because their meanings for the words (concepts) differ from that reality.

Another reason we should remember that our words represent concepts is that it helps keep us from forgetting that language and culture largely create the concepts we develop about the world. In other words, our culture and language organize our experiences, and in so doing, they teach us particular ways of "seeing" the world. Our language encourages us to think certain ideas and discourages us from thinking others. Our culture teaches us certain concepts and doesn't teach us others. When we interact with people of cultures different from our own whose language differs from ours, we often forget that their language and culture may have organized their experiences differently and taught them different thoughts about the world. Many communication problems result from such differences, either because we forget that they exist or were never aware of them.

CATEGORIZING MEANINGS

As we experience events, we develop meanings to explain them, stored meanings called up later and shared, largely through use of language. Thus, to improve our

(Wizard of Id by Parker & Hart; by permission of Johny Hart and NAS Inc.)

skill at communicating, it is useful to understand the role of language in the development of meaning.

Concepts Involve Categories

To develop concepts requires **selection.** We conceptualize by selecting certain elements of a thing to distinguish it from other things. Thus, we focus on some things and ignore others. In this selective process we create meaningful ideas, but to communicate effectively, we need to remain alert to the excluding/including process that occurs. For example, we noted earlier that all of us have a concept of round that lets us see a ball, a roll of tape, and a ring as similar. If we ignored the concept of round, we might see no similarities at all between those items. At the same time, if we concentrated only on the roundness feature of these objects, we'd ignore many of their other important facets.

This characteristic of our language (and our thinking) can lead to major communication problems. For that reason, semanticists suggest we should adopt "etc." thinking. By that they mean remembering the selective nature of our words. Whatever words we select to represent features of any event or object, we leave unmentioned (and perhaps unnoticed) many more things. If we remembered the "etc." characteristic of words used to describe our view of reality, we'd be less likely to forget that the things left unsaid always outnumber those said.

Because of the selective nature of conceptualizing (and thus language) we often forget that *how we categorize experience may differ greatly from how others do.* It is somewhat easier to understand the differences in categories when our languages differ, but we are still often astounded to realize how differently other people see what seems so obvious to us.

Because concepts use a category system acquired as we learned language, that language influences the concepts we learn. We who speak English have a concept of tree. When we hear the word *tree*, we have a meaningful idea of tree. We can see birch, oak, and pine in the same category. And we know that roses and petunias do not fit into that category. Some Australian peoples, in contrast, have no concept of tree. Their language reflects concepts of jarrah, mulga, gum, palm, and so on; but they have no single idea that translates to the English word *tree*. If these people learn no other language, for them the concept of tree does not exist. Without the concept of tree, oak, birch, gum, and palm do not fit into the same category.

More difficult to remember is that those of us who speak the same language also categorize differently, or apply different categories at different times. Remembering the "etc." nature of language would help us remember that, whatever we choose to say about any thing or experience, we have chosen not to say many other things.

Such efficiency is useful, of course, but it can also cause problems. It can lead us to ignore important aspects of things. To describe Jasna as beautiful ignores that she is also a brilliant mathematician. To say a particular television brand has "true" colors ignores its repair records. In using our language to refer to our experiences, we must remember both that whatever the words focus on, they simultaneously ignore other things, and that our choices of focus (our categories) are quite arbitrary.

FIGURE 3–3.

Using Concepts (Categories)

In categorizing, we can focus on many aspects of a reality, the precise number depending on the range of our experiences. A physicist has learned many concepts for analyzing the behavior of matter. But that same person with a stalled car may not have concepts that explain why the car won't run. At the same time, a good mechanic, who would probably have trouble with theoretical physics, has many concepts for dealing with the stalled car (see Figure 3–3).

Especially significant, at least for students, is that the wider our acquaintance with language, the more features of an experience we can focus upon. Anyone who has entered a competition has experienced the feelings that go with victory and defeat. Our vocabulary limits our ability to talk about those feelings, however. We all know people who use a single word, such as *terrific* or *swell*, to describe every good event, or who use *awful* to describe all bad events.

The more language we know, the more different features of an event we are able to recognize and talk about. To know the words *happy, elated, serene, gay, blissful, ecstatic, pleased,* or *joyful* may be the only way to tell someone about the different feelings each term describes. Linguists have shown us that the language of Eskimos allows them to describe snow in many more ways than can people who know only English. The Eskimos' language and experience interact; they have many more experiences with snow than most native English speakers. At the same time, most Americans experience many different types of snow that we describe with a single term.

Similarly, the French who live in the Camargue region have fifty-five words for wind. A resident of another part of France probably wouldn't know all fifty-five terms and might not recognize that many varieties of wind even knowing the words. To fully recognize what each word symbolizes requires both experience and acquaintance with the language.

This principle applies to all languages and all experiences. We generally think about only those concepts we can name. Thus, having a wide vocabulary improves communication in several ways. Certainly it helps us discuss more effectively what we know. Perhaps even more important, the more words we know and use, the *more we know*. We think better and more precisely with a wider vocabulary. Learning language, our own and others, has many advantages.

LEVELS OF MEANING

Specific and General

The categories that language reflects represent various *levels*. Some concepts relate to specific observations. These are applied only to specific objects or events. For example, in describing a particular person, you may say, "Frankie O'Mara is 5'4" tall, has brown hair, green eyes, and is nineteen years old." These words reflect specific concepts. Other concepts are broader and more general. To describe Frankie as young, thin, pretty, or handsome would use more general concepts. It would reflect a higher level of abstraction.

The Ladder of Abstraction   The analogy of a ladder may help explain these levels of abstraction. Using different levels of abstraction, we climb a language ladder—from specific to more general concepts. To illustrate, we'll describe a pet named Muffet. The name, in this case, applies to only one thing. The word *Muffet* refers to a reality, not a concept. But by focusing on different features of this reality, many concepts apply to Muffet. We can say she has short legs and white hair. Short, legs, white, and hair are all fairly specific concepts. Calling Muffet a terrier uses a slightly more general concept. And to refer to her as a dog, a mammal, and an animal would use increasingly general concepts. Each one uses a higher level of abstraction, which means it focuses on less concrete features (see Figure 3–4).

The "higher" a concept is on the ladder of abstraction, the farther it is from what can be verified by observation. To prove that Muffet has short legs and white hair, you need only look at her and know the words. On the other hand, to verify that she is an animal, you must have concepts that distinguish between plants and animals.

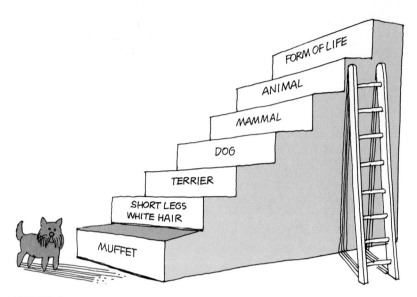

FIGURE 3–4. A Ladder of Abstraction.

Abstraction and Ambiguity   The higher a concept is on the abstraction ladder, the more things it can refer to. Words representing concepts high on the ladder are very general. They are also described as abstract. The more general (abstract) a word, the more ambiguity in its use. To illustrate, look at another abstraction ladder (see Figure 3–5). We have a friend named Joe. He is 5′10″ tall and has

FIGURE 3–5. Another Ladder of Abstraction.

brown hair and green eyes. Moving higher on an abstraction ladder, he is a Croatian-American. At a still higher level, he's labeled as a human being. Then, you guessed it, another level joins Muffet's ladder. Both Joe and Muffet are mammals and forms of life.

Muffet and *Joe* are words that refer to one object. But the labels "dog" and "human" accurately describe many different things and many different kinds of things. The concept *animal* includes some features of both dogs and humans. It is even more general and abstract than the concept *dog* or *human*. That means it is more ambiguous. It is not clear what object or idea an ambiguous word (concept) refers to.

In short, the higher on the ladder of abstraction, the more ambiguous the concept represented by a symbol. Abstract concepts can accurately refer to many different things. What is the importance of this? Higher levels of abstraction in language use increase the possibility that people will not attach the same meanings to the symbols. Even when using the same words, people often mean different things.

Abstract and Concrete Words

Much of our everyday talk involves concepts high on some ladder of abstraction. These **abstract words** *refer to features or concepts that people cannot see.* They refer to intangible things. If a term refers to an object that can be seen, it's called a **concrete word.** *Legs, hair, Muffet,* and *Joe* are all concrete words. They *refer to tangible things, things that can be seen* and described with specific, visual terms. In contrast, *animal, human,* and *mammal* are abstract words. They refer to concepts we cannot see.

Many common words are abstract, and much ambiguity exists when we talk about these concepts. Words like *love, friendship, home, fear,* and *honesty* are abstract. Since what they refer to is not tangible, people using these terms often mean quite different things. Such abstraction in language is the source of many communication problems. The next time you find yourself in an argument, analyze the words being used. Are you really arguing over what a word means instead of the concept itself? You will find that ambiguity causes many disagreements and misunderstandings, when real differences of opinion do not exist.

EXERCISE 3.1   LADDER OF ABSTRACTION

OBJECTIVE   To practice recognizing successively higher levels of abstraction when using language.

DIRECTIONS   1. Do Part I before class on the assigned day.
    2. Part I.
        a. Choose a word from the following: *tree, bird, nation, city.*

b. Using the form below, create a ladder of abstraction related to the word.

c. You may use words, phrases, or both for your ladder.

3. Part II.

a. In class, your instructor will form groups of those who created a ladder of abstraction using the same word.

b. In groups, compare your ladders and discuss until all agree that the ladders are appropriate.

c. You may use these criteria to guide your discussion:

1. Is the word on each riser less specific than the one below it?

2. Can the word on each riser properly be used to refer to the words below it? (Look at the ladder in Figure 3–4: Muffet is a terrier; terriers are dogs; dogs are mammals; mammals are animals; animals are forms of life.)

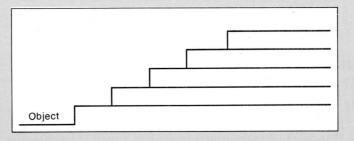

Object

REVIEW **Provide brief answers that may be a writing assignment or the basis for class discussion.**

1. What does the ladder of abstraction illustrate about the use of language?

2. How do abstract terms affect the differences between intended and perceived meanings?

3. Explain the most important communication principle illustrated or learned from this exercise and why you found it important.

TYPES OF MEANINGS

Denotation (Identifying)

As noted above, words often have different meanings. The same word can refer to several different things. This type of meaning is described as a denotation. The **denotations** of a word are *the objects or concepts referred to, the actual "things" the word symbolizes.* One denotation for the word *fire*, for instance, is the rapid oxidation of organic matter. Another denotation is the flame itself. Other possible denotative meanings for the word *fire* are the acts of discharging a gun, dismissing an employee from a job, and igniting a skyrocket. You could add other denotations.

We often forget that most words, even simple concrete words, have several denotations. *Chair*, for instance, can refer to thousands of different kinds of objects.

Have you ever tried to define *chair*? Try it. A chair is _____. Fill in your definition. Compare it with the definitions of others in class. Are there differences? Of course there are. Denotative meanings often differ greatly from user to user. The 500 most commonly used English words have over 14,000 different definitions.

Words with many denotations are ambiguous, which can cause intended and perceived messages to differ. Remembering that most words have several denotations can help you know when to check whether you have the same concepts in mind as others do when you communicate using ambiguous words.

Connotation (Valuing)

Another type of meaning people have for most symbols is connotative. The term **connotation** refers to *the attitudes or feelings a user has about a symbol or the object or concept it symbolizes*. For the word *fire*, for instance, you probably have several different connotations, depending on the denotation you think of. The idea of a fire in a fireplace on a cold day or of a campfire usually has favorable connotations. Most of us like those things. The idea of a fire in the attic or basement, however, produces negative connotations. We dislike that kind of fire. To the firing of a gun, you may have mixed connotative reactions. Is it being fired at a mallard or pheasant? If you like hunting, your connotation is positive. If you think hunting is a cruel pastime, then you probably have a negative connotation.

Connotative meanings reflect the valuing process of interpretation. As people respond to and talk about things, they evaluate. People like things or don't like them, think something is good or not. These feeling (valuing) responses provide the connotative meanings. Indeed, this valuing process may provide the most important meanings we attach to words, and we have negative or positive reactions to most words. Often children acquire these connotative meanings before they develop denotative meanings for the same words. Connotative meanings are thus more basic, more deeply rooted, and more likely than denotations to determine how we respond to words.

Sometimes a connotative reaction occurs in response to a concept. Some ideas remind us of pleasant experiences: love, mother, apple pie, ice cream, and so on. In these cases, we respond positively to a word because we like the idea or concept it reminds us of. We dislike other concepts, such as fear, and thus have negative connotations for the word.

At other times, the connotative reactions are to the words themselves. If you have a female dog as a pet, for instance, you probably don't like to have her described as a *bitch*. You probably don't care what denotation the person using the word meant. It's the word you don't like. We react negatively to many words in this way. Obscenities may be the best example. Negative responses to "four-letter words" are not to the sexual or physical act symbolized, but to the words themselves—or to the place or time the words are used.

Connotative meanings can cause difficulties in communication if we forget or are unaware that others' connotative meanings for words differ from ours. We may have no negative reactions to words others find offensive and find that we offend

(Beetle Bailey cartoon; reprinted with special permission of King Features Syndicate, Inc.)

people and never know why. We may react negatively to what someone says, assuming that their connotations are the same as ours. We may assume a person intended to insult or offend when they didn't. We may conclude a person is crude or ill-mannered when their connotative meanings simply differ from ours. Words that are acceptable to receivers in some settings, arouse negative reactions when used in other settings.

Sensitivity to connotative meanings can greatly improve communication. By using language that calls up positive connotative meanings, we can greatly improve how receivers react to us. By associating negative connotations with people or causes we are opposing, we can influence receivers positively toward our own goals.

Cultural differences become important in relation to connotative meanings. That's especially true with the cultural differences that exist among people who speak the same language. A word (or vocal tone) that has no negative connotations in one culture might be quite negative in another—"correct" grammar, for example. Or a culture might approve of some people using certain language (for example, profanity) but find it inappropriate for other people to use the same words.

LANGUAGE AND SHARING MEANING

We use word symbols as tools to structure and share meanings with others. But for adult communication, language—not just words—is necessary. Words are the building blocks, but grammar and syntax (language) permit us to go beyond childlike message sharing.

Rules of Word Arrangement (Grammar)

Grammar makes word symbols useful. By this we aren't referring just to the rules of subjects, verbs, and so on, introduced in elementary schools. We learned most of the grammar of our language long before entering school. These rules, which for most of us are unwritten and unconscious, enable us to know that a string of words makes sense.

A series of words has little value unless combined in a meaningful arrangement. You recognize the symbols *the*, *is*, *on*, *fire*, and *house*. Individually, they make sense to you. But *The is on fire house* communicates little. It doesn't fit your code, your grammar. However, *The house is on fire* does. As does, *Is the house on fire?* These arrangements are meaningful because they follow rules of word combination (grammar) that you recognize.

Grammar characterizes every human language. Speakers decide the meanings of sentences using grammar. For example, *The is boy running* wouldn't be considered sensible by a native speaker of American English. But *The boy is running* would. *The boy be running* would also be considered meaningful but not "correct" according to the grammar of Standard American English. It is, however, grammatical in another dialect system.

Knowing the grammar of your language helps you interpret word relationships and sentence meanings. You know the two sentences, *A detective hunted down the killer*, and *A detective hunted the killer down*, mean essentially the same because you know the grammar. And *The detective down hunted the killer* won't make sense. A person who knows English grammar will know what the sentence *Flying planes are dangerous* refers to. However, it doesn't make clear what the speaker intends. The arrangement of the words makes sense for a different meaning even if the grammar is not correct.

Some sentences are ambiguous even when the grammar is correct. For example, *The man decided on the train* and *They fed her dog biscuits* can have several perceived meanings that make sense. You need more information to know the intended meaning.

Language Differences

A language involves the organized use of all types of symbols, and each language has many variations. People who use the different versions are described as belonging to different speech communities.

Dialects   Dialect distinguishes among some speech communities. We are all aware that English as spoken by a person from England differs from English in the United States. We also know that U.S. English differs from Atlanta to Boston. We may be less aware of other differences in language that are also called dialect. Dialects vary from urban to rural areas, from one social class to another, and from one ethnic group to another.

We define **dialect** as *a language variant used by a group of speakers that is different from the language of the general community*. Dialects involve differences in the use of words, sounds, syntax (the way words are arranged in a sentence) and style.

Why is it important to be aware of these differences? Partly for clarity. If one group uses words in ways others don't, unclear communication between the two will result. But the most important reason is that dialects lead to evaluations. Not only will our dialect influence how people perceive us; the dialect we speak leads us to react to others in certain ways. For example, hearing a person talk, you may infer that he or she is from the South. Depending on your attitudes, this

TABLE 3-1 Language Differences

DIFFERENCES IN THE USE OF LANGUAGE

Indicator	Marker	Stereotyped Elements
A speech or language element that is used in a distinct manner by a particular speech community without either natives or nonnatives knowing that it is different. For example, according to the specific area of the country, eggs are cooked in frying pans, skillets, or a spider.	An element both natives and non-natives are aware of, even though the use varies among natives. For example, the "Southern" accent varies greatly from Virginia to Tennessee to Louisiana, but it clearly marks Southerners as different from "Yankees."	Stigmatized word uses that are noticed, especially by people outside the speech community. They are prejudiced against the word or phrase usage. For example, use of the verb *to be*, as in *I be going*, is stigmatized as substandard by many people.

leads you to other inferences. If the speaker is a woman and you believe Southern women are coy and empty-headed, you'll tend to see these qualities in her. If the speaker is a politician or a sheriff, your beliefs about Southern politicians or sheriffs will influence how you view the person.

The influence of dialects may be strongest when we identify other dialects as different from that of our own speech community. People within a particular region or community may not be able to describe exactly how another person's speech differs, but they know when it's not native. Nor should we think these differences apply only to large geographical distances. In many metropolitan areas, natives of one community can tell those from another part of town simply by listening for a while. Once perceived, differences in language activate the listener's attitudes or prejudices toward the area the speaker comes from.

Evaluations based on dialect affect communication in another way. People commonly believe one American grammar is "correct." It is described as Standard American English. Many people believe all other dialects or variations of English in this country are not "correct" and are therefore "substandard." These people conclude that people who use a nonstandard dialect lack education and, often, that they are stupid.

Those who study languages do not hold this view of dialects. To them, language dialects are different, but none is superior to another. As students of communication, we should feel the same way, but we must remember that many people with whom we communicate do not agree. Many receivers judge personalities, intelligence, and competence based on language use, including dialect. In one study that illustrates this, listeners rated speakers on an audio tape. The speakers used language of five different speech communities. Those perceived as Eastern were rated high on intelligence and competence and low on warmth and friendliness. The opposite was true of speakers with Southern speech.[4]

Related to these perceptions are ideas about the appropriateness of roles. Some people perceive that various educational, ethnic, social, or sex characteristics

[4] Unpublished manuscript by Wayne Dickerson, professor of sociolinguistics, University of Illinois, 1974.

cause different abilities. Then they apply these perceptions based on language use. In a study similar to the one cited above, speakers of various dialects were rated in terms of the highest occupational level each could achieve. Few women who spoke a language identified as Black, Southern, or lower class were perceived as capable of becoming a bank president. These ratings, of course, were due to other things as well as speech. Most people, however, will perceive a Black female with speech characteristic of upper-class New England as more competent than her sister who speaks the language of Chicago's South Side or the Mississippi Delta.[5]

[5] Ibid.

EXERCISE 3.2   DIALECT AND COMMUNICATION

OBJECTIVE   **To assess the influence of language differences (dialect) on communication.**

DIRECTIONS   **In groups, discuss and answer the following questions:**
1. In which area of the country are people believed to talk most slowly?
2. In which area is speech believed to be the fastest?
3. What characteristics of personality do you tend to expect from persons who have the speech patterns identified in 1 and 2, above?
4. How would you describe the dialect used in your part of the country? Be specific. Think of both social and cultural dialect differences, not just geographic.
5. What characteristics do you believe people from other groups or areas expect of you due to your dialect?
6. Describe the aspects of speech and the related expectations you would have of people from:
    a. California
    b. Illinois
    c. New York
    d. Tennessee
    e. Texas
    f. Wisconsin
7. If you live in, or know well, the states identified, can you cite specific differences in dialect within various regions within the state? Do you tend to expect different characteristics of people who reflect those different dialects?

REVIEW   **Write brief answers to the following questions that will form the basis for a writing assignment or class discussion.**
1. Explain why dialect frequently leads to generalizations about people.
2. As a receiver, what can you do to prevent dialects from distorting your perceptions of those with whom you communicate?
3. Identify aspects of your speaking dialect that may contribute to conclusions others might draw about you.
4. Explain the most important principle you learned from this exercise and why you found it important.

To be effective, communicators must learn to deal with attitudes toward dialects. Many natural languages are not "approved" or associated with desirable characteristics. To achieve the best results, people who speak such dialects need to become *bicodal*. They need the "approved" dialect when talking with people who are negative toward their natural language. They need to become bicodal not because one code is better, but because it helps them communicate more effectively in some situations.

Style   **Style** also affects the way people perceive speakers. *Style differences range from word choices to nonverbal characteristics and relate primarily to differences in the degree of formality in a situation.* Styles vary depending on culture, the speech community, the relationships among communicators, the situation, and other factors. Using a style that receivers perceive as inappropriate for you or the situation will influence how they perceive you.

Style can be considered by level of formality. Five such styles are:[6]

Frozen   Casual
Formal   Intimate
Consultative

These styles range from highly formal to very informal. Frozen style is used with strangers or in ritual situations, formal style most often in speeches or work situations. At the other extreme, among family and close friends, people use an intimate style. Using any of the five styles requires the speaker to make many choices. The choices involve differences in words used, the degree of formality of the expressions (whether sentences are completed or not, how carefully the words are spoken), and appropriate changes in nonverbal behaviors.

The Five Styles of Variable Formality (spoken by a receptionist to a client of a company)

Frozen: Good morning, Sir. May we be of assistance?

Formal: Yes, Mr. Marcus, Dr. Clementi is expecting you for a three o'clock appointment. Let me tell her that you have arrived.

Consultative: Mr. Marcus, Dr. Clementi just took a long-distance call. She won't take long. Can you wait just a minute?

Casual: Jerry Marcus, how great to see you again! Why haven't you been to see us lately? We've missed you.

Intimate: Luv—you're early. It's not three yet, and you know the boss never sees anyone before the appointment time.

How we refer to people illustrates this point well. Using titles (Dr., Mr., Ms., Professor, Captain, Lieutenant, Sir) is necessary in the frozen and formal settings. Depending on the social rules, titles may also be used in consultative settings—that is, among associates in some work settings or among acquaintances. Among friends, titles will be dropped and first names or nicknames used. Among intimates, special forms of address (babe, dear, honey, sweetheart) common only to them will be used. Yet when an argument or the formality of the situation calls

---

[6] The names for the five styles are from Martin Joos, *The Five Clocks* (New York: Harcourt Brace Jovanovich, 1967).

for it, intimates drop the special address and use the same form of address as for friends, sometimes even reverting to titles. We well remember a friend who addressed her husband as Mr. when she was angry.

Toward the more formal end of the continuum, speakers choose words with special care, paying attention to grammar and pronunciation. Formal styles also call for more elaboration because the speakers share less previous information. Formal styles cause more hesitations in speakers who are not comfortable in such settings, and they usually require controlled emotions, with moderate pitch, rate, and volume. All these factors vary from speaker to speaker and situation to situation. But the relationships among language, speech, and situation are generally those reflected in Table 3–2.

When we use the "appropriate" style, others infer accordingly. They see us as competent, at least to the extent that they accept our ideas as competent and other prejudices do not interfere. What if we use a style considered inappropriate to our relationship with the receiver(s) or to the situation? Others' opinions of us will depend on how important *they* think it is to use an appropriate style. The perceiver decides whether the choice of style is deliberate and why, or whether our "error" is accidental due to ignorance or incompetence. Whatever the listener concludes, perceptions of us will be influenced—positively or negatively. Choice of style, like that of dialect or grammar, affects the effectiveness of our communication. We need sensitivity to culture, to situation, and to the individual as well as comfort with our language in order to use a variety of styles to our advantage.

Shared and Unshared Codes

Speaking a common language permits communication because the language permits speakers to *share codes*. That is, it permits them a degree of reliability in attaching similar meanings to symbols, vocal systems, and grammar. Recall from Chapter 1

TABLE 3–2   Relations of Speech Communication Style and Other Variables

Situation	Style	Concern for Speech	Syntactic Complexity	Vocabulary	Nonverbal	Comfort and Ease
Unknown receivers	Frozen	High	High	Wide	Low Use	Low
Important receivers (one or many)	Formal	↑	↑	↑	↑	↑
Acquaintances or associates	Consultative					
Friends	Casual	↓	↓	↓	↓	↓
Intimates and family	Intimate	Low	Low	Limited	High Use	High

SOURCE: Adapted from Wayne Dickerson, unpublished manuscript, University of Illinois, 1974.

EXERCISE 3.3   STYLE AND CONTEXT

OBJECTIVE	**To become aware of the relationships among language use, degree of formality, and situation.**
DIRECTIONS	1. The instructor will assign you to work in pairs or ask you to choose a partner outside of class.
	2. Before working with a partner, state what you would say and do in each of the situations outlined below.
	3. Ask your partner to role play a response in each of the situations below.
	4. Compare your responses to your partner's and analyze how the comments and other responses differ.
SITUATIONS	1. You meet a friend in the local grocery store. You say . . .
	2. You meet a friend upon entering the room at a dinner party. You say . . .
	3. The friend you meet at the dinner party has just applied for the same promotion you seek. You say . . .
	4. The friend you meet at the dinner party just got the job. You say . . .
	5. Your friend is now your boss and you need to keep your job (at least for a while) and the party is to celebrate her/his new job. You say . . .
	6. You believe the friend undercut you in getting the promotion. You say . . .
REVIEW	**Write brief answers to the following questions that will form the basis for a writing assignment or class discussion.**
	1. Describe the ways in which the formality of the situation influences language use.
	2. Note other aspects of style that are influenced by formality.
	3. Explain the most important communication principle you learned from this exercise and why you found it important.
	Note: Your instructor may ask you to describe, in a writing assignment or class discussion, the differences you found in your style in the situations presented in the exercise.

that a speaker (source) *encodes*—assigns meanings to words; uses the rules of word arrangement to form sentences; and uses verbal and nonverbal message carriers to communicate. A receiver *decodes*, creating perceived meanings from the message carriers. If source and receiver share a language, they share codes—at least partially.

If people do not share codes, they can't communicate with language. If one speaks Spanish and the listener *no habla Español*, the meanings aren't shared—not well, at least. That's obvious. What's often forgotten, though, is that people who speak the same language do not fully share codes. We usually recognize when someone uses a word for which we have no denotation. But we don't always keep in mind that the speaker may mean denotations we aren't thinking of. *More often, we don't realize that other aspects of the code may not be shared.*

What you use a word to mean may not be how someone else uses the word at all. When a bricklayer calls for *mud* or a West Virginian says, *I don't care to,* most receivers will not decode as the source intended. These parts of the code are not widely shared. Colloquial uses, slang, and technical terms (sometimes called *jargon*) are not the only cases of unshared codes, but they clearly demonstrate how such variations create misunderstandings.

Slang and Jargon   People create and use slang words for many functions: vividness, evoking specific emotional connotations, and identification among the users by creating an in-group clearly distinguished from others who do not share this part of the code. Media attention focused on a particular version of such in-group language through a movie and song about the speech of "valley girls." Coining slang terms by young people is not new; it will continue as long as each new generation needs to establish its separation from (and often rejection of) the "given" culture.

Nor is the process limited to young people. Groups of all types use "private language" to establish identification, create solidarity, and define outsiders. Virtually every work group has its own technical vocabulary and ingroup language. Sometimes such terms create vivid images and evoke connotative meanings so well that they are adopted beyond the originating culture. Many common terms in standard English dialects today originated as slang and such additions to the language will doubtless continue.

Similarly, speech communities may adopt technical terms because the existing language has no words that serve their needs. The new words may be more precise or refer to concepts not previously known. The language of today's "high-tech" engineer may be the most visible example of this process. We have all noticed (and may even have begun to use) the vivid additions to our language from the electronic revolution. *Bits*, *bytes*, *uplinks*, *network feeds*, macros, and *modems* are only a few of the terms it has spawned. We may no longer even remember that common phrases like *feedback* and *update* came from the early days of the electronic age.

Using Codes   When considering how to use language to improve communication, remember the language processes just illustrated. Words are created to talk about and explain experience, and they are adopted by a speech community because they are functional, having one or more important effects. Effective communicators consider the impact of words they use. How precisely do the words chosen denote an experience? How vivid is the image created in the receiver's mind? How appropriate are the emotional responses elicited? Do the word choices establish solidarity with or separation from your receivers? Answering these and other questions can significantly improve the impact of what you say.

Each of us "received" a way of viewing our experiences as we learned our language. Recognizing this may be the most important lesson of the study of language in communication. As we learned the meanings attached to words and phrases by members of our speech communities, we acquired complexes of attitudes.

These attitudes toward things, people, and ideas are heavily influenced by our language. Attitudes toward certain dialects were mentioned above. Many other examples exist. What one language community considers appropriate in a particular situation, another may find offensive. Profanity, slang, and many nonverbals are acceptable in one community but not in another. Or, some language uses are acceptable in only some situations or by some people—with profanity again the best example. Language OK for a carpenter at work won't do for a college student in class, even if it is the same person! Many people react strongly if they hear a woman say words they wouldn't notice a man saying.

Effective communicators will be alert to these effects of language, keeping two perspectives in mind. They will choose language most appropriate to accomplishing their goals, and they will be sensitive to how attitudes learned through language influence reactions (theirs and others) to people.

Language Evolution   Another principle of language has also been illustrated, language evolution. As terms or dialects or styles become associated with negative or positive meanings in a code, their use may change completely. The term *spinster*, originally used largely without emotional connotations, had no link to the sex of the person referred to; today, the term is sex-specific and has negative connotations. A companion word, *bachelor*, similarly sex-specific, is not at all negative; indeed, to many people, *bachelor* is quite a positive concept. In the colonial United States, taverns included sleeping accommodations and patriots gathered there. Some 150 years later, no one could respectably stay overnight at a tavern, nor were they places frequented by "respectable" women, even to eat or drink.

Some terms, indeed, are coined to counter just such changing attitudes. Often these terms are described as *euphemisms*, but whatever the label, the process is constant. Not too many years ago, businesses advertised and sold used cars. Today one rarely hears a "used car" advertised; they are "pre-owned," or even "pre-driven," though it will be surprising if buyers ever adopt those terms. In this country few people get "old," though some admit to aging.

Societal changes force some language changes. Women on the police force made it difficult to use the term *policeman*, but previous custom only partly influenced the choice of police *officer* as the substitute. Men in the aisles of airliners made *stewardess* inappropriate; *flight attendant* became a common substitute term. One airline "elevated" such jobs with the title "customer service managers," though again it's doubtful the term will be used much by passengers.

Racist and Sexist Language   Occasionally a social group will create language evolution. Leaders of the civil rights movement of the 1960s objected to the devaluation of Blacks in the English language. In an effort described as the "Black is beautiful" movement, activists argued that the euphemism "colored" and the pejorative "nigger" demeaned the people to whom such terms referred. In response to this intentional effort to change the language, the habits of many people changed. As Black became the term many preferred to describe themselves, its use became widespread.

Such efforts have not been totally successful. As negative attitudes toward Black people persist, so do the derogatory terms of reference. And English still has many more negative than positive terms for Blacks.

Women who object to the use in English of the male singular pronoun as generic have made a similar, though less successful, effort.[7] In the past two or three centuries, educators have taught that use of the male pronoun was "correct" for the generic singular. This pronoun is identical to that used for a sex-specific reference; that is, when the referent of the pronoun is actually male. In recent years, some language scholars have pointed out that this male generic is not natural English grammar, that it was a convention created as a part of a general effort to "clean up" and systematize the English language in the eighteenth century. They cite the widespread use of "they" as the generic pronoun in the writing of both learned and popular writers from Shakespeare to the present as evidence that this "correct" use of *he* is not natural English grammar. They also question why matching the number of people referred to is more important than matching the gender.

By now, those of us concerned with effective communication do not need to argue over when and how the "proper" masculine generic originated. Research demonstrates that over 70 percent of the time that the word *he* is used in English, it refers to a male person, not a group. Moreover, when a singular pronoun refers to a generic class or group that is sex-stereotyped female (nurses or secretaries, for example), even scholarly writers will not use the "generic" *he*, though it is "proper" to do so. For example, read the following sentences:

> When a nurse takes a blood sample, he is careful to avoid collapse of old patients' veins.
> When an elementary schoolteacher makes homework assignments, he always provides a worksheet.
> The secretary is very loyal; he always is sure the office is clean and inviting for the boss to work in, dusting the furniture and adjusting the blinds himself if necessary.

In these sentences, did you think of the generic nurse, teacher, or secretary? If you spoke these sentences referring to the general class of nurse or schoolteacher or secretary, you'd use the pronoun *she*, as would all who speak a natural English.

If it still isn't obvious that the male pronoun isn't fully generic, then compare the images you had of the nurse, schoolteacher, and secretary described above with the image provoked by the following sentences:

> When good nurses take blood samples, they are careful to avoid collapse of old patients' veins.
> When elementary schoolteachers make homework assignments, they should provide worksheets.
> Loyal secretaries make offices comfortable and inviting for their bosses.

Some people, confronted with similar examples, respond that these are exceptions because most nurses, schoolteachers, and secretaries are female. That, however, confuses the function of a generic pronoun. Because *some* nurses, schoolteachers,

---

[7] *Generic* is the term to be used when the sex of the referent is unknown or unimportant since the entire class of humans is supposed to be included.

and secretaries are men, the words are not sex-specific, even though much sex-role stereotyping of these jobs exists. Therefore, a generic pronoun should be used when these terms are referred to. A truly generic term does not exclude even minority members of a category. The problem for speakers of English is that our language has no singular generic pronoun.

The key point for students of communication is to learn how to talk with sensitivity to the images our language creates in our minds and others. If we do that, we will remember that racist and sexist talk is racist and sexist behavior. Most of us choose not to behave in either a racist or sexist fashion. Therefore, we will, when a generic pronoun is appropriate, choose terms that do not exclude—unless exclusion is, indeed, our goal.

The examples above serve one further purpose. They demonstrate that learning to write and speak in a nonsexist manner is not as difficult as some might think. We don't like writing that has many "he or she," "him or her" references in it. We find such writing awkward and, more important, it is not necessary. A generic pronoun, by definition, refers to a category or group of persons. Therefore, we rarely need a singular pronoun. Whenever a specific case is cited, a sex-specific pronoun should be used. Whenever a group is referred to, a plural reference is actually more accurate.

EXERCISE 3.4   DENOTATIVE AND CONNOTATIVE MEANINGS

OBJECTIVE   To recognize the variety of meanings that may be attached to words and become sensitive to how such variety affects communication

DIRECTIONS   **PART I—Denotations**
1. List as many denotations as you can think of for the word, *frog*.
2. Ask a friend (or members of a group in your class) to do the same.
3. After comparing your lists to see how many referents for the word, *frog* you collectively have, look up the word in a large unabridged dictionary. What were the definitions found there you did not have?
4. Explain the reasons that your personal lists did not include all the items that were in the dictionary list.

PART II—Connotations
1. As you read the words in the list below, write both your denotative meaning and your emotional response to each.
2. Next read the list to at least four other people, asking them to write their emotional response to each word.
3. Compare the five responses and discuss the review questions.

Word	*Referent (Denotation)*	*Emotional Response (Connotation)*
1. conservative		
2. grockett		
3. pig		

   4. Black
   5. ham
   6. effish
   7. liberal
   8. era
   9. plaque
   10. grass
   11. Italian
   12. crack
   13. Anglo
   14. nigger
   15. Spic

REVIEW   **Prepare to answer the following in writing assignment or class discussion.**
   1. What is the difference between connotative and denotative meanings?
   2. State how you can reduce communication problems resulting from differing denotative and connotative meanings?
   3. What is the most important communication principle illustrated or learned from this exercise?

SUMMARY

Communicating effectively requires shared meaning between communicators. Meaning refers to the entire set of reactions people assign to symbols. Meanings are not directly related to the symbols that stand for them, though it is a common myth that words have meanings. On the contrary, it is people who have the meanings; only the user connects a symbol to the meanings it calls up.

Words are symbols people use to represent concepts, and concepts are the ideas people have to explain their experiences. People develop concepts by synthesizing, or combining, the mental images of experience into ideas. This is called conceptualizing, and to do it, people must be able to abstract. Abstraction refers to the process of selecting an element from a reality to distinguish it from other elements. In abstracting, people develop a category system of concepts. The complexity of a category system depends on the number of features on which a person can focus about any reality.

To use a category system to identify realities, people have to exclude some things. Whatever is said or whatever ideas are thought about any reality, some things are not said or not thought. Words also reflect different levels of meaning or abstraction. Concepts, and thus words, vary from specific to general, and the higher the level of abstractness, the more ambiguous words become.

The more possible things a word can be applied to, the more possible misunderstandings can occur in communicating. When the term *abstract* is applied to words, it refers to words symbolizing a concept that cannot be seen. The word *concrete* refers to features that are specific and can be seen.

Words also represent different types of meanings. Denotative meanings are the actual objects or concepts referred to; connotative meanings are the values people attach to the concept—a negative or positive reaction to the symbol itself or to the thing or experience the symbol stands for.

Communicators also share the system in which symbols are used. Language is described as a symbolic system involving verbal and nonverbal, vocal and nonvocal symbols. Grammar is what makes language systematic. Grammar consists of the rules of word arrangement and inflections that make individual words useful. Knowing grammar helps people interpret word relationships and word and sentence meanings.

Each language system has differences of dialect and style. A dialect is a language variant used by a group of speakers that is different from the language of the general community. Dialects may be ethnic, geographical, or social, and they involve differences in word choices, grammar, and sound. Dialects influence communication because they activate biases communicators may have in favor of or against the group or community with which they identify the dialect. Style differences are primarily related to the degree of formality in language use. Styles vary according to situations as well as the relationships among the communicators. There are five styles of formality: frozen, formal, consultative, casual, and intimate. All these factors are involved as language concepts and experiences interact, resulting in language evolution and uses of language that reflect widespread attitudes in the society. Sensitive communicators are alert to these subtle racist and sexist effects of language.

QUESTIONS FOR DISCUSSION

1. What does it suggest to say "People, not symbols, have meaning"?
2. What is symbolization?
3. Explain this statement: Concepts are ideas created by experience.
4. To create concepts, we must abstract. What does that tell us about communicating?
5. What does the "ladder of abstraction" illustrate about communicating clearly?
6. What good does it do to realize the difference between denotative and connotative meanings?
7. Can you give an example of each of the types of symbols?
8. Can you explain the ways grammar influences communication?
9. What are the effects of dialect in communication?
10. If you talk with an inappropriate style, what are the likely results?

SUGGESTIONS FOR FURTHER READING

Bonah, R. Brent, and Sheila Shively. *The Language Lens.* Englewood Cliffs, N.J.: Prentice-Hall, 1973.

Brown, Roger. *Words and Things, An Introduction to Language.* New York: Free Press, 1958.

DeVito, Joseph. *Language: Concepts and Processes.* Englewood Cliffs, N.J.: Prentice-Hall, 1976.

Farb, Peter. *Word Play.* New York: Bantam, 1975.

Giglioli, Pier P., ed. *Language and Social Context.* Baltimore: Penguin, 1972.

Hayakawa, S. I. *Language in Thought and Action,* 4th ed. New York: Harcourt Brace Jovanovich, 1978.

Goffman, Erving. *Forms of Talk.* Philadelphia: University of Pennsylvania Press, 1981.

Joos, Martin. *The Five Clocks*. New York: Harcourt Brace Jovanovich, 1967.

Lakoff, George, and Mark Johnson. *Metaphors We Live By*. Chicago: University of Chicago Press, 1980.

Langacker, Ronald W. *Language and Its Structure*, 2nd ed. New York: Harcourt Brace Jovanovich, 1973.

Lindsay, Peter H., and Donald A. Norman. *Human Information Processing*, 2nd ed. New York: Academic Press, 1977.

Newman, Edwin. *Strictly Speaking*. New York: Warner Books, 1975.

Safire, William. *On Language*. New York: Times Books, 1980.

Spender, Dale. *Man Made Language*, 2nd ed. London: Routledge & Kegan Paul, 1985.

Thorne, Barrie, and Nancy Henley. *Language and Sex*. Rowley, Mass.: Newbury House, 1975.

Thorne, Barrie, Cheris Kramarae, and Nancy Henley. *Language, Gender and Society*. Rowley, Mass.: Newbury House Publishers, 1983.

Wolfram, Walt, and Ralph Fasold. *Study of Social Dialects in American English*. Englewood Cliffs, N.J.: Prentice-Hall, 1974.

Whorf, Benjamin Lee. *Language, Thought and Reality*, ed. John B. Carroll. Cambridge, Mass.: M.I.T. Press, 1956.

Wood, Barbara. *Children and Communication: Verbal and Nonverbal Language Development*. 2nd ed. Englewood Cliffs, N.J.: Prentice-Hall, 1981.

4 Nonverbal Message Carriers: Sharing Meanings

> Don't say things. What you are stands over you the while, and thunders so that I cannot hear what you say to the contrary.
>
> RALPH WALDO EMERSON

GOAL

To improve receiving and sending skills of nonverbal communication

OBJECTIVES

The material in this chapter should help you to:
1. Describe a "category system" that will help you analyze and understand nonverbal communication.
2. Identify basic nonverbal messages sent by overt and covert actions and the use of face and eyes.
3. Use physical appearance variables effectively.
4. Recognize effects of objects in communication.
5. Use personal space more effectively.
6. Intentionally use various vocal characteristics to improve communication.
7. Develop a better understanding of "touch" as communication.
8. Recognize how using time is nonverbal communication.
9. Identify situations in which nonverbal communication is an effective substitute for verbal communication.
10. Use nonverbal means to complement, not contradict, verbal message carriers.

Nonverbal message carriers add much to our words. They substitute when words are inadequate or inappropriate. They often make words unnecessary. With touch, vocal tone, and pleasant facial expressions we can show love and understand that we are loved in return. With our bodies we can signal strangers we want to meet, tell a lover we're finished, tell people when we are bored, angry, sad. You can easily extend the list.

When you stop to think about it, we all know how much meaning is carried by nonverbal signals. Yet, for most of us most of the time, nonverbal message sources function at the level of marginal attention. If communicators focused more directly on nonverbal sources of information, the messages received would be less ambiguous. This chapter can help you do just that.

(Andy Capp cartoon by Reggie Smythe; reprinted with special permission of NAS, Inc.)

INTERPRETING NONVERBAL CUES

Limiting Factors

Three cautions should be kept in mind as you read this chapter and any other materials discussing nonverbal communication. First, though nonverbal communication has recently been the subject of intense research, many of the conclusions remain tentative.[1] We can state with certainty only that much, if not most, of the meaning in communication situations comes from nonverbal message sources. Beyond that, there are many hypotheses we will share with you. But few unqualified generalizations about nonverbal communication are accurate. Like words, nonverbal signals are ambiguous message carriers.

Second, the ambiguity is particularly important with reference to appropriate generalizations drawn from the research. Recent work has shown that many people

---

[1] A thorough survey of research into nonverbal communication is Mark Knapp's *Nonverbal Communication in Human Interaction*, 2nd ed. (New York: Holt, Rinehart and Winston, 1978) and Judith Hall's *Nonverbal Sex Differences* (Baltimore: The Johns Hopkins University Press, 1984).

perceive nonverbal messages differently based on sex-role expectations. Perhaps that explains why research has also found differences between men and women. Conclusions that may be accurate for women might not be appropriately applied to men, and vice versa.

Third, *situation* provides an essential framework in which to interpret nonverbal cues. Indeed, interpreting nonverbal cues out of context makes no more sense than attempting to decide what a writer means by looking at individual words instead of sentences. We risk serious error to conclude what any behavior, appearance, or other nonverbal element means without knowing the situation.[2] Whether men and women actually behave differently or are simply perceived as doing so, the "differences" influence how both are interpreted.

Using a Baseline

In interpreting the "meaning" of nonverbal cues, a *baseline* concept is helpful. Behavior and other nonverbal cues may be much more idiosyncratic than language. As a result, interpretations of any particular factor usually rely on a known baseline. To know what it means that someone is shouting and red-faced may depend on knowing how common such behavior is for that person. Depending on context, of course, that type of behavior would lead most of us to infer that the person is quite angry. But we need to know that particular individual to decide *how* angry. What is baseline or usual behavior for the person will help us interpret other behavior because it lets us know how unusual, how different a particular behavior is. Indeed, in interpreting messages from those we know well, if a particular behavior fits our expectation (our baseline for that person) we infer, because of no difference, that little is new.

This concept of baseline is useful not only in applying information from context. It helps make sense of our concepts of *categories* of people. We noted above that researchers have found some differences in nonverbal behaviors between men and women. We also know that in some important respects cultural expectations for men and women differ. Similarly, our attitudes have created in each of us expectations regarding the behavior of many different groups or categories of people. Thus, within each culture (and subculture) there is a kind of *cultural baseline* that we use to interpret the behavior of people perceived to fit into the categories. In many cultures, for example, men are expected to be aggressive and women submissive; men to speak boldly and with a strong voice, women to speak more softly. We expect Italians to be voluble and expressive, Scandinavians reserved and cool, and so on. It matters little how accurate the expectations are. If we have them, and a person perceived to fit within the category behaves in a way that counters the expectations, we notice the exception.

Two baseline effects may occur. First, due to selective attention, we tend to

---

[2] This chapter relies heavily on the research and analysis reported there. For a summary of gender-related nonverbal communication, see Marianne LaFrance and Clara Mayo, *Moving Bodies: Nonverbal Communications in Social Relationships* (Monterey, Calif.: Brooks/Cole Publishing Co., 1978), or Judy Pearson, *Gender and Communication* (Dubuque, Ia.: William C. Brown Co., 1985).

ignore behaviors that do not meet our expectations. Since we tend to perceive what we expect to perceive, we often do not notice behavior that differs slightly. An almost reverse effect occurs when we do note behavior that contrasts with expectations. Behavior that we didn't expect becomes magnified in importance precisely because it differs from our baseline. Thus, a woman who is not submissive may be perceived as aggressive, a negative characteristic for women, while a man who speaks softly is described as a "wimp." When perceptions violate our expectations, our attitudes about "proper" behavior come into play. As a result, the baseline we consider applicable to the situation and the people strongly influences our interpretation.

Sources of nonverbal communication can be categorized by the senses that receive the messages. Using this system, we can study nonverbals in groups: those that arrive through visual sensations (eyes), those that come through the auditory channels (ears), those received through touch, those from other channels (taste, smell, time), and such special combinations of the senses as environment.

Keep in mind that any category system is a function of the language, not of the realities it tries to describe. Any of several category systems could be used to discuss nonverbal communication. None perfectly represents reality. That is partly because language cannot re-create nonlanguage phenomena. It's also partly because scholarship in nonverbal communication is relatively new, and there is still much to learn. Providing some structure for study of nonverbal systems is useful as long as you understand that any category system is imperfect. Watch for overlap and interaction among the sources of messages. It will help you understand the reality in spite of the verbal boxes.

VISUALLY RECEIVED MESSAGE CARRIERS

For most of us, nonverbal information is gained from four categories of things we see: actions (overt and covert), appearance, objects, and space (environment).

Actions

Physiologists estimate that the human face can produce more than 20,000 expressions. One researcher noted 7,777 distinct gestures in a study of classroom behavior; another catalogued 1,000 different body postures. These figures may surprise you— but probably only because someone spent the time counting. Most of us are well aware that the human body can assume an almost infinite number of positions. The question is: Do the differences in actions grow from different intended messages and lead to different perceived messages? The answer is yes, even though there can never be total uniformity of meaning, either intended or perceived.

Gestures and Movements (Overt Actions) Many actions are overt (out in the open) and readily observable. Examples are numerous and familiar: shaking a fist, waving, pacing the floor, holding up and using objects, pounding a table, gestures of all kinds. We're all familiar with these gestures and the messages we infer from them. If we heard Mike say to Toni, "You will be sure to get that done, okay?" with a smile and a handshake, it would be quite different from hearing him pronounce the same words with a steady glare and a gesture toward the door. We all know the two intended messages are very different. And if Mike said, "You will be sure to get that done, okay!" with a clenched jaw, while shaking a fist in front of Toni's nose, the meaning would be still different. Other aspects of overt gestures are less well known.

Probably the most important thing to know about large body movements is that they are often inconsistent with verbal messages. A person who says, "Oh, no, I'm not upset," but cannot sit still and whose fingers tap nervously on the table sends contradictory messages. *When verbal and nonverbal messages contradict, people tend to believe the nonverbal ones.* If you want to send messages effectively, be sure your verbal and nonverbal behaviors are consistent.

One significant aspect of the large body movements is general body inclination, or posture. Perhaps the most widely understood gesture is leaning toward or away from a person. We lean toward a speaker if we are interested or we want to close the gap between us. Leaning away is a subtle avoidance signal. Yet these conclusions are not always valid. Sometimes a listener will lean back in a soft easy chair, showing relaxed, comfortable participation in a conversation. But if listeners combine leaning backward with folded arms and eyes on the ceiling, it may be a signal they're not very interested in the conversation.

Body positions can include or exclude others as well as reflect our feelings.

The point is that *nonverbal message carriers, like words, must be interpreted in a total context*. When you hear the sound *rehd* you don't know what is meant without the context. Without the whole sentence, you don't know whether it's a verb, as in "I read it," or a color, red. The same is true of body language. Without the total context, you can seldom say what any single gesture means.

In context, overt body movements send generally accurate messages. An example is crossing the legs as part of general body inclination. When people are in a seated position, crossing the legs is a common gesture. Legs crossed toward the person you are talking with can combine with body posture to indicate interest and warmth toward the person. Indeed, two people can use this posture to indicate to others that they do not want to be interrupted. Crossing the legs away from the person sends a different message. This easily combines with the body posture of leaning away. When a communicator is trying to control body posture or finds it too obvious or impossible to lean away, crossing the legs can form a barrier to make up for the inability to lean or move away.

Arm positions also can send messages. Arm positions are described as open if the elbows are not held close to the body and the arms and hands are free. Arm positions are closed if elbows are tight against the body, arms are crossed, and/or hands are folded.

Closed arm positions can signal several things. They may suggest that the person is cold—figuratively or literally. They may suggest that the person is closed to the ideas or other people present. They may suggest that the person wants no new information ("My mind is made up. Don't confuse me with facts"). Indeed, many people conclude that others are dogmatic, aggressive, or closed-minded due to habitual closed arm gestures.

Remember, this gesture does not occur in isolation. Persons standing with

Overt and covert gestures lead to many possible conclusions.

no support nearby may find the closed arm position more relaxed than having their arms hanging at their sides, and less closed or aggressive than putting hands on hips. When people are seated, however, the opposite is true; and when people are forced into crowded situations, one defensive movement is to cross the arms as a "barrier" against others. It makes up for too little space. So note the context before interpreting. Have elements in the environment caused the closed positions?

Speakers who want to convey warmth should use open arm and body positions for several reasons. Not only do crossed arms suggest coldness and rigidity, but they also prevent spontaneous hand and arm gestures. Some research has shown that warm body postures have a positive effect on persuasiveness, so open postures are usually preferable.[3]

Muscle Tension (Covert Actions)   Covert actions are harder to see than larger gestures but sometimes communicate more. Covert behaviors are not easy to control, so they send very honest messages. Muscle tension that reflects nervousness or anxiety is covert action. So are a blush, hands that tremble or sweat, and muscles that are tight because of impatience or anxiety. These, and many other covert actions, can be very informative if we pay attention to them. Body movements can tell us much about how people feel. We often know when people are sad, angry, or tense, even when they don't say so or try hard not to show it. That is partly because many of our conclusions are based on covert gestures.

Facial Expressions   To illustrate the communicative power of facial expressions, including eye behavior, imagine each of these faces saying "no."

FIGURE 4–1. Nonverbals Add Meanings to Verbal Messages.

Sketch some faces yourself. How many different "no's" can you devise?

Facial expressions are probably the primary communicators of feelings. Expressions reflecting extreme emotions appear to suggest fairly similar meanings to people in all cultures. People across the world describe pictures of smiling or frowning faces in the same ways. Smiles and unhappy expressions are seen on faces of blind children as well as those who see.

[3] Several studies analyzing relations of persuasion and attitude change to nonverbal cues are reported in Judee K. Burgoon and Thomas Saine, *The Unspoken Dialogue* (Boston: Houghton-Mifflin, 1978), pp. 279–96.

People seem to judge facial expressions according to whether they are pleasant or unpleasant, active or passive, intense or controlled. Yet people differ greatly in their ability to judge emotional states from faces. This ability seems to depend on two things: (1) how much attention the observer pays to others' facial expressions, and (2) the observer's personal emotional state. Some never learn to read faces well. One reason is that facial expressions are very complex. Study of photos has shown that faces seldom show one pure emotional state. At the same time that one part of a face appears surprised, another might show anger; or an expression in one part of the face might show sadness at the same time that another part looks surprised.[4]

A frame-by-frame study of films reveals that many people control their overall facial expressions but show micro (very small) changes.[5] A person of this type, told of failing a test, may still smile or seem to show no expression, but if we closely examined a film of that person, we might see a flash of anger or despair cross the face before the smile or blank expression returns. While talking, we notice such changes only marginally, if at all. They happen too fast. The importance of this study is that it shows how well many people have learned to control their facial expressions. Though facial expressions are very meaningful, they are among the nonverbal behaviors most likely to deceive. We learn facial display rules very early in life, often developing our own styles of facial response to feelings and ideas. Observers often read too much into a facial expression.

The Eyes   One primary element in facial expression is use of the eyes. Eye contact is another area about which there are many misconceptions. Many people believe, for instance, that if speakers do not have eye contact, they are uneasy or not telling the truth. Although this conclusion is often accurate, it is not always so. Eye behavior varies greatly depending on the sex and age of those involved, how close the communicators are, what they are discussing, and whether the person is a speaker or a listener, wants to be involved in the situation or not, or has higher or lower status than the other communicator. Differences of culture also account for differences in uses of eyes.

FUNCTIONS OF EYE CONTACT   Eye contact has several functions. One is *cognitive* (having to do with *knowing*). Speakers tend to look away from listeners when they are trying to think of what they want to say or of words they want to use. Direct eye contact shows interest and receptiveness—a willingness to *know*—so it is not surprising that in conversations listeners use more eye contact than speakers. Direct eye contact invites involvement. When people are concerned and involved with what they are trying to say, they may reduce eye contact. That way, they reduce involvement with receivers and can concentrate on what they're saying.

[4] The most recent summary and analytical report of their extensive research is *Unmasking the Face* by Paul Eckman and Wallace Friesen (Englewood Cliffs, N.J.: Prentice-Hall, 1974). You will want to read this book if the material about use of face and eyes is especially interesting to you.

[5] E. A. Haggard and F. S. Isaacs, "Micromomentary Facial Expressions as Indication of Ego Mechanisms in Psychotherapy," in L. A. Gottschalk and A. H. Auerback (eds.), *Methods of Research in Psychotherapy* (New York: Appleton-Century-Crofts, 1966), cited in Knapp, *Nonverbal Communication*, p. 270.

"Wipe that opinion off your face."

(George Dole; reprinted courtesy *Parade* magazine, June 30, 1974.)

Eye contact can *regulate interactions* among communicators. A glance can signal even to strangers that a communication channel is open and that conversation may begin. Indeed, under certain circumstances, such as meeting an acquaintance on the street, eye contact almost obligates us to speak. Sometimes, such as when an instructor looks at students who are talking, eye contact can suppress communication. Extended eye contact—a stare or glare—often cuts off others' talk. Later in this chapter, we discuss these regulatory uses of eye contact in more detail.

Eye contact is *expressive*. The eyes can show how aroused or involved we are in the situation. The muscles that control the eyebrows, as well as eye movements themselves, may be why the face is a primary communicator of emotions. The emotions most accurately communicated by facial expressions are surprise, fear, and disgust. Each of these is seen best in the eyes, eyebrows, and nose near the eyes. The next most accurately expressed emotions are anger, happiness, and sadness.

Another way eyes are expressive is that they show interest in a person or object. As we have already noted, eye contact can signal that the communication channel is open. This is often how interactions begin. But beyond that, we look longer and more often at things and people that are rewarding to us. Except for the long, hard stare at something we disapprove of, long eye contact with something usually means we're attracted to it.

Eyes *monitor*. When people are talking, they use eye contact to see how much impact their remarks are having on the listener. Watching a speaker is consid-

Eye contact is among the most meaningful of nonverbal message carriers.

ered a sign of listening. Many students know this very well. They sit in a class—thinking about last night's date or the exam in their next class—with their eyes fixed intently on the instructor.

Eye behavior can *adapt* for changes in physical distance and space. If people are communicating over a longer distance than is comfortable, they have more eye contact than they do if they are close together. In fact, reducing eye contact is one way people create distance when they must be closer to others than they like. Think back to the last time you sat in a crowded car or room. How much did you look directly into the eyes of people close to you? When you get on a crowded elevator, do you look into the eyes of the people with you? Probably not. If you are on the elevator when others get on, you try to avoid catching their eyes as they enter. And when the door closes, everyone stands rigidly with eyes fixed on the floor indicator. Lack of eye contact is one way to add distance when physical space is limited.

EYE BEHAVIOR: A SUMMARY   There are no "rules" that tell what any particular eye behavior reveals. Nevertheless, the following list summarizes much that is known about the use of the eyes. As long as you remember that these are tendencies and not rules, you may find the list helpful.[6]

Eye contact is increased when:

[6] This list on p. 100 is from Mark Knapp, *Nonverbal Communication in Human Interaction*, 2nd ed, p. 313. © 1978, 1972 by Holt, Rinehart and Winston. Reprinted by permission of the publisher.

You are physically distant from your partner.
You are discussing easy, impersonal topics.
There is nothing else to look at.
You are interested in your partner's reactions—interpersonally involved.
You are interested in your partner—that is, like or love the partner.
You are of a lower status than your partner.
You are trying to dominate or influence your partner.
You are from a culture that emphasizes visual contact in interaction.
You are an extrovert.
You have high affiliative or inclusion needs.
You are dependent on your partner (and the partner has been unresponsive).
You are listening rather than talking.
You are female.[7]

Eye contact is reduced when:

You are physically close.
You are discussing difficult, intimate topics.
You have other relevant objects, people, or backgrounds to look at.
You are not interested in your partner's reactions.
You are talking rather than listening.
You are not interested in your partner—that is, dislike the partner.
You perceive yourself as a higher-status person than your partner.
You are from a culture that imposes sanctions on visual contact during interaction.
You are an introvert.
You are low on affiliative or inclusion needs.
You have a mental disorder like autism, schizophrenia, and the like.
You are embarrassed, ashamed, sorrowful, sad, submissive, or trying to hide something.

Appearance

Physical characteristics are body communicators that do not involve movement. They include physique; size; arrangement, color, and length of hair; skin color and texture; personal decorations; and so on. Physical characteristics are commonly used to draw conclusions about people and personality.

Stable Characteristics   Stable physical characteristics cannot easily be changed. Body type, for example, is a stable element that is assigned meanings by others. When we meet a man with an athletic build, we may be surprised if we find he doesn't like sports. One of the authors was recently hustled into thinking he had an easy tennis game when he was challenged by an overweight man with long gray hair and eyeglasses. The expectations turned out to be mistaken assumptions based on a stereotype; the challenger was an excellent tennis player and won easily.

---

[7] The differences between men and women in eye behavior as well as other uses of nonverbals may be largely due to power and status differences.

There are three major body types: athletic, frail, and obese. Among these body types, you can easily tell which individuals would be expected to be aggressive, jolly, serious, nervous, intelligent, lazy, or slow. Some people expect an attractive, well-built woman to be sexy and not very bright. They act surprised if she speaks intelligently. These expectations influence some perceptions so strongly that some intelligent, educated, and attractive women report they are not listened to in committees or groups.

Most of us realize how important these stable personal appearance characteristics are. People with the "wrong" body types work hard to change their appearance and avoid these interpretations. Thousands diet constantly so they won't be fat, and others try hard to gain weight or add inches in strategic places. Hucksters make fortunes by promising to create a Mr. Universe from a skinny man or a Raquel Welch from a flat-chested woman.

Personal appearance plays an important role in initial attraction between people, but the impact of appearance extends beyond first impressions. There is a correlation between good looks and good grades in school, between good looks and persuasiveness, between good looks and higher starting salaries for college graduates, between good looks and number of teacher-student interactions, between poor looks and being convicted of crimes, between size and being elected to office.[8] Except in 1976, the winner of every presidential election since 1900 has been the taller of the two candidates.[9] When we look at people, most of us create distortions of appearance in favor of those who are tall and those who are light-skinned.

All this is more than a little disturbing to those of us who think that the inner person, not outer appearance, should influence how others respond to us. But whether we like it or not, we must recognize the unconscious (and for many people conscious) desire to interact positively with people the culture defines as attractive. Nor is it important only for women to be attractive. The studies showing relationships between positive outcomes and attractiveness include people of both sexes.

Let's be sure we're being clear here. We are not suggesting that good looks cause positive outcomes. No evidence supports or refutes that kind of causal link. What a student of communication should realize is that the stereotype affects the communicators. The athletic person is stereotyped as stronger, more mature, more self-reliant. The obese person is seen as older, shorter, more old-fashioned, more talkative. Those with a frail body type are stereotyped as more ambitious, suspicious, stubborn, difficult, and pessimistic. Unfortunately, the question is not whether the stereotypes are true or not. If you fit one of these body types, people may perceive you as the stereotyped personality, regardless of your actual self.

This effect of appearance demonstrates the principle that people tend to perceive what they expect to perceive. And, as we noted in Chapter 2, we tend to fulfill the prophecy. That is, each of us tends to respond to others as they expect us to respond. So the stereotypes are important in communication. If you look athletic

---

[8] Knapp, *Nonverbal Communication*, pp. 153–75.

[9] As this book went to press, the outcome of the 1988 presidential election was not known.

but are not strong or mature or self-reliant, if you look frail but are not ambitious, suspicious, stubborn, difficult, or pessimistic, people may still respond to you as if you were.

Unstable Characteristics Unstable physical characteristics are easier to change. These include length or color of hair and/or beard and the way we decorate our bodies with clothes, jewelry, and cosmetics. A man with long hair may choose to ignore whether people consider him a liberal or a rebel. But if he wants a job that requires it, he can cut his hair or put on a wig. He can manipulate all the unstable characteristics to give himself the desired appearance.

The power of the relationship between unstable characteristics and impressions is shown by the impact of uniforms. The uniform itself often conveys status, power, authority, and good looks. We've always seen police, airline pilots, flight attendants, and soldiers in uniform. Today we also see uniforms on bank officers and tellers. Not only do waiters in restaurants and Playboy bunnies wear uniforms, but so does every person who works in a fast food chain. Even places without formal uniforms have informal uniform policies. IBM may no longer be a world where all the suits are gray flannel, but IBM's executives do wear suits, and they are not denim. At the other extreme, students who come to night classes still wearing their business suits often feel compelled to explain that they didn't have time to change their clothes after work.

We all know that clothes identify us with groups or classes of people. What we may not realize is how important appearance is in the way people respond to (that is, communicate with) us. John Molloy, who commands upward from $1,500 a day in consulting fees, advises corporate clients how to dress for advancement in the business world. He suggests that if you don't wear the right clothes the right way, you won't advance.[10] Michael Korda points out that for men to be perceived as important in the office, they have to carry the proper size briefcase.[11]

Personal appearance characteristics, whether stable or unstable, affect how people perceive us. People attribute to us skills, personality traits, and abilities based on how we look. These advance expectations may be crucial to whether we ever have a chance to know people better or to demonstrate personal qualities beyond what they expect us to have.

Use of Objects

Objects are important nonverbal message carriers. Many visually received impressions come from objects, and by controlling the environment, they often affect how people communicate. We have already mentioned how many messages are drawn from one kind of object: clothing and personal decorations.

[10] John T. Molloy, *St. Louis Globe Democrat*, September 6–7, 1975. Those interested in a further discussion of "dress codes" in businesses may want to see Molloy's *Dress for Success* (New York: Warner Books, 1978); and *The Woman's Dress for Success Book* (New York: Warner Books, 1977).

[11] Michael Korda, *Power! How to Get It, How to Use It* (New York: Random House, 1975), pp. 226–27.

Nonverbal communication results from a variety of sources acting in combination.

Objects that are part of the environment affect communication because they influence how people are able to talk to each other. Conversations can be influenced by the way furniture is arranged. Classroom chairs arranged in straight rows facing the front, for instance, guide interactions back and forth between instructor and students—not among students themselves.

Chairs arranged in a circle enhance communication among members of a group. This arrangement is even better than seating people at tables. For instance, seating a group of fifteen people at a table almost automatically eliminates some persons from the interactions—whether they want to be excluded or not. The same people at a round table, or on chairs in a circle with no table, will all have an equal opportunity to interact. In that setting, the people, not the environment, will influence who may participate in the discussion.

People are free to arrange the furniture in their houses and, usually, their offices. Therefore, we can tell a lot about how people like to interact with others from the way they arrange objects in their homes and offices. The objects people choose enable us to draw many other conclusions about them. The cars people drive, the houses and neighborhoods they live in, and the ways they furnish and decorate their houses and offices can all tell us much about their personalities.

Space

The nonverbal messages we draw from how people use space are related both to their actions and their use of objects. Two aspects of space influence communication: personal distance and territoriality.

Personal Space   The study of personal space is often called proxemics. **Proxemics** deals with *the distances among people as they communicate.* It primarily involves how close to people we stand or sit when we are talking with them. The basic theory is that we all carry around us an invisible bubble, which expands and contracts depending on the circumstances. Anyone invading our personal space bubble makes us uncomfortable and influences our communication. How much space we want between ourselves and others (how large our bubble is) depends on the situation and our relationships with the people to whom we're talking. It is also influenced by habits approved by culture and family.

Generally, people prefer larger spaces for strangers or formal situations. We reduce the distance according to the informality of the situation and the intimacy of the relationship. If we feel warmth toward people, we allow them to get close; we keep our distance from those we do not like or people from whom we sense disapproval.

To illustrate this bubble, you might try some experiments. After one of your classes today, ask your instructor a question while standing closer than you would normally. Observe the reaction. We don't recommend trying this on your boss, because it's considered an intrusion, and the "right" to do so is usually reserved for persons of high status. Moreover, you should explain to your instructor immediately afterward that you were doing this for a class experiment. Intrusions of this kind usually create negative reactions.

Try this with some friends: Engage in conversation standing at what feels to you a normal distance apart. Then move in as close as you can before someone backs away. Next, walk two or three feet farther away and try to continue the conversation. Does that seem inappropriate for personal conversation? Talk with your friends about how they felt in the different spatial relationships. You might then try the same things with your parents. You'll find it interesting to compare the reactions of different people.

Anthropologist Edward Hall has studied the personal distances as well as voice volumes that seem appropriate to people in the United States. Though comfortable personal distances vary greatly from person to person and situation to situation, his guide to the various uses of personal space is appropriate for most people:[12]

	Distance	Voice
Intimate	1. Very close (3–6″)	Soft whisper; top secret
	2. Close (8–12″)	Audible whisper; very confidential
Personal	3. Near (12–20″)	Indoors, soft voice; outdoors, full voice, confidential
	4. Neutral (20–36″)	Soft voice, low volume, personal subject matter
Social	5. Neutral (4½–5′)	Full voice; information of nonpersonal matter
	6. Public distance (5½–8′)	Full voice with slight overloudness; public information for others to hear

[12] Edward Hall, *The Silent Language* (Greenwich, Conn.: Fawcett, 1959), pp. 184–85.

| Formal, impersonal | 7. Across the room (8–20') | Loud voice; talking to a group |
| | 8. Stretching the limits of distance (20–24' indoors, up to 100 ft outdoors) | Hailing distance, departures |

Use of personal space is closely tied to relationships, but other factors are also involved. Age, sex, and ethnic background make a difference. Mixed sex pairs, for instance, communicate at closer distances than do pairs of females or pairs of men. Women generally communicate at closer distances than do men. Peers (people with equal status) generally interact more closely than do people with different status. This may explain why young people will establish closer distances with each other than with someone older.

Differences among cultures are striking. Hall found, for instance, that Arabs communicate at much closer distances than do people reared in the United States. Yet, even within each society, great variances exist. Within the United States, various ethnic groups seem to have different patterns of using space. For instance, Blacks interact more closely with other Blacks than will most white pairs. This may be caused by differences in social and economic status, not to the ethnic identification. It may also be because Black communicators tend to move and gesture more than whites do. More study is needed before we can draw any sure conclusions about differences among ethnic groups.

Territoriality   The other way space influences communication is territoriality. **Territoriality** refers to *staking out a space or a territory that people believe is their own.* You show territoriality, for instance, when you sit in the same chair in class every day, or when you park in the same place, or ask the waiter for "your" table in a restaurant. Try this: Go to class early today and sit in "somebody else's" chair. Watch the person's reactions when she or he enters. You could also observe this phenomenon by parking in the boss's parking spot today, but we don't recommend it.

Territoriality may have the most effect when you fail to recognize what others claim as their territory. It affects both the way they relate to you and what you say to each other. Being aware of your and others' territoriality can help improve your communication.

Each of us claims different types of territory. First, we have *primary* territory. That is space exclusively ours. It might be our side of the bed, our bedroom, our closet, our bathroom, our chair. No one else uses these, at least not without our permission. We also have *secondary* territory. It is less central to our lives, but we have a sort of claim on it, by unspoken agreement or by habit. A good example is "your" chair in a classroom. No one else sits there after the first day or two of class.

Finally, there is *public* territory. It belongs to no one. In this category, what counts is temporary occupancy. If you are sitting on a park bench, it's unlikely people will come by and say, "That's my seat!" If they did, you'd consider them eccentric. On the other hand, if several people eat lunch in a park near your office building every day, you probably concede certain seats to each other. You have a kind of secondary territory among yourselves. But if strangers in the park take "your" seat before you arrive, you probably accept their temporary occupancy, even though you don't like it. How much distance you give them will depend on how full the park is, how close the other benches are, and the attitudes you and your companions hold.

Once people have staked out a territory, different levels of encroachment can occur. Outright *invasion* is the most serious. When people actually come within your bubble of space or use your primary territory, they are invading. It would be an invasion if you were sitting on that park bench alone and a stranger sat right beside you when there were other empty benches nearby. If a member of your family went to sleep on your side of the bed, that would be invasion, too. Less serious, though still disturbing, is *violation*. It's a violation if someone sits an acceptable distance from you but carries a portable radio playing loud music you don't like. If someone rustles papers or watches you, it's violation. Finally, space is sometimes *contaminated*. People do not actually enter your space, but mess it up. Someone leaving beer cans on your lawn or smoking in your office contaminates your territory.

Reactions to encroachments depend on who did it, how they did it, why, and for how long. People with higher status feel freer to invade, and we permit it. Also, we accept more encroachment from those with whom we have close relationships. Emergencies or work are often permissible invasions. You can be having a personal conversation with someone at the office and not be bothered if the boss interrupts. A janitor can enter an office during a conference to pick up trash, and no one objects. But in either case, if you didn't think that the person who entered had acceptable reasons, your responses might be very strong.

In response to encroachments, we often engage in preventive behavior. We stake our territory. We build fences around our yards, put nameplates in our offices, sit in the middle of the park bench, scatter objects around us. In public situations (for example, at a concert in the park), if we want to leave temporarily we may ask the person sitting next to us, "Will you save my seat?"

If we can't prevent encroachment, we might move or ask the other person to move. More likely we'd make several defensive movements. We might give the invader a hard stare. We might cross our arms or move objects to build a sort of wall between us. Purses, umbrellas, briefcases, papers, and books can all be used for this purpose. We can shift posture to lean away, and we can hold our bodies rigid, as we do in elevators or crowds. We can scratch our necks, extending our elbows toward the person as a kind of defense.

Most people do not like to invade any more than they like to be invaded. If two people are talking in a hallway where others must walk, they are the ones who are really intruding. Yet when people want to walk down that hallway, they say, "Pardon me," bow their heads, and hunch as they pass. This happens even though they are using public territory. They know they may be invading, so they do not like to do it.

AURALLY RECEIVED MESSAGE CARRIERS

Besides hearing verbal elements in speech communication, we get other information through our ears as well. These messages are drawn from the sounds of voices and from other sounds.

Voice Qualities

Voice includes several distinct elements: pitch, volume, rate, rhythm, and a distinctive sound usually described as quality. We use many of these elements to draw conclusions about people and about what they mean by the words they use. (Due to the importance of these elements, we discuss them in some detail in Chapter 13.)

Listening only to voices, people can quite reliably judge a speaker's sex, age, level of energy, enthusiasm, ethnic group, and region of the country. They are also relatively successful in assessing status, emotions, moods, and how aggressive a speaker is. But people aren't terribly reliable in deciding from voice alone whether or not a person is extroverted, honest, law-abiding, or healthy.

We use both verbal and vocal cues to identify a person's dialect. Then, as noted in Chapter 3, once we have identified social, educational, ethnic, or regional status, our attitudes affect the interactions. If we have either negative or positive attitudes toward the group with which we identify the dialect, these attitudes are often triggered by voice alone.

Other effects of sound are caused by voice quality. Many words used to describe vocal qualities show negative reactions; the words *strident*, *harsh*, *nasal*, and *weak* refer to vocal qualities for which most of us have negative connotations. When we hear someone whose voice has one of those qualities, our impressions are often negative.

Not only do we perceive many types of voices negatively, we think many more are appropriate only to a certain sex, a certain type of person, or specific situations. When people hear voices they consider inappropriate for either the situation or the person, they draw negative inferences about the person. For instance, a high, thin voice in a man will influence people to assign certain personality traits to him, whether he really has them or not.

We often infer other personal qualities from the pitch of a voice. Circumstances such as anger, tension, or fear raise the pitch of the voice. When we hear a higher than normal pitch, we infer that the speaker is angry, tense, or afraid. Many characteristics of mood and feeling are also inferred from pitch. Similarly, when people talk quickly or slowly (rate), loudly or softly (volume), we have opinions about both their personalities and their attitudes.

Vocalizations

Vocalizations are another way voice carries information. **Vocalizations** are *elements of voice other than words that convey very specific information*. Some obvious examples are laughing, crying, whimpering, yelling, screaming, and groaning. None of these sounds is a word, but from each we infer very specific meanings.

Other aspects of vocalization directly affect language by adding information to the words. For example, think of the word *no*. We noted earlier how facial expressions can change meaning. With only your voice, you can also change the meanings communicated by *no*. Say *no*, letting your voice rise in pitch on the *o* sound. That makes a question mark. Now, say *no* loudly. Then say *no* at a high pitch. Each varies the intensity of the word. Say *no* with a long *o*. Depending on the intensity of your voice, that can be a very firm *no* or a quite uncertain one, especially if you allow a slight rise in the pitch at the end of the *o*. Finally, add a vocalization. Say, *uh, no*. Again, with a sound that is not language you have added meaning. Many of these vocalizations help us decide what speakers mean by their words or how they feel about the ideas or the people they're speaking to. We can often judge moods and attitudes quite accurately from a person's vocalizations.

Some common vocalizations are sounds used by speakers to fill silences: *uh, um, and uh, you know,* and *you see.* These vocalizations are often just fillers. They fill quiet spaces for the speaker. The fillers may say, "I'm not finished talking; don't take your turn yet," "I'm not sure what I want to say here," or "I don't really want to have to say this." The use of such fillers may be mere habit but tends to increase with the speaker's discomfort.

Environmental Sounds

Many environmental sounds are sources of information, and many affect communication in other ways. One of the most obvious effects is the impact of a loud sound. Too much noise can destroy the ability to communicate by talking. When a jet flies over you on takeoff or landing, conversation stops until it passes. In most dance clubs, there is no conversation during the music.

Noise affects communicators' feelings. Depending on the level and kinds of sounds, the results can range from fatigue to irritability. Prolonged exposure to noise may actually damage physical health. Psychologists report that family arguments occur most often when there are loud noises, such as a vacuum cleaner, a dishwasher, or loud music, in the background. The study of noise pollution and efforts to counter its effects relate to these serious results of noise.

In contrast, businesses have discovered that pleasant background music can increase workers' productivity, and that they can achieve specific effects by varying the music. Soothing music, like that heard in a dentist's office, can relax you. More lively music will be heard in places where the goal is to keep people moving. A clothing boutique may have rock music in the background; places specializing in more expensive clothing may feature classical music. Some business people and physicians use *white noise*, a low, continuous sound, something like an air conditioner. White noise can mask or cover distractions. It enables people to work in an environment where irregular noises are distracting.

TOUCH

Touch is a separate category of nonverbal message carrier because it communicates through actions and personal space. For infants, touch is the first source of information. Some evidence shows that extensive touching aids infants in normal development. As we grow older, touch comes to symbolize many different things, depending on our social group and culture. A handshake may be obligatory in some situations for some people and totally out of place in other situations for other people. An arm around a shoulder may be interpreted as aggression, affection, sympathy, or ritual behavior, depending on the people and the circumstances.

The rules of touch are strictly regulated by social norms. For infants and children, there is much freedom to touch. For adults in many social groups in the United States, touch is very limited. Nevertheless, it remains important in all our lives. Touching gives an impression of warmth and helps satisfy our needs for love, belonging, and security. One study showed the power of touch by comparing responses to library clerks when they touched their customers' hands when handing them the card and when they didn't. Customers who were touched rated the clerks as warmer persons.[13]

Society probably regulates touch because of the strong identification of touch with intimacy. Touching another's hand is permissible in most situations (a handshake or clasp), but touching other parts of the body may not be. It can violate social norms or suggest a close relationship or desire for intimacy. Touch is guided by certain criteria. A pat on the shoulder or the arm is more acceptable from a person of higher status to one of lower status than the other way around. Can you imagine walking into work in the morning and patting your boss on the arm, or strolling into class and touching the instructor? Yet the reverse is common. Bosses and supervisors pat employees on the arm or shoulder; police feel free to touch subjects, teachers to touch students, doctors to touch patients. Depending on the circumstances, their doing so can lead people to think of them as warmer persons.

The use of touch varies from group to group in our culture. Players during a football game frequently pat each other on the rear or throw their arms around each other. Similar behavior in other circumstances would cause quite different reactions from both the person who is touched and anyone who happens to be looking. An Italian wedding reception is likely to startle an unsuspecting non-Italian male. In contrast, people from other cultures perceive many U.S. social groups as cold, because they touch very little and employ great personal distances. Understanding these cultural differences may be important. Being unaware of the group "rules" about touching can lead to incomplete information at best and, at worst, serious misunderstanding.

Touching is similar in one important way to most other aspects of communica-

---

[13] J. D. Fisher, M. Rytting, and R. Hestin, "Hands Touching Hands: Affective and Evaluative Effects of an Interpersonal Touch," *Sociometry*, 39 (1976), 416–21, cited in Knapp, *Nonverbal Communication*, p. 242.

Touch is strongly feeling oriented.

tion. We can state no unqualified "rules" about it. Touching behavior is as much a matter of individual style as of culture and situation. Some people find it natural to use a variety of touching behaviors, and for them touching communicates very effectively. However, they are still guided by situation and culture. Other people may try to use the same touching behaviors but not find them natural or effective. They don't fit everyone's individual style. Within the limits of common sense and respect for others, you might experiment with touching behaviors. You may find they will help you communicate more effectively.

MESSAGE CARRIERS FROM OTHER CHANNELS

All the human senses are involved in gaining information. In this section, we discuss the information gained from time, smell, and combinations of several senses.

Time

As a code in communication, time deserves special notice. Rate of speaking is an obvious way to convey meaning by time. But time is also involved when someone pauses before replying to a question, or when someone interrupts another speaker. How long it takes to reply to questions or to return a telephone call tells you a great deal about the answer. Time is concerned with sounds and silences and with combinations of them. Time may even be the reason that rhythm, both of voice and of music, is such a potent communicator.

Time is an element in communicating relationships. How important it is to be "on time" for an appointment, for instance, depends on who the appointment is with, who made the appointment, who you are, and the culture. In the United States, success of an interview could be jeopardized if you appear fifteen minutes late, while in some Latin American cultures that would be acceptable. In those cultures, to be "on time" according to the U.S. definition would damage your chances of succeeding. But even in this country, the boss—and others of high status—can be late without much penalty. A professor, for instance, can come late to class but penalize students for doing the same thing.

A sense of the time of day also affects communication. Some events are better suited to the evening than to the morning, and vice versa. You can easily see how time can influence a meeting if it is scheduled shortly before mealtime. Or how about a meeting at work at 4 P.M. when quitting time is 4:30?

Use of time is one of the most culturally bound of the nonverbal codes. We can all improve our communication if we learn the time-use codes of our group or society.

Smell

The sense of smell is an important communicator, though one we are often not aware of. Smell sends basic messages. Think, for instance, of your response when you walk in the door at home and smell a roast cooking, or when you enter your favorite Italian restaurant. Compare that to how you feel when you open a container and smell spoiled food.

People in the United States seem anxious to suppress natural body smells. Some suggest this is because labor is "lower class," and the smell of sweat suggests that a person has to do physical labor for a living. Probably the identification of body smells with dirt, as well as social class distinctions, are involved in our reactions to such smells. It is more than that, however. We do respond positively to pleasant smells: flowers, a cool forest, perfume. Yet socialization certainly influences what we consider a pleasant smell. Arabs conversing feel that to communicate effectively they must smell each other's breath. To most Americans that is distasteful, not only because the space is too close, but also because we don't like the smell. Differences of this type are important to effective communication in many situations, as any person who wants to hold a white-collar job in the United States will soon find out.

Environment

Earlier we discussed some of the influences of environment on communication under the headings Use of Objects and Space. Other aspects of the environment also affect us. The color or size of a room can influence the interactions that take place within it. (Designers of public and private places try to take this into account, or they should.) These aspects of environment affect communication not so much through the messages people draw from the objects—though that happens—but in

Environment shapes the communication within it.

how people are affected. As Winston Churchill said, "We shape our buildings, and afterward our buildings shape us."

Colors influence our moods and behavior. Blue and green (except for very intense shades) tend to relax people and create a cool feeling or enhance security. Yellow and orange, on the other hand, are energizing. Red is a hot color. Red and black combinations are sensuous. (Think how often in fine restaurants you see combinations of red and black.) Brown and orange combinations are warm. Gray and brown are serious, somber colors. Can you recall the number of older banks that give you a predominant impression of gray? And have you noticed how many new banks are bringing color into their total image? Their employees wear warm-colored uniforms, and their walls are covered with many brightly colored art works.

Another important influence of environment is the air. High humidity and high temperatures negatively affect communication, because they lead to irritability and unpleasantness. Cool temperatures are more efficient and more productive. Temperatures seem to influence not only the efficiency with which people work, but also the effectiveness of their interactions. For example, police report increases in crowd fights, family disturbances, and other kinds of hostile outbreaks in hot, humid weather.

Textures in the environment also influence how we perceive situations. Soft, plush textures give us a warm, relaxed feeling. Hard, bright, angular textures create energy and perhaps even anxiety. Think of the differences between a fine hotel lobby or a cocktail lounge and the admitting room of a hospital. Compare an executive's office, with its plush furniture and wood desks, with a clerk's office outfitted with typewriters and steel desks and chairs.

Textures create varied tactile images, particularly if they are mixed. Designers use such mixtures to create interesting buildings and homes. Isn't it true that the most pleasant buildings you can remember do not have walls of all the same kind? Mixtures of wood, brick, stone, and plaster are more attractive than just plaster or sheetrock.

Light also makes a difference in how we react to the environment. Brightness makes us feel that it's time for work or activity, and we respond accordingly. Low and diffused lights lead to relaxed feelings and enhanced conversation. This probably explains the bright lights in fast food restaurants and the dim lights in expensive restaurants and bars.

EXERCISE 4.1   NONVERBAL SYMBOLS

OBJECTIVE   **To recognize nonverbal symbols in varying communication situations.**

DIRECTIONS   **1.** Complete the chart in Table 4–1.
  a. List at least one symbolic communication you received in each category.
  b. Briefly describe the nonverbal message carriers and state the conclusion you drew (example: Dad smiled; he was glad to see me).
2. Your instructor may have you discuss the following with a group of your classmates:
  a. Were any of the categories more meaningful than others as sources of information for you? Why? What kinds of information did you receive?
  b. Did members of your group vary according to which categories were most meaningful to them?
  c. Was there any ambiguity in the symbols you cited?
  d. In which categories was there little ambiguity? Why?

REVIEW   **After completing the chart, answer the following questions in preparation for class discussion or a writing assignment.**
  1. Note possible ambiguities in the interpretations you made of the nonverbal messages you recorded in the chart and use these as examples to explain why nonverbal messages are difficult to interpret accurately.
  2. State the most important communication principle you learned from this exercise.

USES OF NONVERBAL MESSAGES

Now that we have identified the many sources of nonverbal messages, let's examine some of their uses for both sources and receivers.

TABLE 4–1 Nonverbal Symbols

		SITUATIONS		
Nonverbal Category		Instructor in One of Your Classes	Wife/Husband/ Mother/Father/ Roommate at Dinner Today	Employer at Work Yesterday, or Salesclerk Last Time You Went Shopping
Action (includes face and eyes)	Observed Nonverbal		Dad smiled.	
	My perceived message		He was glad to see me.	
Voice	Observed Nonverbal			
	My perceived message			
Time	Observed Nonverbal			
	My perceived message			
Personal space	Observed Nonverbal			
	My perceived message			
Touch	Observed Nonverbal			
	My perceived message			
Physical characteristics	Observed Nonverbal			
	My perceived message			
Objects	Observed Nonverbal			
	My perceived message			

Interpreting Verbal Messages, Source Feelings, and Attributes

Receivers use nonverbals to draw conclusions about people and about what they intend to say. Since verbal messages are often ambiguous, effective listeners use nonverbals to clarify what speakers mean as well as how they feel about it.

Vocal influences are especially useful. Different types of sentences have particular inflections. Questions, for instance, usually end with a rising pitch. Exclamations are spoken loudly and emphatically. Emphasizing words with pitch, volume, and changes in voice quality can convey sarcasm and irony. The words, "Oh isn't that great," can suggest two very different meanings, depending on the speaker's tone. Vocal emphasis can suggest several different meanings from exactly the same words.

> "*I* did not tell Jimmy to go" (someone else did).
> "I did *not* tell Jimmy to go" (positive I didn't say it).
> "I did not *tell* Jimmy to go" (perhaps I merely suggested or implied it).
> "I did not tell *Jimmy* to go" (maybe I told someone else).
> "I did not tell Jimmy to *go*" (perhaps he was to stay).

If you are having trouble understanding what a person means, listen carefully for nonverbal cues.

Speakers' movements give other clues to word meanings because words and movements are usually coordinated. Changes in body position often accompany changes in ideas. Head and eye movements mark sentences. Finished thoughts are signaled by eye contact and often a shift in posture. Voice inflections and pauses also indicate changes in thought. Larger changes in ideas (such as major changes in subject matter or a shift from one point of view to another) are indicated by larger movements. For instance, when we're talking we often lean forward. Then we lean back and gesture toward the other person when it is time for an answer. A shift of posture signals that a long statement is about to begin, and the speaker may hold that same posture throughout, even though many arm and hand movements occur within the sustained "speech."

Assessing how strongly the speaker feels is another way receivers use nonverbal signals. Face, voice, and body movements are the best—often the only—way to know how speakers feel about what they are saying. Attitudes toward both ideas and others present are shown through behaviors. Our heads and faces tend to reflect *how* we're feeling (anger, joy, sadness); body cues reveal the *intensity* of feeling. Eye, hand, and head movements usually reflect specific emotional states. Postures show general emotional states (avoidance, interest, passivity).

Almost every category of nonverbal message carrier discussed earlier can be used to interpret how speakers feel. Postures, movements, facial expressions, eye contact or lack of it, degree of muscle tension, appearance, use of objects, time, and space all can help us know how people feel—both about what they're saying or hearing, and about the people involved.

With regard to gestures, especially with the arms, people often raise questions about habitual behaviors. People say, "I do that all the time; it doesn't mean I'm not interested." Certainly, many of us have movement habits. We cross our arms, rest hands on hips, tap pencils, drum fingers, jingle coins in a pocket, pull on a beard, swing our feet. These habits may reflect basic personality traits or general attitudes toward people.

To interpret such invariables, use the baseline concept. Even habitual mannerisms vary. Such behaviors may be described as *adaptors*, and they tend to increase when we are under pressure or are anxious. As our discomfort in a situation increases, adaptor behaviors increase, at least until we reach a state of extremely high anxiety. Then we may freeze and have no movement at all.

Body touching seems to suggest that a person is self-interested. If we see people doing a lot of arm clasping, pulling on hair or beard, and so on, we may decide they are quite concerned with self. This concern may be caused by anxiety or rejection of people or ideas. Even behaviors that popular body language literature describes as "preening" or courtship behaviors are self-interested. Smoothing hair, stroking sideburns, smoothing a skirt or a pants leg, and similar behaviors attract attention. Even if these behaviors display courtship, as claimed, they are self-interested because they seek to call attention to themselves.

Many nonverbals discussed throughout this chapter relate to interpreting people. We have cited only a few here to illustrate our point. Nonverbal message carriers, though ambiguous, help us understand the people we communicate with.

Supporting or Replacing Verbal Messages

As sources in communication, we consciously and unconsciously use nonverbal message carriers to reinforce our verbal messages, to substitute for them, or to regulate the behaviors of those with whom we communicate.

Reinforcement Perhaps the most common source use of nonverbal message carriers is to emphasize or reinforce our ideas and feelings. You've doubtless seen speakers say, "I see three reasons why this should be done," and hold up three fingers. Or you've said "I'm sorry" by sending flowers or a gift. Or perhaps you've extended sympathy to others by putting an arm around their shoulder and saying, "Can I do anything?"

We commonly use our appearance to reinforce the perception we want others to have of us. A professor who wants to be seen as free of conventional social rules may wear jeans and a tee shirt to classes. In contrast, an executive at IBM will wear a stylish, expensive suit.

We all surround ourselves with emblems that we want to send messages for us: houses, cars, clothes, jewelry, attaché cases, and so forth. The list is almost limitless. Politicians drape the halls of meeting rooms with flags. Democrats hang pictures of Franklin Roosevelt, Harry Truman, and John Kennedy; Republicans, of Abraham Lincoln, Teddy Roosevelt, and Dwight Eisenhower.

One of the terms used to describe this use of nonverbal communication is *strategic presentation of self*. All people do this, and we do not use the word *strategy* to connote anything negative about the process. *Strategic presentation of self* simply emphasizes that we actively make efforts to affect the images others have of us—whether we are conscious of what we do or not. What image we try to present, of course, depends on our concept of self and the situation. The point here is that we use nonverbal as well as verbal means to reinforce whatever image we try to present.

Substitution   Often, words seem inappropriate. In moments of extreme emotion, we may feel a need to substitute nonverbals for words. Grief or passionate disappointment are difficult to express with words, so we use touch or do something other than talking. Lovers greeting after a long absence will fall into each other's arms and hug and kiss. A lover, trying to make up after a quarrel, may send a dozen roses instead of calling or writing. All of us at times wear clothes we know some other person will like. We use perfume and after-shave, sit close to people, lean toward them, use constant eye contact—all to say without words, "I like you; I want to interact with you."

Control or Status   Another way we use nonverbal signals is to control other people or express status. For many reasons, a source may want to assert status in a situation or control the behavior of others. Words are not usually used for this purpose. Nonverbals can substitute for the words, and they are usually quite sufficient.

One way to display status is to use time. Taking longer to answer (whether a telephone, a letter, the door, or in person) can express superiority. Executives may keep employees or salespeople waiting, but they wouldn't do that to their superiors or members of the board of directors. A good illustration of time and status relationships is the difference in the attitude of people as they buy services. If you were buying insurance, you'd be pretty irritated if you were kept waiting by the salesperson. But purchasing the services of a physician or attorney is quite a different matter. The difference is status, expressed through use of time.

Space also can be used to control others' behavior or express status. Higher-status people "have" more territory. They have larger offices, bigger desks and chairs, larger and more luxurious cars. They also have more personal space. People do not closely approach persons higher in status than themselves, but the person of higher status feels free to invade the personal space of those with lower status. Higher-status people sit and stand in control positions. They take seats at the head of a table, use papers, briefcases, and aides to expand their personal space.

Dress and movement also express status. Persons of status dress and walk in ways that give an impression of height and good looks. Uniforms are often instrumental in conveying the status of those wearing them. Classic examples are found in the armed services, of course, but are not limited to them. Compare, for instance, the uniform of an airline pilot with that of the flight steward. Then compare the airplane mechanic's uniform to the steward's. You can supply many other examples from your own experience.

Masking and Contradiction

In the process of strategically presenting ourselves, we often send verbal and nonverbal message carriers that contradict each other. When sources actively try to create perceptions of themselves that may not fully square with the reality, they do not always succeed. This can happen when we say what we don't really mean or when we are trying not to say something.

Perhaps the best example is a person in a job interview. In this situation, people are often anxious. Job interviews are situations where people would naturally be expected to be nervous. But employers expect job applicants to be poised and confident enough not to show that they are nervous. Therefore, when most people interview for a job, they try not to appear anxious. They are masking.

When we attempt to mask feelings or beliefs, nonverbal and verbal messages often contradict each other. When this happens, we usually believe the nonverbal messages because they are less controllable, and we are less conscious of sending them. If you are embarrassed, for instance, you might blush even if you don't want to show the embarrassment. Anger can also result in a red face, even if the angry person controls facial expressions and hand movements.

The degree to which people are aware of and control their nonverbal messages varies. It varies with the people, the situation, and the specific kind of behavior. Though most of us believe eye contact is related to honesty, many people have learned to control facial expressions and eye contact. If we want to know whether a person is trying to deceive us, we must consider more than eye contact. Other nonverbals may be less under control. One researcher illustrated this by having observers study films of patients in a mental institution. The observers knew these patients were trying to deceive their psychiatrists. Some observers were directed to watch only the head of the patient. Others watched only the body of the patient, and a third group watched all parts of the body. People who watched the head thought that the patient was mature, stable, and doing well. Those who watched the body found much less control and concluded the patients were not stable.

All this makes at least two points about masking and contradictory nonverbals. First, if you are looking for deception, look most closely at the whole body, especially the feet and legs. They are often a source of nervous movements described as *leakage* when deception is intentional. Second, if you are trying to present a specific image to others, work to control all parts of your body.

Regulating Interactions

Nonverbal communication can regulate interactions among communicators. We have already noted that:

1. People use space and posture to exclude others from a conversation.
2. Use of eyes can signal that communication channels are open or closed.
3. Postures and eye contact can also indicate the degree of desire to communicate.
4. Nonverbal cues as feedback can regulate a speaker.

In addition, behaviors regulate how we take turns in conversations. Voice, eye contact, and body movements are the primary regulators. To yield a turn, we let our voice inflection rise or fall. When we're nearly finished talking, the rate will diminish and body movements will stop or pause. Body relaxation and direct eye contact indicate that the listener should now become the speaker.

To request a turn, we may draw in our breath loudly enough for someone to hear it. If a person is anxious and doesn't want to wait, he or she may interrupt. A kind of stutter start—*uh, er*—may occur, which is almost an interruption. A person might speed up the feedback, using what is sometimes called back-channeling. A listener saying *uh huh* or nodding the head usually indicates interest, a willingness to keep listening. The *uh huh*'s and *yes, yes* or head nods become more rapid when the listener wants to speak. An upraised finger or hand or straightened posture or leaning forward signals that a person wants a turn to speak.

Sometimes people will refuse to yield their turn. Then they do not look at the other person, thus avoiding the feedback requesting the turn. Volume may increase, along with rate of speech. What would normally be pauses in sentences or at the end of sentences are filled in, so no pause will give an opening. Gestures won't stop. Or the speaker will touch the other as a gesture to say "Wait a minute."

EXERCISE 4.2   USES OF NONVERBAL COMMUNICATION

OBJECTIVE   To practice identifying the uses of nonverbal symbols in a conversation.

DIRECTIONS
1. During a discussion with friends or in class, watch for uses of nonverbal communication. Remember to look for both source and receiver uses.
2. Use Table 4–2 to record the uses you noted. (See first row for example.)

REVIEW   **Write brief answers to the following questions that will form the basis for a writing assignment or class discussion.**
1. Explain how nonverbal messages perform the functions identified. Is it possible for one behavior or object to perform more than one function? How?
2. Why is nonverbal communication sometimes perceived as more credible than verbal messages?
3. In the interpretations of nonverbal messages you recorded, either in this exercise or in Exercise 4.1, did you find the concept of baseline expectations influencing your conclusions about what a particular behavior or object meant?
4. Explain the most important communication principle you learned from this exercise and why you found it important.

TABLE 4–2 Uses of Nonverbal Communication

RECEIVER USE OF NONVERBALS	INTERPRET MESSAGE	INTERPRET SOURCE FEELINGS	INTERPRET AS PERSON	CONTRADICTIONS	REGULATE
EXAMPLE: "Friend doubled her fist and pounded the table."		She feels strongly about this.			
SOURCE USE OF NONVERBALS	REINFORCE	SUBSTITUTE	CONTROL	MASK	REGULATE
EXAMPLE "Doubled my fist and pounded the table."	Emphasize verbal message.				

SUMMARY

Communication messages other than words come from nonverbal communication. Although they account for much, if not most, of the meaning we get in speech communication, nonverbals are ambiguous message carriers. To understand nonverbal messages, we have to become aware of them. Classifying nonverbal symbols and learning the meanings usually attached to each major category can help us understand what they mean, as long as we are alert to the limitations that apply to our interpretations.

One way to categorize nonverbal message carriers is according to the senses that receive them: sight, hearing, touch, smell, and interactions among several senses. There are four major types of visually received nonverbals: actions (including face and eye movements), appearance, use of objects, and space. Actions include both covert and overt movements of arms, legs, and body. Appearance includes physical characteristics, both stable and unstable. The use of objects includes elements we use intentionally to communicate (such as wearing a wedding ring) and objects that limit or direct communication by being part of the environment (such as the way furniture is arranged). Communication through space includes using personal distance and territoriality.

We also receive nonverbals through our hearing. Voice quality, nonverbal vocalizations (such as crying or laughter), vocalizations that relate directly to language (such as pitch), and fillers or adaptors are all nonverbals received through hearing. Environmental sounds, such as background music or loud noises, affect communication by interfering with vocal messages as well as affecting our feelings.

Touch is another nonverbal message carrier. It includes elements of both movement and space. Our society has strict norms governing touch among communicators, although how much and where we can touch vary according to age, sex, social groups, individual characteristics, and the situation. Other senses are also important carriers of communication messages. These include smell and such environmental factors as color, design, light, atmosphere, and temperature.

We can understand nonverbal messages better if we know how they function. Both receivers and sources use nonverbals. Receivers use nonverbal communication to help them interpret both intended messages and how sources feel about them. Receivers also use nonverbals to draw conclusions about sources or personalities. Sources use nonverbals to reinforce verbal messages, to substitute for words in some situations, to assert status or control, or, sometimes, to mask feelings. Occasionally a source's verbal and nonverbal messages will contradict. When that happens, receivers usually believe the nonverbal.

Both source and receiver use nonverbals to regulate interactions. Through voice, eye contact, and body movements, communicators indicate to each other their interest in opening or continuing communication, whose turn it is to speak, and when they think a conversation should end.

QUESTIONS FOR DISCUSSION

1. What are the types of visually received information?
2. What is the difference between overt and covert actions?
3. How do we generally communicate our feelings?
4. What are the several functions of eye contact?

5. Describe body communicators that do not include movement.

6. In what ways do objects communicate?

7. What influence does space have on communication?

8. How does information we receive through the ears influence communication?

9. Why is touch so important as a communicator?

10. What are the uses of nonverbal messages?

SUGGESTIONS FOR FURTHER READING

Argyle, Michael. *Bodily Communication*. London: Methuen, 1975.

Burgoon, Judee K., and Thomas Saine. *The Unspoken Dialogue*. Boston: Houghton Mifflin, 1978.

Fast, Julius. *The Body Language of Sex, Power and Aggression*. New York: M. Evans, 1977.

Frye, Jerry. *FIND: Frye's Index to Nonverbal Data*. Minneapolis: University of Minnesota Computer Center, 1980.

Hall, Edward T. *The Silent Language*. New York: Doubleday, 1973.

————. *The Hidden Dimension*. Garden City, N.Y.: Doubleday, 1966.

————. *Beyond Culture*. New York: Anchor Books, 1977.

————. *Dance of Life: The Other Dimension of Time*. New York: Doubleday, 1983.

Hall, Judith. *Nonverbal Sex Differences*. Baltimore: The Johns Hopkins University Press, 1984.

Harper, Robert, et al. *Nonverbal Communication: The State of the Art*. New York: John Wiley, 1978.

Henley, Nancy M. *Body Politics: Power, Sex, and Nonverbal Communication*. Englewood Cliffs, N.J.: Prentice-Hall, 1977.

Knapp, Mark L. *Nonverbal Communication in Human Interaction*, 2nd ed. New York: Holt, Rinehart and Winston, 1978.

Korda, Michael. *Power! How to Get It, How to Use It*. New York: Ballantine Books, 1975.

LaFrance, Marianne, and Clara Mayo. *Moving Bodies: Nonverbal Communications in Social Relationships*. Monterey, Calif.: Brooks/Cole, 1978.

Lamb, Warren, and Elizabeth Watson. *Body Code: The Meaning in-Movement*. London: Routledge and Kegan Paul, 1979.

Lorenz, Konrad. *On Aggression*. New York: Harcourt Brace Jovanovich, 1974.

Malandro, Loretta, and Larry Barker. *Nonverbal Communication*. Reading, Mass.: Addison-Wesley, 1983.

Mehrabian, Albert. *Silent Messages*. 2nd ed. Belmont, Calif.: Wadsworth, 1980.

Montagu, Ashley. *Touching: The Human Significance of Skin*, 2nd ed. New York: Harper & Row, 1978.

————. *The Nature of Human Aggression*. New York: Oxford University Press, 1976.

Morris, Desmond. *Intimate Behavior*. New York: Random House, 1971.

————. *Gestures*. New York: Stein & Day, 1980.

Rosenthal, Robert, et al. *Sensitivity to Nonverbal Communication: The Pons Test*. Baltimore: Johns Hopkins Press, 1979.

5 Thinking: Intrapersonal Processing

> It is the capacity of organizing information into large and complex images which is the chief glory of our species.
>
> KENNETH BOULDING

> Eloquence is the child of knowledge. When a mind is full, like a wholesome river, it is also clear.
>
> BENJAMIN DISRAELI

GOAL

To learn how to use thinking (intrapersonal communication) to communicate with others more effectively.

OBJECTIVES

The material in this chapter should help you to:

1. Explain the major difference between sensory information storage and long-term memory.
2. State why it is important to know that long-term memory involves interpretations, not sensory information.
3. Improve your use of the processes for recall.
4. Identify the following processes of reasoning:
   Generalization
   Deduction
   Cause to effect
   Comparison and contrast
   Creative thinking
5. Explain how failure to distinguish facts from statements about facts can affect communication.
6. Distinguish among statements of observation, of inference, and of judgment.
7. Explain why a statement of judgment tells more about the person who said it than the object or idea being evaluated.
8. Recognize and avoid using each of the following types of fallacies:
   Hasty or unrepresentative generalization
   Faulty deduction
   Faulty causal reasoning
   Inappropriate comparison
   False alternatives

The term *thinking* may be the simplest description of intrapersonal communication. As receivers, we process perceptions to draw meanings from what we see, hear, or otherwise experience. As sources, we consciously or unconsciously use thinking to choose verbal and nonverbal message carriers to express our ideas and feelings. Both sources and receivers must think to communicate.

What actually happens as you think? Don't you often say, "Let me think about that a little"? When you "think about it," what do you do? Do you consciously make a list of pros and cons for every issue? When thinking through a problem, do you systematically gather data, analyze the problem, establish criteria, consider all possible solutions, and choose a solution on the basis of which best meets all the criteria? Most of us do not—at least not most of the time. We think less systematically and do so most of our waking hours. Thought is the intrapersonal communication that helps us survive.

In thinking, we examine possible explanations of external and internal realities and choose the explanations that seem best. Thinking relates existing concepts to new information received. Thinking is how we choose among the many possible meanings for sensations received. Thinking is use of an existing store of meanings to draw conclusions about external and internal realities.

In thinking, we examine the possible explanations and choose the one that seems best.

Very often, maybe even most of the time, thinking is an unconscious process. We believe or disbelieve and act on our conclusions without much conscious attention. We could all improve our interpersonal communication if we used thinking (intrapersonal communication) more consciously. To help you do that is the goal of this chapter. Memory, reasoning, and thinking errors (fallacies) are the topics we will cover.

MEMORY

Thought requires memory. Indeed, memory may be our most important process in interpreting sensations received. Without the ability to remember, neither perception nor symbolization would be very useful. The term **memory** describes *the brain's ability to store and use information* based on sensory input. Memory enables us to use words to communicate about things that are not present or about ideas we cannot see or touch.

Storage

The brain interprets the sensory input it receives, stores information, and retrieves information from storage. Three different types of storage exist: sensory information storage, short-term memory, and long-term memory. *Sensory information storage is the impression of actual sensory reception you retain for a limited time.* To illustrate it, press your fingers against your arm and then lift them off. You briefly retain the sensation of touch. Wave a pencil back and forth in front of your eyes while you stare straight ahead. Notice how an image of the pencil trails behind as the pencil moves. These are examples of sensory information storage. When people talk, the sights and sounds are sensory information. But to have lasting impact, at least some of the information must enter short- and long-term memories.

Short- and long-term memory differ from sensory information storage because we do not retain actual sensory input. *Interpretations, not sensations, are stored in long- and short-term memory.* For example, when someone talks to you, you do not remember the sounds unless the person has an unusual way of pronouncing familiar words, or uses strange words. Generally, you remember only some of the words; mostly you remember ideas. You remember your interpretations, what the actual sensations meant to you, as reflected in Rod McKuen's poem "Thirty-Six."

> *I'm not sure what it means.*
> *Why we cannot shake the old loves from our minds.*
> *It must be that we build on memory/and make them more than what they were.*[1]

Remembering that short- and long-term memory contain interpretations, not sensations, can improve communication in at least two ways. First, you'll be less likely to engage in useless arguments over what someone "actually" said. Keeping in mind that what you remember is what you interpreted requires you to focus on

[1] *Listen to the Warm* (New York: Random House, 1967), p. 56. Reprinted by permission.

what really counts in communication: *intended and perceived messages*. The best way to clear up a misunderstanding is to find out what a source meant to say and what a receiver understood them to say. That will avoid fruitless and emotional hassles over what someone actually said.

Remembering this quality of memory also reminds us how language influences communication. When talking with others, we don't remember words; we remember what we decided the words meant. And since both language structure and words reflect a cultural perspective about reality, our culture affects what we remember. Thus, our cultural values and perspectives partly create our memories. For example, most people who grow up in the United States value cleanliness, but they rarely focus on it as a value. Yet when they talk with people, that value influences both what they hear and how they interpret their talk. If it is an election year and someone knocks on our door, giving us reasons to vote for a candidate, our memory of the arguments will differ according to whether the campaign worker was clean and neatly dressed or dirty and disheveled.

Finally, we need to remember that our memory system is more than a pile of stimulus-response blocks. *It is a dynamic system that grows as we interact with our environment.* Think back to when you were learning about the Pilgrims landing at Plymouth Rock. Can you remember what you first learned about the event? Probably not. And whatever it was, certainly your concept of the event is different now. You've learned about other settlers, other religions, other reasons the Pilgrims came. You've learned more about the Indians and their relations to settlers both before and after the Pilgrims arrived. Each memory continually builds onto earlier concepts. When you now recall the Pilgrims, even if you never studied their landing after grade school, you will take into consideration what you have learned since then. This same process applies to all concepts you learn. As you gain more knowledge, each memory is modified and elaborated, as well as expanded. Thus, *recall involves reconstruction.*

The evolution of stored knowledge affects how we process new information. Obviously, the way adults and children take in information differs. Young children memorize a great deal. With more maturity, they want to understand the sensations received. After early childhood, memory primarily fits new concepts into a preexisting memory structure. If adults don't understand information, they will often reject it instead of storing it. The existing store of knowledge interprets, organizes, and integrates new information.

Recall

The process of recall involves more than pulling something out of a storage system. The major memory difficulty for most people is retrieving stored information. Most of us have stored much more than we can easily recall, as McKuen notes in another poem.

> *The mind is such a junkyard;*
>   *it remembers candy bars*
>   *but not the Gettysburg Address,*

> *Frank Sinatra's middle name*
> *but not the day your best friend*
> *died.*[2]

We all have experiences that illustrate McKuen's point. Some events, both important and trivial, we recall quite vividly and in great detail. Other events, also both important and trivial, seem to fade from our minds.

Though recall processes usually operate without conscious direction, we can all improve our recall ability. Recall processes seem to resemble those of problem solving. Let's illustrate. What did you have for dinner on the first Sunday of last month? Though it would be easier to recall what you had for dinner yesterday, your brain uses similar operations for both answers. The first thing you do is eliminate information you know you never had. If the question asked about breakfast and you always skip breakfast, you'd have a quick response. If you were asked, "What kind of car did Thomas Jefferson drive?" you'd say, "Nonsense—Jefferson never had a car." But if asked, "In what kind of car was John Kennedy killed?" your mind could search for answers. The question about Jefferson sought information you know you never had. The other question asks for something you may have known, so you will not automatically reject it. In many situations that require recall, the elimination processes happen quickly and efficiently. You never notice them. In other cases, you must, step by step, eliminate incorrect answers and develop correct ones.

To recall events you seem to have forgotten, you combine fragmented recollections with conclusions about what could have happened. This is a logical reconstruction process. You first eliminate what was never known, then seek bits of memories. You combine the fragments of memory with conclusions about what events were possible. This thinking often results in further recollections that provide more elements to eliminate or more conclusions about what was possible. Conscious application of logical reconstruction can help you learn to recall more efficiently.[3]

Since remembering involves reasoning, it's appropriate here to review the thinking processes in more detail.

REASONING

First, let's restate that perceptions and the statements made about them are two different things. Some of these statements reflect association. For instance, look at the picture on p. 128. You see a woman, grass, and a frisbee, among other things.

---

[2] Ibid., p. 40. Reprinted by permission.

[3] The subject of recall is one most of us find fascinating because forgetting is so common and so inconsistent for us. If you would like to read more on the subject of recall, good sources include Norman Spear, *The Processing of Memories: Forgetting and Retention* (New York: John Wiley, 1978), and Geoffrey Loftus and Elizabeth Loftus, *Human Memory: The Processing of Information* (New York: John Wiley, 1976). An interesting examination of research directions is the report of a 1978 symposium in M. M. Gruneberg, P. E. Morris, and R. N. Sykes, eds., *Practical Aspects of Memory* (New York: Academic Press, 1978).

We can infer some conclusions about the unknown based on the known.

You recognize the objects and associate labels and concepts with the objects. This is one type of information processing. It uses perception, symbolization, and memory.

Now look again. Is it summer? Is the woman in a competition? Is she having fun or expecting to? To answer those questions, your mind does more than recognize and recall. You must **infer**—that is, *draw conclusions about the unknown based on the known*. More formally, this is called *reasoning*. Since effective communication requires accurate inferring, understanding the reasoning processes is useful. Four processes are introduced here: generalization and deduction, comparison and contrast, cause and effect, and creative thinking.

Generalization and Deduction

We infer (or reason) in two basic directions. **Inductive thinking** draws general conclusions from specific events (inductive thinking may also be called **generalization**). In generalizing, we make predictions about a group of objects or events based on information about part of the group. For example, driving around town three or four times at 5 P.M. may lead you to conclude that traffic conditions are bad at 5 o'clock. Your generalization predicts, on the basis of three or four experiences, that the general conclusion is probably true. The *reliability* of a general conclusion depends on the repeatability of the cases. Were you driving only on days when there was a ball game? Then maybe traffic isn't always bad at 5 P.M. If the conditions are repeated every day, the generalization is reliable.

Generalizing classifies concepts; it puts things into categories.[4] Perceiving objects, persons, or experiences as similar creates a category. The conclusion of similarity is the generalization. We generalize: "All balls fit into the class of round" or "It

---

[4] From one point of view, the process of concept formation on which language is based (as discussed in Chapter 3) is generalizing.

snows every winter." The classifying process is not especially a matter of being accurate. Generalizations are simply a result of what features of an object or reality we attend to or perceive to be similar. Often, what we infer in a generalization depends on our language.

Another basic reasoning process is **deduction.** Using deduction, we apply a generalization to a specific case. A deductive inference draws a conclusion from two related statements. Here is an example of deduction:

> All humans are mortal (generalization).
> I am a human (specific case).
> Therefore, I am mortal (application).

This deductive reasoning involves:

1. A generalization
2. A specific case inferred to belong in the category of the generalization
3. A conclusion that the essential element of the generalization applies to the specific case

Using the example of driving, you could reason deductively. Start with a generalization: "Driving is difficult at 5 P.M." Note: "It's now 5 P.M." Conclude: "Driving now would be difficult."

Look back at the picture of the woman with the frisbee. Whether you answered "yes" or "no" to any of the questions we asked about the picture, you used both generalization and deduction. Take a close look at your thinking. If you concluded she was having fun, you may have used this deduction:

1. Playing frisbee in spring is fun (generalization).
2. The woman is playing frisbee with friends (specific case).
3. Therefore, she is having fun (conclusion: the generalization applies to the specific case).

Here are some other deductions. If you decided it was spring, you may have thought, "Trees have heavy foliage in the summer; these trees aren't fully leafed out yet; therefore, it's not summer." Or perhaps, "People wear short sleeves in the summer; she is wearing long sleeves; therefore, it's spring." In each case you took a general belief, looked at a specific case, and decided that the general conclusion applied to the specific case. In other words, you reasoned deductively.

Your previous experiences led you to the generalizations. Therefore, you were also reasoning inductively. Why do you believe people wear short sleeves in the summer? Because you have experienced a few (or many) summers, and you have seen it every summer. You could make a similar analysis of each of the deductions. If you think she's having fun, it's because your previous experiences with frisbees lead you to generalizations about people who are playing with them. Other thought processes also enter into your inferences about summer, spring, and frisbees.

What generalizations might you make about this career for a woman?

Comparison and Contrast

We use comparison and contrast to draw inferences of similarity or difference. We see things as similar to or different from something else. For example, if we tell a child who is swimming in a lake that an ocean is like a lake but much larger, we're asking the child to use comparison and contrast. **Comparison** concludes how concepts are *alike*. **Contrast** concludes how they are *different*. We use contrast if we say that the average size of cars made today is much smaller than that of cars made ten years ago.

Look at the picture above. How does it compare to the one of the woman with the frisbee? To answer, you automatically use comparison and contrast. If you thought, "How rare for a woman to be working on telephone line work," you used generalization and deduction as well. See if you can identify the steps of inference involved in such a conclusion.

Cause and Effect

Look at the picture of the woman telephone worker again. Did you wonder how she got the job? If so, you were searching for a cause of the effect. **Cause to effect**

thinking involves inferring that one event occurs because of something else. Suppose we contrasted the average size of a car made in 1984 with those built in 1974. We might note that average gas mileage in 1974 was 13.65 miles per gallon, and in 1984 was 17.05 miles per gallon. This could lead to the inference that the decrease in car size led to the increase in gas mileage. This is cause-effect thinking. The conclusion is that one event caused another.

Causation is not nearly as simple as most of us believe. *For one thing to cause another, two conditions have to be true.* One is that the cause never occurs without the effect following it. The other is that the effect never occurs without the cause. Cigarettes alone, for instance, do not cause lung cancer. Some people who smoke don't get cancer. Moreover, some people with lung cancer never smoked. For smoking cigarettes to be the *cause* of cancer, people who never smoke must never get lung cancer, and those who smoke must always get it. Clearly, smoking is a predisposing factor or a contributing cause of cancer, but it's over simplifying to say, "Cigarettes cause cancer."

To be clear about causation, we need to distinguish between *necessary* and *sufficient* causes. Some elements, like viruses that lead to colds, are necessary causes. This means you will not get a cold without the virus. *A necessary cause is one that must be present or the effect will not occur.* But often the necessary cause won't result in the effect. For instance, often a virus is present, and a cold doesn't occur. The virus is not a sufficient cause. Other conditions must be present before you will get the cold. *Sufficient cause will include any necessary factors plus whatever additional factors must be present for the effect to occur.* Smoking, for instance, may be a sufficient cause for lung cancer.

Creative Thinking

A fourth inferential process is **creative thinking.** Creative thinking *enables us to add, subtract, and combine experiences to create new ideas.* This form of thinking, sometimes called *imagination*, is more than recalling and reconstructing experiences. Creative thinking involves the reworking, reforming, and remodeling of abstractions.

Creative thinking goes beyond experience. For instance, imagine a purple terrier with green stripes. You've never seen one, but you can imagine it. We all can think creatively. We can (and do) extend imagination beyond simple abstracting to create thought beyond experience.

Certainly some people use their imaginations better than others, but we can all use and improve this style of thinking. Not only can we daydream or fantasize, we can imagine with direction, which is the reason for most human progress. For example, having observed birds flying, people used imagination, tried lots of things, and today, men have visited and returned from the moon. We have received television images from Saturn, and with appropriate funding, a space shuttle could some day operate on a regular schedule.

Creative uses of language can combine *denotative* and *connotative* meanings with vivid effects. Imaginative uses of words often create powerful images. For example, look at this image from T. S. Eliot's "Love Song of J. Alfred Prufrock":

The yellow fog that rubs its back upon the window-panes,
The yellow smoke that rubs its muzzle on the window-panes
Licked its tongue into the corners of the evening,

. . . .

Slipped by the terrace, made a sudden leap,
And seeing that it was a soft October night,
Curled once about the house, and fell asleep.[5]

Eliot's imagery is forceful and especially meaningful to anyone who has experienced a foggy night in a city. We're not all as skilled with words as Eliot, but each of us can learn to "see" and think in new and imaginative ways. Doing so, we'll perceive more, understand our experiences better, and learn to use language in ways that help others better understand our ideas and feelings.

EXERCISE 5.1   CREATIVE THINKING

OBJECTIVE   **To practice thinking creatively.**

DIRECTIONS   **1.** Give five explanations for the women in the pictures on pp. 128 and 130. Why are they where they are? What will they do when they leave?
2. Compare your explanation with those of a group of your classmates.

REVIEW   **Write brief answers to the following questions that will provide the basis for a writing assignment or class discussion.**
1. Why is creative thinking a useful approach to practical problems?
2. Cite examples from your own life to illustrate how creative thinking can contribute to effective communication as well as how it sometimes creates difficulty in communicating.
3. Explain what you see as the most important communication principle learned from or illustrated by this exercise and why you found it important.

THINKING ERRORS (REASONING FALLACIES)

In reviewing the types of thinking, you may have thought of examples of inaccurate conclusions. That's not uncommon. We all reason carelessly at times, with resulting communication problems. A study of some common thinking errors (or reasoning fallacies, as they are often called) can help avoid such problems.

Inference-Observation Confusion

Throughout this book, we have stressed that *facts* and our *perceptions* of them differ. Now let's note some differences among statements about perceptions. Some

---

[5] T. S. Eliot, *Collected Poems 1909–1962* (New York: Harcourt Brace Jovanovich, 1963), pp. 3–4. Reprinted by permission.

statements only report perceptions or observations. Other statements report **infer-ences,** which are *conclusions about what we perceive or feel.* One of the most common thinking errors is confusing our observations (perceptions) with the conclu-sions we draw from the perceptions. To illustrate, complete Exercise 5–2. People often miss many items in this exercise. Indeed, some people have such difficulty distinguishing inference from observation that they don't understand why some answers are wrong even when the explanations are provided.

Let's look more closely at the problems involved. Inferences usually do one of the following:

1. Relate the present to the future
2. State relationships
3. In some other way connect the known or observed to that which has not been, or cannot be, observed

Inferring is necessary. We could not survive or do most of the things that make humans different from other animals if we did not infer. Problems occur when we fail to distinguish between our inferences and our observations, as Figure 5–1 illustrates.[6]

In this situation, car A is moving with the right of way and a right-turn signal blinking. Car B is at the stop sign; its driver wants to make a left turn. The driver of car B *observes* the right-turn signal of car A and *infers* that it's going to turn right at the intersection. Acting on this inference, car B's driver pulls into the path of car A, whose driver had been intending to turn into a driveway 100 feet past the intersection. In this case, confusing inference and observation cost time and money. Other cases result in more serious accidents.

Our daily lives contain many examples of communication problems caused by confusing inferences and observations. Often we draw an inference and act on it without checking its accuracy. Forgetting that we are acting on inferences subject to error, we often do or say something that gets us into trouble, as the following example illustrates:

> A foreman walking down the line told a machine operator, "Better clean up around here." Ten minutes later, the foreman's assistant phoned, asking, "Say boss—that bearing Sipert is working on—isn't it due up in engineering pronto?"
> "You bet your sweet life it is. Why?"
> "Well, Sipert claimed you said to drop it and sweep the place up. I thought I better make sure."
> "Listen," the foreman flared, "Get the idiot back on the job. It's GOT to be ready in twenty minutes."[7]

By not confusing inferences with observations, we can communicate more effectively. To do so we must remember that facts differ from statements about

---

[6] This example is found in William V. Haney, *Communication and Interpersonal Relations*, 5th ed. (Homewood, Ill.: Richard D. Irwin, Inc., 1986), pp. 213–214. © 1955 and 1983 by William V. Haney.
[7] "The Foreman's Letter," February 8, 1950, published by the NFI, a division of VISION Incorporated.

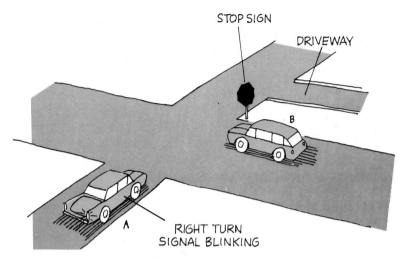

FIGURE 5–1. Inference-Observation Confusion.

them. This statement makes sense to all of us, but our language encourages us to forget it. "That's a fact" we all say, about statements. This is a common use of our language.

We will better avoid confusing observations and inferences if we use the word **fact** only when referring to a *direct, observable reality,* and use the term **statement of observation** when referring to *statements that report our perceptions of facts.* This would help us remember the differences between facts and statements about them and also to distinguish between statements of observation and those of inference. For example, think of a friend who has red hair. To say "My friend's hair is red" is not a fact. The existence of your friend's hair and its color are facts, as are several other things about it, but the statement was not a fact. It reported an observation—which means that it reported some perceptions of aspects of the reality. Whatever you say about an event or object (a fact), you do not say many other things. To report that your friend's hair is red says nothing about its length, texture, style, shade of red, or many other things.

Try making some other statements of observation about your friend's red hair. Compare your statements with those of a group of your classmates. See how many different observations are possible. Then check whether any of the statements are inferences.

To infer about your friend's red hair, you would use your perceptions or stored information to draw conclusions. For example, you might conclude that red hair makes your friend look like Lucille Ball; you might think your friend is like other people with red hair and has a hot temper; you might assume that red hair will make it hard for your friend to get jobs in management because many people have prejudices based on appearances. You can make dozens of inferences about your friend and the red hair. What is important to remember is that an inference requires a conclusion. It may be based on a perception or an observation, but it also involves a mental operation that cannot be observed. It may be accurate or inaccurate, but it is tested by the quality of a reasoning process, not the correctness of a perception.

After reviewing your list of statements about red hair, ask your instructor about any statements that you're not sure whether to classify as inference or observation. Learning to make these distinctions will improve your communication skill.

Judgments   A special kind of inference is a **statement of judgment.** Such a statement appears to be about something else, but actually reports *the reaction of the observer to objects or events.* Judgments, like all inferences, involve a mental leap. They assert what has not or cannot be observed. The difference about a statement of judgment is that it reports an assessment of value. Judgments are reactions. A statement of judgment reports that something is right or wrong, good or bad, according to the values of the person making the statement.

A statement of judgment really tells more about the person talking than about the thing being discussed. For example, suppose someone visited a museum, saw an abstract painting, and said, "That's not art! How foolish to spend money on that silly thing." This statement tells nothing about the painting. But it tells a great deal about the reaction of the person who saw the painting.

Let's return to the example of your friend's hair. Judgmental statements about it might include: "The hair is too long." "It's a foolish style for an adult." "It's a beautiful shade of red." "It would look better if it were curly." In each case, the statement reflects a value assessment—an evaluation. None of the statements tells much about the hair.

At this point we need to introduce an important distinction. Earlier we defined a statement of observation as a statement reporting one's perceptions of facts. We discussed those perceptions in terms of observing external realities. You may have thought about another kind of perception—the recognition of internal realities. When we observe facts (including people and events), we usually react to them. Our reactions often, if not always, involve feelings, not just opinions and actions. When we talk about these feeling reactions, however, habit and language lead us to report *opinions*—evaluations, or what we have here labeled as judgments. Under most circumstances, it would be better to talk about those reactions differently— to report what the feeling or reaction is, instead of hiding or burying it in an opinion or judgment statement.

Let's extend the earlier example to clarify this concept. Instead of just talking about your friend's red hair, imagine that friend using your hair dryer to style his or her hair without asking your permission. Different people respond quite differently to this "fact." To some people the friend's behavior would be only a fact; nothing more would be perceived, and the reaction would be only a perception. To someone else, however, the behavior would be perceived as rude or an invasion of privacy, and the reaction would include anger or disappointment. If that person wanted to discuss the behavior, he or she would make statements of judgment about it: the friend was irresponsible; the friend used poor judgment; the friend's behavior was immature. In each case, the statements reflect an evaluation by the source, but are framed in language that makes the statements appear to describe something outside the speaker.

It is possible, however, for this person to talk in a way that reports perceptions. Such statements might be: "I am angry you borrowed my dryer without asking." "I feel belittled, as if I'm not important enough for you to ask my permission." "I am disappointed when you behave in a way that I describe as immature." Each of these statements reports a feeling, a reaction of the source. Each of these statements takes responsibility for the receiver's reaction and does not project an evaluation of something outside. The feelings (reactions) reported in the statements occurred because of the way the perceiver evaluated the behavior. But the perceiver has "owned" the evaluation and not projected it outward on the object. The person who talks this way accurately reports reactions and feelings. This person has made a statement of observation about an *internal reality*.

A final point about statements reporting internal realities: We often disguise them. In recent years, mainstream culture in the United States has recognized the value of incorporating feelings into our thinking about reality. As a result, we have modified (somewhat) our way of talking. Now you often hear someone say, "I feel . . ." Unfortunately, however, you usually hear, "I feel that . . ." In the extended example given above, such a statement might be, "I feel that you were irresponsible in using my dryer without my permission." The person who talks this way responds to a cultural change (recognizing the importance of feelings) without making a significant change in mode of thinking (or perhaps, of talking). Such a statement does *not* share a feeling at all. It says, "I feel," but then it reports a judgment (you were irresponsible). The *feeling* is not reported. A listener must infer what the speaker's reaction is; the speaker has not reported it. If we conclude that this person is angry, disappointed, or irritated, that is our inference—the speaker did not report it.

In learning to spot such disguised judgment statements, you have an easy cue. Almost every such statement will involve the word "that." If the speaker is actually reporting a feeling, the word "that" does not fit. For example, the statement, "I feel that I am angry that you used my dryer without my permission," isn't natural. When native speakers of United States English report anger, they say, "I'm angry." They might say, "I'm angry that you did that," but such a sentence would be rare. A natural English sentence would be, "I'm angry you did that." So, when listening to people for whom English is their native language, you can be certain their saying, "I feel that . . ." introduces a statement of judgment. It does not openly report a reaction.

In later chapters, this concept becomes important as we discuss listening and interpersonal communication. At this point, we want you to understand the distinctions among these ways of talking and to recognize the thinking/talking duality that our communicating habits and our English language tend to obscure.

Now, look back at your earlier list of statements and at those of a group of your classmates. Did some of the statements report judgments? Did some disguise opinions as "feeling" statements? Can you see how some of the judgment statements tell more about the person talking than about the friend's hair? If not, be sure to ask the instructor to discuss this concept more in class. Table 5–1 can help you keep in mind the differences among these kinds of statements. Exercise 5.2 can help you learn to distinguish among the statements.

Faulty Generalizations

Hasty Generalization   One of the most common errors of generalization is *drawing a conclusion on the basis of too few cases.* Some generalizations require only a few cases to support an inference. To conclude that all green apples are sour because you tested two or three that were sour might be appropriate. Green apples don't vary much; that is, the elements generalized about are quite similar.

If the cases are more variable, however, you need many instances to generalize. Otherwise, you commit the error of **hasty generalization.** If you encountered three red-haired people with hot tempers, you might generalize that red-haired people

TABLE 5–1   How to Distinguish Types of Statements

FACTS	STATEMENTS OF OBSERVATION	STATEMENTS OF INFERENCE
1. Exist or happen in physical world 2. Can be verified by one or more senses	1. May describe facts but are not themselves facts 2. Are limited to what can actually be observed 3. Can be verified by other observers 4. Cannot be made about the future	1. Go beyond describing 2. Are not limited to observation; usually involve interpretation of something observed; involve mental processes beyond perception, symbolization, and memory 3. Often use abstract language 4. Cannot be verified by one or more senses; are tested by whether they meet logical standards or criteria

	STATEMENTS OF FEELING (Type of Observation)	STATEMENTS OF JUDGMENT (Type of Inference)
	1. Describe "internal reality"; describe reactions that are not overt; report feelings of observer 2. Are limited to the observer; describe reaction of only one person 3. Cannot be verified (or questioned) by others 4. Cannot be made about the future	1. Go beyond describing 2. Are not limited to observation; usually involve interpretation 3. Often use abstract language 4. Cannot be verified; result from personal value system 5. Attach value to things referred to 6. Tell more about the source than about what is judged

are hot-tempered. This is an example of hasty generalization. Three cases aren't enough to draw inferences of similarity when you're talking about something as variable as people. You might qualify the generalization and conclude that many red-haired people are hot-tempered. But even then, using only three cases makes your conclusion weak.

Unrepresentative Instances Generalizing on the basis of unrepresentative cases is another error of generalization. The classic example of this was the big win predicted by the polls for presidential candidate Alf Landon in 1936. Thousands of people were called, so the generalization wasn't hasty. But the polling was by telephone, and in 1936, only high-income people had telephones. The cases weren't representative.

This kind of error is common in our conclusions about people. We tend to generalize about people on the basis of those around us. But since most of us have limited social contacts, it is easy to be guilty of generalizing from *unrepresentative cases*. People from different social systems or cultures believe and behave differently. So to draw conclusions about people in general on the basis of the few we know is both a hasty and unrepresentative generalization.

Faulty Deduction

Deduction applies a generalization to a specific case. But if a case doesn't fit into the general category, the deduction is faulty. This error also often occurs when the generalization is qualified. For example, examine the following deduction:

> Most students want to earn good grades.
> Because Jan is a student, she wants good grades.

Jan, however, may not be in the "most students" category. The conclusion may not apply. Since the generalization is qualified by "most," not enough information is available to apply it. Applying the generalization "green apples are sour" to a Granny Smith apple, for example, would not be accurate. The case doesn't fit within the generalization.

Probably the most common error of deduction is starting with a faulty generalization. Consider the following: Male drivers under twenty-one are irresponsible; since Ian is under twenty-one, he cannot be trusted with the car. The deduction is logically flawless, but the conclusion may be wrong because the generalization is faulty. Not all drivers under twenty-one are irresponsible.

Stereotyping is an example of applying faulty generalizations in ways that cause communication problems. Since the people within any social group differ greatly, it's an error to conclude that all or even most people from the same group or culture have the same characteristics. To draw conclusions about people in a group on the basis of a few we know is to be guilty of both unrepresentative generalization and faulty deduction.

Causal Fallacies

Cause-effect reasoning infers that one event causes another. Perhaps the most common causal reasoning error is *to conclude that because one event regularly precedes another, it causes it*. This is called the **post hoc fallacy.** Two events may be connected by coincidence, or both may be connected to something else; thus, they occur in sequence. One does not necessarily cause the other. For instance, before people knew the causes of malaria and yellow fever, they believed that something contaminated the night air. People were warned not to go outside at night because breathing night air would make them sick. This illustrates how easily a wrong cause can be inferred. The cause of the diseases was not the air, although night does correlate with factors related to the cause of the disease.

Though they're often confused, correlation is not causation. **Correlation** *shows a relation between two elements*. A high correlation indicates that when one event occurs, another is also likely to occur. But that one event regularly happens before another does not mean it causes the other. In the United States, autumn and football games are highly correlated. But autumn certainly does not cause football! Other cases aren't so obvious, and this kind of association is a common causal fallacy.

As you realize from earlier discussion, something besides correlation must establish that one thing causes another. At night mosquitoes come out and bite. But for mosquito bites to be the cause of malaria, everyone bitten must become ill. Such evidence never existed. To find the cure for malaria, scientists had to consider both necessary and sufficient causes. Identifying the cause required finding the anopheles carrier mosquito *and* the disease-causing protozoa.

Inappropriate Comparisons

Reasoning with comparison and contrast often results in inappropriate comparisons. That two items are similar in some respects does not mean they are similar in all respects. We may hear, "British police do not carry guns, and the rate of violent crimes is very low in England. Therefore, police in the United States do not need guns." This assumes that the British and United States populations are enough alike that they could be treated similarly.

When we think other people feel or should behave as we do we often commit this fallacy. We think, "It works for me—it should work for them." Such thinking assumes cultural and individual similarity—a fallacy. Valid comparisons must relate items that are actually similar in the aspects being compared. Having some similarities does not mean things are alike in *all* respects.

False Alternatives

Another common fallacy is "either-or," or **false alternatives** thinking. People will argue, "We must do either this or . . . ," predicting a dire outcome if we don't behave as they wish. Given a truly contradictory situation, a conclusion "either this, or that" is valid. It is either 8 A.M. or it's not. It is either 70 degrees Fahrenheit or it's not. The fallacy occurs when we permit only two alternatives in situations when in fact several options exist. It may be 70 degrees or not, but it's false alternative thinking to say, "If it's not 70 degrees, it's cold." If someone says, "Either you support me, or you're against me," the alternatives are false. Other options exist. Indeed, either-or thinking is invalid reasoning in most cases, because most situations offer more than two possible alternatives.

The prevalence of this fallacy in the United States demonstrates again the influence of language and culture on thinking. Among the most common verbs in the English language are the words "is" and "are." Thus, our mode of talking leads us easily into thinking something "is" or "isn't" whatever we say. When we stop to apply "logical" thinking, we know that isn't so. It's just the way we talk. We know the temperature isn't either hot or cold. Yet we commonly say, "It is awfully hot in here," or "It's sure cold outside today." In ordinary conversation, such a habit causes little trouble. But we so commonly use that pattern of talking that we easily fall into applying dichotomies where none exist.

EXERCISE 5.2   THE INFERENCE-OBSERVATION CONFUSION[8]

OBJECTIVE   **To practice distinguishing inferences from observations.**

DIRECTIONS   1. Read the following story, assuming that all the information presented is accurate.
2. Read the statements, deciding whether they are True (T), False (F), or Questionable (?) on the basis of information presented in the story. *If any part of the statement requires you to infer, mark it "?"*

THE STORY

A businessman had just turned off the lights in the store when a man appeared and demanded money. The owner opened a cash register. The contents of the cash register were scooped up, and the man sped away. A member of the police force was notified promptly.

STATEMENTS ABOUT THE STORY

1. A man appeared after the owner had turned off the store lights.   T F ?
2. The robber was a man.   T F ?
3. The man who appeared did not demand money.   T F ?
4. The man who opened the cash register was the owner.   T F ?
5. The store owner scooped up the contents of the register and ran away.   T F ?
6. Someone opened a cash register.   T F ?

[8] Adapted from "The Uncritical Inference Test" by William Haney, *Communication and Interpersonal Relations*, 5th ed. (Homewood, Ill.: Irwin, 1973), pp. 213–214. Reprinted by permission. © 1955 and 1983.

7. After the man who demanded the money scooped up the contents of the cash register, he ran away.   T F ?

8. While the cash register contained money, the story does *not* state *how much.*   T F ?

9. The robber demanded money of the owner.   T F ?

10. The story concerns a series of events in which only three persons are referred to: the owner of the store, a man who demanded money, and a member of the police force.   T F ?

11. The following events were included in the story: someone demanded money, a cash register was opened, its contents were scooped up, and a man dashed out of the store.   T F ?

3. After you have marked all eleven statements, talk with a friend or class-mate about your answers. Discuss each statement thoroughly to try to be sure you have marked "?" by each statement that requires an inference to be considered either T or F.

4. Now check your answers from the key supplied by your instructor. If you answered any questions incorrectly, it was because you confused the observation reported and the inferences you drew.

REVIEW   **Write brief answers to the following questions that will provide the basis for a writing assignment or class discussion.**

1. Explain how inferences differ from observations and what value it is to a communicator to be aware of the differences.

2. Why are inferences so often confused with observations?

3. Identify the inference-observation confusions that caused you to answer incorrectly any item in the test.

4. Explain the most important communication principles learned from or illustrated by this exercise and why you found it important.

SUMMARY

After we receive and interpret sensations, we must do more mental processing to communi-cate. This process is usually described as thinking. Thinking uses a recall and storage system. There are three types of memory: sensory information storage (which lasts a very short time), long-term memory, and short-term memory. The main difference between sensory information storage and memory is that we interpret sensory information before it is stored. Memory calls up or recalls what has been stored. Recall is a process similar to problem solving although recall is usually done unconsciously.

There are five general types of reasoning. Generalization and deduction are two of them. When we generalize, we infer general statements about a group of items based on experience with a few items. Deduction takes a generalization and applies it to a specific case. The third kind of reasoning is comparing and contrasting. Comparing draws conclusions based on similarities, contrasting on differences among items. Fourth is cause-effect thinking, which concludes that because of one thing, another happens. The final reasoning process we discussed was creative thinking. This is using imagination to extend ideas beyond reality, to create new ideas and thoughts. Imagination is another way to describe the process of creative thinking.

Thinking errors, or fallacies, are common. Perhaps the most common is confusing inferences with observations. A statement of observation is a description of what someone saw or felt. An inference is a conclusion (usually based on other observations) about what we cannot see or know. The third kind of statement about reality, a statement of judgment, reports is a special type of inference that evaluates, using the observer's value system.

Another common thinking error is faulty generalization. There are two kinds of these: (1) the hasty generalization, which is drawing a conclusion based on too few observations, and (2) the generalization based on unrepresentative cases—that is, on items that are not typical of the category the generalization applies to. Causal fallacies, inappropriate comparisons, and applying false alternatives (assuming a situation is contradictory when there are actually many alternatives) are other thinking errors.

QUESTIONS FOR DISCUSSION

1. How does memory function in interpreting sensations?
2. What are the two basic directions of inference?
3. How do induction and deduction differ?
4. Can you give examples of the five inferential processes?
5. Name the fallacies of reasoning and illustrate by citing cases.

SUGGESTIONS FOR FURTHER READING

Brockriede, Wayne, and Douglas Ehninger. *Decision by Debate,* 2nd ed. New York: Harper & Row, 1978.

Fearnside, W. Ward, and William B. Holther. *Fallacy: The Counterfeit of Argument.* Englewood Cliffs, N.J.: Prentice-Hall, 1959.

———. *About Thinking.* Englewood Cliffs, N.J.: Prentice-Hall, 1980.

Haney, William. *Communication and Organizational Behavior,* 5th ed. Homewood, Ill.: Irwin, 1986.

Kahane, Herbert. *Logic and Contemporary Rhetoric,* 4th ed. Belmont, Calif.: Wadsworth, 1984.

Kaplan, Martin, and Steven Swartz, eds. *Human Judgment and Decision Processes.* New York: Academic Press, 1975.

Kruger, Arthur. *Argumentation and Debate: A Classified Bibliography,* 2nd ed. Metuchen, N.J.: Scarecrow Press, 1975.

Lindsay, Peter H., and Donald A. Norman. *Human Information Processing*, 2nd ed. New York: Academic Press, 1977.

Mills, Glen. *Reason in Controversy.* Boston: Allyn & Bacon, 1968.

Ruggiero, Vincent. *The Art of Thinking: A Guide to Critical and Creative Thought.* New York: Harper & Row, 1984.

Sproule, J. Michael. *Argumentation, Language, and Its Influence.* New York: McGraw-Hill, 1980.

Thum, Gladys, and Marcella Thum. *The Persuaders: Propaganda in War and Peace.* New York: Atheneum, 1972.

Whorf, Benjamin L. *Language, Thought and Reality*, ed. John B. Carroll. Cambridge, Mass.: M.I.T. Press, 1956.

Ziegelmueller, George, and Charles Dause. *Argumentation: Inquiry and Advocacy.* Englewood Cliffs, N.J.: Prentice-Hall, 1975.

6 Listening: Receiving Accurately, Responding Appropriately

> To understand people, I must try to hear what they are not saying, what they perhaps will never be able to say.
>
> JOHN POWELL

> Nature has given [us] one tongue, but two ears, that we may hear from others twice as much as we speak.
>
> EPICTETUS

GOAL

To become a more effective receiver

OBJECTIVES

The material in this chapter should help you to:
1. Explain why most of us do not listen well.
2. Respond with appropriate listening levels to different situations.
3. Prepare effectively for important listening situations.
4. Increase skills of listening to understand.
5. Reduce evaluative listening in situations when it is not appropriate.
6. Use feedback more effectively.
7. Listen empathically.
8. Relate three theories of human motivation to improved listening.
9. Assess instrumental, relational, and self-related communication purposes, whether open or hidden.
10. When appropriate, apply the skills of listening to:
    Identify when values are motivating messages.
    Distinguish between facts and statements of observation.
    Distinguish between inference and judgment.
    Be able to decide what inferences are acceptable.

Effective listening may be the most important communication skill. Research has shown that listening is the communication activity most people do most—whether they are students, housewives, or workers in any rank or position.[1] Indeed, one study of chief executive officers demonstrated that they spend from 66 percent to 68 percent of their day listening to someone.[2]

Most of us spend nearly half our time listening; it is important to do it well. Listening well helps us evaluate the messages of those who want to change our behavior or beliefs and helps us understand and relate to people at work or in social situations. Listening probably does more than any other single factor to help us establish and maintain satisfying interpersonal relationships.

Skill at accurately interpreting the messages we receive enables us to be more effective as speakers. When we need to give others information or to affect their behavior, listening helps us know how to choose the best messages, helps us evaluate the effectiveness of our message sending, and helps us know when to try something different in order to accomplish our goals. We can use listening skills to know when others accept our ideas and how to persuade them when they don't.

Yet most of us listen with less than 50 percent accuracy. We mishear or do not hear messages more often than we receive them correctly. And most of us remember less than 50 percent of what we do hear. How sad, when satisfying our needs depends so heavily on listening well.

To help you learn to listen more effectively is the goal of this chapter. First, we examine the types of listening and discuss techniques applicable to all situations—techniques for understanding and remembering what sources say as well as understanding why they talk as they do. Then we'll discuss specific techniques appropriate for empathic and critical listening.

Before discussing listening skills, however, we need to make an important point. In most cases, better listening relies more on having a different *attitude* than it does on improving skills. All of us listen well at some times. Most of us have the skills to listen effectively, but we do not use these skills well all the time. That requires effort and motivation. So, while most of us can improve our skills, it will require changed attitudes for most of us to really improve our listening.

LISTENING SITUATIONS

Levels of Involvement

We must listen in many different kinds of situations. They fall along a continuum that runs from minimum to maximum involvement.[3]

[1] Six studies of students at all levels and of persons in several job classifications are summarized in Larry Barker, *Listening Behavior* (Englewood Cliffs, N.J.: Prentice-Hall, 1971), pp. 3–4.

[2] Henry Mintzberg, "The Manager's Job: Folklore and Fact," *Harvard Business Review*, July–August 1975, pp. 49–61.

[3] For this concept and much of the structure for this chapter, we are heavily indebted to Linda Heun and Richard Heun and their work, which predates their book, *Developing Skills for Human Interaction* (Columbus, Ohio: Merrill, 1975). In addition, anyone who writes about listening skills owes a special debt to Dr. Ralph Nichols, who pioneered the study of how to improve listening. For his landmark work with Leonard Stevens, see *Are You Listening?* (New York: McGraw-Hill, 1957).

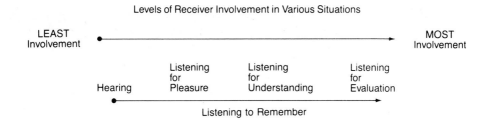

Levels of Receiver Involvement in Various Situations

Hearing   Hearing is little more than *being in the range of and receiving sound.* It requires little personal involvement. You may not even be aware of sounds you hear unless they're called to your attention. Background music and environmental sounds usually are heard, not listened to. If you keep your radio on or become used to typewriters and conversations in the office or to traffic outside in the street, you usually won't even notice hearing the sounds. What comes into your brain on the level of hearing has little effect on memory and doesn't require conscious decoding. That does not mean it doesn't affect you. The effects of environmental sounds, noted in Chapter 4, do influence communication.

Listening for Pleasure   Listening for pleasure involves more personal involvement than hearing: *We receive sounds more consciously and actively decode* (usually by classifying). We hear and note differences, changes, and similarities. Listening to music is a familiar example of this activity, but we often receive speech at this level, too. We may listen to a pleasant voice, to poetry, to television and radio, or we may engage in casual, social, or ritual conversation at the level of listening for pleasure.

Listening to Understand   Listening to understand requires a higher degree of involvement. To understand what we're receiving, we consciously control our decoding. *We try to decode as accurately as possible, seeking to understand all the messages we receive, both verbal and nonverbal.* This level of listening is described as **active listening.** At this level, we consciously focus attention and feedback to bring the perceived and intended messages as close together as we can. Listening to understand may be the most common listening situation. It happens with friends and family in informal settings; at work in dozens of different settings, both formal and informal; in school talking to classmates or listening to professors' lectures; in our roles as citizens receiving political and public communication; and as consumers.

Listening to Evaluate   Listening for evaluation also requires high receiver involvement. It involves many of the aspects of listening to understand. Before we evaluate, we should understand a speaker's verbal message. As with listening to understand, listening to evaluate seeks similarity between intended and perceived messages. But listening to evaluate goes beyond understanding. It involves analyzing messages received to decide how believable and worthwhile they are. We need this kind of listening when someone tries to sell us something or wants us to behave in a certain way. At these times, we need to evaluate the messages before responding.

Listening levels vary by situation and goals.

Listening to Remember   At all levels of listening, we usually want to remember as much as we can. Remembering is necessary for both understanding and evaluation. Remembering requires special effort.

Similarities in Situations

Whatever the level of involvement, listening involves constant intrapersonal and interpersonal interaction. Effective listeners realize that their personal involvement affects what they receive and perceive. Our interpretations of words and actions affect all levels of listening: pleasure, understanding, evaluation, and memory. Thus, all elements noted in Chapters 1 through 5 affect our listening. Indeed, interpersonal communication always involves intrapersonal communication, so you will see in this chapter many applications of the information and principles introduced earlier.

Whenever one needs to understand, thinking of it as active listening emphasizes the receiver's active role. Good listeners are not just sponges, soaking up sounds and information. They participate actively in any listening situation beyond the level of hearing. They seek to answer two important questions: What is that person saying? Why? Good listeners will not be satisfied with answering just one of those questions. In this chapter, we will examine ways to answer both, then turn to the issue of responding appropriately to the messages received.

EXERCISE 6.1   LEVELS OF LISTENING

OBJECTIVE   To identify situations in which different levels and types of listening are appropriate.

DIRECTIONS   **1.** Use the form in Table 6–1 to keep a diary of the situations in which you listen during a day.
2. For each listening event, briefly identify the situation.
3. Use this code to identify the level of listening:
   1. Hearing
   2. Listening for pleasure
   3. Listening to understand
   4. Listening to evaluate
4. When the level is listening to understand (3), use this code to show whether active or empathic listening is appropriate:
   a. Active
   b. Empathic

REVIEW   **Write brief answers to the following questions that will provide the basis for a writing assignment or class discussion.**
1. Why are different levels of listening appropriate for different situations?
2. Based on your diary, identify the most important listening situations for you.
3. Explain the most important communication principle you learned or found illustrated in this exercise and why you found it important.

TABLE 6–1   Listening Diary

	AMOUNT OF TIME LISTENING	SITUATION	TYPE OF LISTENING		AMOUNT OF TIME LISTENING	SITUATION	TYPE OF LISTENING
6:00–6:30 A.M.				3:00–3:30			
6:30–7:00				3:30–4:00			
7:00–7:30				4:00–4:30			
7:30–8:00				4:30–5:00			
8:00–8:30				5:00–5:30			
8:30–9:00				5:30–6:00			
9:00–9:30				6:00–6:30			
9:30–10:00				6:30–7:00			
10:00–10:30				7:00–7:30			
10:30–11:00				7:30–8:00			
11:00–11:30				8:00–8:30			
11:30–12:00				8:30–9:00			
12:00–12:30 P.M.				9:00–9:30			
12:30–1:00				9:30–10:00			
1:00–1:30				10:00–10:30			
1:30–2:00				10:30–11:00			
2:00–2:30				11:00–11:30			
2:30–3:00				11:30–12:00			

1 = hearing   3 = listening to understand
2 = listening for pleasure   4 = listening to evaluate

EFFECTIVE LISTENING: UNDERSTANDING THE WORDS

Be Prepared

Perhaps this is a truism, but it's often forgotten. If you know about a listening situation in advance, you can prepare for it in fairly obvious ways. First, be physically prepared to listen. Active listening is hard work. It takes a lot of energy. So try to be rested physically when you know a listening task (for example, a required lecture) will require a high level of involvement.

Second, be mentally prepared to listen. When possible, think about the situation and the subject that will be discussed. Will it be helpful to gather information ahead of time? Even if you aren't able to get it, you can protect yourself simply by recognizing that you need to know more before deciding. If you are facing a sales pitch, tell yourself in advance not to make final judgments until you have the needed data. This will help avoid hasty responses using inadequate information.

Set Goals

Once we understand a listening situation, the next step is to set listening goals. People rarely set listening goals. That may be one reason we listen poorly. Goal setting improves listening in several ways.

Appropriate Focus   The main value of goal setting is that it helps focus attention. Remember, in any situation we can choose to attend to many different things. Since we cannot possibly focus on everything, we must select from many competing stimuli. Having a goal increases the chances of choosing the right ones. Goal setting helps a receiver ignore distractions and irrelevant stimuli and focus on useful ones.

Appropriate Behaviors   Having a goal can help us avoid behaving in ways that prevent us from achieving what we want. For example, we all know people who frown when they are concentrating. Suppose a supervisor is listening intently, trying to understand an employee explain a complicated interpersonal conflict in the office. While listening, the supervisor had better not frown! The employee could interpret the frown as disapproval. A supervisor who is aware of both goals— understanding the message and being supportive of the person—will avoid frowning, crossed arms, or other nonverbals that might interfere with accomplishing either goal.

Since each person is source and receiver in all interpersonal communication, remember that when you're listening you're sending messages as well as receiving them. Students usually are aware of this. They look alert and attentive while the professor lectures, even when their minds are on tonight's date or the exam next hour. Knowing your listening goals can help you know what behaviors will interfere with reaching them.

Motivation   The nature of attention permits us to attend to any one stimulus only briefly. Keeping mind, eyes, and ears tuned to a single focus is hard work. It requires much energy. Thus, listening well requires constant effort, especially if it lasts longer than two or three minutes. When the listening task is demanding (as it usually is when active listening is needed), goal setting can help you *want* to exert the effort.

Changing Involvement Level   Different listening situations call for different types of receiving behaviors. Setting listening goals helps you know when it's necessary to shift from one level of listening to another. For instance, in a social conversation, you may suddenly realize that the person is trying to change your behavior. Then you must quickly shift your focus and listen to evaluate. Watching television requires changes like this because you see commercials along with entertainment and news. Many other situations call for such changes. During a social lunch, a golf game, or a coffee break, people often try to persuade you to do something. Conversely, what may appear to be a case of someone trying to persuade you may really be a situation calling for empathic listening.

Aids to Goal Setting   Determining goals for listening is not always easy. Situations aren't always clear. Speakers often have several purposes, so receivers may also need more than one goal. Three questions can help you identify your specific needs in each situation:

1. What do I want to get from this situation?
2. What outcome do I need or want?
3. How do I want to affect the others involved?

Deciding the answers can help set appropriate listening goals for each different situation.

Use Listening Speed Efficiently

Humans can decode speech at approximately 400 words per minute, but few people speak more than 150 words per minute. Effective listeners use the time to their advantage. Poor listeners do not. Extra listening time and short attention spans often make concentration difficult. Poor listeners either daydream or waste the extra time. The following pages suggest some ways to use the time better.

Find Self-Interest   Try to find some personal interest or need you can satisfy by listening. People behave in ways that satisfy their needs. If you can identify how to benefit from understanding what is being said, it will help you concentrate.

Determine Speaker Goals   To set receiving goals or to decide what level of listening to use, it helps to understand what the speaker wants. Therefore, when listening, decide as quickly as possible what the source wants.

Both verbal and nonverbal cues can help identify a speaker's goal, even when it's not clearly stated. Listen for cues about goal statements, including remarks in the introduction. Goal statements may be introduced by phrases such as, "What I want you to understand today is . . ." "The point I'm making is . . ." "I'd like to spend a little time talking about . . ." Careful listeners will be alert for these and similar phrases.

People seeking to change your attitudes or influence your behavior will probably not say so clearly—at least not at first. They will move gradually to the subject before stating their purpose. Suppose someone says, "How secure is your home?" You may not know for a while whether the person is just sharing information or selling an alarm system. But if you ask yourself, "What does this person really want?" you will be alert for cues that can help you decide.

The *context* of statements includes many cues to source goals. If the comment about home security was in a conversation or a speech, the goal would not be immediately clear; but if it came from a stranger on the telephone, you'd be fairly sure a sale was intended. Many nonverbals accompany goal statements: pauses before or after a goal is stated, changes in volume or rate, shifts of body position, changes in eye contact. Environment, situation, and previous knowledge about a source can help you make fairly reliable inferences about purpose.

Identify Thought Structure

Look for the Central Idea   Besides identifying a source's goals, search for the main point or idea. An effective listener recognizes that most messages have a major idea—a point the person talking wants the listener to understand or believe. In formal speeches, we call this a *thesis*. A more useful term applies to all types of messages, not just speeches. This is the **central idea.** Most statements have a central idea.

A central idea is often related to goal statements. When you hear one, the other usually follows or is implied. For example, a member of your family might

Preparation improves listening effectiveness.

say, "We ought to think about buying a smoke detector. With it, we'd never be caught asleep in a fire." The goal (influencing your behavior) and main idea (buying a smoke detector is a good idea) are closely related.

Look for the Supporting Ideas When listening, don't try to remember everything a speaker says. Concentrate on the major ideas. Look for a central idea and the points that support it. Distinguish between the main supporting ideas and lesser details. Don't concentrate on the details. Seeking such structure in what you hear will help you remember the important information.

Use Both Verbal and Nonverbal Cues Just as both words and nonverbals can identify goals, they also help identify main ideas. Pauses or body shifts often follow or precede a direct reference to a main point. Verbal and nonverbal cues often occur together. A person may say, "The first important idea is," "Another important point is," "Furthermore," "And finally." These transitions highlight main ideas, usually accompanied by hand gestures and vocal emphasis. Repetition also emphasizes important points. A source who repeats something several times doubtless considers it important.

Review Mentally As you listen, mentally summarize main ideas. When you identify a main idea, use a key word or phrase to remember it. Then use your excess decoding time to restate and summarize as you hear each new important idea. Restating helps you clarify the speaker's overall thought structure and remember the ideas.

Occasionally you may want to take notes, but relate the notetaking to your goals. Don't try to take complete notes. That will interfere with your listening. Moreover, it's seldom useful to write down everything. Much that is said is not worth trying to remember. If for some reason you need a detailed report, get a tape recorder. Usually, it's best to do what journalists do: As soon as you have finished listening, use your memory to expand brief notes.

Listen for What Is Not Said

Sometimes a message can be best understood by careful attention to what is not said. Omission of specific words and phrases or ambiguity can be intentional and quite significant. For example, a well-known advertisement asserts that three out of four doctors recommend the ingredient in Anacin. Naturally, the ad doesn't say the ingredient is aspirin. In other ads, salespersons for the higher-priced products claim, "No other brand has more pain reliever," or "None has a better record of reducing cavities." What these ads do not say may be more important than what they do say.

Minimize Distractions

Listeners often do not understand a source because they allow themselves to be distracted. Effective listeners learn not to let this happen.

Recognize Emotional Responses   The most common distractions in listening are emotional responses. We disagree with what we hear, or we react emotionally to a source's appearance or behavior. Good listeners know that emotional reactions—whether to loaded words, dialect, mannerisms, appearance, or an idea they disagree with—can distort their perceptions.

Understanding others and their ideas requires an open mind and the ability to overcome emotional distractions. Otherwise, perception will be overly selective, and listening less efficient. Research has shown that poor listeners are less open to new ideas than good listeners are.[4] Controlling mental and emotional responses improves accuracy and understanding. Good listeners concentrate on what the source means instead of reacting emotionally to loaded words or an appearance they don't like.

Use Counterarguments with Care   The most common response to any idea we disagree with is to begin thinking of arguments against it. Once we have started this counterarguing, we have quit listening to understand and have begun to evaluate. We may have quit listening altogether, whether we actually say anything in response or not. Haven't you been in many discussions when you heard someone ask a question that had already been answered? That happens because people hear ideas they disagree with and begin mentally arguing. From then on, they hear little that others say. Good listeners keep listening even when they disagree.

Avoid Evaluation Until Necessary   For most of us, evaluation is a habit. It's a behavior we learned early in life. We like or dislike almost everything. We believe things are either good or bad, right or wrong. We evaluate few things neutrally. To most of us, neutrality is the same as no reaction. Yet, as noted in Chapter 1, evaluation itself influences what we perceive. If we really want to understand what a person says, we will not evaluate unless it is absolutely necessary. Many situations don't really call for it. Psychologist Carl Rogers says judgments are the major barrier to interpersonal understanding.[5] Premature or unnecessary evaluation is probably also the major barrier to effective listening to understand.

Sometimes we must evaluate, of course. Later in this chapter we discuss listening in those situations. But even in such cases, we will hear more accurately if we first fully understand the intended messages. *Understand first, evaluate second* is a good rule to follow.

Use Feedback

The only way to be sure messages are perceived accurately (as the source intended) is the use of feedback. Remember, the term feedback refers to a receiver's response as the source perceives it. Listeners use feedback by checking with a source to

---

[4] Charles Kelly, "Empathic Listening," in *Small Group Communication: A Reader*, eds. Robert S. Cathcart and Larry A. Samovar (Dubuque, Iowa: Brown, 1974), pp. 340–47.

[5] Carl Rogers, *On Becoming a Person* (Boston: Houghton Mifflin, 1970), p. 330.

see how close the perceived message is to the intended message. You can do this several ways, and all involve asking questions and paraphrasing.

The techniques for a listener using feedback depend on the situation. Are you listening to a speech? If so, decide what the speaker's goals and main ideas are. After the speech, ask the speaker, "Do I understand correctly that your main point is . . . ?"

Less formal, conversational situations involve give and take. In these cases it's easier to paraphrase. Try to state, in your own words, what you heard the person say. Several lead-in lines are helpful:

"Let me make sure I understand what you're saying. You believe that . . . ?"
"Do I hear you saying that . . . ?"
"You mean . . . ?"

The amount of summary and restatement you need depends on several things, including how complicated and how long the message is and how familiar you are with the ideas.

Paraphrase whenever possible—don't just repeat the source's words. This is important. If you just repeat, the person will simply decode the words as they were originally coded. It's much more useful to restate—that is, to use different

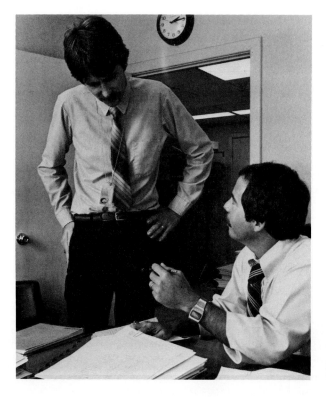

The only way to be sure that you have perceived a message accurately (as the source intended) is active use of feedback.

words to express the idea you heard. This lets you check how accurately you understood the intended message. Repeating does allow you to check how accurately you heard the words. But it won't check how accurately you perceived the message. And as you know, words only carry messages; they aren't the messages. So to check how close your perceived messages are to the ones the source intended, paraphrase.

EXERCISE 6.2   LISTENING TO UNDERSTAND AND REMEMBER

OBJECTIVE   **To practice skills of listening to understand and remember.**

DIRECTIONS   1. Your instructor will give you the opportunity to hear several short speeches. Listen without taking notes, trying to apply the skills of listening to understand and remember.
2. For each speech:
   a. Pick out the central idea and purpose.
   b. Attempt to determine the speaker's main idea or main points, using a key word or phrase to identify them.
   c. Compare what you perceived as the main idea and main supporting points for each speech with what a group of your classmates perceived.
   d. The speeches may be given by students in class. If so, use feedback to check accuracy of your listening by questioning the speakers. Compare their statements of purpose and central idea to what you heard.

REVIEW   **Write brief answers to the following questions that will provide the basis for a writing assignment or class discussion.**
1. List the skills of listening for understanding and remembering and identify those that you most need to improve.
2. How can a listener prevent distractions from interfering with listening?
3. Explain the most important communication principle you learned or found illustrated in this exercise and why you found it important.

EFFECTIVE LISTENING: UNDERSTANDING THE SOURCE

Perhaps the most important tool for good listening is an accurate answer to this question: Why is this person talking—or saying these things? The answer provides the context to interpret the words you hear. An understanding of human motivation can help provide this context.

Theories of Human Motivation

All communication is goal-oriented, whether a source is consciously aware of the goals or not. Being aware of this fact, and of several ways to think about human motivation, can help you listen more effectively. You'll be better prepared to identify

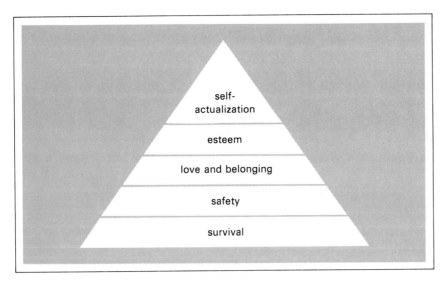

FIGURE 6–1 A hierarchy of needs.

a speaker's goals as well as your own reasons for listening and responding.[6] Three theories of motivation are particularly useful in understanding communication. Let's briefly take a look at all three.

The Maslow Needs Hierarchy   Psychologist Abraham Maslow's analysis of human needs suggests that many needs of varying importance motivate human behavior. Describing the needs as a hierarchy, Maslow argues that what actually motivates behavior in any situation depends on whether needs lower in the hierarchy are satisfied. Figure 6–1 shows his hierarchy.[7]

SURVIVAL   Survival needs form the base of the hierarchy. To survive, certain basic physical needs must be satisfied. These include shelter, food, water, air, reproduction—all the requirements necessary to sustain life. The need to maintain a constant internal environment provides some of our most basic, though often unnoticed, motivations for communication.

Survival motivations underlie many other needs, and under most conditions they must be satisfied before other needs will motivate. A higher-level need seldom motivates a person gasping for lack of oxygen. Yet there are complex interrelations in human motivation. As you know, some people do deny themselves survival to satisfy other basic needs. Parents reenter a burning building to save a child; police officers live with threat of bodily harm; a hero may risk death to stop a mugging.

---

[6] As a source, you can also assess your own goals and the best ways to achieve them. We discuss how sources can use an understanding of motivation in later chapters.

[7] Based on "Hierarchy of Needs," in *Motivation and Personality*, 3rd ed., by Abraham H. Maslow, revised by Robert Frager et al. Copyright 1954; © 1987 by Harper & Row, Publishers, Inc. Copyright © 1970 by Abraham Maslow. Reprinted by permission of Harper & Row, Publishers.

The survival needs are physical. We describe the other needs in Maslow's hierarchy as social and psychological. These factors, though less important to survival, often explain how people respond to physical needs. Each society teaches acceptable ways to satisfy physical needs. In the process, people learn psychological and social needs that motivate behavior. Most of us learn to seek these satisfactions with as much intensity as we seek survival. The next four categories in Maslow's hierarchy involve these social and psychological needs.

SAFETY NEEDS   Safety needs are primarily mental extensions of survival needs. They result from a fear that survival needs will not be met. People "need" a house, for example, because they want to know they will have a place to sleep and won't freeze in the winter. They mentally extend the need to survive.

These needs are often called *security needs*. People are trying to satisfy a safety need when they oppose change because they fear the change will destroy their ability to cope with their environment. People who want insurance for retirement income, who need savings accounts, who work to secure job security, or who want a fire department nearby are all trying to satisfy safety (security) needs.

LOVE AND BELONGING   The next category in the hierarchy includes needs for love and belonging. It may be helpful to think of these in *two subgroups: (1) the need for loving interpersonal relationships* and *(2) the need for identification with something or somebody*. This last is the need for identity.

Some theorists suggest that the need for love and satisfying interpersonal relationships is a survival need. Infants deprived of cuddling and loving in the very early months of life, for instance, die at a higher rate than those who do get it. We think the term *security* describes the relationship better, however. Love and security do not relate invariably. Without oxygen, for example, we all die. Therefore, the need for breath (a physical need) is a survival need. Love—though important, and the need for it a powerful motivator—doesn't correlate totally with survival. A high correlation exists, however, because the need for love strongly motivates.

The need for loving interpersonal relationships explains the need for family found in all kinds of cultures. Cultures define family differently, and families provide different kinds of relationships for their members. But whatever their differences, families supply the close interpersonal relationships we all need, and families exist nearly everywhere. (We caution you to remember, however, that families differ greatly. In this example, we do not define family *only* as it is commonly defined in the United States.)

The other group of love and belonging needs is the need for identity. This is a sense of belonging to somebody or some group. Most of us feel a need to identify with an ethnic group, a neighborhood, a religion, or a national group. In part, the identity provided by sports teams explains the devoted, often fanatical, fans who follow professional or college football teams—or basketball, hockey, baseball, and so on. This aspect, too, helps explain why the concept of family so powerfully motivates. People work hard to preserve families and family traditions. They contribute long hours and much money to neighborhood preservation or college alumni associations. Patriotism, reflecting the need for identity, motivates us to attend parades, display the nation's flag, or support wars that involve invasions of other countries. These and many other behaviors reflect our need to identify with some community, some existence beyond ourselves.

ESTEEM   At the fourth level in the Maslow hierarchy are the needs for esteem. These go beyond the need to identify with something. They involve needs for acceptance and respect by others and self. Efforts to achieve, to accomplish, to gain respect and attention from others and from self reflect needs for esteem.

Needs for esteem can be divided into two subcategories which interact and affect each other: (1) the need for self-respect and (2) the need for respect from others. The more basic need may be for self-esteem. For some people, lack of self-acceptance is the most significant motivator. Such people constantly seek approval from others. Because they lack self-esteem they need others to assure them of worth. Over time, respect and acceptance by significant others help a person gain self-esteem, but both needs continue to motivate behavior.

SELF-ACTUALIZATION   Maslow describes the top of the hierarchy as the need for *self-actualization*, defined as "becoming everything one is capable of becoming." Self-actualization means reaching one's full potential as an individual. For some people, this involves creative activities; for others, manipulating the environment. Some people need to write poetry, others to paint; some need to build or fix things, others to control people. Many different behaviors reflect efforts to satisfy self-actualization needs.

Schutz's Interpersonal Needs   Another useful analysis of human motivation is that of William Schutz. Schutz, concentrating on interpersonal needs, named three primary factors that motivate interpersonal behavior: needs for inclusion, control, and affection.[8]

INCLUSION   Inclusion is the need to have satisfactory relationships with others. While the strength of this need, as with all motivation, varies from person to person, Schutz argues that everyone needs some level of identification with others, some sense of belonging to the human species. Specific reflections of the need for inclusion might be striving for attention, recognition, prominence, prestige, and status, or displaying commitment and participation.

AFFECTION   The need for affection is the need to love and be loved, which also ranges in intensity. Some people have a strong need for closeness with loved ones, while others prize more highly distance and personal freedom. According to Schutz, we can only satisfy this need in a one-to-one relationship.

CONTROL   The need for control is the need to exert influence or power over others—or on the other extreme of a continuum, to be controlled or influenced by others. This is occasionally described negatively as the need to manipulate or be

[8] William C. Schutz, *The Interpersonal Underworld* (Palo Alto, Calif.: Science & Behavior Books, 1966), pp. 13–33.

The need for love and satisfying interpersonal relationships is very strong for most people.

manipulated. People with a strong desire to exert power over others or to be dominated and led by others reflect this need.

Comparing these two analyses of human motivation is useful. Maslow, in presenting the broader perspective, includes motivations that relate to one's environment, not just to other persons. Both analyses look at similar factors from different viewpoints. Each provides a perspective useful in answering the question: Why is this person talking—or saying—these things?

NEED TO INCREASE PREDICTABILITY A third useful analysis of human needs is a theory developed by Charles Berger and Richard Calabrese.[9] They suggest that a primary motivator of much communication is the need to reduce uncertainty— or, to describe it another way, to increase predictability. People generally do not like ambiguity in their lives and want to be able to predict how their interactions with others are likely to turn out. Much communication behavior aims to satisfy this need.

The need appears in two ways during communication: first, during an interac-

---

[9] Charles Berger and Richard Calabrese, "Some Explorations in Initial Interaction and Beyond: Toward a Developmental Theory of Interpersonal Communication," *Human Communication Research*, 1 (1975), 99–112.

tion, especially with strangers, we seek to predict with some accuracy how others will respond; second, after an interaction, we often feel compelled to explain why others talked or acted as they did.

The need for close interpersonal relationships may relate to how strongly one needs to reduce uncertainty. Persons who can tolerate much ambiguity (or lack of certainty) about how others will respond to them have a weak need for predictability. Conceivably, they may need close relationships less than other people.

Communication Purposes and Motivation

Since people communicate to satisfy needs, understanding the various analyses of human needs helps us understand why people talk and act as they do. Receivers who are aware of motivations can clarify the purposes of those they are listening to. However, since human motivation is not simple, several cautions are in order.

Need Structures Are Complex and Variable   The theories must be considered models, not explanations for every event. For example, though generally needs higher in the Maslow hierarchy will not motivate if lower level needs aren't satisfied, it may not always be true. Many people continue to eat high fat diets, smoke, or combine drinking and driving even though they know such behavior threatens their survival. Perhaps it is that what one person perceives as a lower-level need will not be perceived that way by someone else. For example, most starving people will not be greatly concerned with self-esteem or self-actualization. Yet Bobby Sands and others chose to starve to protest Northern Ireland's political situation. Their religious faith satisfied their needs for survival and security.

People often deny apparently lower-level needs to achieve "higher" goals. If asked why, their explanations will show other needs more important to them than survival. What is a primary motivator for one person will not be primary for others. Needs and means of satisfying them are self-identified.

Another reason motivations vary from person to person is that needs may be partially satisfied. Seldom are all physical needs satisfied at any one time. Much less often will all the psychological needs be met. And a person's condition changes. You can feel quite secure, loved, or independent one day, but the next day, with only a few changes in your life, you may feel insecure, unloved, or controlled. Changes in life situations may cause major changes. Primary needs at age eighteen will not be primary at forty-eight or seventy-eight. The interrelations among satisfied and unsatisfied needs create complex motivational patterns.

Interrelations among needs often exist because one behavior can satisfy several needs. The desire to have a house is a good instance. A house gives shelter against freezing in winter, but that doesn't explain the strong desire many people have to own property. Owning a house also satisfies security needs. You know you'll have shelter later even if you don't need it now. Nor can anyone (within limits) tell you what to do with property you own. So having property gives a sense of independence or of control. It may satisfy a need for self-esteem or self-actualization. Having a house may please people you love and help you feel you deserve their love. Houses are identified with homes, and homes are a way to satisfy the need for love, belonging, and affection. Having a house in the "right" neighborhood with a nice lawn and a big lot can satisfy a need for esteem. Working on lawns and landscaping satisfies creative needs for some people. These people gain self-actualization through their houses.

Communication Purposes Are Multiple   One obvious effect of all this is that seldom does a single need motivate any act of communication. Most, if not all, communications have several different purposes.

INSTRUMENTAL PURPOSES (SUBJECT-CENTERED)   Usually, we think of the instrumental purposes as the only purposes of communication. *Instrumental purposes have to do with the behavior or reaction wanted from others.* Suppose someone said, "Please close the door." In this case, the instrumental purpose was that another person would behave in a certain way. Getting receivers to understand something they didn't before, giving them information they didn't have, leading them to believe in some idea, and influencing them to behave in a certain way are all instrumental purposes.

RELATIONAL PURPOSES (OTHER-PERSON CENTERED)   Many times, a particular communication aims to establish or maintain a relationship with the other person. This may satisfy one of the interpersonal needs. A communicator may seek to establish a love relationship, one of control, or one of identification with a group. A relationship can provide self-esteem or security. And in the example of requesting someone in a room to close the door, it is probably not so simple as just wanting the door closed. If it were, why ask someone else to close the door? Why not close it oneself? One goal of such a request could be to establish or maintain a relationship of control.

SELF-RELATED PURPOSES   Much communication aims to satisfy personal needs, such as survival, safety, esteem, predictability, and reduction of ambiguity. But self-related communication purposes also encompass other factors.

Communication may *reinforce our concept of self.* Self-concept, you will remember, refers to the total complex of beliefs and attitudes we have about ourselves. Self-concept involves negative and positive views of self and of self in relation to others. Once we have developed one of these basic ways of viewing ourselves, we often use interpersonal communication to confirm that view. Pay careful attention to your own and others' communication, and you'll see how often this is true. You will also be able to understand why some behavior cannot be explained in rational terms: Many people are reinforcing a negative self-concept.

Another self-related communication purpose is expression. *Expressive speech communicates, but the intent of conveying meaning or influencing others is not its only motivation.* The purpose is to express feelings. If you hit your finger with a hammer, you probably use expressive speech. When you respond with four-letter words to rude treatment by a waiter or a salesperson, you use expressive speech. You speak primarily to express feeling. A nonstop talker deals with a subject, but the main purpose of talking is expressive. Such people talk to relieve tension, to eliminate silence, to express feeling, or to get rid of anxiety.

Expressive speech.

People often engage in expressive speech without realizing it. They think they intend to influence others when the primary purpose is expressive. Have you ever said, "I'm going to give him a piece of my mind," and then did it? Then later you found you didn't achieve your goal? You didn't get what you thought you wanted because of the way you had talked? You had used expressive speech. You said what you thought. But it was the desire to *express* feelings that primarily motivated you, not your desire to influence the other person's behavior. Otherwise, you probably would have chosen your words more carefully.

Purposes Are Often Hidden Samuel Butler once said, "The true use of speech is not so much to express our wants as to conceal them." He was pointing out that many communication purposes are not obvious or open. An open purpose is apparent to everyone who is participating. In the door-closing example we used earlier, the open purpose is instrumental: to get the door closed. But why close the door? The speaker may not tell the person asked to do it. The speaker may not even know all the reasons.

People often have goals they don't disclose. These hidden purposes may simply be unstated. If a communicator is seeking to satisfy some personal need, it may be obvious even if not stated—asking for water on a hot day, for example.

In other cases, purposes are consciously or unconsciously concealed. The communicator may feel that others will not approve if they know what the motivation is. Or the person may not really be aware of the motivation. Often people ask others to do things for them that they could do themselves. They may not be aware of the relationship that such requests imply or create. In these cases, the purpose may be hidden even from the person who has it. Whether unstated, concealed, or unknown, hidden purposes are among the most important in communication.

Listen for What Is Not Said

Too often, we must rely on inferences to understand others' communication purposes. Though sometimes we can ask questions or use verbal feedback to check the accuracy of our conclusions, many times we cannot. Feedback about instrumental purposes can be used more often than people do use it, and good listeners use that strategy every time they can. Similarly, good listeners use direct conversation about the self and relational purposes in communication whenever the situation permits. But all too often we must rely on our ability to infer.

In so doing, listening to the words and to what is *not* said provides a good foundation. We must integrate the verbal messages with relevant nonverbal cues, including the ideas and feelings left unstated. We must remember that feelings are most often communicated through nonverbals. And to understand intended messages completely we must know a source's feelings. Thus, we must note and accurately interpret nonverbal message carriers. As John Powell points out, to understand people, we must try to "hear" what they do not say, "what they perhaps will never be able to say."[10]

Good listeners use all they know about motivation and verbal and nonverbal communication to answer the following questions:

1. Why did the person say that?
2. How does she or he feel about the message?
3. How does the source feel about the listener(s) and the speaker/listener relationship?
4. How does the speaker feel about herself or himself?

[10] *Why Am I Afraid to Tell You Who I Am?* (Niles, Ill.: Argus Communications, 1969), p. 113.

EXERCISE 6.3	MOTIVATION
OBJECTIVE	**To practice identifying motivations.**
DIRECTIONS	1. Choose two advertisements for some product. Select each ad from a different medium: newspapers, magazines, radio, or television.
	2. Identify the needs the advertisers are trying to appeal to in selling the products.
	3. On the assigned day, bring the ads or a description of them to class.
	4. Be prepared to explain the needs you think the advertisers are appealing to, and explain how the advertisers were trying to use them.

REVIEW   **Write brief answers to the following questions that will provide the basis for a writing assignment or class discussion.**
1. Explain how motivation influences effective listening.
2. Using the selected advertisement(s), explain how the appeal attempts to motivate listeners.
3. Explain the most important communication principle you learned or found illustrated in this exercise and why you found it important.

Note: Attach the print ad and a description of the radio or television ad to the worksheet when you turn in a writing assignment.

EMPATHIC LISTENING

To listen empathically requires the sense (or skill) of empathy. We define **empathy** as *a sense of experiencing the feelings of another*. It's feeling as another person feels. Empathy is not the same as sympathy. To sympathize usually means to "feel sorry for." To empathize means to "feel with" another. You can empathize with positive feelings just as with negative ones. Sympathy is usually extended only to persons with problems. To empathize with another is to experience his or her world. When you sense another's feelings and attitudes as if you had experienced those feelings or attitudes, you are empathizing. Empathy is the ability to see as another sees, hear as another hears, feel as another feels. But empathy always retains the "as if" quality, for in reality no one can get "inside the head" of another.

It may be true that you can fully empathize only with internal states you have experienced. If you have never loved, it's probably difficult to empathize with someone who is in love and even more difficult to empathize with someone who has lost a loved one. But a person who has loved could probably empathize with a person who has lost a parent or wife or husband. If you've experienced love, it would be easier to sense how you'd feel without it. To listen empathically, however, you don't really need complete empathy. More important is caring about or wanting to share a person's feelings.

Goals, Limitations, Benefits

The differences between **empathic listening** and other types of listening to understand have more to do with intentions than techniques. *An empathic listener tries to hear the messages as the source is hearing them.* Carl Rogers describes empathy as seeing "the expressed idea from the other person's point of view, to sense how it feels to that person."[11] Empathic listeners use most of the techniques discussed in the preceding pages. They need to be mentally and physically prepared, avoid distractions, pay attention to nonverbals as well as words, identify the source's

[11] Carl Rogers, "Communication: Its Blocking and Its Facilitation," in *Communication Concepts and Processes*, ed. Joseph DeVito (Englewood Cliffs, N.J.: Prentice-Hall, 1971), pp. 182–88.

goals and main ideas, and understand the motivations. The empathic listener does these things *to try to experience the other person's feelings*, not just to understand the messages.

In empathic listening, you want to know more than why a person said something; you want to know what it means, how it feels to that person. Only by understanding others' points of view, by sharing their perspective, can you understand *with* people, rather than understand *about* them. That's what the empathic listener tries to do.

Empathic listening is not easy. Just understanding verbal messages is not simple. Getting "inside" the mind of another person is even harder. As noted, we can only approximate others' perspectives. A more serious barrier is that most of us don't really *want* to see things from a point of view different from our own. If we let ourselves see things as others do, we run the risk of having to change. Entering another's world without evaluating it can threaten our own attitudes and values.

The degree of difficulty rises because we usually need empathic listening in emotional situations. Our emotions interfere with the effort to feel as someone else does. But if we impose our own values—in other words, evaluate instead of understand—we'll find it nearly impossible to empathize with people whose values differ.

Perhaps the major difficulty most of us have in listening empathically is a habit of thinking and talking evaluatively. We respond first to any verbal message by evaluating it or its source. We do it so quickly that this response often prevents our accurate understanding of messages. Even more so does this immediate evaluative response inhibit empathic listening. Indeed, immediate evaluation makes empathic listening virtually impossible.

In spite of the difficulties, we usually benefit from empathic listening. Interpersonal relationships seldom move beyond acquaintance unless people work at relating to others' feelings as well as understanding their ideas. Moreover, if we empathize with others, we'll understand them better. Then, if we *must* evaluate what they say, we can do so more accurately and sensitively. Empathic listening is the best way to assess motivations and to discover hidden purposes. Nothing prepares us better to fully understand the entire message than empathic listening.

Nonverbals in Receiving and Responding

Empathic listening requires us to interpret nonverbal message carriers with special care. As noted earlier, nonverbal communication helps one understand the full message. One should: watch source behaviors (eyes, face, overt and covert gestures); listen to the voice; pay attention to appearance; note aspects of time, personal space, use of objects, and the impact of the situation. All these clarify both what speakers say and what they feel—whether about words, ideas, the listener, the situation, or themselves.

Nonverbal cues are also important in empathic listening for two reasons discussed in Chapter 1:

1. Perceived messages are not always what the source intends.
2. Receivers are sources of messages, even while they are listening.

Let's apply those principles to the concept of feedback.

Unintentional versus Intentional Messages   Because feedback exists only as a speaker perceives it, what is intended by a response may not be what the feedback is. Remember, the feedback is what the originating source perceives of a response—which often differs from what is intended. Thus, much feedback is unintentional. When we listen to others, we respond nonverbally, even if we say nothing. When perceived, our responses become feedback, and the perceiver infers what we think. Often their inferences don't match our intentions and differ from what we mean. To avoid such differences in intended and perceived messages, and to achieve our goals, we must attend carefully to our own nonverbal responses as we listen.

Empathic Behaviors   Since our nonverbal messages can become unintended feedback, our bodies show it if we are really empathic. The following list identifies some behaviors of empathic listeners. These nonverbal responses can improve listening because they help communicate empathy to the source.

> *Empathic Behaviors*
> Nodding head
> Natural eye contact (not extended stare)
> Pleasant facial expression
> Slower body movements
> Same elevation
> Close personal distance
> Pleasant background
>   sounds
>   textures
>   temperature
> Legs crossed toward
> Leaning toward
> Open (not folded) arms
> Touch
> Natural (soft) voice

A reminder is in order here. Remember, nonverbals usually display feelings more honestly than words. If you are attempting to appear empathic and do not really feel that way, you will probably send inconsistent messages. Your voice or body will betray your real feelings. The point here, strongly emphasized in the next chapter as well, is: Honesty is essential to listen with empathy.

Directive and Nondirective Responding

A listener can respond either directively or nondirectively. **Directive feedback** communicates an evaluation of either the source or the message. Suppose, for example, you go shopping with a friend for new clothes and ask for your friend's opinion of a suit you've tried on. If your friend replies, "It's terrific," that's a directive response.

Directive feedback can be positive or negative. The reply "terrific" was positive. A frown would have been negative but still directive.

Directive feedback may be rewarding or punishing. Usually positive feedback is rewarding—but not always. A teacher picking out one student to praise might intend to give rewarding feedback. But the student, knowing classmates will resent the special treatment, might not perceive the positive feedback as rewarding. Similarly, a teenager who enjoys a reputation as the "boss" in the neighborhood will consider it rewarding to receive negative feedback from the police. We can determine whether feedback is positive or negative from the verbal content of the statement. Whether it rewards or punishes depends entirely on the perceiver.

Any response perceived as evaluative is directive feedback. No matter what you actually do or say, if the source perceives the response as an evaluation, it is directive feedback. Questions, failure to answer, or simple repetition can all be perceived as evaluations, whether you intend that they are or not.

Empathic listening often calls for nondirective response. **Nondirective feedback** *refers to responses perceived as nonevaluative.* It describes and stays as close as possible to the "facts." Nondirective feedback avoids judgment. It relies on questions and statements of observation; it focuses on "how I see it" rather than "how it is." Phrases such as, "It appears to me . . ." or "Here's what I heard . . ." or "My feelings are . . ." respond nondirectively.

Questions that seek more information are nondirective, as are several other things. You can encourage a source to talk more or think further about what's being discussed; verbally give encouragement to continue talking—say, "Yes," "Go on," "Uh-huh"—while nodding with an interested facial expression. Paraphrase what the other person says to check accuracy by asking, "Is this what you mean?" or "Do I hear you saying that . . . ?" Repeat part of the original message: "Only two people got an A?" "You want to quit school?"

Here let us reemphasize the difference between response and feedback. Remember that response isn't feedback; it becomes feedback only when perceived

Appropriate responding involves both verbal and nonverbal message carriers.

by the source of the messages to which it is a response. That distinction is needed to differentiate between a nondirective response and nondirective feedback.

Nondirective feedback doesn't necessarily mean a listener stays uninvolved. Nondirective feedback may include reporting your reactions. You describe, not evaluate, when you make clear you are reporting your feelings, not your opinions. To do this, however, you must concentrate on your own reactions and not describe your feelings about the other person and his or her behavior. For example, if you react to someone's behavior by saying, "That sure was a dumb thing to do," you would be giving a directive response. But if you say, "I felt angry about that," you are describing a reaction. If you go on to say, "I was angry about that because it was irresponsible behavior," you have moved from a nondirective to a directive response. Recall the discussion of reporting observations and internal realities in Chapter 5. To remain nondirective, you must limit yourself to reporting reactions. Reporting an evaluation, even as part of or reason for a reaction, will make the statement directive.

Again, however, we must emphasize that whether a nondirective *response* becomes perceived as nondirective *feedback* depends on the perceiver. Whenever feelings are involved, what you intend as nondirective will probably be interpreted as directive.

All responses—verbal and nonverbal—influence whether the feedback is directive or not. The words may not be evaluative, but the voice can clearly convey a judgment. Voice, tone, and emphasis can make, "Is *this* what you mean?" into a suggestion that the speaker said something really dumb. People can interpret body language and use of space and time as evaluative. Since feedback is a perception, not the response itself, sending nondirective feedback requires real skill.

Directive or Nondirective: Making a Choice   How do you decide what form of response to use? In some communication situations, the decision is simple. If someone asks, "What time is it?" the appropriate answer is easy. If you know, you say. Most often, however, it's not so simple to decide the best response to a message. Suppose Ben is dating Emily, a full-time college student who also works twenty hours a week. On Saturday night, they're going to the biggest dinner-dance of the year together. Saturday afternoon she spends her entire week's paycheck to buy new clothes. When he arrives that night, she asks with anticipation, "How do you like my new outfit?" Now, if he likes it, the answer is easy. But suppose he doesn't? Does he give his opinion just because it's asked for? The decision involves a lot of factors. What is their relationship? Will his words, even if nondirective, be perceived as evaluative and negative? Will his nonverbals contradict the words? Was her question really a request for his opinion, or was she seeking reinforcement? Ben must consider all these things, and quickly, before he responds—for even his silence will be directive.

Your goals for listening give the best guidelines for how to respond. What do you want to accomplish? Having thought of that, you can decide which response behaviors will most likely help you do it.

Nondirective responses are useful when you want to learn more about the source or help the person draw conclusions without relying on your opinions. Nondirective responses often help a source open up and think through ideas. If you want others to make their own decisions and rely on their judgments, not yours, use nondirective feedback.

A directive response may often be your first, impulsive reaction. And to respond honestly is important. Nonverbal communication easily contradicts a nondirective response you don't really mean. The best guidelines for deciding when to use directive feedback are: (1) be sure you understand the message before you respond; and (2) before you give your opinion, make sure that giving it will accomplish your purpose. Learn to recognize when evaluation will interfere with the goal you're seeking.

Whatever their initial response, empathic listeners concentrate on understanding the source's feelings and ideas. When responding, they avoid evaluating the other person and seek to experience the other's feelings. If you do this, you can worry less about whether to be directive or nondirective. Most situations calling for empathic listening do not involve a need to evaluate. When that need does exist, understanding the distinctions between response and feedback, directive and nondirective, and positive and negative can be useful.

EXERCISE 6.4   **USING FEEDBACK**

OBJECTIVE   **To practice identifying goals for sending feedback and choosing appropriate responses to achieve those goals.**

DIRECTIONS   **1.** For each of the three situations below:
  a. Identify a goal for responding.
  b. Indicate whether you would use a directive or nondirective response to achieve the goal.
  c. Indicate what you would say to achieve the goal, using the type of feedback you chose.
2. Be prepared to share your responses in class.

Situation I: Your supervisor has given you a task to complete. After looking it over, you decide it will take at least 10 hours of work; it is now noon and you are expected to have the job completed by 10 A.M. tomorrow.

Situation II: You and a friend have just met for a Friday night of relaxation. You had planned that the two of you would go to one or more of the local places for an evening of dancing, but you hope not to spend more than two or three dollars for the whole night. Your friend greets you with, "Hi, there's a great movie downtown. Let's go to that, O.K.?"

Situation III: You are shopping with a wife/husband/girlfriend/boyfriend who has just tried on an outfit that you do not like at all. She/he says, "How do you like this? Doesn't it look great?"

REVIEW   **Write brief answers to the following questions that will provide the basis for a writing assignment or class discussion.**
  a. What is the difference between directive and nondirective feedback and give an example of when you might choose to use each type?

b. Explain why feedback is an essential element of the communication process.
c. Explain the most important communication principle you learned or found illustrated by this exercise and why you found it important.

LISTENING TO EVALUATE

Often, our goals as receivers require us to do more than understand a message. We must decide a number of things: Is the information accurate? Are the conclusions reasonable? Should I believe or behave as this person wants? In these cases, we need to analyze and evaluate.

Listening to evaluate involves the ability to:

1. Determine whether the message really calls for evaluation.
2. Assess the values motivating the people we listen to.
3. Distinguish among facts, observations, and inferences in the messages we receive.
4. Use relevant criteria to evaluate inferences.

To explain the first step, we need only restate earlier comments. Many communication situations do not really call for evaluation. Good listeners break years of habit and resist the pressure applied by the English language. Good listeners ask: Does this situation *require* that I evaluate either the messages or their source(s)? Only when they are certain the answer to the question is "yes" do they proceed with the next steps in listening to evaluate.

Assessing Values

Values anchor each person's perceptual system, and even though we take them for granted most of the time, these values strongly influence behavior. As discussed in earlier chapters, values influence how people feel, what they believe, and what they do, as well as how they perceive and interpret messages. Therefore, listening to evaluate involves assessing the values that motivate the message.

First, the values must be identified. They are seldom stated; they are implied. Sometimes we can use feedback to determine the source's values. In a conversation we can ask, "Why do you believe that?" In other situations, we have to infer. One way to make these inferences is to ask, "What would I have to believe to say that?"

Sometimes values differ so from our own that we cannot understand them. Some experiences are so foreign to our way of life we can't even imagine them. In these situations we must work at listening to understand. We need to learn more before we evaluate. In assessing messages based on values different from ours, we often prejudge and do not listen at all. But by rejecting messages from people whose values differ from ours, we miss opportunities to grow and expand our horizons.

*Listening to evaluate involves
assessing values, inferences,
and sources.*

The reason for deciding what values motivate others is not to reject everything based on values that differ from ours. As we've said, an open mind may be the strongest quality of good listeners. Rejecting anything just because it is based on new or different values robs us of much valuable information.

Discovering the values that motivate messages helps identify differences among people that might not otherwise be clear, and it can explain differences for which the reasons aren't clear. Discussing differences of values contributes to more open communication. It can lead people to consider an idea or behavior they might otherwise have rejected. For example, suppose you don't like the idea of labor strikes. But if you find that the strike occurred because the employer abused the child labor laws, you might listen to a message you would otherwise have rejected.

Conversely, identifying the values underlying messages can lead you to reject messages you'd normally accept. For instance, you may respond positively to advertisements that claim clothing "made in America" costs less than competing products. But when you ask questions about the company because you wonder why it is less expensive, you discover that the employer has hired illegal aliens, refused to pay them adequate wages, and made them work in barely heated and poorly lighted rooms. Then, when they complained about the wages and substandard working conditions, the employer threatened to turn them over to immigration authorities. Knowing the values (profit above all) that motivate such advertising may incline you to refuse the purchase.

The following three questions can aid in assessing the values on which messages are based:

1. On what values is this message based?
2. How do these values differ from mine?
3. How appropriate is it for me to act on a message based on these values?

Distinguishing Facts, Observations, and Inferences

Listening to evaluate requires distinguishing facts from statements about them and sorting out statements of observation from inferences. Remember, a statement of observation differs from the object or event observed, and no statement can report all that is knowable about an object or event. Moreover, observations vary due to selective attention, perception, and retention. So statements of observation may be inaccurate.

To verify observations, check with other observers of the same facts. If you cannot verify observations, then you must decide: Can I accept these observations as accurate? This really asks: Am I willing to trust this person's perception? In these cases, assess the qualifications of the person making the statements. Ask yourself:

1. Is the observer reliable?
2. Is the observer biased?
3. Was the observer in a position to see what is claimed?

If people were not able to see or hear what they claim to have seen or heard, the observation is not acceptable. Acceptable witnesses in an auto accident case must have been where they could see it happen. When Abraham Lincoln was a lawyer, he used this principle in a classic defense. A woman claimed to identify a defendant as the burglar she saw in her backyard at night. Lincoln proved the woman couldn't have seen the defendant's face because it was the night of a new moon. With no moonlight, she couldn't have seen what she claimed to see. Her testimony was rejected on the grounds that she was not qualified.

Using Criteria to Evaluate Inferences

Most people evaluate messages through "good-bad," "right-wrong" evaluations based on some unstated standards. These abstract evaluations are not very useful. They tell little except "I liked it" or "I didn't agree." More useful is to evaluate inferences using one or more of these standard criteria:

1. The source should be qualified to draw the conclusions.
2. An acceptable authority should be unbiased.
3. The inference should be based on adequate evidence.
4. The evidence should be relevant to the conclusion.
5. Contrary evidence invalidates a conclusion.
6. The reasoning should be valid.
7. Too much reliance on propaganda techniques may signal weak evidence or reasoning.

Listening to evaluate is an important and necessary skill.

To evaluate inferences, choose whichever of these standards is most appropriate in each situation, and phrase the criterion as a question. Answering your own question either "yes" or "no" will provide the evaluation and the reasons for it.

Qualified Source? To most messages we ought to apply the criterion that a source should be qualified. For example, a successful actor is qualified to discuss theater or movies, but what qualifies that person to give opinions about politicians?[12] Yet it is common for candidates to present a lineup of stars to persuade the voters. All people have a right to their own opinions, but we should avoid accepting inferences by those who have little or no background in the area under discussion.

Biased Source? This question applies the criterion that an acceptable authority should be unbiased. It asks: Does the speaker have anything to gain personally by taking a position on an issue? A "yes" answer to this question should make us suspicious of the speaker's conclusions. Be properly skeptical of everything a salesperson says about a product, for instance. Having a stake in the outcome doesn't automatically disqualify a person as an authority. But it does suggest a bias, even if unintentional. Be aware of and guard against these source biases. Believing sports stars who advertise products when you know they've been paid for the endorsement is not good evaluation.

On the other hand, if you find a person testifying against a viewpoint of personal benefit, it is important evidence. This is called *reluctant testimony,* and it is usually worth listening to. Speaking against a point of view that would bring personal benefit is strong evidence of a speaker's sincerity.

Sufficient Evidence? An inference implies that observations exist on which the conclusion is based. Therefore, the observations must be adequate. Is there enough basis for the inference? If evidence isn't adequate, you should reject the

---

[12] The presidential election of Ronald Reagan does not dispute this conclusion. Years of writing, speaking on public issues, and executive experience intervened between his career as an actor and his election as governor of California and as president.

inference. For example, in attempting to convince us to support a law to ban smoking in public places, one might argue that nonsmokers are irritated by smoke. Some people will reject this as insufficient evidence. These listeners require the source to give evidence that smoking is harmful to nonsmokers' health. These people believe much harm must be proved before government should regulate individual freedom.

This case shows how complex some critical listening is. How much harm should be proved? Whose freedom should be valued most? Such questions take listeners back to values assessment. Simple "right-wrong" evaluations are inadequate in situations like these.

Relevant Evidence? Often statements offered as evidence have no relevance to the conclusion. For example, in asking you to vote for a senatorial candidate, a person may say the candidate has a lovely family. Is that information really relevant to the issue of becoming a senator? Should it influence a decision to vote for the candidate? Applying this criterion will help you reject all inferences based on irrelevant data.

Contradictory Evidence? Is there any information that would qualify or negate the inferences in the message? Take the senatorial candidate as an example. Suppose you knew that the candidate's children were vandals who were kept out of juvenile court only by the politician's influence, and that the candidate's family got money from organized crime. You might feel this evidence negates the claim that the candidate has a lovely family. You've heard people say, "Why shouldn't I smoke? I see no harm in it. No one I know got cancer from smoking." This fails to mention people the person didn't know who died of cancer. When you reject inferences because of contrary evidence, you have applied the criterion that contrary evidence invalidates a conclusion.

Valid Reasoning? Inferences require a mental leap. Is the leap logically sound? If it's not, you should reject the conclusion. It does not meet the criterion that reasoning should be valid. Identify the kind of reasoning you are hearing. Is it generalization? deduction? cause-effect? comparison and contrast? Once you've identified the basis for the conclusion, assess it, using the guidelines for reasoning given in Chapter 5. Reject conclusions based on the fallacies discussed there.

Excessive Use of Propaganda? Much advertising and other persuasion relies too much on propaganda devices. You've probably already been introduced to these devices. If not, Table 6–2 reviews them. The problem with propaganda is excessive use of emotional appeals. When you see or hear such techniques, you should "see" a *Caution* light in your mind. Emotional appeals are necessary and useful in persuasion, but they should not circumvent sound reasoning and good evidence. Relying almost entirely on emotion may spring from weak logic. For this reason, when you hear highly emotional appeals, apply the first six criteria in Table 6–2 even more strictly. Don't reject an emotional message just because it's emotional, but don't let emotional appeals and propaganda make you forget to look carefully at the evidence and reasoning either.

TABLE 6–2   Propaganda Devices

DEVICE	METHOD
Bandwagon	Argues: "Since everyone else is doing it (or buying it) you should, too."
Half-truths	By telling only part of the information, leaves an impression that is inaccurate; for example, advertising that "three out of four doctors surveyed recommend the ingredient in Anacin," without pointing out that the recommended ingredient is common aspirin.
Card Stacking	Presents only the favorable side of the evidence to support the source's position.
Glittering Generality	Applies concepts that have powerful positive connotations—for example, "motherhood," "morality," "decency," "fairness"—to the idea being urged.
Name Calling	Uses words in a manner intended to arouse powerful negative connotations, usually to depict another person or a group as inferior or bad; for example, calling busing a conspiracy or attacking the opponents of busing as racist.
Labeling	Uses words to categorize a person or a group under a single heading, frequently negative; intentionally selects one aspect of the person or group being labeled.
Transfer	Introduces one subject or topic that is highly respectable or popular, and then moves into other areas in an effort to transfer the positive attitude onto the new topic.
Testimonial	Uses a source of authority as evidence for ideas and positions, often in areas in which the person is not really an authority; for example, Bob Hope advertising Texaco products.
Plain Folks	Presents the source or authority as a person who is really simple and humble, a person just like your neighbors, a person who is innocent and trustworthy.
Loaded Words	Uses words that will stir strong emotional responses either to support the position of the advocate or to attack the position of opponents.

EXERCISE 6.5   CRITICAL LISTENING

OBJECTIVE   **To practice the skills required to evaluate messages.**

DIRECTIONS   1. Below are three messages. For each of them, answer the following questions:
   a. What is the speaker's goal?
   b. What are the basic values on which the message is based?
   c. What are the important inferences I am expected to accept if I do or believe as the speaker wants?
   d. What are the appropriate criteria to evaluate this message?
   e. Applying the criteria, is the message acceptable?
   f. What further information do I need to fully evaluate the message?

Message I: A student who sits next to you in history class meets you for a few minutes before class starts. "Hey, have you voted in the student senate elections?" When you say you haven't, the person replies, "Well, you'd better. You know the senate is working very hard to get the pass-fail system adopted here at the college, and the Barker candidates haven't come out very strongly in favor of it. The Brinkman party, however, has an entire slate that supports pass-fail grading strongly. You wouldn't have to take all your classes pass-fail, but you would at least have that option, which is more than we have now. Come with me after class. Let's go vote for the Brinkman candidates."

Message II: You are talking with a friend about what classes to take during the next semester. You may take one elective and must decide which English teacher to take composition from. The friend says, "Listen, this ecology course is great. We go on field trips and visit places, and we haven't had a single test all semester. It's a breeze, nothing to it. And as for English—well, I don't know. This prof I have makes us write a theme every week. What a drag. You sure don't want to get Jones."

Message III: You are listening to a speaker who is urging you to support the Right to Life constitutional amendment. The speaker's basic argument is that abortion is murder because any fetus is a human life. Therefore, the speaker argues, abortion should not be acceptable under any circumstances.

REVIEW   **Write brief answers to the following questions that will provide the basis for a writing assignment or class discussion.**
   1. How do you decide which criteria are appropriate for evaluating different messages?
   2. What distinguishes situations in which critical listening is appropriate from those in which the listener's goal is to understand and remember?
   3. Explain the most important communication principle you learned or found illustrated in this exercise and why you found it important.

SUMMARY

To listen effectively, we have to understand the differences among listening situations and respond appropriately. Listening situations vary from merely hearing through listening to understand, to remember, and to evaluate. Techniques of active listening are useful in all situations requiring understanding, remembering, and evaluating. They involve understanding the words and the source. In improving the ability to understand the words they hear, good listeners prepare to listen, set goals, use listening speed efficiently, minimize distractions, and effectively use feedback. To use listening speed efficiently, find self-interest in the listening situation, identify the personal value of listening, pick out and recognize the speaker's goals, and identify the speakers' main ideas by using key words to summarize and restate while the speaker is talking. The most common distractions are emotional reactions to what a speaker says. These emotional reactions lead us to quit listening while we prepare a rebuttal and thus to misunderstand. If listeners paraphrase to check their understanding of speakers' ideas, feedback is most effective.

To understand the source in communication, one recognizes that communication is goal directed and tries to apply an understanding of some theories of motivation. Maslow's theory suggests that human needs are arranged in a sort of hierarchy. Physical needs, at the base of a pyramid, need to be satisfied *before* the higher-level, culturally defined (or social and psychological) needs will motivate behavior. The physical needs are described as survival needs. The others, in ascending order, are safety (or security), love and belonging, esteem, and self-actualization. Schutz' analysis of interpersonal needs suggests that all people have a need for some degree of inclusion, for affection, and for control. Berger and Calabrese argue that much communication is motivated by a need to be able to predict what will happen in the future. Since human need structures are complex and variable, purposes for communicating are multiple. Most messages are motivated by three purposes: instrumental, relational, and self-related. In addition, the purposes of many communicative messages are hidden, even from their source. Thus, the effective listener pays careful attention to verbal and nonverbal messages, including words that aren't spoken, to decide source goals and motivations.

A special type of listening to understand is empathic listening. This is an effort to understand the speaker and how the speaker feels about what is being said. Empathic listeners want to understand more than verbal messages. Nonverbals help interpret the message and the speaker and provide a supportive atmosphere that will help the person who is talking be more open. To listen empathically, be aware of intentional and unintentional messages, and control nonverbal responses. Empathic listening also involves understanding the difference between responding directively and nondirectively and knowing when to use each response.

Listening to evaluate involves (1) assessing the values that motivate messages; (2) distinguishing among facts, observations, and inferences; and (3) using criteria to evaluate inferences. To assess values, identify the values a message is based on and determine their appropriateness. To distinguish facts, observations, and inferences, you have to know that a fact is not the same as a statement about it. If observations cannot be verified directly, evaluate by asking three questions: (1) Is the observer reliable? (2) Is the observer biased? and (3) Was the observer in a position to see what he or she claimed to see?

Seven criteria are recommended to evaluate inferences: (1) The source should be qualified to draw the conclusion; (2) An acceptable authority should be unbiased; (3) Inferences should be based on adequate evidence; (4) Evidence should be relevant to the conclusion; (5) Contrary evidence invalidates a conclusion; (6) The reasoning should be valid; and (7) Too much reliance on propaganda techniques may signal weak evidence or reasoning.

QUESTIONS FOR DISCUSSION

1. How do listening situations differ?
2. What are the benefits of goal setting in listening?
3. What specific things can a receiver do to use listening speed efficiently?
4. How can knowing theories of motivation improve listening?
5. What three purposes motivate most communication?
6. What are the benefits of empathic listening and why is it so difficult to do?
7. Distinguish directive from nondirective responses and indicate when and how to use directive and nondirective feedback.
8. What steps are involved in assessing values as you listen to evaluate?
9. What questions help assess whether to accept observations?
10. List the questions asked in using criteria to evaluate inferences and indicate how the questions would have to be answered for inferences to be acceptable.

SUGGESTIONS FOR FURTHER READING

Anastasi, Thomas. *Listen! Techniques for Improving Communication Skills.* New York: Van Nostrand Reinhold, 1982.

Atwater, Eastwood. *I Hear You: Listening Skills to Make You a Better Manager.* Englewood Cliffs, N.J.: Prentice-Hall, 1981.

Barbara, Dominick. *The Art of Listening.* Springfield, Ill.: Charles C Thomas, 1971.

Barker, Larry L. *Listening Behavior.* Englewood Cliffs, N.J.: Prentice-Hall, 1971.

Brockriede, Wayne, and Douglas Ehninger. *Decision by Debate,* 2nd ed. New York: Dodd, Mead, 1978.

Duker, Sam, ed. *Listening: Readings.* Metuchen, N.J.: Scarecrow Press, 1966.

Erway, Ella A. *Listening: A Programmed Approach,* 2nd ed. New York: McGraw-Hill, 1979.

Fearnside, W. Ward, and William B. Holther. *Fallacy: The Counterfeit of Argument.* Englewood Cliffs, N.J.: Prentice-Hall, 1959.

Nichols, Ralph G., and Leonard A. Stevens. *Are You Listening?* New York: McGraw-Hill, 1957.

Thum, Gladys, and Marcella Thum. *The Persuaders: Propaganda in War and Peace.* New York: Atheneum, 1972.

Weaver, Carl H. *Human Listening.* Indianapolis: Bobbs-Merrill, 1972.

Wolff, Florence, et al. *Perceptive Listening.* New York: Holt, Rinehart and Winston, 1983.

Wolvin, Andrew, and Carolyn Coakley. *Listening,* 2nd ed. Dubuque, Iowa: Brown, 1985.

7 Developing and Maintaining Personal Relationships

> People carry around with them a complicated set of aspirations, the central focus of which is developing an intimate and enduring relationship with another human being.
>
> PHILIP BLUMSTEIN and PEPPER SCHWARTZ

> I was angry with my friend/I told my wrath,
> my wrath did end.
> I was angry with my foe; I told it not,
> my wrath did grow.
>
> WILLIAM BLAKE

GOAL

To understand the factors involved in improving personal relationships

OBJECTIVES

The material in this chapter should help you to:

1. State how the study of perception is related to improving interpersonal communication.
2. Distinguish between role performances and expectations and demonstrate an awareness of how roles and norms affect communication by citing personal experiences.
3. Illustrate the four major sources of interpersonal attraction by describing how those conditions influence your relationships with friends and with those you do not like.
4. Define trust and describe how it can develop in a relationship.
5. Explain how acceptance and empathy contribute to the development of trust, and why, by themselves, they will not create trust.
6. Given specific situations, phrase statements that demonstrate skills at taking others' perspectives.
7. Distinguish among the ways of talk classified by level of self-disclosure and relate to the types of statements introduced in Chapter 5.
8. Explain how defensiveness interferes with effective communication, giving examples that show effects of defensive climates.
9. Use the I Message formula to disclose positive and negative feelings.
10. Demonstrate communication skills that help to build and maintain long-term interpersonal relationships.

We can never walk twice in the same river, even though we may return each day to the same spot on its bank. The water there yesterday is gone today, and that now here is leaving even as we stand in it. As you know, the process view of communication sees people as much like that river. Though each of us has the same name and much the same appearance from day to day, we change, in perhaps imperceptible ways, from one moment to the next. So too do our relationships with others. It is this complexity we confront as we seek to learn to communicate more effectively within important personal relationships.

Interpersonal communication, like all behavior, is goal-directed, aimed at satisfying important needs and motivations. Much of the discussion in Chapter 6 sought to emphasize that people establish and maintain relationships with others in order to satisfy basic needs. Knowing that is fundamental to understanding interpersonal communication. Other factors, however, also affect interpersonal communication. In this chapter, we first discuss some of those factors, then turn to specific suggestions for improving interpersonal relationships.

FACTORS IN PERSONAL RELATIONSHIPS

Interpersonal Perception

Perception affects both development and maintenance of personal relationships. In Chapter 1 and elsewhere we have stressed the importance of knowing that communication is based largely on perceptions. The effects of perception are as strong, if not stronger, in interpersonal relationships as in any other aspect of communication.

Interpersonal perception differs in no essential way from any other perceptual process, except that people are infinitely more complex than objects. Thus, perceptions of people vary more than other kinds of perceptions. Recall the communication problems in talking about abstract phenomena discussed in Chapter 3. Then note that though a person's body may be concrete, the person is not. Interpersonal relationships are even more intangible. In communicating *we interact with our perception of the whole person constrained by our perception of the relationship.* The communication situation, inherently abstract and thus ambiguous, directly and concurrently affects how we perceive those we communicate with.

Interpersonal perception can be defined as attributing characteristics to people as we interact with them. For example, a colleague tells about something that happens to him with some regularity. Often he stops at a nearby store on his way home after work. Because he is wearing a suit, other customers in the store mistake him for a store employee and ask for help with a purchase. They have attributed the characteristic of store employee to him (an interpersonal perception) on the basis of their perception of his appearance. We all do this, usually totally unaware of having done so.

The process increases in complexity because interpersonal perception involves attributing characteristics to people while we interact with them. We perceive an "object" and we decide what characteristics that "object" has, even as we make other choices about what to say, what is the appropriate relationship between us, and many other things.

We need to remember that *we communicate, not with other persons, but with our perceptions of those persons' personality and the relationships between us*. When people talk, they consider their perceptions of the receiver's goals, intentions, attitudes toward them and others, and so on—or at least they should do so.

We do not wish to overcomplicate the issue here, but we do want to be sure you understand that what you perceive in a person you are talking and listening to is just that—your perception. And, as with any perceived message, it may be quite different from the other person's intentions or the "reality" itself.

Roles and Role Performance

Communicating in relationships involves social factors. Social groups, whether an entire culture or a family or group of friends, expect certain behaviors from persons within those groups. Whether one adheres to the expectations of those groups or not influences the communication. Of importance is understanding how roles and norms affect communication.

Roles　Role, an important concept in understanding communication, is a word used with many different meanings. One search of journals and books revealed forty different uses of the word.[1] Sometimes *role* refers to position in social relationships; for example, you commonly hear of the roles of mother, father, husband, wife, son, daughter, parent, student, teacher, and so on. More accurately, we think, the word **role** refers to *a set of behaviors expected of people who occupy specific positions in a social relationship*.

Roles involve expectations. Because expectations differ, one cannot state precisely what a particular role is. Only those holding the expectations can identify a role. For example, what is the role of parent? Many parent roles exist, related to both general and specific situations. All include behaviors, part of the concept of role. *What a person does in a social position* is called **role performance.** Understanding the effects of role in communication involves recognizing both role expectations and role performances.

Only in stable social structures will role performances conform closely to role expectations and will members agree on role expectations. Think about the social position called "parent." We might agree on how to divide the population into two groups, parents and nonparents. We would not easily agree on the role of a parent. How is a parent to act? What behaviors are expected of parents? What should they avoid doing? Most of us have expectations regarding a parent's behavior, but we will rarely agree with everything others expect parents to do.

But that people do not agree on role expectations makes them no less real. Each person, each group, and each society expect certain behaviors from people they call parents, and each reacts strongly to people who violate the expectations.

[1] Lionel Nieman and James Hughes, "The Problem of the Concept of Role—A Resurvey of the Literature," *Social Forces* 30 (December 1951), 141, 149.

Norms   Some expected behaviors are standardized into norms. **Norm** refers to *a standard of expected behavior for the violation of which people must pay a social penalty.* An entire society or subgroups within the society establish norms which then greatly influence communication. You may choose to follow, ignore, or flout social norms, but in every case your actions relate to them. Even when you attempt to show that the larger society's norms don't restrict you, they influence your communication.

Choosing to ignore social norms leads to penalties from people who adhere to them. The penalties vary according to the strength of the norm, how much it was violated, and how much it applies to a particular situation. Nudity, for example, can get people arrested in some places, but it brings customers to a movie or burlesque house, and it brought a fortune to the creator of *Playboy*. Arriving at work, at school, or at your neighborhood supermarket in your pajamas won't get you arrested, but you'll have a hard time engaging anyone in a conversation, even about the weather. Even though the pajamas might be attractive and more modest than many commonly worn clothes, social norms do not permit you to wear them to the supermarket. If you arrive dressed according to the norm for that situation, however, others will ignore or talk to you depending on your wishes.

The degree of pressure to conform to roles and norms depends on the individual and the situation. Usually people participate in social situations, either formal or informal, because they feel a need to. The need doesn't have to be strong. For instance, a decision to join a group of classmates standing in the hall before class doesn't usually reflect a strong need, and violating the expectations of that kind of group brings little penalty. But a strong need for approval increases the pressure to conform. How strongly a group feels also affects how they react to those who don't conform to expectations. If people feel strongly about norms, they ostracize or reject violators.

If a social group holds attitudes strongly enough, people who disagree have a choice: giving in to the expectation (at least to some extent) or not belonging. In less extreme situations, one can learn to disagree in tactful ways and still be accepted.

In all cases, role expectations and norms help define the communication situation. They become part of each communicator's perceptual screen, affecting how messages are perceived and identifying the choices for what can be said and done or what the penalties or rewards for different words and behaviors will be. When you are attempting to understand any communication event or to decide what to say or how to behave, you ignore these factors at great potential cost.

EXERCISE 7.1   **ROLES**

OBJECTIVE	To become aware of the roles you perform and of the role expectations of people you associate with.
DIRECTIONS	1. List all the roles you perform in a typical day. 2. Choose the two roles that most influence your daily behavior.

3. Identify the most significant people who communicate with you in that role.
4. State the norms associated with these roles.
5. List the expectations you perceive these people have of your behavior.
6. Show the list you made in question 4 to the people. Ask them to confirm your listed expectations or to explain to you how their actual expectations differ.

REVIEW   **Write brief answers to the following questions that will provide the basis for a writing assignment or class discussion.**
1. Distinguish among role expectations, role performance, and norms.
2. What are the consequences of violating social norms?
3. Explain the most important communication principle you learned or found illustrated in this exercise and why you found it important.

Interpersonal Attraction

Another element important in establishing and maintaining personal relationships is interpersonal attraction. **Interpersonal attraction** *describes the positive regard people have for other people.* When persons are "attracted" to each other, they feel a bond. They have a positive "feeling" toward each other. Many factors attract people to each other. The major sources of interpersonal attraction are appearance, proximity (closeness), reciprocal liking, and attitude similarity.

Appearance   The first information we process when we interact face-to-face with someone is that person's appearance. Appearance largely determines initial impressions, but even if we are interacting for the hundredth time, we interpret the appearance and make evaluations about feelings, personality, and character.

As noted in Chapter 4, people stereotype physical characteristics, and the stereotypes vary from culture to culture. Thus, cultural norms in part dictate what makes a person attractive. Moreover, what is considered attractive varies from person to person. But whatever one perceives as a pleasing appearance affects the development of relationships. It helps open channels of communication and positively affects the interactions.

Strength of the influence of physical appearance depends on how important appearance or cultural stereotypes are to the perceiver and on how accurately the perceiver has assessed personality and feelings in the past. But rarely is physical appearance unimportant.

Proximity   A second source of interpersonal attraction is accidental or intentional use of proximity. Distances between people influence interpersonal attraction. *Accidental proximity* is physical closeness over which we have little control, such as with neighbors or coworkers.

The rules of living dictate these and other associations, and frequently those associations result in liking. The more often we interact with people, the more likely we will be attracted to them. Research has shown that, on the average, people who live near or work with minority group members have more positive attitudes about them. Similarly, men who have worked under women managers respond more positively toward the idea of women in management than do men who have never worked under a woman's supervision.

Two factors explain this effect of accidental proximity. First, it is just easier to get along with those we work with or live near. One coping reaction to those you dislike is to ignore or stay away from them. Keeping close contact with enemies is a stressful situation people usually try to avoid. We have more opportunities to know those we are close to, so we replace prejudices with opinions based on experience.

More significantly, closeness offers opportunities for shared experiences and exchanges of personal information. Notice yourself in classes. You become acquainted with people whose seats are next to yours or who are assigned to group projects with you. Out-of class friendships may develop simply because closeness gives you the opportunity to know each other. You will become less well acquainted with someone who sits on the other side of the room—unless, that is, you create intentional proximity.

Intentional proximity results when you make a special effort to be near someone you find attractive. If you've seen someone in class who appeals to you, you may change seats so you can get acquainted. Or you may try to leave the room at the same time or request work reassignments to be near someone you would like to get to know.

It's difficult to create relationships without some proximity. Some people develop close friendships through letters or computer networks, but generally people need face-to-face contact for liking to develop and relationships to continue.

Reciprocal Liking Reciprocal liking affects interpersonal attraction. If you become aware that someone likes you, then your evaluation of her or him moves toward liking. A positive evaluation from one person encourages a similar response from the other person. Liking people can prompt you to focus attention on them; their liking of you becomes the catalyst for you to consider liking them. How often have you heard, "He (or she) likes you," and then paid more attention to that person than you otherwise would have?

This reciprocity hinges on two factors. First, the person extending the reinforcement (liking) must be someone you are willing to be attracted to. If not, you will rationalize or justify your dislike. Second, the recipient of liking must not have a negative self-concept. People with low self-esteem often regard people who dislike them more favorably than those who like them.

Attitude Similarity Similar attitudes also produce increased liking. Attitude similarity relates to interpersonal attraction in two ways: First, people are attracted to those who share their attitudes. When we meet someone who shares our interests, we find it pleasing. Conversations with strangers are less awkward when you discover

People are attracted to people who share their attitudes.

you have something in common. Talking to someone who doesn't share your attitudes and interests can be boring, while discussing shared interests is fun.

The relationship of attitude similarity and liking is unpredictable. People don't require similar attitudes to like each other. People of opposite interests can be attracted to one another because they appreciate the differences. However, long-term relationships require some similarity, even if it's only a similar tolerance for variety. Once liking occurs, it's a "chicken-egg" argument: Were the people initially similar, or did the interaction create similarity?

Liking itself can create perceptual distortion in favor of similarities. When people like each other, they often assume similarity in interests and attitudes. We find it disappointing, for example, if our friends dislike a musical group, political candidate, or cause we believe in. We tend to rationalize their attitudes, thinking, "He may dislike that particular song, but would like their other music if he heard it." Or we perceive the attitudes as less different than they actually are, thinking, "Well, she may not like Senator X, but when she gets more information, she'll probably approve."

Another way attitude similarity begins is that we often start developing interests in things we perceive to be of interest to someone we are attracted to. Many women, for instance, have little interest in hockey or drag racing—until they begin dating men who participate in such activities. Then they learn about these things and develop interests and positive attitudes toward them.

These four factors vary from one relationship to another, and at times within one relationship. Appearance and proximity more strongly influence the establishment of relationships; reciprocal liking and attitude similarity have more effect in maintaining them. Knowing about these factors can help you understand why some relationships develop and others decay. They can also help you know how to communicate in ways that develop or maintain relationships.

EXERCISE 7.2   **WHY DO I LIKE PEOPLE?**

OBJECTIVE   **To examine how the factors of interpersonal attraction affect you.**

DIRECTIONS
1. Pick out a person you like very much and one you do not like.
2. Using the items listed here, assess how many of the factors of interpersonal attraction are involved in each relationship.
3. Discuss the following questions with a group of your classmates:
   a. Do your ratings confirm the relationships we discussed in this chapter between attraction and (1) appearance, (2) proximity, (3) reciprocal liking, and (4) attitude similarity?
   b. If so, how?
   c. If not, why not?
   d. Can you think of other factors involved in interpersonal attraction?

The Person I like:

PHYSICAL APPEARANCE
Is pleasing to me.	_____	Is not pleasing to me.

PROXIMITY
I associate whenever I can.	_____	I avoid whenever I can.
I must be around a lot at work/home/school.	_____	I don't need to be around very much.

ATTITUDE SIMILARITY
Religion is like mine.	_____	Religion is different.
Is interested in same things.	_____	Is not interested in same things.
Political views are like mine.	_____	Political views are not like mine.

RECIPROCAL LIKING
Likes me.	_____	Doesn't like me.

The Person I do not like:

PHYSICAL APPEARANCE
Is pleasing to me.	_____	Is not pleasing to me.

PROXIMITY
I associate whenever I can.	_____	I avoid whenever I can.
I must be around a lot at work/home/school.	_____	I don't need to be around very much.

ATTITUDE SIMILARITY
Religion is like mine.	_____	Religion is different.
Is interested in same things.	_____	Is not interested in same things.
Political views are like mine.	_____	Political views are not like mine.

RECIPROCAL LIKING
Likes me.	_____	Doesn't like me.

REVIEW   **Write brief answers to the following questions that will provide the basis for a writing assignment or class discussion.**
1. Explain how the factors of interpersonal attraction affect interpersonal relationships, long and short term.

> **2.** Identify the factors of interpersonal attraction that seem most important in your relationships.
> **3.** Explain the most important communication principle you learned or found illustrated in this exercise and why you found it important.

IMPROVING RELATIONSHIPS

Most factors of personal relationships vary in degree or amount. And as they vary, the quality of the relationship varies. In this section we discuss some concepts you can use to develop and maintain healthy interpersonal relationships. Again, however, we make the point that much of your success in interpersonal communication relies more on attitude than it does on skill. We will suggest many skills you may use, and some you can encourage those who share relationships with you to try themselves. The techniques that improve communication in relationships are not difficult; motivating yourself to *want* to use them often is.

Taking Others' Perspectives

Learning to take another's perspective contributes to improved personal relationships. To take a perspective different from our own involves concepts and skills previously discussed in this book. It requires understanding that each person's communication behaviors rely on that person's perception of the situation, including the people and relationships in it; it involves effective use of feedback, especially paraphrasing, to increase a communicator's ability to "see" as does the communication partner; it involves empathy; and it requires sensitivity to the impact of culture on how one perceives and values. Perhaps most important, it requires a conscious effort to enter into another's perceptual world.

Each of us knows the information in the paragraph above, and we are able to apply these skills. Too often, however, we don't. What usually prevents us is that we focus on ourselves and our own goals in a communication situation. As we talk with those with whom we share interpersonal relationships, our attention centers on our own feelings and beliefs. This is natural. It is, after all, what we want and need that motivates us to communicate. What the skilled communicator does that most of us do not is remember that *accomplishing goals in interpersonal relationships requires considering the wants and needs that motivate our communicating partners.*

The skills of taking the other's perspective differ little from those previously discussed. We must remember to use verbal and nonverbal feedback to answer the following questions:

1. How is this person perceiving this situation—including me, our relationship, and what has occurred between us prior to this point?
2. What values are motivating this person's communication?
3. What goals is this person seeking?

In answering these questions, we must avoid the tendency to substitute our own perceptions for those of another person. We must remember that culture, language, experience, perspective, emotions, and physical state influence perceptions. This will remind us that how we perceive may differ from how others perceive.

We want to emphasize another concept discussed earlier. Taking the perspective of others does not mean we discard our own viewpoints or agree with others' values or opinions. It does mean knowing and trying to "enter into" another's values and basic assumptions. When we can "role play" the perspectives of those with whom we communicate, we have the foundation for improving our relationships with them.

One final caution: In long-term interpersonal relationships, do not assume that you understand another person's perspective simply because you have known the person for a long time. On the contrary, efforts to take the other person's perspective must be ongoing to successfully maintain the relationship.

Building Trust

A relationship rarely develops to the level of true intimacy without trust. More important, maintaining long-term, healthy relationships requires trust. Therefore, understanding what trust is and what causes it are important.

A trusting situation exists when a quarterback accepts criticism from the coach, or when a department head takes a suggestion from an employee. In both cases, one person is confident about the intentions and abilities of the other. Trust involves having a confident belief in someone. But more specifically, a belief in what? We define **trust** as having confidence in someone's behavior under the following conditions:

1. Another person can behave in ways that can have either positive or negative outcomes for you.
2. Those outcomes depend on the behavior of the other person (not on fate or something you do).

When under those conditions you have confidence that the other person's behavior will have positive results, that is trust. Suppose you have an important job interview at 8 A.M. the next day. At 10 P.M. you discover your alarm clock is broken. You know you will not wake up without the alarm. You ask your parents to awaken you at 6 A.M., the time at which they normally rise. If you go to sleep, sure they will call you at 6 A.M., you trust them—in this situation. If they failed to wake you up, the outcomes would be negative for you. They are the ones with the clock, so they control the outcomes. The two conditions are present. Therefore, if you believe their behavior will result in the positive outcomes, you trust them.

The effects of trust may be most obvious when it does not exist. The title of a popular book, *Why Am I Afraid to Tell You Who I Am?*,[2] describes such situations. The author analyzes the many ways people use "masks" to keep others from knowing their innermost feelings and thoughts. He relates a friend's answer to the title

---

[2] John Powell, *Why Am I Afraid to Tell You Who I Am?* (Niles, Ill.: Argus Communications, 1969).

Trust is a confident belief in another's behavior; it involves predicting that others' behavior will affect you positively.

question: "I am afraid to tell you who I am because if I tell you, you may not like who I am, and it's all that I have." The friend's answer shows the absence of trust. He wants to be liked (condition number 1). Liking is the author's to give or withhold (condition number 2). The speaker's refusal to "be himself," to communicate feelings openly and honestly, shows that trust is missing. Lacking confidence that the other person will like the "real" person, the speaker reveals only what he thinks the other person might like.[3] Since trust does not exist, communication is not honest.

Trust plays an important role in personal relationships because it permits people to share information that leads to liking. Without trust, people rarely share their feelings openly or feel comfortable with one another. Two additional factors should be noted. First, trust is NOT something that either exists or does not. It varies in degree. You can trust someone a lot, not very much, or not at all. The degree of trust affects how it influences behavior, a factor we return to later in this chapter. Second, it should be obvious that trust is not always appropriate. Not everyone is trustworthy. People often have good reasons to avoid being fully

[3] Recall the discussion of masking or "face making" in Chapter 2.

open with others. But since trust leads to the most satisfying relationships, let's examine the sources of trust.

The Situation   Most people develop trust on the basis of specific experiences. They have learned to expect certain types of persons to be trustworthy. For example, generally ministers and doctors are considered trustworthy, and some people also trust teachers, police, and counselors. Other people have had experiences that created the opposite expectations. They do not trust ministers, doctors, police, or teachers, and would never go to a counselor for fear of being betrayed. Trust is also person-specific. We expect the police to come when we report a burglary, even though we might not trust the officer to refuse a bribe if someone offered it. We might trust a police officer we know personally but not the police generally, or vice versa.

Propensity to Trust   For trust to develop, communicators must perceive each other as trustworthy. For some, that is easy. Some people believe everyone is basically "good." This type of person tends to trust everyone until specific experiences prove some individuals not trustworthy. Others are much less likely to trust anyone. They believe all people are basically "bad" and if given the opportunity will behave in selfish ways that harm others. This type of person will distrust everyone until specific experiences demonstrate that a few people are exceptions. Naturally, these mistrustful persons watch their words very carefully.

Simply put, most of us develop trust when we have communicated with a person or group of people and found our confidence in the positive outcomes of their behavior justified. Less simply, we develop trust when we have constructed attitudes about individuals or groups based on our experiences, and we extend trust to others whom our attitudes lead us to perceive as trustworthy. Three factors make it likely for individuals to be so perceived: acceptance, empathy, and honesty.

Acceptance   We define **acceptance** as *the ability to relate to another person without judging or trying to control that person.* Acceptance is the attitude that the other person is a worthy individual as a human being. Carl Rogers describes the attitude of acceptance as positive regard. A person with positive regard prizes an individual "regardless of his particular behavior at the moment."[4] An accepting person believes other people are worthy as individuals simply as what they are. If you are an accepting person, you perceive others realistically and accept all their characteristics, both the ones you like and the ones you dislike.

Accepting others does not mean you like their behavior. Acceptance is of people, not behavior. When you accept people, you do not judge them just because you dislike how they act. You relate to others with acceptance when, even if you disapprove of their behavior, you communicate regard for them as persons. Acceptance contributes to trust because it increases the chances that people will be confident your behavior will have positive consequences for them.

Acceptance is not common. Most of us find it very difficult. Earlier chapters have noted how quick most of us are to pass judgment on others. Perhaps that's

[4] Carl Rogers and Barry Stevens, *Person to Person* (New York: Pocket Books, 1971), p. 91.

why many of our interpersonal relationships work less well than we would like. Absence of acceptance quickly reduces open communication. Unaccepting people tend to evaluate and criticize—unpleasant behaviors that constrict channels of communication.

Empathy   Empathy also helps create trust. As discussed in Chapter 6, to empathize is to experience the feelings of another person. To develop trust, you don't need complete empathy. Often it's enough to communicate that you're trying to empathize. Just caring about or wanting to share a person's feelings is often as important as actually sharing that person's world.

Empathy differs from much that passes as empathy. Often you've heard people say, "I understand what the problem is" or "I understand why you behave as you do." And perhaps they do understand. But that's not empathy. This kind of "understanding" involves evaluation, judgment. Empathy as a response "knows." It feels with another; it doesn't evaluate.

Empathy contributes to trust because it helps communicate the attitude of acceptance. Acceptance without empathy could be perceived as indifference, an "I-don't-care-about-you" attitude. To most people, indifference is undesirable. To create trust, acceptance of another person includes empathy.

Honesty   Even when you are accepting and empathic, trust may not develop. Other factors are involved, and one of the most important is honesty. Acceptance and empathy may be offered but not *perceived*. Or they can be perceived wrongly—acceptance can be seen as uncaring, uninvolved, or unreal, and empathy as pretence or sarcasm. Nothing insures against such perceptions, but honesty comes closest. *Honesty in interpersonal relationships is the foundation of trust.* Not responding to others as you really are is "face making" or "masking." Being honest removes the mask, freeing the relationship from deception.

Honesty leads to trust because it helps one predict an outcome. For instance, don't you often find yourself trusting a person who is outspokenly biased more than you do one who refuses to express an opinion? If so, it's because knowing the strong opinions increases the accuracy with which you can predict the person's behavior. You can have confidence the person will behave as you expect. Given a predictable set of behaviors, you know when you can expect beneficial or harmful consequences. Honesty helps create predictability.

Now we should be honest with you. Honest interpersonal communication is not easy. Many situations seem to require deception. Often, total honesty will hurt someone, or limit our ability to achieve some goal. With some people and some goals, honesty may not be possible. But those situations are rarer than you think. Usually, in interpersonal relationships, we can be more open with others than we are. We fear outcomes and avoid taking the risks that could improve our interpersonal relationships for two reasons. First, acceptance and empathy are missing in the relationship, either on our part or that of the other person involved. Second, we don't know how to engage in appropriate self-disclosure, the next subject of discussion.

Using Appropriate Self-Disclosure

In many relationships, total openness in communication will not achieve trust. Indeed, sometimes it hurts relationships more than it contributes to their maintenance. The key is appropriateness, which depends partly on how we talk and partly on how we listen.

Virtually all of Chapter 6 relates to this point. Many failures in achieving communication goals in interpersonal relationships stem from poor listening. We set ourselves up for failure when we inaccurately understand the message or its source, or inadequately consider the best response. Beyond listening well, we must also know how to talk about our ideas and feelings when the goal is to improve an interpersonal relationship.

Ways of Talking   In Chapter 5, we classified statements in four categories: (1) statements that report an observation of external reality (facts); (2) statements that report a perception of internal reality (feelings); (3) statements that report a conclusion (inferences); and (4) a special type of inference that reports a value judgment, even though phrased as if reporting a conclusion about an external reality. We'll now introduce a way of classifying talk according to how much self-disclosure it includes. Then we'll show some similarities between these two classification systems.

RITUALS   *Ritual communication involves the least self-disclosure.* Rituals are patterned types of talk that often follow prescribed forms. In rituals people communicate with each other, but the words don't matter very much. Following the form of the ritual is more important than the content. We have a maintenance person, for instance, who comes to our building every day. When greeted with a "Hi" or "Good afternoon," his response is always "All right." A security guard answers the same "Hi" with "Fine, thank you." The responses are ritual. It's irrelevant that no one asked about their health. The greetings acknowledge our presence. The ritual— the acknowledgment—is important, but the words are not.

People often belittle ritualistic communication, but we think this attitude is a mistake. *Rituals are important.* When you meet someone with, "Hi, how are you?" you seldom want information; yet the greeting is important. It acknowledges the existence of and makes contact with the other person. A problem is that people often rely on ritual when more sharing would improve the relationship.

Ritualized communication includes many social situations that require us to speak and interact with people in prescribed ways. At church, at home with friends, and at work, rituals serve valuable functions. Using a ritual communicates that you know the prescribed forms and by participating you show belonging. But the ritual shares little of your perceptions or relations to the people or the situation.

REPORTS   Reports, as descriptive statements about external realities, also involve little self-disclosure. Reports share observations and perceptions of the environment, as in a doctor's diagnosis or a police officer's report. The subject may be terminal cancer or murder, but the speaker will use objective statements as if the content were a bruised knee or bent fender.

Since our personal interpretive system shapes our perceptions, some disclosure comes through when we describe or talk objectively about the world around us. But compared to other types of talk, reporting involves little personal sharing. This kind of talk does not include personal reactions.

INFERENCES AND JUDGMENTS   Inferences, opinions, and evaluations involve a somewhat greater amount of self-disclosure. Even though these statements are oriented toward others, objects, and ideas, they share what a person thinks. As you recall, inferences draw conclusions about the unknown or the unseen or predict the future. A statement of judgment is a special type of inference which implies the speaker's personal values or reactions. Judgments and inferences reveal what the person making them thinks or believes, but additional self-disclosure is not usually intended.

A perceptive listener can figure out a lot about what people feel and many of their values by analyzing evaluative and inferential statements. But the speaker did not intentionally disclose these feelings and values. Evaluative statements only indirectly reveal the feelings of the person making them.

Opinions and evaluations are probably the most common type of talk in this country. Our society values rationality, and we consider ideas important. We are reinforced for talking in a way that intentionally focuses outside us. Many cultural factors—religious, social, and educational—encourage this type of communication. As a result, most of us are quick to evaluate, and we state our opinions often. Other forms of talk, however, serve better to maintain personal relationships.

SHARED FEELINGS   Statements that share feelings involve the most self-disclosure. These tell how we feel about situations, events, ideas, and people. Such statements are I-centered. They focus inside the person speaking. Instead of saying, "Your taste is terrible," a statement that shared feelings would say, "I am irritated by how you dress," or "It embarrasses me when you wear that." These statements focus more clearly on the speaker and the speaker's feelings.

Because most of us hear little of this kind of talk, the examples below may be helpful. They contrast statements of judgment and of feeling.

Judgment	Feeling
"You're not thinking clearly."	"I am puzzled by what you just said."
"You shouldn't behave that way."	"I feel angry when you act that way."
"You are bothering me."	"I need to concentrate on my work right now and an interruption upsets me because it breaks my train of thought."
"You are beautiful."	"I feel good when I look at you."

In each case, the judgment concentrates on the other person and evaluates her or his behavior. In contrast, sharing feelings tells the speaker's reaction.

For almost every judgment remark, many more feeling responses are possible.

Judgment	*Feeling*
"I think you are beautiful."	"I feel ugly."
	"I feel inadequate."
	"I feel jealous."
	"I am proud of you."
	"I am suspicious of you."
	"I like to be with you."

When making statements to share feelings, pay careful attention to the structure of the sentences. Recall the Chapter 5 discussion of what it means to say, "I feel that." A statement such as, "I feel that you shouldn't behave that way" doesn't really share feelings at all. It is a judgment introduced by the words, "I feel that." If you listen to yourself and others carefully, you will often hear this "I feel that" phrasing. Almost always such statements share an opinion, not feelings.

COMMANDS   Other statements can be described as commands. They give orders. Clearly, such statements intentionally do not contribute self-disclosure. They contribute nothing positive to healthy interpersonal relationships. Such statements express a relationship of ownership or authority and are not consistent with maintaining good personal relationships.

Unfortunately, in a book about how to improve interpersonal relationships within the reality of most students' daily lives, we cannot ignore such statements. Some people talk as if they had ownership or authority in personal relationships, and you may encounter such individuals. When you do, perhaps all you will need to do is identify for that person what kind of relationship such talk suggests. By pointing out how inappropriate it is, you may influence the person to behave differently. If that doesn't work, perhaps you must decide not to participate in the kind of relationship command talk implies.

You may need to learn to recognize commands when the form of talk disguises them. Statements of judgment—or even other kinds of statements—may imply a command: "I wouldn't do that if I were you." "You just can't keep hanging around with that crowd." Shortly, we'll suggest a model for discussing how to confront problems in relationships you don't wish to end but would like to alter.

Sharing Appropriately

In general, appropriate sharing of feelings helps establish, enrich and maintain close interpersonal relationships. Look back at the first three statements on p. 192. Ask yourself, How would I respond to the different statements? It's obvious, isn't it, which would lead to a better relationship?

We think it hard to overstate the change in relationships that can result from changed ways of talking. All of us tend to respond with self-defense when blamed for something negative. Even when we are at fault, our first reaction is to defend ourselves instead of examine our shortcomings. Since any relationship involves some negative feelings, talking about them in a framework that reduces the amount of blaming will contribute to achieving a positive outcome.

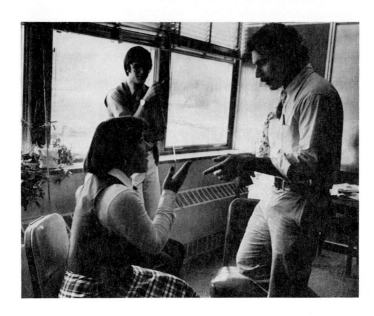

Appropriate talk about negative feelings can help improve relationships.

Appropriate talk about negative feelings provides opportunities to "unload" them in nondestructive ways. If something happens you don't like, you have an emotional response—whether you talk about it or not. When you feel angry, inadequate, threatened, or hurt, the feeling is real. It exists, and even if unstated, it becomes part of the framework for any subsequent interaction with the person by whom you felt threatened or hurt. When such feelings are not stated, especially between two people who must interact often at work or at home, the negative framework builds up. This backlog of unexpressed feelings creates enormous emotional loads in relationships which we carry into each new interaction. This load creates explosive situations in even simple interactions.

A popular poster accurately states, "When I repress my emotions, my stomach keeps score." Repressed emotions cause more than ulcers and physical ailments; they can destroy personal relationships. When feelings are not shared, much that is positive in a relationship can be destroyed as the negative factors grow. This causes communication problems, ends friendships, and can lead to continual conflict.

Remember, however, shared feelings must be appropriate—both to the person involved and to the situation. We all know the person who embarrasses or drives others away by talking too much or in the wrong places and times. An endless narrative of feelings, hurts, and hopes can harm relationships as much as appropriate sharing can improve them.

Even in close relationships, if both people do not want to share, the sharing person may meet some resistance. Some people cannot or do not want to handle others' feelings. Many people prefer evaluative, objective, or ritual interactions; they will not or cannot relate on any other level.

When we want to improve a relationship by sharing feelings, we should be sensitive to the ability of those with whom we want to share. Usually, a change by one partner in a relationship leads the other person also to change, especially if the relationship involves caring. But it won't always happen, and if it does, the changes achieved may not be what we expect.

GUIDELINES FOR SELF-DISCLOSURE

We offer three guidelines for appropriate self-disclosure, but first several factors deserve mention. Most important, different cultures define what is appropriate quite differently. Some groups encourage expressiveness and openness; others are more restrictive. Cultures identify subjects or topics as appropriate for discussion or specify particular situations or audiences for personal disclosures. Therefore, these guidelines should be applied carefully, noting appropriate cultural constraints. This does not mean you must always follow cultural "rules." But you should always consider cultural rules before deciding what behavior will best accomplish your goals.

Usually, but not always, concern about sharing feelings relates to expressing negative feelings. Most of us share positive feelings relatively well. In many relationships that last a long time, however, people begin to take the relationship for granted and state positive feelings about each other less often than at first. This factor often appears as an impact of gender in communication. Women fairly consistently express concern about the feeling aspect of relationships and complain that long-term partners do not express positive feelings often enough. Men often respond that their continued presence in the relationship demonstrates their positive feelings. Women want positive feelings expressed; men tend to measure the health of the relationship by the absence of negative feelings. Sensitivity to this difference can help both men and women improve their communication in long-term relationships.

Our first guideline is that *talk should use the highest appropriate level of shared feelings and the lowest level of judgment.* Reporting feelings, rather than opinions or judgments, generates positive outcomes. First, people tend to reciprocate. They respond to you more openly because, as you tell them things about yourself, you exhibit a degree of trust in them. Trust increases with reciprocal expression of trusting behaviors. Second, even in cases where your negative feelings come from reacting to another's behavior, both you and the other person respond more positively when you talk in a way that "owns" your feeling rather than blaming it on the other person.

Using "I Messages"

Our second guideline for appropriate self-disclosure is *talk that shares feelings should use the "I Message" Formula.* This model for talking about feelings with others can increase the appropriateness of self-disclosure. We developed this model using the work of Thomas Gordon as a foundation.[5] Using the I Message Formula, you

---

[5] Gordon presents this idea in *P.E.T.: Parent Effectiveness Training* (New York: Wyden Books, 1970), pp. 115–120. He develops it more fully in *Leader Effectiveness Training, L.E.T.* (New York: Wyden Books, 1977), pp. 101–120.

can tell others how you feel and why in a way that encourages you to *own* your own feelings. It also provides a way for you to think through situations clearly so that you understand the potential outcomes of your talk.

The I Message Formula includes six parts, the first three of which are essential. The remaining three should be used if initial attempts do not resolve the problem. The first three parts are:

1. "When you . . ."   (DESCRIBE the other's behavior to which you have reacted.)
2. "I feel . . ."   (Use a FEELING WORD; opinions or "I feel that" constructions are not permitted.)
3. "Because . . ."   (State a TANGIBLE effect on you.)

The First Three Parts   Several items are crucial to this formula. First, you must phrase the behavior of the other person descriptively. You must use statements of observation or reports. The formula does not permit inferences, whether in sentences or single words. If, for example, you are concerned about the mess left each morning by the person who shares your bathroom, the formula does not permit you to say, "When you leave a mess in the bathroom each morning . . ." The term "mess" reports either an inference or judgment; it describes nothing. The formula would require you to say, "When you leave hair in the sink, the cap off the toothpaste, soapy splashes all over the counter top . . ." These are descriptions. They are concrete. They do not suggest inferences.

Second, you must describe your feelings accurately, not disguise them with an opinion. Your reaction to the "messy" bathroom may be anger, irritation, disappointment, disgust, or any number of other feelings. But the formula does not permit you to say, "I feel that you are irresponsible," or "You are a slob." You must say, "I am angry . . ." "I am disappointed," etc.

For many people, the third element in the formula is the most difficult. Stating the "because" requires a description of the tangible effect of the other person's behavior *on you*. In making you focus on the source of your anger, the formula does not permit you, even at this point, to blame your anger or irritation on the other person's behavior. You cannot say, for instance, "The messy bathroom makes me angry because it shows how irresponsible you are." That is not a tangible effect on you. The time it takes you to clean up the mess is a tangible effect. If your bathroom partner leaves hair in the sink, the tangible effect is easy to state. After sufficient instances, if someone doesn't clean each time, the drain will become clogged and the bathroom unusable, and you will encounter delay, disruption, and expense. In other situations, finding a tangible effect is more difficult.

Confronting Problems Early

The third guideline is *use the I Message Formula to confront and deal with problems as soon after they occur as possible.* If you don't—as all too often people do not— the result is a heavy load of negative emotions that explode at inopportune times. When a bathroom mess first occurs, if you clean it up yourself and don't say anything, you probably swallow a small irritation. But when the same thing happens morning after morning, the small irritation grows into anger or rage.

We all recognize the inappropriateness of flying into a rage over soap splashes on a counter and hair in a sink. Yet that explosion often happens because the first few times the person who was irritated said nothing and cleaned the sink. Using the I Message Formula the first time you encounter the messy bathroom usually permits a talk free of anger. The tenth time the sink is left in that condition, irritation has turned to rage, and a calm, nonblameful discussion is nearly impossible.

We separate the first three parts of the I Message Formula from the others because many situations can be resolved using only these. Since you should always use the simplest message required to accomplish your communication goals, the rest of the formula shouldn't be used unless necessary.

In some cases, however, additional parts of the I Message Formula can be helpful. All six parts are illustrated below.

1. "When you . . ."   (Describe behavior.)
2. "I feel . . ."   (Describe feeling.)
3. "Because . . ."   (State tangible effect.)

4. "And because I think your behavior means . . ."
5. "I would like you to . . ."
6. "If you are unwilling to do what I ask, I will . . ."

Part Four   Step 4 applies when it is useful to discuss what motivation you attribute to the other person's behavior. This step may help in cases where your interpretation of another's behavior motivates your response more than the tangible effect does.

We vividly recall an example from a student, Bill, who completed an I Message Formula about his brother during a class exercise in the following way: "When you leave the cap off the toothpaste every morning, I am enraged . . ." But Bill found the "because" part nearly impossible to complete in a way that even he found reasonable. As he searched for a way to state a tangible effect of his brother's behavior upon himself, the only thing Bill could come up with was that the toothpaste had dried somewhat by the time he used it the next day. Reviewing this situation in the classroom, Bill recognized that the tangible effect should not generate a reaction of rage. The recognition led him to examine his own reactions—a major benefit of using the formula. Bill had to ask himself, "Why did I become enraged over something that affected me so little?" This question led to a series of other questions.

Clearly, his brother didn't cause Bill's intense anger over the toothpaste. It was Bill's *definition of what that behavior meant.* When we permitted Bill to use the fourth part of the formula, he began to see how he had defined the situation in a way that created his own anger. Bill then wrote, "When you leave the cap off the toothpaste every morning, even after I have asked you many times not to do that, I am enraged, because each time I use the toothpaste I am reminded that I think you don't care about my opinions and feelings." Bill had now framed the problem quite differently from what would have been his initial reaction without the formula: "I am enraged because you are so irresponsible."

Many situations benefit from use of this "because I think it means . . ." part of the formula. When you share your reasoning with the other person without blaming, you accept the responsibility for the inference you have drawn. When you say, "because I think it means . . ." you make clear that you have only inferred what it means. The other person might infer the behavior means something quite different.

Using this formula requires you to recognize that the inference is yours, and it permits you to discuss what the other person thinks the behavior means. When two people are in a caring relationship, such sharing can lead to changes in thinking or changes in behavior. And when such discussions occur before irritation or disappointment grows to anger or shame, people can discuss the inferences fairly easily with positive results. In contrast, postponing such a discussion until feelings become intense places a heavy emotional load on the talk, reducing the likelihood of a positive outcome.

Part Five Using the fifth part of the formula, you complete the sentence, "I would like you to . . ." by stating clearly, in concrete, specific terms, what you want the other person to do. As with the other steps, the largest benefit of this step may be that it helps you think the situation through clearly. You can't just say, "I want you to be more responsible," or "You must quit being so messy." The formula requires that you make a direct request for a *specific* behavior. You thus avoid assuming the other person knows what you want. You must specify what behavior will reduce your negative feeling. You must say, in specific, concrete terms, what you want the other person to do.

Another benefit of talking specifically is that you and the other person *negotiate* what each behavior means to each person. Talking with descriptive, concrete language makes this kind of give and take less difficult than using the inferences and judgments that usually permeate such talk.

Part Six Part 6 of the formula applies only in situations where all five of the other parts have been unsuccessful. It is, so to speak, a last resort. As such it requires very careful consideration. But it is sometimes necessary. Indeed, it is something we all do when the negative aspects of a relationship grow to intolerable proportions. The formula here merely provides a framework for talking about the situation that may moderate the outcome. This part of the formula should be used only when you have made a direct request and, after an appropriate amount of time, are not satisfied the request has been met.

Part 6 involves repeating your request and stating what you will do if the person doesn't do as you ask. The formula requires you to describe *your* behavior, not the other person's. Using this part of the formula reflects your recognition that you control only your own behavior. All other parts of this formula have involved your talking about your reaction to someone else's behavior, usually some behavior to which you have reacted negatively. In part 6, you describe what your own behavior will be. It requires you to recognize that you cannot actually change other people's behavior. They must do the changing. And if, for any reason, they choose not to behave differently, then you must decide what *you* will do.

This again shows a major benefit of using the I Message Formula. In thinking through a situation, you clarify for yourself how important the problem is to you. You must quit concentrating on trying to control the other person's behavior and focus instead on what you will do and potential consequences of your behavior.

To use again the example of Bill's reaction to his brother and the toothpaste cap, thinking through the formula and being honest about his own reaction clarified an easy solution. Each would buy his own toothpaste. A toothpaste cap in fact made no real difference in the relationship. Most likely, the problem was not really the toothpaste cap. Once Bill identified the real source of his anger, he could request changed behavior appropriate to the cause.

This illustrates the values of clarifying problems using the I Message Formula. Conversations can take place without blame, and with timely confrontation, issues can be discussed at a level of low emotional intensity. Analysis clearly identifies real sources of negative emotions. The person initiating the discussion recognizes his or her own role and responsibility in the situation and accepts others' right and responsibility to be responsible for their behavior. Both parties may negotiate the meaning of behaviors and the appropriateness of changes requested.

Reducing Defensiveness

Some situations do not involve trust or appropriate ways of talk. Instead, attitudes and behavior that lead to **defensiveness** characterize many relationships. Defensive behavior results when a person perceives a threat in a situation. Degrees of defensiveness vary, but generally people who are defensive devote so much attention to protecting themselves that they have little time or energy left for understanding others. In long-term relationships, such defensiveness can become an ongoing problem. Therefore, to maintain good relationships, we need to know how to reduce defensiveness.

Causes of Defensiveness   Jack Gibb's research in small group behavior revealed six kinds of behavior that cause defensive reactions in others.[6] As we discuss them, you'll see why defensiveness is so common.

EVALUATION   **Evaluation** is *passing judgment on others, assessing blame or praise.* Evaluation involves making moral assessments of others, questioning their standards, values, and motives. It suggests that differences in behavior and ideas are unacceptable. Some people judge a married mother who works as a poor mother. She may even evaluate herself as less effective a mother than she could be. If so, even a look or question by others may cause her to respond defensively.

CONTROL   To **control** is *to try to get others to change themselves or to change their attitudes, opinions, or behavior.* When we try to restrict the choices available to others or to influence their behavior in making choices, we are controlling. Control behaviors imply evaluation, because the effort to change others implies

---

[6] The first publication of this research was in Jack R. Gibb, "Defensive Communication," *Journal of Communication* 11 (September 1961), 10–15.

that they are not adequate. Trying to control others also displays a lack of acceptance. If we accept people as they are, we won't try to change them. We'll behave in ways that allow them to decide what changes in themselves they want to make. Parents usually believe they need to control their children. By the time the children become teenagers, the parents' control behaviors can result in much defensiveness.

SUPERIORITY   A person who displays **superiority** communicates *an attitude of being better than others in some way*: more status or power, higher economic or intellectual levels, and so on. Actual superiority in any respect usually results in some defensiveness in those with whom you communicate. Combine this with an attitude that the differences are important, and you increase the defensiveness. A person with actual superiority can balance it with empathy and acceptance. But if others sense that you feel superior and it's important to you, they are not likely to perceive acceptance from you.

CERTAINTY   **Certainty** is *the attitude that the speaker has all the answers*. A person with certainty appears dogmatic, usually needs to win arguments rather than solve problems, and sees ideas as "truths" to be defended, not hypotheses to be explored. A person with certainty seldom listens to others' ideas and is usually sure that others are wrong.

STRATEGY   **Strategy** involves *using tricks or manipulation to influence others' behavior*. People who use strategy have hidden purposes or private, unrevealed motives, or they use communication for unstated personal benefits. Gibb defines strategy differently from most people. Most people use the word *strategy* to mean what Gibb used the word *control* to mean. In his context, strategy refers to trickery and hidden manipulative behaviors. A comment of the television character Archie Bunker is an excellent illustration of strategy. When asked how he'd accomplished a particular feat, Archie said: "You get others to do what you want by promising to do something you ain't got no intention of doing."

NEUTRALITY   **Neutrality** is *the communication climate of impersonality*. It expresses a lack of concern for the other person, a detached "other-person-as-object" attitude. *Neutrality* is another word that is used distinctly in this context. People often use *neutral* to mean objective. Objectivity may or may not be neutrality as we define it. To be neutral is to have no empathy.

Effects of Defensiveness   Often defensive communication distorts perceptions. If preoccupied with defending ourselves or our own point of view, we'll only half listen to others. When defensiveness is high, intended messages differ greatly from perceived messages; communication accuracy is low; aggressiveness spirals.

Defensiveness can reach extremes of hostility. Often, communication is not just impaired, but hostile and aggressive. Hostility may bring complete separation, or even physical violence. Our students who are police officers tell of repeated family arguments that break into violence. Indeed, approximately 25 percent of police calls are in response to family disturbances. Long periods of defensive behaviors by all family members precede most cases in which hostility erupts. Acceptance, empathy, honesty, and appropriate self-disclosure were missing. Evaluation, control, superiority, and certainty were present. Serious communication problems were predictable.

Supportive Climates Reduce Defensiveness   Some people are extremely defensive. They almost always feel threatened. They perceive threats in situations even when no one shows superiority, control, or other behaviors that cause defensiveness. This is because of their past experiences, negative self-concept, and fear, among other things. Few suggestions can help if you must deal with persons of that type. But most of us encounter (and experience ourselves) less severe defensiveness. It relates directly to a situation and the presence of one or more of the behaviors discussed before. For these situations, alternate ways of communicating can help reduce the defensiveness.

During his research, Jack Gibb also identified characteristics of groups that did not display significant defensive behavior. Each of these characteristics is a communication style opposite the behaviors that cause defensiveness. We describe these characteristics as supportive, meaning the behaviors lead to a supportive climate.

Awareness of and ability to use supportive styles of communicating can help you learn to reduce, though probably not eliminate, defensiveness in people with whom you communicate.

Behaviors Resulting in Defensiveness	Supportive Behaviors that Reduce Defensiveness
1. Evaluation	1. Description
2. Control	2. Problem orientation
3. Superiority	3. Equality
4. Certainty	4. Provisionalism
5. Strategy	5. Spontaneity
6. Neutrality	6. Empathy

Let's look more closely at the supportive behaviors.

DESCRIPTION   **Description** is the opposite of evaluation. *To be descriptive is to be nonjudgmental.* Asking questions that are perceived as genuine requests for information, and reporting feelings, events, and perceptions are description. This style of communicating does not ask or imply that others should change their behavior or attitudes. To be descriptive is to be *perceived* as accepting. We emphasize *perceived* because evaluation is so common that what may not be intended as evaluation is often perceived that way. "Did you say that?" might be perceived as an attack, not a simple request for information.

The recommended descriptive behavior may seem to contradict the earlier suggestion that reporting statements share less about people than evaluative or inferential statements or those that share feelings. Therefore, we need to add two comments about descriptive communication and defensiveness. First, it's *appropriate* self-disclosure that improves relationships. When descriptive communication is needed to reduce defensiveness, sharing feelings may be no more useful than evaluation. Second, and perhaps more important, *description*, as Gibb classifies statements, includes those that share feelings. If you report your own perceptions and feelings—about external or internal realities—that would be description as the word is used here. A statement such as, "I am uncomfortable in this situation," or "I am angry about that," reports (describes, in the Gibb terminology) though it might well be perceived as evaluation.

PROBLEM ORIENTATION **Problem orientation** is the opposite of control. It involves *communicating a desire to work together to define problems and seek solutions.* With problem orientation, you don't suggest that you have all answers. Instead, you indicate that you have no preconceived solutions. To be problem-oriented is to allow others to set their own goals, to make choices, and to evaluate their own progress toward those goals. In a situation with people who share common goals, problem-oriented people work together. They share goal setting and decisions about how to meet the goals.

EQUALITY **Equality** is the climate that counters superiority. Equality is *willingness to interact with mutual trust and respect and to attach little importance to differences.* Differences in skill, status, wealth, power, beauty, and other things among communicators are inevitable. People are seldom truly equal in any qualities. But a climate of equality deemphasizes differences. If we recognize the value of the qualities all parties bring to the situation, we can reduce the defensiveness superiority causes. A climate of equality stresses people's similarities and does not degrade the value of people who are less able, poorer, or less attractive.

PROVISIONALISM **Provisionalism** is the opposite of certainty. To be provisional is to be *willing to reconsider behavior, to consider the possibility of being in error.* The basic attitude of provisionalism is investigation, not advocacy. Provisionalism is a willingness to say, "Well, I could be wrong" and to do something about it.

SPONTANEITY **Spontaneity** is the opposite of strategy, and the essence of spontaneity is honesty. *To be perceived as straightforward and free from deception is to be perceived as spontaneous.* People who show spontaneity demonstrate that they have no hidden motives. Behaving spontaneously gains all the benefits of honesty we discussed earlier.

EMPATHY **Empathy,** which we defined earlier, is the opposite of neutrality. Empathy respects the worth of people by "knowing" their feelings. It is accepting behavior, accepting that the feelings, emotions, and attitudes people express are real and believable from their own perspectives.

Mixed Climates Several observations about communication and defensiveness are now in order. First, behaviors do not usually occur unmixed. In most interpersonal interactions, both the causes of defensiveness and their opposites show up. When they do, they partially neutralize the effect of each other. For example, a person

---

EXERCISE 7.3   DEFENSIVE AND SUPPORTIVE COMMUNICATION

OBJECTIVE   **To practice identifying behaviors that create and reduce defensiveness.**

DIRECTIONS
1. For a week, keep a journal of communication situations you've been in in which defensiveness has occurred. Describe each event briefly.
2. Identify what behaviors in each situation seemed to cause or increase defensiveness. Note if you saw one or more of the six categories identified by Gibb as likely to cause defensiveness.
3. Identify which behaviors seemed to reduce defensiveness. Which of the six supportive behaviors did you notice?
4. What else do you think could have been done in those situations to reduce defensiveness?
5. Your instructor may ask you to share some items from your journal with others in the class.

REVIEW
1. Review your journal and provide a summary addressing the following questions:
   a. Overall, which supportive behaviors do you use most effectively?
   b. Which defensiveness causing behaviors do you do most often?
   c. Which behaviors by others are most likely to provoke defensive reactions on your part?
2. Relate the 12 behaviors that Gibb describes to the conditions and attitudes leading to trust.
3. State a personal plan to improve how you deal with defensiveness, both that you may create in others and that you feel in response to others' behaviors.
4. Explain the most important communication principle you learned or found illustrated by this exercise and why you found it important.

---

you respect and believe to have your best interests at heart may criticize, but you might not react defensively. Instead you may listen and talk the ideas over.

Second, words themselves may not reduce defensiveness. How messages are perceived is what counts. You might intend to be supportive, but unless your behavior is perceived that way, you're not being supportive. You may think you are trustworthy—indeed, you may *be* trustworthy, but if a receiver doesn't see you that way, you won't be trusted.

Constantly check the perceptions of those you communicate with. Only by use of feedback can behavior become consistent with intentions. Communicating supportively will usually reduce defensiveness, but the total situation affects the outcome. The results of any interaction depend on the participants' level of defensiveness and concept of self, as well as on the influences of time, setting, previous experiences, and previous specific interactions.

We have added a column to Gibb's list. It shows how a defensive person might perceive what you intend as supportive communication. Someone who doesn't believe you are honest might react the same way.

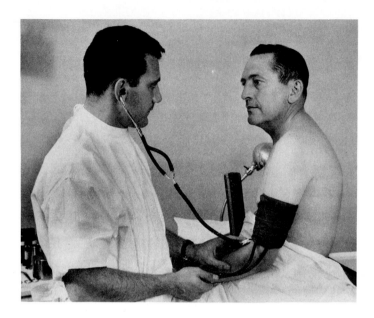

Some communication situations involve mixed climates.

Supportive Behaviors	*Supportive Behaviors Perceived by Defensive Person*
1. Description	1. Paternalistic, condescending
2. Problem orientation	2. Crisis-ridden
3. Equality	3. Patronizing
4. Provisionalism	4. Indecisive, sneaky
5. Spontaneity	5. Rude, overbearing
6. Empathy	6. Sarcastic, insincere

To reduce or avoid creating defensiveness, supportiveness must be genuine. Otherwise the words may be supportive, but the nonverbals will contradict them. And recall that nonverbal messages are usually perceived as more honest than verbal ones. It is possible to be verbally descriptive while sending evaluation messages nonverbally. You can display dogmatic actions, such as crossing your arms or standing with your hands on your hips, while saying things that are provisional. Saying, "It's up to you" in a voice that indicates only one sensible choice communicates judgment, not provisionalism. Saying you feel equal while sitting at the head of the table, dominating the conversation, constantly interrupting, or invading others' personal space will convey an impression of superiority, not equality.

Maintaining Long-Term Interpersonal Relationships

Many people have difficulty in developing and maintaining long-term interpersonal relationships. Sociologists have identified numerous possible causes, including career conflicts, unrealistic expectations, and inability or unwillingness to make the commitment. Yet the need for such relationships persists. They help us function effectively within society, and more important, to satisfy some of the most basic personal needs.

A long-term interpersonal relationship may be defined as a close personal relationship that lasts and involves frequent communication. It can include friendships and family relationships. While some relationships are long term, they are neither as significant nor as personal as others. The most important long-term interpersonal relationships are those that permit expression of our basic human needs. Self-disclosure is an essential part of a long-term interpersonal relationship; acceptance, empathy, and trust are necessary to keep the relationship healthy.

Realistic Expectations One of the most difficult problems with maintaining good long-term relationships is that partners have unrealistic expectations from the relationship. No single interpersonal relationship can satisfy all of a person's needs. But many people expect their lasting relationships to do just that. After a period of time, such people begin to feel frustrated because some of their needs remain unmet. At this critical point, many people decide to move on instead of adjusting their expectations. And the cycle repeats itself.

A realistic assessment of what one can reasonably expect from a long-term relationship is essential for it to be maintained. Certainly, each of us is unique and has different specific needs, but it is also true that the development of healthy, long-term interpersonal relationships is difficult without commitment and willingness to adjust expectations to a realistic level.

Another common unrealistic expectation is that the people or the relationship will not change over time. Yet all of us change as time passes; relationships change as they mature, as do the expectations each person has for the other and for the relationship itself. To expect no change is unrealistic and inevitably results in problems.

Unstated Expectations Another factor that causes problems in maintaining long-term interpersonal relationships is unstated expectations. Often, in the beginning of such a relationship, the partners have a strong desire to please each other. Attempting to do so, they fail to state clearly their expectations for the other's behavior, and they behave in ways they will not and do not expect to continue throughout a long-lasting relationship. As time passes, events ensure that conflicts develop because the changed behavior patterns violate the unstated expectations. Suppose, for example, that both members of this relationship expect to share important financial decisions, but they never discuss or agree upon what is an "important" decision. Surely, both will agree that buying a house is important. But is a new couch important? A car? What is not important? What things can each buy without the other's agreement?

Over time, members of long-term relationships must expect to clarify unstated expectations. We cannot hope such differences will never occur. And when we understand that these differences of unstated expectations are inevitable, we can deal less emotionally with the conflicts that are certain to arise when events force the unstated expectations to the surface.

To maintain an interpersonal relationship, all expectations must be dealt with openly and honestly. We cannot assume that others should be able to recognize our expectations for them just because we have developed a long-term relationship. We need to be able to state our own needs and wants and to listen empathically to similar statements of needs and wants from the other(s) involved.

EXERCISE 7.4   SELF-DISCLOSURE STATEMENTS

OBJECTIVE **To practice making statements varying in self-disclosure.**

DIRECTIONS 1. For each of the following situations, prepare three different responses: one that would be classified as ritual or objective, one that gives an inference or evaluation, and one that shares feelings.

Situation I: You are shopping with a friend who has just tried on a suit that costs $150. The friend says, "How do you like it?"

Situation II: You and your husband/wife/girlfriend/boyfriend are planning an evening out. She or he suggests you eat at a place you do not like.

Situation III: Your instructor has given you a take-home final exam. A classmate who has been having trouble in class asks if he or she may see yours after you have finished it.

2. For each of the judgment statements in the list on p. 192, make five different statements that share feelings.
3. Your instructor may ask you to report and discuss your responses to 1 and 2.

REVIEW 1. Explain why statements of self-disclosure are necessary in some interpersonal relationships.
2. Why is appropriateness the key to using self-disclosure effectively?
3. Cite an example in which particular statements of self-disclosure could hurt a relationship more than help it and state the principle which would allow you to generalize from that situation to others.
4. Explain the most important communication principle you learned or found illustrated by this exercise and why you found it important.

SUMMARY

Understanding the factors involved can help in building and maintaining satisfactory interpersonal relationships. At the foundation of interpersonal communication is the perceptual process, which becomes more complex when it involves interpersonal perception, the attribution of personal characteristics to an individual during interaction with them. Also involved in personal relationships are roles and norms and the processes of interpersonal attraction, which is influenced by four factors: appearance, proximity, reciprocal liking, and attitude similarity.

Roles, the behaviors expected of persons in specific social positions, are meaningful largely in reference to specific groups because they differ from group to group. To understand the effects of role on communication, both role expectations and role performances must be considered. Norms are standards of expected behavior for which a violator pays a social penalty. Norms are both internal and external. Both kinds of norms affect communication.

Improving interpersonal relationships involves the skill of taking another's perspectives, and that of building trust, which is having confidence in another person's behavior when that person's behavior can affect you either negatively or positively. Trust is in large part situation-dependent, and also depends on an individual's propensity to trust. Trust is enhanced in situations characterized by acceptance, honesty, and empathy.

Interpersonal relationships can also be improved by appropriate amounts and methods of self-disclosure. Ways of talking vary from rituals, to reports, to inferences and judgments, to commands, and to shared feelings. Self-disclosure is appropriate when the way of talking shares feelings at the highest amount appropriate. This sharing works best when the I Message Formula is used, the first three parts of which are essential in all situations.

Many relationships are characterized by defensiveness. Defensive communication results when a person perceives a threat in a situation and interferes with relationships by causing distorted perceptions. Six kinds of communication are likely to cause defensive reactions: evaluation, control, superiority, certainty, strategy, and neutrality. To cope with defensiveness, use supportive communication. Six specific styles of communication are described as supportive: description, problem orientation, equality, provisionalism, spontaneity, and empathy.

In most communication situations, a combination of defensive and supportive communication styles is present. An effective communicator must frequently check the perceptions of others and take appropriate action to maintain a supportive, open climate. To maintain relationships over a long period, realistic expectations are important, and unstated expectations must be clarified.

QUESTIONS FOR DISCUSSION

1. How does the fact that communication is directed to satisfy needs affect interpersonal relationships?
2. Can you cite situations in which you performed roles differently from what others expected, and describe how the differences affected the communication in that situation?
3. How do the factors leading to interpersonal attraction affect your interactions with both strangers and intimates?
4. What recent situation in your life illustrated the presence or the absence of trust? Identify the conditions that resulted in the trusting or nontrusting relationship.
5. What seems to you, in your important personal relationships, the limit of self-disclosure? Can you cite a recent situation in which you encountered (or displayed) inappropriate disclosure?
6. Can you phrase statements that share feelings, not opinions?
7. How does the I Message Formula contribute to understanding of self-disclosure and effective communication?

8. What have been your experiences with behaviors that cause defensiveness?
9. Have you tried supportive communication? With what result?
10. Can you cite a recent example in your life where changes in relationships resulted from changed patterns of communication?

SUGGESTIONS FOR FURTHER READING

Argyle, Michael. *Social Interaction.* New York: Methuen, 1973.

Babcock, Dorothy, and Terry Keepers. *Raising Kids OK.* New York: Avon Books, 1977.

Brown, Charles, and Paul W. Keller. *Monologue to Dialogue,* 2nd ed. Englewood Cliffs, N.J.: Prentice-Hall, 1979.

Byrne, Donn. *The Attraction Paradigm.* New York: Academic Press, 1971.

DeVito, Joseph. *The Interpersonal Communication Book,* 4th ed. New York: Harper & Row, 1985.

Goffman, Erving. *Interaction Ritual.* New York: Pantheon Books, 1982.

———. *Strategic Interaction.* Philadelphia: University of Pennsylvania Press, 1970.

Harris, Thomas. *I'm OK—You're OK.* New York: Avon Books, 1973.

Hocker, Joyce H., and William Wilmot. *Interpersonal Conflict.* Dubuque, Ia.: William C. Brown, 1985.

Howell, William. *The Empathic Communicator.* Belmont, Calif.: Wadsworth, 1982.

Jaffe, Joseph, and Stanley Feldstein. *Rhythms of Dialogue.* New York: Academic Press, 1970.

Johnson, David W. *Reaching Out: Interpersonal Effectiveness and Self-Actualization,* 3rd ed. Englewood Cliffs, N.J.: Prentice-Hall, 1986.

Kramarae, Chris. *Women and Men Speaking.* Rowley, Mass.: Newbury House Publishers, 1981.

Laing, Ronald D., et al. *Interpersonal Perception.* New York: Springer, 1966.

McCall, George, et al. *Social Relationships.* Chicago: Aldine, 1970.

———, and J. Simmons. *Identities and Interactions.* New York: Free Press, 1978.

Miller, Gerald, ed. *Explorations in Interpersonal Communication.* Beverly Hills, Calif.: Sage, 1976.

———, and Mark Steinberg. *Between People: A New Analysis of Interpersonal Communication.* Chicago: Science Research Associates, 1975.

Phillips, Gerald, and Nancy Metzger. *Intimate Communication.* Boston: Allyn & Bacon, 1976.

———, and H. Lloyd Goodall. *Loving and Living: Improve Your Friendships and Marriage.* Englewood Cliffs, N.J.: Prentice-Hall, 1983.

Powell, John. *Why Am I Afraid To Tell You Who I Am?* Niles, Ill.: Argus Communications, 1969.

———. *The Secret of Staying in Love.* Niles, Ill.: Argus Communications, 1974.

Stewart, John. *Bridges Not Walls,* 4th ed. Reading, Mass.: Addison-Wesley, 1987.

Sudnow, David. *Studies in Social Interaction.* New York: Free Press, 1972.

Tagiuri, Renato, and Luigi Petrullo. *Person Perception and Interpersonal Behavior.* Stanford, Calif.: Stanford University Press, 1958.

Tavris, Carol. *Anger, The Misunderstood Emotion.* New York: Simon & Schuster, Inc., 1982.

Warr, Peter B., and Christopher Knapper. *The Perception of People and Events.* New York: Wiley, 1968.

8 Making Decisions in Groups

As for the best leaders, the people do not notice their existence. . . . When the best leaders' work is done, the people say, "We did it ourselves."

LAO-TZU

"What is not clear is whether power always goes automatically with top rank, with elite position, with defined authority to make decisions. . . . In fact, it often does not. There is a striking difference between privileged position and the ability to make anything happen. This is the first and most central paradox of leadership. . . .

ROSABETH KANTER and BARRY STEIN

GOAL

To learn the factors that enable groups to improve decision making

OBJECTIVES

The material in this chapter should help you to:
1. Explain how each of the following factors affects decision making in group situations:
   Group purpose
   Group maturity
   Relationship to outsiders
   Interdependence and cohesiveness
   Attractiveness and satisfaction
2. Explain the values of agendas as groups make decisions.
3. Given a specific situation, prepare an appropriate agenda.
4. Define the words *leader* and *leadership* and distinguish a leaderless group from one without leadership.
5. Be able to identify the functions of leadership.
6. Improve your ability to manage conflict in group situations.
7. Assess your personal leadership skills and know how to perform those functions for which you are best suited.

At school or at home, at work or play, in worship or in pursuit of some hobby, most of us are involved in groups. And in most of these situations, we must work with others to reach decisions. Thus, group decision making is important to us. Indeed, it is so important that a survey found many college graduates wanted more training at making decisions as members of groups.[1]

This chapter introduces that aspect of group life. Note one major exclusion: We confine the discussion to *small* groups, those in which members face each other and interact directly on a personal basis. Many such small groups exist within larger groups (a study group in a class, for example, or the budget committee in a sorority or church). In these groups, the larger group affects the decision process, but it is an "external" influence.

Large groups operate through parliamentary procedure or representative bodies, such as an executive committee. We mention representative groups in this chapter, but we do not cover parliamentary procedure.[2] We will look at some factors affecting group processes, then examine group goal setting, leadership, and the management of conflict.

FACTORS AFFECTING GROUP PROCESSES

Many factors affect group processes. We'll discuss purpose, goals, maturity, relation to outsiders, member involvement, and methods of deciding.

Purpose

Groups vary according to purpose. A school environment involves many different types of groups. Some are primarily social, as a fraternity, sorority, or chess club. Learning groups may be used in classes or develop among people who study together. The faculty is divided into work groups within departments, as are many people on their jobs. These work groups, or task groups, exist to accomplish a specific task or tasks.

In this chapter we focus on task groups, but much said here applies to all kinds of groups. Even social or learning groups must make decisions, and most have tasks to accomplish even though the task is not why the group exists. As we discuss the purpose of a group, keep in mind that the reason a group exists may differ from the reason people belong to it. When we distinguish a group by purpose, we mean the reason the *group* exists, not the reasons people join it.

---

[1] Edward Foster et al., "A Market Study for the College of Business Administration, University of Minnesota, Twin Cities," in Samuel L. Becker and Leah R. V. Ekdom, "That Forgotten Basic Skill: Oral Communication," *Bulletin of the Association for Communication Administration*, October 1980.

[2] To cover parliamentary procedure would require more space than permitted here. If you need work in the subject, the standard authority is *Robert's Rules of Order Newly Revised*. Several briefer guides for quick reference in meetings are available. One of the best is O. Garfield Jones, *Senior Manual for Leadership: Parliamentary Procedure at a Glance* (New York: Irvington Publishers, 1980).

Group versus Individual Goals   One reason purpose is important is that people belong to most groups voluntarily. They choose to associate with others to accomplish personal goals or purposes. These personal goals may differ from those of others in the group and from the group's goal. A church, for example, exists as a center of worship, but members' reasons for belonging may vary widely. Such differences affect the level of members' commitment to the group, how much stress or disagreement they will endure and still remain members, and how satisfied they are with membership. Such factors greatly affect the process of decision making, as well as the decisions themselves.

Complementary versus Antagonistic Goals   Member goals can be either complementary or antagonistic. **Complementary goals** exist when each member can achieve her or his individual goals only if other members achieve theirs. **Antagonistic goals** exist when one member can reach individual goals only when others do *not* reach theirs. Your instructor could create complementary goals in the classroom if you were divided into groups for a task and told that none of your group could get an A on the project unless all did. Antagonistic goals could be created if the instructor said that only one member of each group could get an A, only one a B, one a C, and the others would flunk. Antagonistic goals cause competitive, often defensive communication.

Though not all members in a group need to have identical goals, some degree of agreement is necessary. The greater the agreement, the more likely members will work together effectively. Individual goals that differ from or conflict with group goals, or that are antagonistic to other members' goals, can reduce or eliminate chances of accomplishing the group goal.

Maturity of the Group

How long a group has or expects to exist influences group processes. Groups may be casual, temporary, or permanent. Casual groups often occur by accident and exist only a few minutes or hours. A group that has met to hear a speaker and suggest solutions to a community problem would be a casual group, as would a marketing or political candidate's focus group. This type of group will tend to reflect the patterns and decision-making habits of the dominant person. There will be little or no effort at establishing group procedures.

Groups that expect to exist for some time, even if they are temporary (such as an ad hoc committee), will spend time developing structure and procedures. If the expectation is that the group will exist only long enough to complete a task and then disband, structures will be informal and one or two dominant people will influence the decision-making processes.

Permanent groups expect to last. Churches, corporations, fraternities, and service clubs are permanent groups and continue to exist even though members change through the years. Outside the family, small groups tend to be temporary rather than permanent, though important exceptions to that generalization exist—

groups within larger organizations, executive or budget committees of voluntary organizations, boards of churches, teams in work places, for example.

Permanent groups usually establish rules (often written) by which they operate. By-laws, corporate rules, union contracts, or a history of procedures and precedents will guide decision-making processes. Indeed, in many such groups, members change more often than the rules or procedures. Newcomers must learn the "rules," whether written or unwritten. Dominant individuals can affect how established groups operate, after such people have achieved positions of power or influence, ordinarily a while after joining the group. Established groups tend to close ranks against "outsiders," which is what newcomers are perceived to be.

Even in small groups without written rules, maturity develops over time. Mature groups have norms, roles, and patterns of interaction that include habits of dominance, submissiveness, division of labor, and so on. Maturity tends to improve the efficiency of decision making. It makes communication among members easier and more comfortable. In immature groups, members must devote much more effort to maintaining the group and to developing needed roles, norms, and interaction patterns. People must get acquainted, develop trust in one another, and grow accustomed to a pattern of relationships. With maturity, more time can be spent on the substance of the issues.

Relation to Outsiders

The relation of a group to outsiders influences group processes. Groups may be public or private. In *private groups*, the members do not interact in front of audiences. Most task groups are private, but the term does not imply closed membership. By private, we mean groups whose member interactions are not open to observation by outsiders. Such groups often interact with outside people. But they do not conduct their business in front of audiences.

In *public groups*, interactions among members are "open" to outsiders in the sense that the outsiders observe the group in action. Examples of this kind of group might be a panel of experts discussing a question on a television program; a company board of directors meeting in open session; a board of education holding its monthly meeting; or a city council meeting. In such a group, the audience frequently interacts with group members. Communicating in public groups is complex because both interpersonal and public communication are involved.

An important aspect of relationships to outsiders is whether or not the group is independent. An outside group may actually be a "parent" group that prescribes how certain decisions are to be made or limits the options available to group members. This relationship influences how much control the group has over members' behavior, its own environment, and its task. Control affects members' morale and commitment to the group. If members can decide the task of the group and are free from environmental restraints, their communication will differ from that in a situation in which external or internal forces limit their freedom. The amount of control relates directly to satisfaction, productivity, and communication patterns.

Perceived competition with outsiders also influences groups. If members per-

How long a group expects to last may affect the process of communication.

ceive themselves as working together to achieve a goal in competition with outsiders, it tends to promote a sense of cohesiveness. Such a situation leads to perceptual distortions of both insiders and outsiders. Members of such groups will see the insiders as more alike than they actually are, and the outsiders as more different. Such relationships may increase the productivity of a group and help achieve decisions that might otherwise be impossible to achieve. We all know of coalitions of people who work together to defeat a disliked incumbent; but if they are fortunate enough to win and no longer have the outsider for an enemy, they cannot find basis for agreement among themselves. You may have experienced class situations in which the teacher uses this competitive element between groups to achieve greater results from each group.

Member Involvement

The level of involvement by each individual member strongly influences group processes. The involvement may result from commitment to group goals, or from ways in which the group and its interactions fulfill personal needs. Specifically, note the elements of interdependence, cohesiveness, attractiveness, and satisfaction. The communication processes used in decision making affect each of these factors— while in turn each factor also affects retention of members and efficiency of decision making. Similarly, the processes of deciding can affect the level of member commitment. In short, the effects of member involvement and group processes strongly interact.

Interdependence and Cohesiveness **Interdependence** refers to *the extent members need each other to achieve group and individual goals.* Some interdependence is always needed or a group will not exist, but the amounts can vary. High interdependence usually results in cooperative task-oriented communication. Low interdependence among group members reduces the amount of communication among them and many also result in less cooperation among the members.

Cohesiveness *describes the forces that influence members to choose to remain in the group.* Cohesiveness gives group members a sense of belonging, a feeling that the group is a unit and not merely a collection of individuals. If cohesion is high, members want very much to be part of the group. They derive satisfaction from group membership and devote energy and time to earn and defend that membership. If cohesion is low, members of a group do not feel close to each other and have little attachment to the group.

As with all group characteristics, interdependence and cohesiveness are variables—they can change. Although the two characterists affect each other, they do not cause each other, nor are they caused by the same factors. The presence or absence of either, however, will affect the amount and quality of communication within a group.

Group members obtain satisfaction and a sense of belonging.

Factors leading to interdependence and cohesiveness may be external to a group, and members may have little or no control over them. Other factors affecting both characteristics may be internal—for example, personal attitudes, perspective, and values. These personal characteristics may also be beyond control, but communication processes can affect many of them.

Attractiveness and Satisfaction   Attractiveness and satisfaction, both related to cohesiveness, also affect and are affected by group processes. Either an individual in the group or the group itself may be attractive to members. Whatever the cause, attractiveness leads people to join and remain in the group. A person may want to belong to a certain country club because of the others who belong to it. Or people may be attracted to those in a church, a bridge club, or a service organization. In other cases, the group itself may be attractive. Members may believe in a group's goal or be impressed by what it is or what it has accomplished, and join for those reasons.

Group members must have at least minimal satisfaction—with the group, with others in it, or with its product—to remain in the group. How much satisfaction one needs to stay in a group varies according to the purpose for belonging, personal needs, and the situation. Satisfaction, perhaps more than the other factors discussed here, directly relates to the method of decision making used.

Methods of Deciding

Each time a work group meets, members must agree on many things: agendas, procedures, issues. Rarely will any group use a single method of making decisions. The method used will vary according to what kind of decision is being made, how important the decision is, changes in membership, and how members feel or believe at a particular time. Each method for reaching decisions affects members' attitudes and group outcomes differently. You can benefit from knowing the different methods and their impacts.

Follow the Leader   Some groups, and most groups at some times, use a "leader" type of decision making. An influential person, an opinion leader, or a person who for some other reason has power in the group says, "This is the way it ought to be," and the others follow. This behavior may not really deserve the label of group decision making, except that group members decide to follow the decision of the leader. More commonly, one of the following methods is used.

Voting   In the United States, we often decide by voting. When two or more opposing viewpoints exist, the group chooses one of them according to the number of members who favor each alternative. When only two choices exist (and no tie results), this voting method results in a decision based on *majority rule*.

When more than two choices exist, voting procedures are often structured so that if no alternative receives a majority when the first votes are cast, the two alternatives receiving the most votes are voted upon again. In some cases, groups simply select the alternative with the most votes. If no option is favored by a majority, this is deciding by a *plurality*.

Though voting is a common procedure, it has serious disadvantages. Losing members seldom feel involved in or responsible for the decision. They usually have no commitment to carry out the decision. In fact, they may have personal agendas, hidden or open, to see that the decision does not work. Then they can say, "We told you so."

Majorities often consist of people on the same side of an issue for different reasons. Using majority rule can mask this disagreement and result in a decision hard to implement. Majority rule leads to polarization—creation of two sides who see themselves as quite far apart. Polarization often decreases member involvement and group productivity.

Compromise In groups with two or more differing points of view, another common way to decide is *compromise*. When politicians do this, it's often called porkbarreling. The compromisers say, "I'll give you a little of what you want if you will give me a little of what I want, and we'll both come out with something." Politicians aren't the only ones who use compromise, although they may be the only people accused of selling out when they do so. This process may be most common when members of the deciding group are responsible to outside constituencies and have to have something to show them. When group members represent others outside the group, they need to show that no constituent group clearly lost. Collective bargaining uses compromise by necessity.

Deciding by compromise, often used by necessity, has some disadvantages. Short-range benefits may justify or require the compromise, but often at the sacrifice of long-range goals or benefits. From the long-range viewpoint, compromise often results in poor decisions. The conclusion may not have been based on logical procedure or on ideas that members thought "best." Reasons that have little to do with the problem, such as political influence or the power of the groups represented, lead to the decision. Moreover, because all members gave up something they wanted and accepted some things they didn't want, they may not work very hard to implement the decision.

Consensus When time, circumstances, and member skills permit, consensus is the best mode of decision making. *Consensus* exists when all members of a group agree that a decision is the best that can be reached. In reaching a consensus, not all members must agree the solution is the best choice. What they agree on is the *best choice that can be achieved*. Using this mode of deciding, group members have considered the ideas supported by everyone and the members' objections to all alternatives. Using analysis and cooperation, members combine ideas, seek new ideas, and find ways to create the best outcome that meets all objections and achieves support in the group.

Consensus, the most difficult and time consuming way to decide, in the long run is usually the best. Members feel more committed to and responsible for decisions reached by consensus. They are all more likely to work at implementing the decisions.

Consensus also contributes to cohesiveness and increases productivity because it eliminates a losing side.

Disadvantages of deciding by consensus include the difficulty of achieving it and the great amount of time it requires. If enough time is available and some group members are skilled at leadership, consensus can usually be achieved. The benefits are usually worth the effort. At times, however, groups are so polarized that censensus can't be reached. In these cases, compromise or voting may be needed. But in many situations, increased productivity, member satisfaction, and commitment to implement the decision justify the effort of deciding by consensus.

EXERCISE 8.1   REACHING CONSENSUS

OBJECTIVE   **To experience the process of reaching decisions by consensus.**

DIRECTIONS
1. Individually rank the items in the list below according to the directions in the narrative.
2. Next, discuss and agree upon a group ranking. Use consensus to decide. Do not take votes.
3. Assess your group's process. What did this exercise illustrate about the factors affecting group process?

NARRATIVE

An anonymous donor has decided to make two annual $1000 Good Citizen- ship awards, one each to the man and woman in your city whose lives best exemplify the phrase, "a good citizen." The donor's only restriction is that both must be at least fifty-five years old. Your group is a committee appointed by the city government to establish the criteria by which nominees for the awards will be judged. The following items are the ones suggested as standards. Your committee's task is to rank the items from most to least important as standards against which to evaluate the nominees. You may have one ranking, or a different one for the man and the woman winner.

PROPOSED CRITERIA	YOUR RANKING	YOUR GROUP'S RANKING
Has a happy family	___	___
Has a good income	___	___
Is a church leader	___	___
Is an elected city, state, or national officeholder	___	___
Has achieved distinction in local civic organizations	___	___
Has well-educated, mature, employed children	___	___
Is a distinguished civil servant	___	___

Has achieved distinction in a career	___	___
Is liked and respected by neighbors	___	___
Is a happy, stable, loving person	___	___

REVIEW   **Write brief answers to the following questions that will provide the basis for a writing assignment or class discussion.**
1. Explain the advantages and disadvantages of consensus as a mode of group decision making.
2. What demands are placed on individual members of a group when consensus is sought?
3. Explain the most important communication principle you learned or found illustrated in this exercise and why you found it important.

ESTABLISHING GROUP GOALS

We have noted that when members agree on goals, it improves decision making. To achieve this, an agreed upon **agenda** is a great help. We think of an agenda as *a plan or procedure the group agrees to follow.* An agenda can improve both the speed and quality of decision making. Failure to agree on such a plan is perhaps the most common reason group discussions wander aimlessly and fail to achieve goals efficiently. Groups need agendas for several reasons.

Advantages of Agendas

To Clarify Group Goals and Procedures   Agendas help groups by clarifying group goals. Individual members' personal goals may not be the same as those of others in the group. Agenda setting provides time to discuss and agree on group goals. It also helps members to become aware of and/or agree to a plan to follow in achieving that goal. The agenda will guide the use of time throughout the discussion. It also aids in focusing attention on relevant and important issues and in excluding talk related to irrelevant issues.

To Cope with Hidden Purposes   When members' personal goals differ from group goals, it is usually not revealed. The *unstated personal goals* are called **hidden agendas.** Hidden agendas exist when individuals belong to a group for the purpose of using the group to achieve personal aims. They use the group as a vehicle for personal purposes.

Sometimes personal goals are open and do not interfere with group goals. For example, at work Frank may say to the two people who occupy desks next to him, "Hey, Bett, Mel—I need your suggestions. I'm having some trouble getting this drawing done today. I can't seem to get it started. Can we brainstorm some ideas?" In other cases, unrevealed personal goals constitute hidden agendas. Suppose Frank wants Bett's job. Then he may engage in efforts to downgrade her work, cause her to perform less effectively, and make her appear unreasonable. This kind of hidden agenda can interfere with the group process. One way of coping with hidden agendas is to have the group discuss and set agendas together.

To Avoid Hasty Conclusions   Another problem often arises if agenda setting isn't done at the outset. Sometimes everyone quickly agrees when a solution is introduced at the outset. Then they may overlook important considerations about the cause of the problem or implications of the decision. Quick agreement usually results from superficial consideration of the total situation. If the group jumps immediately to a conclusion, they fail to examine important aspects of the total situation. Sometimes this hasty consideration is described as *groupthink*. Agenda setting alone won't eliminate groupthink or poor decisions, but it can help.

To Reduce Debate over Pet Solutions   Quick debate over conclusions also can result from not setting an agenda early in a meeting. Some people always want to begin by suggesting their pet answer. That causes others to state opposing conclusions, and a debate over everyone's favorite idea results. Instead of a cooperative effort in seeking a decision, competition to win begins. The worst thing about such debate is the failure to examine causes first. Arguing over the best solution without first deciding the sources and dimensions of a problem wastes time and needlessly polarizes groups.

Setting Agendas

Plan and Secure Group Agreement   Once aware of the importance of agendas, you can exert a positive influence. Take the initiative before the meeting by planning an outline for the group to follow. State a goal or goals for the group and outline a tentative procedure to follow during the discussion. In cases where you haven't had time to prepare in advance, start the session by saying: "Let's begin by clarifying what exactly is our goal and how we plan to go about making this decision. Perhaps we should establish an agenda."

Introducing a tentative agenda can increase the speed with which the group clarifies its goal and decides on a plan for the discussion. Be careful, however, not to be defensive or possessive about your plan. Remember, the agenda should be a *group* plan, not one an individual imposes. Don't be defensive about suggestions for changing it before the group adopts it. You should, of course, be able to explain the value of following the plan you outline, but don't let the agenda-setting portion of the meeting degenerate into needless argument.

Reassess Agendas Periodically   Even when all members agree, agendas should never be cast in concrete. The group should review any adopted agenda periodically. The group may decide an adopted agenda is no longer helpful, and change it.

Agendas are like planning for a trip. You read a road map and plan a route to follow. But along the way you may decide the plan is no longer appropriate. Perhaps the road has too much traffic, or is under construction. So you choose an alternate route. Similarly, groups plan agendas and then at times change their plan. But having the plan gives a rational base for the changes.

A Suggested Agenda

Depending on the circumstances, several standard agendas can be used. If the group needs to solve a clearly defined problem, it can benefit from using the problem-solving agenda. The problem-solving agenda is sometimes described as a reflective thinking outline. This format is useful for either group or individual problem solving. We describe it here as used by groups, but you can easily adapt the outline to a method for analyzing personal problems.

The Problem-Solving Agenda The problem-solving agenda (the reflective thinking outline) involves six major steps:

1. *Awareness-ventilation:* Group clarifies goal; establishes agenda and climate.
2. *Description:* Group determines current status of the situation or problem.
3. *Analysis:* Group examines causes of the problem and sets criteria for evaluating solutions or decisions.
4. *Proposals:* Group suggests as many alternative solutions and decisions as possible.
5. *Selection:* Group chooses the best solution or decision by evaluating alternatives using criteria.
6. *Implementation:* Group decides how to implement, who is to be responsible for doing what.

Each of these steps involves important considerations. During the first, the *awareness-ventilation* stage, a group examines the questions of agenda setting discussed previously. As a group, members answer the following questions: What is the specific goal of this group? Of this session? Will research be necessary? What kind and how much? How will we do it? Are there specific barriers that will hinder this group? Do strong individual member attitudes exist that will prevent reflective thinking? How will we deal with preconceived notions? Are important points of view not represented? How can we be sure minority views are represented? What will be the best procedures to ensure full participation?

Factors of time, place, and physical arrangement should be considered, along with issues of leadership and individual responsibilities. During this stage, members become acquainted and establish the climate for all remaining interactions.

During the *description* step, the group fully examines the problem or situation. Any unfamiliar or ambiguous terms need to be defined. Members must learn of existing policies, identify the persons affected, and review what has happened to date. If a solution to a problem is sought, members should find out exactly what is wrong and if any previous efforts at solution have been tried, and the results. They should determine how large or serious the problem is.

At the *analysis* stage (step three), the group decides why the situation has developed into a problem. If a group or person has a goal and nothing prevents reaching it, that situation is not a problem. A problem exists only when something or someone (or both) prevents reaching the desired goal. Analysis involves identifying barriers to goal achievement and causes for what's wrong.

During the analysis step, the group should agree on criteria for a solution. This step is commonly overlooked, and the concept of *criteria* is hard for many people to understand. **Criteria** are *standards that any solution must meet in order to be acceptable.* For example, suppose a group of medical researchers is seeking a cure for the common cold. One criterion for a cure might be that it not have side effects worse than the illness itself. Others are that it not be addictive and that it not reduce doctors' ability to treat more serious illnesses. A group could use these three possible criteria to evaluate any possible solution.

The fourth, or *proposal* step is another commonly underused step. At this stage members should offer as many possible alternative solutions or decisions as possible. For this, **brainstorming** is recommended. Brainstorming involves setting aside *time during which members give many ideas without criticism or evaluation.* The aim is to be creative and to think of as many ideas as possible. The goal is *quantity* of ideas, not quality.

The advantage of brainstorming is that people will suggest ideas they would hesitate to mention if they expected evaluation. This way the group gets many ideas. What often seems a ridiculous suggestion may encourage someone to combine previous ideas and come up with a completely new idea that isn't so far afield. So in addition to getting many different suggestions, the group often finds one idea generating another, leading to fresh and untried solutions.

To use brainstorming, start by declaring: "For the next _____ minutes (amount of time depends on group, problem, and situation) we will list all possible options we can think of. No criticism or evaluation of ideas is allowed—not even by the person who makes the suggestion. No idea is too absurd. Mention anything you think of. The aim is to get as many ideas as possible."

Then appoint someone to act as recorder. The recorder should list all ideas, no matter how silly they sound. Ideally, write the suggestions on a chalkboard or flip chart so everyone can see them. Enforce the "no criticism" rule. Don't let anyone forget and begin to evaluate. Brainstorming is a time for creative thinking. Evaluation will take place later, when people run out of ideas.

Brainstorming can be used at many points in the decision-making process. Though commonly associated with listing all possible solutions to a problem, the process applies to choosing goals for a group as well. It also is useful for selecting criteria to evaluate alternatives and for finding means of implementing decisions. Use brainstorming any time that a wide variety of ideas can improve decision making or whenever group creativity needs to be stimulated.

The fifth step in the problem-solving process is *selecting the best proposal.* This step is much easier if the previous two steps have been done carefully. When the causes of a problem are known and criteria for solutions agreed upon, evaluation of possible decisions can be done rationally. Simply ask the question: Which solution or decision eliminates the problem and meets the criteria? If more than one alternative does both, other criteria can be helpful: Which option does not create other problems? Which creates the fewest other problems? Which option costs the least? Which is more acceptable to people it will affect?

Finally comes *implementation*, another step often overlooked in group decision making. At this stage, the group asks and decides on answers to: How can the proposal be put into effect? Who will have to be involved? What will need to be done? By whom? When is the best time to do it? What should be done first? What obstacles may interfere with implementation? How can those barriers be overcome?

Other Agendas In some situations a group doesn't need to solve a problem, but it does need to make a decision. In such cases the group will benefit from using a different agenda. Developing an outline to fit the particular situation may work. Using any particular outline is less important than following some agreed upon plan for achieving the group purpose.

Short meetings or those that continue the work of earlier sessions involve simple agenda-setting steps. In other cases or the first time a group meets, agreeing on the agenda may require considerable time and thought. But whatever agenda the group uses, it must include a step for clarifying the group purpose and agreeing upon a plan to accomplish that purpose. A useful agenda to guide decision making follows.

   I. *Awareness-Ventilation*: Group clarifies goal, eatablishes agenda and climate.
  II. *Statement of Objectives*: Group lists all possible objectives (brainstorming).
 III. *Ranking Objectives*: Group agrees on importance of objectives; divides objectives into two classifications:
    A. Identifies MUSTS—what MUST be accomplished for goal to be met
    B. Identifies WANTS—what would be nice to accomplish but is not essential
 IV. *Identify Obstacles*: Group states what, if anything, now prevents their reaching the goals.
  V. *Identify Alternative Ways to Reach Objectives*: Group lists all possible alternatives (brainstorming).
 VI. *Analysis*: Group assesses alternatives:
    A. Which alternatives will work?
    B. Which can be implemented?
    C. Which alternatives will achieve the objectives?
      1. Meet the MUST objectives?
      2. Meet the WANTS?
    D. Which alternatives have negative consequences? How serious?
    E. Which alternative is most cost effective?
    F. Which has fewest obstacles to implementation?
 VII. *Select Alternative, Test and Plan Implementation*:
    A. Group chooses alternative that best achieves goal.
    B. Group agrees on steps for implementation.
    C. Group establishes evaluation plan.

EXERCISE 8.2   BRAINSTORMING

OBJECTIVE   **To practice brainstorming in a creative situation, and to secure as many answers as possible to each problem.**

DIRECTIONS   1. The class will be divided into groups of six or more.
2. One person will be recorder and one will be process observer.
3. Taking each of the problems in turn, group members are to brainstorm responses. The recorder is to list everything suggested on a chalkboard or flip chart, and the process observer is to stop any person who starts to evaluate any suggestion.
4. At the end of the class period, groups may be asked to share their lists to compile a total class list of possible answers.

Brainstorm Problem 1: Suggest solutions (practical, imaginative, and scientific) to the problem of getting students registered in school each semster.

Brainstorm Problem 2: Suggest uses (actual, potential, imaginative) for an out-of-date car license tag.

Brainstorm Problem 3: Suggest possible consequences (whether immediate, long-range, probable, improbable) that might occur if your instructor decided not to teach but just to attend class.

Brainstorm Problem 4: Suggest possible solutions to the energy shortage in the world today.

REVIEW   **Write brief answers to the following questions that will provide the basis for a writing assignment or class discussion.**
1. Describe the process of brainstorming.
2. Why is it important that each member of the group thoroughly understand the brainstorming process before engaging in it?
3. Explain the most important communication principle you learned or found illustrated in this exercise and why you found it important.

LEADERSHIP

Perhaps the most important element in the quality of decision making is leadership. Exactly what results in effective leadership, however, is not easy to determine. Much research into this important group variable has not yet led to definitive answers to the question: What makes good leaders?

In one popular classification system, group leaders follow one of three basic styles. One is authoritarian. An *authoritarian* leader determines policies, identifies necessary tasks and assigns them, sets timetables, and in general acts as the group authority. Another style of leadership is described as *democratic*. A democratic leader guides group members as they all participate in deciding group goals, priorities, policies, and procedures. The third type, a *laissez-faire* leader, provides no direction to the group. We think this more accurately describes a group without a leader.

This three-part distinction is attractive, but too simple to be helpful in learning how to provide leadership. Many classifications of leader types can be found in research about leadership. You can find several included in the reading list at the end of this chapter.

A Functional Approach

We believe a more useful approach to understanding leadership begins with identifying what functions must be performed for a group to accomplish its purpose. To us, **leadership** is *any behavior that aids a group in accomplishing its goals.*

What functions are necessary will vary according to the group. Therfore, what leadership is varies from one group to another. Generally, leaders do two kinds of things. The first involve accomplishing the tasks that must be done—the **task leadership** functions. The second type of functions help maintain the group. These are **climate leadership** functions. They include the interpersonal interactions that help satisfy the needs that brought members and keep them in the group.

Usually all group members do some leadership functions. Rarely does one person perform them all. Though the concept of a single leader is popular, it is seldom what actually happens. Even though groups usually designate a leader, this person doesn't perform all the leadership functions a group needs. That person may chair a meeting, head a department, or speak for a committee. But leadership involves more than these functions. This designated head is more likely only one of several group leaders.

We think of a **leader** as *one who performs more leadership functions than others in the group.* Thus, we can identify leaders by observing groups. Or by asking members, "Who contributes most to accomplishment of the task?" or "Who contributes most to an effective working climate?" or "Who contributes most to keeping members satisfied?"

Some groups have only one leader, but most have **shared leadership.** This is when several people perform significant amounts of leadership. Many groups have one person who is task leader and one who is climate leader. Groups often have separate **opinion leaders.** By opinion leaders we mean people whose ideas are listened to with respect and accepted uncritically by others in the group. The task or climate leaders may be opinion leaders as well and the reverse may also be true. Nor is it uncommon for a group to have two or three leaders in each category. In these cases, two or three people contribute much to task accomplishment, and two or three others do more to establish a good working climate.

Sometimes, especially in mature groups that are fairly homogeneous, no one performs more leadership than others. We call these leaderless groups. This need not be a laissez-faire situation. A laissez-faire group is without leadership. By leader*less*, we mean a group in which all members contribute equally to accomplishing the purposes. No one person stands out as recognizably more valuable than anyone else. Leaderless groups usually have shared leader*ship.* That is an important distinction. To be without leadership means that the important task or climate functions are not performed. To be without leaders means that no one performs more leadership functions than anyone else. A leaderless group may be without leadership, or it may have shared leadership.

We make this distinction between leader and leadership to emphasize that learning to provide leadership means learning to do what groups need to accomplish their goals. We urge students who want to learn how to become good leaders to study the functional approach. Learn to recognize what particular groups need, and concentrate on learning to perform the needed functions.

Task and Climate Leadership

Now let's be more specific about leadership functions by describing what leaders do. The following lists introduce both task and climate leadership.

Task Functions

1. *Goal setting*: proposing goals, seeking clarification and agreement on goals, determining significance and priorities of different objectives.
2. *Planning*: assessing needs, setting agendas, preparing for sessions, making physical arrangements, providing for special resources, arrangements for publicity when necessary.
3. *Guiding*: attending to procedure, keeping group attention on agenda, summarizing when necessary, keeping or seeing that necessary records are kept.
4. *Giving information*: giving needed data, opinions, experiences.
5. *Seeking information*: seeking needed data, opinions, experiences.
6. *Analyzing*: clarifying ideas; testing information; assessing inferences and judgments; examining implications; seeking standards for assessment; relating procedures, information, and conclusions to goals; being devil's advocate; reality testing.
7. *Synthesizing*: summarizing, bringing related ideas together, testing for consensus, seeking compromises when necessary.

Climate Functions

1. *Encouraging*: supporting others, building status and confidence of members, building status and confidence in group.
2. *Mediating*: suggesting middle or common ground when differences among members arise; harmonizing; maintaining emphasis on issues, not personalities.
3. *Opening communication*: maintaining permissive atmosphere, encouraging shy or reluctant participants, preventing dominance by one or two, counteracting private or subcommunication patterns.
4. *Reducing tension*: resolving conflicts, diverting attention when there is tension, seeking catharsis when helpful, improving interpersonal relations.
5. *Following*: listening to others, accepting group decisions.
6. *Directing self-oriented behaviors toward group goals.*

We have included the sixth climate function because we recognize that satisfaction of individual members' personal needs may have negative effects. This is especially true when individuals' goals are antagonistic, not complementary. Listed below are some behaviors that satisfy personal needs and usually cause goals to be antagonistic. Good climate leadership minimizes these negative effects. Destructive personal actions include:

1. *Aggressing*: lowering status of others, building personal status.
2. *Obstructing*: blocking progress by irrelevant digressions or dwelling on points already covered, rejecting ideas without adequate consideration.
3. *Seeking recognition*: claiming credit for ideas, demanding to be heard on all points, dominating.
4. *Withdrawing*: remaining silent and nonparticipative, engaging in side conversations, going off on tangents.
5. *Competing*: trying to outdo all others, needing to win.
6. *Distracting*: clowning, diverting attention to tangents, disrupting.
7. *Pleading special interest*: supporting personal projects and interests, supporting vested interests, pressing others for support.

Providing group leadership involves getting the needed climate and task functions done. It doesn't necessarily mean doing them yourself. Because the composition and task of groups vary, not all groups need the same things. Only through careful attention to what is happening in a group will you know what needs to be done. And only through practice will you know which functions you do best. Attention to the group processes identified in this chapter and practice in doing what groups need can improve your leadership skills.

A Situational Approach

Another useful approach to understanding leadership is Fred Fiedler's. He analyzes leadership as situational, suggesting that effective leadership depends on the circumstances in the situation. It depends primarily on the *proper match between the leader's style of interacting with other group members and how much control and influence the situation gives to the leader.*[3]

Fiedler distinguishes between leaders who are primarily task-oriented and those who devote more time and concern to relationships between leader and members. He also distinguishes groups along a continuum of high to low power by leaders (powerful leaders can fire, hire, discipline, and reprimand members). He found that task-motivated leaders perform better in situations that are either highly favorable or unfavorable. Relationship-oriented leaders tend to perform better in only moderately favorable situations in which leaders have only moderate control or influence. Fiedler concludes: "It makes no sense to speak of a good leader or a poor leader. There are only leaders who perform well in one situation but not well in another."[4]

---

[3] Fred Fiedler, "The Trouble with Leadership Training Is That It Doesn't Train Leaders," *Psychology Today* (February 1973), p. 26.

[4] Ibid. Those interested in Fiedler's concept can learn much from Fred Fiedler, Martin Chemers, and Linda Mahar, *Improving Leadership Effectiveness: The Leader Match Concept* (New York: Wiley, 1977), a programmed introduction to the situational approach to leadership.

This research is important to the study of group leadership because it shows that answers to the question of how to lead groups are never easy. More important, Fiedler emphasizes that the situation always influences the answers. The principles in this chapter can help you develop leadership skills, but only as long as you remember to consider the situation when you choose leadership behaviors. No single behavior works in every case. The skills are many and the situations differ widely. Probably the only task that doesn't change is the need to communicate accurately and effectively.

MANAGING CONFLICT

Groups that make decisions effectively manage conflict effectively. Indeed, at times this skill distinguishes groups that work well and survive from those that don't.

People often think of group discussions as situations in which conflict should be avoided and in which cooperation is the ultimate goal. Certainly, to achieve consensus requires a cooperative spirit, but not all conflict is harmful. In the first place, it is unrealistic to believe conflict can be avoided. In addition, it would be unwise. Conflict can be valuable.[5]

Value of Conflict

Conflict within a group is often healthy. A group with no conflict probably will not thoroughly examine ideas, or consider different points of view. Untested decisions will emerge. Groups without conflict may reach consensus quickly, but in doing so may fail to consider all the alternatives. They need the valuable person who plays the "devil's advocate." This person says, "Wait a minute—there's another side to this issue. Let's look at it from that perspective." The existence of competing ideas or factions may be required to avoid groupthink.

A major advantage of group over individual decision making is that the group includes different points of view. Each additional member increases the potential informational resources available. *Without conflict, the potential may remain untapped, and the major advantage of group decision making lost.*

Types of Conflict

Of course, conflict within the group should be constructive. If it is not, it will interfere with what the group accomplishes. Two main types of conflict exist. The first relates to task. *Conflict about different points of view encourages thorough examination of all sides of issues.* To have confidence in its conclusions, the group

---

[5] Some writers distinguish between conflict and competition. We do not think this is necessary in an introductory book. Both occur when people are seeking different goals. One can lead to the other. Both can interfere with group decision making or benefit it. We suggest ways to cope with the effects of competition and conflict, not to eliminate them, and see no need at this point to be concerned with the differences between them.

Open disclosure of differences generates benefits from conflict.

should thoroughly test its ideas. Task conflict is so valuable that when no disagreement exists, someone should take a devil's advocate role. On the other hand, interpersonal conflict can be damaging. Competition among members because of personal dislike or hidden agendas can interfere with task accomplishment and reduce both member satisfaction and productivity. *Interpersonal conflict leads to defensiveness*, almost always damaging in task groups.

Many groups have members with adversary relationship. Adversaries are people who come to a group with either hidden or open agendas to reach goals antagonistic to those of others in the group. The extreme case of this kind of group may be collective bargaining situations.

We do not have space to discuss adversary relationships here. Groups with adversaries within them present a different situation from those in which members begin with similar goals. If you need to learn how to cope with these situations, you'll want to study group communication in depth. We have included some suggested readings that can provide more insight, and most colleges provide advanced study in the area. In this introductory book, we limit our suggestions to those helpful in coping with conflicts in groups that *begin* as cooperative.

Avoiding Destructive Conflict

The differences between destructive and helpful conflict in groups are largely differences in attitude. With certain attitudes, members will communicate with each other competitively and in destructive ways. In contrast, other attitudes reduce conflict as they result in more effective communication.

Supportive Communication   The most harmful attitudes are those related to *defensiveness*. Because people get defensive when they perceive a threat, it causes much conflict in groups. Recall from our discussion in Chapter 7 that defensiveness results partly from attitudes and partly from specific behaviors. *Evaluation* is an attitude, and it is communicated by verbal and nonverbal behaviors. Evaluation of ideas is necessary in task groups, but evaluation of people is not. If you approach a group with evaluative attitudes toward the other members, it usually creates defensiveness.

Control is another example. If you think you should be able to control others in the group, both verbal and nonverbal behavior will cause conflict. Similar comments could be made regarding each behavior that leads to defensiveness. *Superiority*, *stategy*, *certainty*, and *lack of empathy* are attitudes reflected in communicative behavior. If someone displays these attitudes during group decision making, a source of destructive conflict is present.

In contrast, creating supportive climates can help develop trust and reduce defensiveness. Description, problem orientation, equality, honesty, provisionalism, and empathy can help you reduce excessive competition and interpersonal conflict.

Neutralize Adversaries   Another way to cope with conflicts is to neutralize the effect of members who think of others as adversaries. Many people regard decision situations in groups as win-lose situations. They think, "If I don't achieve this result, I lose." To prevent this adversary attitude from interfering with group process, members must realize that the group need not be a win or lose situation. Everyone can gain something. Members must see the benefits of hearing conflicting ideas and sharing different points of view. They need to see that the product of the group can be better than if each individual worked alone. This "better" quality may be because a decision will be more readily accepted and implemented, or it may be a better decision. In either event, all can benefit from the group effort—a win-win situation.

Not everyone shares the everyone-win attitude. Some people cling to the win-lose perspective. They may have commitments outside the group that make the decision-making task for them an actual win-lose situation. Personal or vested interests, promises to constituencies, and strong biases are only a few reasons that for some people group decision making is a win-lose situation. Coping with these people is not simple. The next suggestion can help, but no solution is perfect.

Focus on Process   A third way to deal with conflict is to *focus openly on group processes*. During the awareness-ventilation step, members should emphasize the necessity to be as critical of their own suggestions as of others' and remind one another that ideas are no one's personal possession. If a general discussion of group process occurs early, reminders are probably all that will be necessary later.

Sometimes when conflict arises, the discussion must be stopped long enough to focus on group process. Bring the conflict or problem into the open. You can say, "Can we stop a minute and focus on what's going on here? We seem to have a conflict that doesn't relate to the issues. I think we might be better off to get it on the table and resolved. Then we can return to talking about the subject." State what you are hearing, describe what you perceive the conflict to be, and then ask the parties involved to comment. Remember the guidelines from earlier chapters. Keep your language descriptive. Don't judge; just report what you are hearing and ask for others' perceptions. This kind of focusing on process is not easy or pleasant, but it usually clears the air. Members can then continue the discussion with better focus and less disruption.

The Cooperative Spirit

Groups that best deal with conflict display a cooperative spirit. Having such an attitude does not mean the absence of conflict. It does reflect a way of looking at conflict.

Most important is to *recognize the value of conflicting ideas*. Group members need to believe that conflict of ideas is healthy. If members believe people can disagree without being disagreeable, the group will probably have healthy conflict that contributes to improved decision making. If, on the other hand, members interpret disagreements over ideas as personal attacks, or if they react to evaluation of ideas as if they were evaluations of themselves, the situation can quickly deteriorate into interpersonal conflict. When members realize that the processes of interaction generate most of the ideas in a group, they will respond positively to task conflict and reduce their idea possessiveness.

When members approach group decision making with an awareness that everyone perceives things differently, it helps them see the value in conflict. They will recall that each person has a view of the world based on individual life experiences, and that no one has all the facts, or all the relevant information, or all the truth. When disagreements exist, members should remember that the conflicting ideas are all probably partly right and partly wrong. If they do, they are less likely to react with defensiveness when someone disagrees with them.

The cooperative spirit, in summary, results from the following beliefs:

1. It is valuable to express conflicting points of view.
2. No one has a monopoly on the accurate perspective of the world.
3. The group needs everyone's perspective to develop an accurate view of the world.
4. Group processes can improve decisions.

When groups display this cooperative spirit, interpersonal conflict is less likely to develop from competition over ideas.

SUMMARY

Decision making in groups is a skill most people need. It can be improved by knowing the influence of several factors: that individual goals are not the same; that members having complementary goals enhance the process, while antagonistic goals interfere; that maturity improves group efficiency by establishing roles, norms, and interaction pat-

EXERCISE 8.3   PROBLEM SOLVING

OBJECTIVE   **To practice deciding on solutions to a problem in a group.**

DIRECTION   1. In groups of five to six you will meet to choose a problem to discuss in a later class session.
   a. Decide on the problem by consensus.
   b. State a goal question for the discussion (such as: What should be the city council action regarding the rezoning of the Queeny District? or, How should the college reduce operating expenses to meet its budget?).
   c. A goal question for a problem-solving discussion should be specific, limited, and unbiased.
2. Check with your instructor to be sure your goal question is specific, limited, and unbiased. The instructor will assign a date for the group to discuss the chosen question.
3. The group may decide to assign specific research tasks to individuals.
4. Each group member should individually prepare for the discussion by planning specific steps within the agenda suggested on page 220.
5. On the assigned day, members of the group should attempt to agree by consensus to an answer to the goal question. The discussion should follow the steps of the problem-solving agenda.
6. After the discussion, members should individually answer the following questions and then share their analysis of the discussion.
   a. What characteristics discussed in the text did our group display?
   b. Was the group goal clear? Were members' goals complementary or antagonistic? (Respond with specifics.)
   c. Was group communication defensive or supportive in nature?
   d. Assess each individual's contribution to the group. What leadership functions were performed by each member?
7. Your instructor may ask you to present steps 5 or 6 or both to the class.

REVIEW   1. Explain the differences between complementary and antagonistic goals.
2. What values have agendas?
3. Describe the problem solving agenda and explain what should happen at each step.
4. Why is conflict a positive factor at times and desctructive at other times?
5. Explain the differences between task and climate leadership functions?
6. Explain the most important communication principle you learned or found illustrated by this exercise and why you found it important.

terns; that the relationship of a group to outsiders can affect member interaction positively and negatively; that member involvement can increase interdependence, cohesiveness, attractiveness, and satisfaction.

Most groups benefit from adopting agendas to guide their decision making. Agendas assure that all members of the group know its goal, provide a means for focusing attention and a way to organize the discussion, and help avoid overlooking important considerations.

Groups may use the problem solving format, a decision making agenda, or an individual plan, depending on their purpose. Groups should pause periodically to assess the agenda and be prepared to change when it is no longer appropriate.

Several modes of decision making are possible, and each has advantages and disadvantages. Majority rule, though common and efficient, has the disadvantage of polarizing a group and making some members feel they have lost. Compromise is a form of decision making in which supporters of every side give a little to create a result in which everyone gains a little. The advantage, especially in groups responsible to other constituencies, is that of having no losing side. We recommend consensus decision making. Though it usually requires a great deal of time and leadership skill, it is best because it makes everyone committed to implementing the decision. Members are more satisfied, the group is cohesive, and as a result more productivity exists.

Leadership in groups comprises those actions that help the group accomplish its purposes. These functions are of two types: task and climate leadership. Leaders are people who perform more leadership functions than others in the group. Most groups have more than one leader, often one a climate leader and the other a task leader. Task functions are goal setting, planning, guiding, information giving, information seeking, analyzing, and synthesizing. Climate functions include encouraging, mediating, opening communication, tension reducing, following, and directing self-oriented roles toward group goals. Leaders need to prevent the personal need satisfaction behaviors of members from disrupting group progress. Destructive personal-oriented behaviors are: aggressing, obstructing, recognition seeking, withdrawing, competing, distracting, and special-interest pleading.

Competition and conflict are useful in groups as long as task conflict does not become interpersonal. Conflict helps ensure that all viewpoints are examined and that hasty, ill-considered decisions are not made. A cooperative spirit can help prevent conflict over ideas and tasks from becoming interpersonal conflict. With a cooperative spirit, members believe that no one has sole possession of any idea; that no one has a monopoly on the accurate perspective of reality; and that the group needs widely varied perspectives to generate the best decisions.

QUESTIONS FOR DISCUSSION

1. What are the effects of purpose, maturity, and relationship to outsiders in group communication, especially decision making?
2. Can you explain four variables affecting and affected by member involvement in the group?
3. What are the advantages and disadvantages of the different kinds of decision making in groups?
4. Why are agendas valuable in group decision making?
5. Outline the problem-solving agenda. How does a group choose an appropriate agenda?
6. Can you become a task leader? a climate leader? an opinion leader? How?
7. What are your conclusions about the research of Fred Fiedler?
8. How can conflict be useful to groups? What steps prevent interpersonal conflicts from arising?

4

SUGGESTIONS FOR FURTHER READING

Argyris, Chris. *Increasing Leadership Effectiveness*. Melbourne, Fla.: Krieger Publishing Co., 1983 (reprint of 1976 edition).

Bales, Robert. *Interaction Process Analysis.* Reading, Mass.: Addison-Wesley, 1967.

———— et al. *Symlog: A Manual for the Case Study of Groups.* New York: Free Press, 1979.

Cartwright, Dorwin, and Alvin Zander, eds. *Group Dynamics*, 3rd ed. New York: Harper & Row, 1968.

Cathcart, Robert, and Larry Samovar. *Small Group Communication: A Reader*, 5th ed. Dubuque: William C. Brown, 1988.

Fiedler, Fred, Martin Chemers, and Linda Mahar. *Improving Leadership Effectiveness: The Leader Match Concept.* New York: Wiley, 1977.

————. "The Trouble with Leadership Training Is That It Doesn't Train Leaders," *Psychology Today* (February 1973), pp. 23–29.

Fisher, B. Aubrey. *Small Group Decision Making: Communication and the Group Process*, 2nd ed. New York: McGraw-Hill, 1980.

Fisher, Roger, and William Ury. *Getting to Yes: Negotiating Agreement Without Giving In.* Boston: Houghton Mifflin, 1981.

Harnack, R. Victor, Thorrel Fest, and Barbara Jones. *Group Discussion*, 2nd ed. Englewood Cliffs, N.J.: Prentice-Hall, 1977.

Hocker, Joyce, and William Wilmot. *Interpersonal Conflict*, 2nd ed. Dubuque: William C. Brown, 1985.

Jandt, Fred. *Conflict Resolution Through Communication*. New York: Harper & Row, 1973.

————. *Win-Win Negotiating: Turning Conflict into Agreement.* New York: Wiley, 1987.

Johnson, David W., and Frank Johnson. *Joining Together: Group Theory and Skills*, 3rd ed. Englewood Cliffs, N.J.: Prentice-Hall, 1987.

Korda, Michael. *Power! How to Get It, How to Use It.* New York: Random House, 1975.

Likert, Rensis. *The Human Organization: Its Management and Value.* New York: McGraw-Hill, 1967.

Likert, Rensis, and Jane Likert. *New Ways of Managing Conflict.* New York: McGraw-Hill, 1976.

Luft, Joseph. *Group Processes: An Introduction to Group Dynamics*, 3rd ed. Palo Alto, Calif.: Mayfield Publishing, 1985.

Miller, Gerald, and Herbert Simons, eds. *Perspectives on Communication in Social Conflict.* Englewood Cliffs, N.J.: Prentice-Hall, 1974.

Phillips, Gerald, and Julia Wood. *Emergent Issues in Human Decision-Making.* Carbondale, Ill.: Southern Illinois University Press, 1984.

Tubbs, Stewart. *A Systems Approach to Small Group Interaction*, 3rd ed. New York: Random House, 1988.

Weick, Karle. *The Social Psychology of Organizing*, 2nd ed. Reading, Mass.: Addison-Wesley, 1979.

Zander, Alvin. *Groups at Work: Unresolved Issues in the Study of Organizations.* San Francisco: Jossey Bass, 1977.

9 Communicating in the New Workforce

> We now live in a very new economy, a service economy, where relationships are becoming more important than physical products.
>
> KARL ALBRECHT AND RON ZEMKE[1]

> . . . the understandings of the greater part of men are necessarily earned by their ordinary employments.
>
> ADAM SMITH

GOAL

To learn how to apply communication skills more effectively in the new workforce.

OBJECTIVES

The material in this chapter should help you to:
1. Develop positive relationships with peers, supervisors, and subordinates in the new workforce.
2. Improve your ability to follow and give directions related to work responsibilities.
3. Prepare relevant information for an effective employment interview.
4. Conduct interviews to gather information for reports and other job-related purposes.
5. Explain how structures and channels influence communication in organizations.
6. Describe the factors that influence intercultural communication in the new workforce.
7. Adapt to male/female communication situations in the new workforce.
8. Develop a plan to use communication skills to achieve important career goals.

---

[1] *Service America,* Dow Jones-Irwin, 1985, p. v.

Work is an important part of daily life. For most of us, being at work, getting ready for it, getting there, and getting home take up most of our waking hours at least five days a week. So communicating at work is critically important for most of us. And for most of us, communicating at work means becoming a part of the new workforce. That almost always places us within an organization, either large or small, and usually a formal organization with corporate officers and structure.

In this chapter we look at several aspects of communication that can help you improve your effectiveness in this new workplace. The "new workforce in the United States" is more than current jargon. It represents a new network of interpersonal and business relationships. It includes nearly equal numbers of male and female workers, and it stresses the importance of good communication skills. Communicating in the new workforce touches everyone: majority and minority groups, males and females of all ages, people from a variety of cultures. Job requirements at the entry level and at advanced positions in the professions demand that we adapt our skills to the needs of this new workforce.

This chapter first discusses the communication setting at work and some of the common problems that people experience in their jobs: getting along with other people, giving and following directions correctly, understanding work responsibilities. Next we consider some specific suggestions for dealing with the new workforce, and then we turn to an examination of interviews and how communication is affected by organizational structure.

COMMUNICATING IN THE NEW WORKFORCE

Value of Communication

Employment normally requires skills in two primary areas. One area relates to the procedures, products, and services of the company or organization. Formal training and on-the-job training usually provide the employee with the necessary background in this area. This knowledge is important to job success; in the language of Chapter 5, it is necessary for such success, not a sufficient condition. Skills in the other area more frequently affect work effectiveness, promotions, and career satisfaction. This is the area of communication skills. You may think of exceptions where isolated work is involved, but these are rare. Even the stereotypical white-coated laboratory scientist now generally works in a team.

What are the communication skills needed to be effective in the new workplace? What can you do to enhance your chances of career advancement? These questions and their answers are related. Though frequently overlooked in career preparation, communication skills often distinguish the person who advances in a profession or trade from those who do not.

The skills required for effective communication in the new workforce have largely been presented throughout this book. Only a few concepts and skills that apply directly at work differ from those necessary for good communication anywhere.

Perhaps this sounds obvious, but it is those people who *apply* these ideas in the new workforce who will succeed.

Your ability to process the information you receive (intrapersonal communication) and to work effectively with other people (interpersonal communication) will determine your career success. Skill at presenting ideas clearly or at persuasion in small and larger groups (public speaking) will also affect your career advancement. You may believe that you will never need public speaking skills in *your* work, but most people moving up the career ladder soon learn differently.

Common Problems in the New Workforce

The most common problems in the new workforce derive from poor communication. Employers and supervisors complain that workers "can't follow simple directions" and "can't express themselves clearly." Your own experience probably adds validity to these observations. And unfortunately, the problems aren't easily solved. No reliable cures exist. People peddle easy formulas and prescriptive step-by-step approaches, and companies buy them because the need is great. But the variables in communication are too dynamic to yield effective solutions to simple formulas. The principles of effective communication, the key concepts and theories, provide insight into many situations. Applying these principles on a regular basis will provide significant improvement. But the problems remain resistent to solution. They do so because, just as with poor listening and ineffective interpersonal communication, the solutions lie as much in changed attitudes as in skills. Thus we will give you much information that can improve your communication at work, but only you can supply the motivation to apply this information to your work situation.

Interpersonal Relationships In Chapter 7 we discussed communication in developing and maintaining personal relationships. Applying these ideas in the new workforce will prove challenging. At work, most of us have an interdependent relationship with coworkers. We work together effectively to achieve organizational goals. At times we may have trouble "getting along" with others at work. These problems can interfere with our ability to function well. In extreme cases, such problems create stress that interferes with other aspects of personal life.

We probably won't ever prevent all interpersonal problems at work; what we must learn is how to keep them from interfering with our ability to work effectively. That different people have different attitudes and values is a basic cause of interpersonal problems in the workplace. Since people attach different degrees of importance to issues, inevitably we encounter people whose attitudes and values conflict with ours. When they do, problems result.

Away from work, we are free to choose acquaintances with similar attitudes and values. At work, we don't usually have that choice. Because the new workforce is increasingly multicultural, we can expect to work with people from diverse backgrounds. And people who work for an organization are expected to adapt to the people and goals of that organization. Simply put, this means the job obliges us to work with people whose attitudes and values may differ markedly from our own.

The new workforce is increasingly diverse.

Moreover, in an increasingly regulated and competitive service economy, even creating our own business does not free us from that obligation. Since Benjamin Franklin, the motto has been, "The customer is always right." For an entrepreneur, whether in a large or small business, modern life has not changed that!

To develop effective relationships in the workplace under these circumstances, we must start with the recognition that each individual has the "right" to differ from you in many ways. Such acceptance alone will reduce many interpersonal problems at work. Beyond that, remember that all workers, however different, share the goals of the organization. Though a tension exists in all work life between personal goals and those of the organization, when disagreements or problems develop at work, focusing on the organizational goal provides a means of dealing with others whose values differ from our own. This point implies some tough decisions. At times, people must choose their own personal goals over those of the company, as numerous whistle-blowers have learned. Making such choices is not easy and the consequences seldom pleasant. Some of these cases make dramatic reading or television, as the cases of Karen Silkwood or Marie Ragghianti demonstrate.[2]

Getting along at work essentially means getting the job done. While all the communication concepts and skills in this book are necessary to be effective in the new workforce, two areas are especially useful in handling problems with other people: self-concept (Chapter 2) and personal relationships (Chapter 7).

Giving and Following Directions   A supervisor's complaint that an employee "can't follow simple directions" usually reveals one of two things: poor listening by the employee, or the supervisor's poor use of feedback when the directions were

[2] *Silkwood,* Mike Nichols and Michael Hausman, Producers, Mike Nichols, Director (1983); Peter Maas, *Marie: A True Story* (New York: Random House, 1983).

given. Although it can be argued that the person giving the directions has primary responsibility for clear explanations, it is the employee who usually suffers the greater damage when there is a failure to follow directions.

How can this situation be handled? Whether you are giving or getting directions, remember to use feedback to verify accuracy and understanding. Feedback is the receiver's response as interpreted by the source. In these situations, the interpretation must be accurate, so both repetition and restatement may be needed. To verify directions repetition may be necessary: "Use exactly 5 ounces of oil, no more." If the response is, "OK," the source has no way to be sure the message is understood. Whether you are source or receiver, repetition should be demanded, especially if 4 ounces or 6 ounces can cause damage. You're certain that 5 is what was said and heard, but if there is any chance you're wrong, it may be an expensive cost for the few seconds it would take to say, "That's 5 ounces, right?" In addition to verifying, repeating will reinforce memory. In other kinds of situations with more complicated directions, paraphrase may be required.

Occasionally, you may hesitate to ask for clarification because you fear it will reveal a lack of ability to understand what was said. Such an interpretation is possible. But far worse is beginning a task without being sure of what is expected. More likely, the supervisor's interpretation of your question will be that you are conscientious about doing the job right.

From the viewpoint of giving directions, we often just don't take time to seek feedback to be sure we are understood. At other times, we don't ask for repetition or restatement because we're not skilled enough as communicators to know how to ask for it without making it sound as if we think the person receiving the directions is stupid. Both responses are understandable, but the long-range costs rarely justify the behavior. You can establish a routine during which everyone understands the importance of clarity. You can model a way of communicating that encourages everyone on the job to use repetition and paraphrase to verify directions. Just as pilots of both large and small airplanes carefully complete a checklist of very routine behaviors to make sure nothing is missed, so can work situations benefit from adding routine use of verbal feedback procedures to the job.

In short, the reason most people don't follow directions is usually that the directions are not adequately understood or reinforced sufficiently to be remembered. This can occur when neither supervisor nor employee use feedback well enough. Knowledgable communicators find the problem easy to correct.

Clarifying Areas of Responsibility   Another common problem in the new workforce is failure to clarify what is expected of the employee. This is a problem of role definition, and it exists in many situations.

Unclear role definitions confront many people who work in situations without clear or strong contractual arrangements. Usually, this happens in nonunion situations, increasingly the predominant work situation in the United States. It characterizes almost all white collar jobs, especially those in management and professional roles. The major problem with unclear role definitions is that job limits are not clear. In these situations, employees may be expected to do things they do not believe they were hired to do. Many of us cause this problem for ourselves. Overanxious to secure a job, we accept an unwritten, open-ended contract. We thus permit the employer total freedom to set and alter our working conditions.

Sometimes the solution is simple. Ask for a written job description or clarification of your tasks from a supervisor. Or write out what you think your job involves, and ask the supervisor to edit it. As the two of you discuss the written description, it will clarify the ideas you both have about the role. If your problem is a supervisor who expects too much, simply writing it down may solve nothing. Most people are reasonable, however, so writing all their expectations in a single list can reveal that unreasonable demands exist.

Written job descriptions can solve another problem: inconsistent expectations. You may be expected to do one thing one time, yet at other times be reprimanded for doing exactly that same thing. Inconsistency may be more frustrating than excessive demands. With specified job limits, inconsistent expectations can usually be identified and eliminated.

Recognize, though, that unclear job limits have some advantages. You have more freedom when work roles are ambiguous. Written job descriptions can limit individual effort and initiative. Perhaps you choose to go beyond what is expected of you so you can demonstrate that you are capable of doing another job, are worthy of promotion, or are really invaluable to the company. A job description won't tell you when to exceed the limits and when not to. These are matters of personal judgment, dependent on particular situations. Still, having clear job limits can make it more obvious to you and your supervisor when you perform better than the average worker.

In the new workforce, with its greater emphasis on relationships and communication skills, clarifying areas of responsibility can be difficult. In many situations, a person can clearly identify specific tasks but must decide how to achieve them. For example, a bank gives a teller specific instructions on how to process each type of customer transaction. But how the teller interacts with customers is quite individual. The bank expects tellers to be friendly and courteous, and will certainly evaluate them on these behaviors. Though tellers are rarely given explicit instructions regarding these communication skills, such skills largely determine their success and promotion.

In situations like this, and there are many, the part of the job that can be clarified is less important than the other part. Advancing in a company requires that employees go beyond the minimum level required for a job. They are expected to build relationships that will assure the future success of the company or organization. Thus, effective communication skills, especially effective interaction with others, determine overall success more than the specific tasks of the job.

Preparing and Delivering Reports Reports that you may need to give at work vary in importance and degree of formality. A manager may simply request, "Check this out for me, please," or a vice-president may request a report for the Board of Directors. Either requires careful attention to communication to do the

Preparing and presenting reports is a major part of the job in the new workforce.

job properly; both provide an opportunity for you to demonstrate skill and perform for the organization.

As in all cases involving directions, first make sure you *clearly understand the request or assignment*. A few questions (or a lengthy discussion if necessary) to clarify directions can prevent wasted energy and unsatisfactory results.

After achieving a clear understanding of the assignment, you may find that investigation and research are required. Use your interviewing skills and develop a plan of attack. Gather information from all relevant sources, and *make notes* as you gather information. Don't trust your memory! Thoroughness is recognized and appreciated in the new workforce.

Organizing your report—whether it's an informal, short report or a major presentation—is important. How you present information reveals your effectiveness and potential value to your employer. Generally, the simplest organizational pattern is the best, because reports should be to the point and easy to follow. Whatever the length, the information about organizing speeches in Chapter 11 will be useful.

The informal report frequently requires talking to one or more persons to gather information. Two important communication skills are necessary in this situation: one is to know how to ask questions; the other is to make effective use of listening skills.

Reports frequently require information about facts and attitudes. To gather this information, you may want to use factual questions (closed) and value questions (open-end). Factual questions are used to *gather factual data* about a particular situation. They are frequently closed questions, starting with phrases such as: "How much . . . ?" "How often . . .?" "When did you . . . ?" Value questions try to gather information about how a person *feels* about a particular situation or product. Value probes frequently begin with "How do you feel about . . .?" The respondent, as in most open-end questions, is asked to give personal reactions to the question. When gathering information about opinions and attitudes, value questions are essential tools in the process.

Listening skills are critically important. In gathering information for reports, every situation has a clear purpose: to understand, remember, and evaluate the information. As you approach the interview, keep in mind your specific listening purpose. What information do you need from this person to prepare your report? Organize your interview and phrase your questions to get the necessary information. Listening is an active communication skill, requiring energy and concentration. Good listening skills are not only important in gathering information for reports; they are a major factor in your overall career satisfaction and success in the new workforce.

Achieving Career Goals through Communication

It is hard to overstate how important communication will be in achieving career goals in the new workforce. How you perform in almost every case means knowing the details of your job and knowing how to communicate effectively with all of the people with whom you come in contact.

Establish Appropriate Goals To advance within an organization, your goals must be compatible with those of the organization. They must fit within the overall function and goals of the organization. You should establish goals both for short- and long-term career objectives. These goals, like a group's agenda, serve as a map to a destination. They give you checkpoints along the way. To assure your goals are compatible with the organization and that they serve your purpose, review them periodically with your supervisor. The evaluation interview provides a setting for such a discussion. Be sure you prepare for it as you would for any important interview.

Analysis may show your goals are incompatible with your position or the organization. That is important to know. It faces you with choices: modify or redefine your goals, or change positions or organization. Doing either requires careful thought, planning and communication. Talk with others can clarify both your goals and attitudes.

Establish a Career Advancement Plan Career advancement benefits from a systematic plan to improve and apply your communication skills to specific situations. Honest analysis of your skills and of responsibilities at work can yield valuable information to develop an appropriate plan. Although a plan will not guarantee that you will achieve the desired results, it will enhance your chances of success.

Models and Mentors   Study those who have already achieved advancement in your organization or career. Try to observe specific behaviors that led to career advancement. Note how they talk, dress, what they do.

Try to interview successful people in your field. Ask their "secrets" and advice for succeeding. Such an interview can help you in a number of ways. The information and ideas you will receive can be invaluable, especially if you don't limit yourself to a single such interview. The combination of experience and knowledge that successful people share with you can be gained in few other ways. These interviews, some of which should certainly be done with people within your organization, can help you identify a mentor. Such a person can provide ongoing advice and assistance in moving up within an organization.

Finally, such interviews can help important people know who you are. Then later, when you do good work, your name and face will not be unfamiliar to them. In most organizations, many good people are competing for fewer and fewer open positions as they advance. Thus, you can use every available advantage. Having important people know who you are is one such advantage.

Seek to become part of the organizational networks. Develop interests compatible with those successful in your field. This isn't advice to form yourself totally into a corporate "mold," but rather to study people who achieve in order to decide which of their characteristics and behaviors "fit" you. You'll also identify things you do, ways you talk and other communication behaviors that don't match the style of people who succeed in your organization. Such analysis will help you know what elements of your own style to enhance and what to change—or conversely, you'll know when it's time to seek a new job or organization.

RELATING TO DIVERSE POPULATIONS

Intercultural Communication

The new workforce is frequently an international social structure. Many organizations are multinational companies, and more are becoming so all the time. Organizations increasingly hire people from cultures other than the mainstream United States. Increasing diversity in our workforce and social environment decreases the pressure on those of "other" cultures to adapt to United States patterns. Thus, the workplace is now an intercultural setting requiring that even those from the dominant United States culture understand the basic factors of intercultural communication.

Need to Accept Differences   Intercultural communication usually includes people shaped by different cultural values as well as different experiences. Communication between people from different cultures reflects these differences. When we talk with someone of our own culture, we expect at least minimal sharing of meaning in our language codes, nonverbal messages, and values systems. For effective intercultural communication, we must totally reverse this expectation. In fact, neither expectation is totally realistic. Those from the same culture are never totally the same, while those from different cultures are not totally different. Yet the fundamental expectation of difference, in values and attitudes as well as language and history, is the appropriate expectation with which to approach communicating with people from different cultures. Moreover, effective intercultural communication requires that we approach such situations with an attitude that accepts such differences.

Two factors are most important in improving communication with people from another culture. First, remember that the most important differences between cultures are not seen and are seldom discussed. These are the fundamental value systems that motivate behavior. You could compare communication between two people of two different cultures to the meeting of two icebergs. What the two people see and hear of each other is comparable to the part of the iceberg above the water. What remains unspoken and yet has trememdous importance compares to the part of the iceberg below the water. Where cultures collide, as they often do, is like two icebergs meeting in the water. The differences are usually both unseen and unspoken because they are fundamental value systems that generate beliefs and attitudes so essential to our language and way of thinking we never even notice them.

In communicating with people of different cultures, it is essential to remember the impact of unspoken values. One such value relates to the second factor that can improve our communication with people from another culture. This is to recognize and minimize the impact of **ethnocentrism**. People from most cultures tend to be ethnocentric; that is, their *attitudes involve a sense that their own culture is superior to others*. Those of us from the United States, however, tend to be more ethnocentric than most. We are justly proud of our governmental system and way of life. We are perhaps less justly confident that our culture has created our wealth or that our affluence is a deserved reward for our diligence and ideal way of life.

Adding a natural cultural tendency to a hubris generated by a generally weak knowledge of economics and history results in a population that exhibits two characteristics that limit our effectiveness at intercultural communication. First, we are excessively ethnocentric. We tend not to see the positive qualities in other cultures. We tend to believe our own culture so perfect that although others may be interesting, there is little we have to gain by understanding theirs. Second, we generally believe that any others who have the opportunity will want to become like us, and (more seriously) we expect them to. We expect people of other cultures, especially if we encounter them in the United States, to adapt to mainstream United States culture. We become offended when they don't, and we attribute many negative characteristics to them.

Under these circumstances, it is hardly a surprise that we don't communicate particularly well with people of other cultures. Not only do we tend to create United States enclaves when we live overseas, we become irritated by excessive need to interact with people of other cultures here in the United States. Such communication requires more work than ordinary communication, and our attitude is generally that those of the other culture should do the work, not us. Thus, as with so many things in improving communication, the best way to improve our intercultural communication involves a change of attitudes.

Need to Develop New Communication Habits Once we have corrected the underlying attitudes, however, some specific attention to intercultural communication skills can benefit us. First, we should recognize that a restricted vocabulary or strong accent often interferes with effective communication. Thus when communicating with people of other cultures, we need to use feedback extensively, even with simple messages. Repetition may often be needed since words will be pronounced in ways neither party is familiar with. Paraphrase becomes essential. The phrases "Did you say . . . ?" or "Let me be sure I understand. You mean . . ." should frequently punctuate intercultural communication.

People with limited experience with other cultures show a lack of awareness of the important differences in intercultural communication. Though it's obviously simplistic, almost all of us respond to people with restricted use of our language by talking more loudly. We do it even with people who are native speakers of English. If someone doesn't understand us, we don't just repeat. We do so with higher volume (usually including a touch of irritation). In most cases the problem was not that the person didn't *hear* us. It was they didn't *understand* us. And higher volume, by distorting sounds, may actually make things worse. For better results try clearer articulation, slower rate, and more frequent use of feedback. Each will produce better results than increased volume.

On the nonverbal level, communication skills are also more difficult to use appropriately. Nonverbal communication is culturally defined, and an understanding of the nonverbals in a given culture requires extensive experience in that culture. We tend, however, to forget that. We often think others mean the same in their use of nonverbal communication as do we. They do not. Other cultures use time, space, body and eye gestures, clothes, and other artifacts quite differently from the way we do. We must remember the differences. We must use verbal feedback to check our interpretations of nonverbals and must rely more on verbal channels. Above all, we must reduce our tendency to negatively evaluate that which is different from our own culture.

Male-Female Communication at Work

The new workforce in the United States includes women in numbers that nearly equal men. More important, the increased numbers of women are outside traditional female jobs. Women are now succeeding in traditionally male occupations. No longer are female managers and executives rare. The number of women in law school nearly equals that of men; women constitute over one half the students in business schools. Though few women are found in some of the sciences, engineering, and top management positions, the workforce is no longer male dominated. Communication within organizations is changing as a result.

Certainly, many traditional feminine communication patterns will change as well. To meet the demands of a competitive market-based economic system, women in most work situations can no longer be submissive, passive, or always gentle. The organizations must change as well. The newly discovered value of androgynous management stresses the need for managers who listen and support their employees. Businesses in a service-based economic sector need workers who relate well to customers. These and many other jobs now need traditionally feminine communication skills: behavior that is cooperative, supportive, and nurturant. Men are learning these skills as organizations adapt to their new workforce.

Both men and women will need to learn communication patterns that are free of previously held stereotypes. Appropriate behavior in the workplace is neither exclusively masculine nor exclusively feminine. Good management today involves some of both the traditionally masculine and the traditionally feminine behaviors. This creates a new work environment for both men and women. Men must learn to adapt to women in places where the culture previously taught that women did not belong. Women must learn to adapt to the demands of an environment where many people still believe, at least on an emotional level, that women do not belong. To accomplish these goals, both men and women must abandon stereotypes and stereotypical behavior. Both men and women must learn to apply to individuals and situations the communication principles taught throughout this book, whether they are dealing with men or women.

INTERVIEWS

Interviews serve many purposes in the new workforce. This section examines a few of the typical uses of interviews: the employment interview, the information interview, and the evaluation interview. By the time most people enter college today, they have already experienced one or more employment interviews. These interviews usually serve the purpose of assessing the qualifications of the person interviewed and providing an opportunity for the person to learn more about the organization. A few basic guidelines may be helpful to achieve the maximum benefit from the employment interview.

The Employment Interview

Getting a job is something most of us don't do very often, but it is terribly important when we do. And to get good jobs in the new workforce we need to use the communication principles discussed through the early chapters of this book. Whether you are an interviewer or interviewee, you need to accurately interpret information received, use verbal and nonverbal messages so receivers interpret you as you intend, build trust, avoid defensiveness, and effectively use feedback and listening skills.

Additional suggestions helpful for an employment interview will be covered in this chapter. If you have already gotten a few jobs, you have used some of these suggestions. But even if you already are familiar with these ideas, a review can be beneficial; you may decide to look for a better or a different job at some point.

Interviews require effective communication.

Apply in Person   When you can, make an appointment and apply for a job in person. You can learn about available positions and the job requirements, as well as learn something about the organization. By seeing the setting and layout, by talking to people who work there, you can learn much about the organization to help in the interview. If you cannot apply in person, the next best alternative is to use the telephone to gather more information. Learn who might do the interviewing, and ask questions about the job opening, its requirements, and so on. Whether you telephone or apply in person, a letter confirming the conversation helps you be sure the arrangements are firm.

Letter of Application   Sometimes you can neither phone nor go to the company or institution. Then you must write for a job interview. When you must do so, the letter is critically important. It will be only one of many an employer receives, so you must try to increase the chances it will be read and responded to favorably. To be noticed, originality is imporant, but don't be "cute." Your authors have received such letters, and they rarely present candidates with a favorable image.

Your letter must be personal. Never send form letters. The resumé that accompanies a letter may be printed, but the letter must not be. If possible, direct the letter to a specific individual, and check carefully that you use the proper title. Women who receive letters addressed as "Dear Sir" will be unlikely to view your letter favorably. *Your letter must be free of error.* Proofread it carefully to make all necessary corrections. Have others double check it. Just one mistyped word can make the difference in whether you even get a chance for an interview or not.

The resumé you send is important as well. Most colleges provide assistance in preparing employment letters and resumés through a job placement office. Use this service. Well-prepared application materials can permit you opportunities that ineffective ones can prevent. These materials, especially the letter, probably will be your first contact with the people who might hire you. They are often the first item in the file studied by all who participate in the hiring. More than most other initial interactions between two people, the first impression made by your letter may be lasting; indeed, it may be the last.

Preparing Questions and Answers   Interviewers will want to learn how you feel about your career and the potential job. They will probe for your attitude toward the organization, its products, and services. They will be trying to assess how your personality and character might fit into the job or situation. In the new workforce, they will assess your communication skills to determine your potential ability to contribute to the goals of the organization.

Think about questions in advance. You can't write out answers to prompt you during the interview, but you can prepare to answer questions completely and confidently. Some of the following are sure to be asked. Decide how you would answer them and others. Have a friend role-play the interview to help you prepare for it.

Questions You May Be Asked in an Interview

1. Why do you believe you are qualified for this position?
2. How have your previous jobs or experiences prepared you for this situation?
3. What are your attitudes toward this organization? Its product? Its policies? Its public image?
4. Do you see this position as long-term?
5. What are your career goals? (Commonly asked as, What do you see yourself doing in ten years?)
6. How do you feel about punctuality? Absenteeism?

Too often applicants think of interviews as a time when only employers ask questions. Not so. Interviewers usually expect applicants to ask questions. Some of the following questions may be useful when seeking to learn more about the position and the organization.

Questions You May Want to Ask in an Interview

1. What is the potential for advancement for this position?
2. Does the organization usually promote from within its own ranks?

3. What is the organizational climate and morale?
4. What are the long- and short-term goals of the organization?
5. How is job performance evaluated?
6. What are the most important aspects of this position?

Questions of this kind show that you have thought about the position and organization and that you are interested enough to want to know more than wages, hours, and pension plan. The questions you ask employers show your interests, your intentions, and the seriousness with which you have approached the interview.

The next sections include some information about types of questions, which is, of course, relevant to the discussion of interviews. Earlier sections on nonverbal communication and self-presentation are also relevant in knowing how to effectively interview for a job. Be sure to review those earlier chapters, especially Chapter 2, 3 and 4.

Information Interviews

In the new workforce, additional information is frequently required from other persons in order to complete specific tasks or on a broader level, to achieve career goals. Information interviews, either formal or informal, serve this purpose.

Planning the Interview In all kinds of interviews, planning is important. The person who initiates the interview should set a goal for the session and have a plan for achieving it. Interviews should be conducted with a definite structure, one planned with time constraints in mind. The people involved are busy and will not want their time wasted.

At the outset, the interviewer should make the purpose clear and, in a general way, what the procedure will be. This is an agenda, really, and as in any discussion, it should be followed as long and as closely as it is useful. As with all agendas, it should be changed when necessary. Finally, interviews should have an ending—a point at which the goal is achieved, or when it becomes clear that it cannot be reached. Who has follow-up responsibilities and what they are should also be clarified.

In short, interviewing compares to other forms of discussion. It has the elements of roles, norm and status relationships, organization, nonverbal communication, and interpersonal relationships. Whether you are questioner or respondent, you can apply most principles and skills of communication to interview situations.

Using Questions Interviews are primarily question-and-answer sessions. Since the answers depend on the questions asked, interviewers should think carefully about how to ask questions and what they should accomplish. Many questions are too long and imply how the interviewer thinks they should be answered. As you plan for an interview, make sure your questions accomplish what you want.

Types of Questions Questions in interviews fall into two categories: open-end and closed. An open-end question has no restrictions on the answer. It seeks a response, but the one responding must provide the structure for the answer. "How do you feel about the new policy?" and "What do you think about the new reorganization plan?" are examples of open-end questions. Closed questions are restrictive. They indicate specifically what type of answer is wanted. The most closed question asks only for a yes or no, as in "Will you do it?" Others ask for a less restrictive but still limited response, for example, "How often did you report under the old policy: daily, weekly, or semi-annually?" or "Is the new schedule acceptable, or do you think it should be changed?"

Combining questions is common. Suppose the person answered a closed question such as the above, "It should be changed." A follow-up such as "How?" or "In what ways?" is natural. Interviewers should plan the questions to include just such questions to follow up a variety of possible answers.

Purposes of Questions   More valuable than simply knowing the types of questions is knowing which to use for what purposes. Open-end questions ask a respondent to elaborate, to give more information. They also require respondents to assess the questioner's intentions. Before answering, respondents must decide: "What is that person getting at?" Then they must decide how to respond.

Before answering open-end questions, you should often probe to learn the sense of the question. If asked for opinions about a new company policy, for example, you might respond, "Do you want to know if I think it's workable? Or if I like the idea? Or do you want me to estimate its cost?" This is a good use of feedback before answering to try to clarify what the questioner wants. Also appropriate is trying to learn the intent of the questioner. One of the worst things in an interview is to waste time. And time is wasted if the answer differs from what a questioner wants. Finally, the answer to an open-end question should provide some structure in the response. Once you decide what the question means, your answer should be organized accordingly.

From a questioner's point of view, open-end questions are useful because they tell much about the attitudes and thought patterns of the person answering. Answers reveal point of view, feelings, and ability to structure thoughts.

The major disadvantages of open-end questions are that they result in subjective responses and are time-consuming. Respondents may fail to address the question and often ramble. Many people cannot structure their answers well. If that ability is what the questioner wants to assess, (as in a job interview) the time may be well used. Otherwise, much time may be wasted.

Evaluation Interviews

In the new workforce, evaluation interviews frequently include assessments of a person's communication skills as well as the specific task requirements of the job. Both parties often find these interviews distasteful. Too often they mean that the supervisor, usually much too late, sits down and tells subordinates what they are not doing right. Carried out effectively, an evaluation interview does far more. It gives the subordinate an opportunity to see how the supervisor perceives job perfor-

EXERCISE 9.1   EMPLOYMENT INTERVIEWS

OBJECTIVE   To become aware of the differences in roles, power, and use of communication in various interviewing situations.

DIRECTIONS
1. Construct interview questions that you would plan to use both as interviewer and interviewee in the following situations.
2. In class, you will be assigned in groups of two to role play the situations.
3. For a few minutes before each role-playing session, discuss with your classmate to agree upon the missing data in each situation: for example, the company, the specific job, the sex or ethnic background of both parties.
4. After each role-playing situation, discuss:
   a. What preconceptions regarding each role did each person bring to the situation?
   b. What communication skills could you use to improve the outcome?

Situation I: A white male personnel director is interviewing a prospective female fork-lift driver for a position in a plant that now has all men employees.

Situation II: An owner of a small business is discussing possible employment with a black college student. The business is a retailing establishment with several outlets in a metropolitan area.

Situation III: A sales manager is conducting an interview for a sales position with a high school dropout.

Situation IV: A young mother is interviewing a twenty-year-old male college student for employment as a babysitter for her four- and five-year-old children for five hours every morning during the summer.

Situation V: A female advertising supervisor is interviewing a newly graduated male advertising major for a job.

REVIEW   Write brief answers to the following questions that will provide the basis for a writing assignment or class discussion.
1. Describe the basic steps in preparing for an employment interview.
2. Explain the importance of nonverbal communication in interviewing.
3. State specific steps you can take to improve your ability in interview situations that are important for you.
4. Explain the most important communication principle you learned or found illustrated in this exercise and why you found it important.

mance, including strengths, weaknesses, and the future of the job. At the same time, it gives the supervisor an opportunity to learn how the subordinate sees these same things. The evaluation interview is often the best opportunity to find out what the supervisor expects.

An effective evaluation interview usually involves a written evaluation of the subordinate's work by the supervisor and a self-appraisal by the employee. Each then reviews the assessment of the other, and they discuss the two views. Discussion is focused on job-related factors. Performance, not personality, is the topic for effective evaluation interviews.

One useful way to direct this discussion is for supervisor and subordinate to agree upon some goals or objectives for a specific period of time. Then the two meet periodically (and regularly) to assess progress toward these goals. This is called *management by objectives*, and it provides an ideal way to combine evaluation with goal setting by the person being evaluated.

A major problem in the evaluation interview is that it tends to be conducted in a defensive climate. If the total climate of the organization or the relationship between the two individuals involved is open, permissive, and supportive, defensiveness can be reduced. This is why focusing on anything other than task-related factors is inappropriate. Discussing non-job issues such as personality can be confusing and can make both parties less objective. When personality factors are mentioned, the person being evaluated has the right to ask the supervisor how these factors relate to job performance. It is probably a good time to use open-end questions to determine the evaluator's real concerns in the situation.

Evaluation interviews frequently include comments about the employee's attitude. Sometimes the comments are direct and open, especially when they are positive. In many cases, however, the supervisor will not make direct comments about attitude, but will reveal a concern by other questions and comments.

Although attitude is difficult to assess, employers place a high value on a positive attitude that supports the goals of the organization. Employees are well advised to show a positive attitude at all times by cooperating in all efforts to achieve organizational goals. Supervisors interpret employees as having a positive attitude when they show individual initiative, do work exceptionally well, are thorough with all assignments, and attend to details.

EXERCISE 9.2   INTERVIEWS

OBJECTIVE   **To practice communication skills required for interviews in work settings other than entrance-employment interviews.**

DIRECTIONS   1. Construct interview questions and plans for the following situations. Plan as if you were both interviewer and interviewee in each situation.
2. In class, you will be assigned to groups to role play the various situations.
3. For a few minutes before each role-playing situation, decide with your classmate(s) about the missing specific data needed to complete the role play—age and sex of participants, location, and other necessary details.

Situation I: A plant manager conducting a problem-solving interview with a good engineer who is almost always late for work.

Situation II: A teacher discussing a motivation problem with an eighth-grade student and his or her parents.

Situation III: A concerned citizen arguing for stricter controls over public relations advertising by oil companies. The citizen is talking with a local television station manager.

Situation IV: A welfare caseworker discussing a housing problem with an elderly couple.

REVIEW **Write brief answers to the following questions that will provide the basis for a writing assignment or class discussion.**
1. What types of interviews, other than employment interviews, are likely to be important to you?
2. What specific information and skills will you need to succeed in those situations?
3. Explain the most important communication principle you learned or found illustrated in this exercise and why you found it important.

Note: When presenting a written assignment, attach the interview questions and plans you prepared.

UNDERSTANDING THE ORGANIZATION

In the new workforce, the communication network within an organization may determine its continued survival and success. Communicating within organizations involves most of the principles and skills discussed throughout this book. In addition, communicating within organizations involves some specific factors not found in other situations. In this section, we focus on some of those factors.

As a beginning, it helps to understand the nature of the organization itself. We think of **organizations** as *complex systems that intentionally coordinate the actions of their members to accomplish specific purposes.* What does this concept suggest? First is the interrelatedness of the organization. Not only do the parts fit together to form the whole, they directly affect each other. Each part has a function intended to help the organization reach its goals.

Effects of Organizational Structure

The structure of an organization influences how communication functions. Every worker in an organization functions within its structure and channels. By understanding the overall organization, you will be in a better position to effectively advance your career.

Organizations usually try to accomplish their goals by dividing tasks and functions through a structure of authority and responsibility. The structure aims to coordinate members' behaviors toward achieving organization goals. Organizational and individual goals often differ, and the differences commonly create communication problems. If the organization is to continue to exist, however, members must work toward the system's goals. The formal organization coordinates individuals' behaviors with the system's goals; the informal organization manages interpersonal relationships.

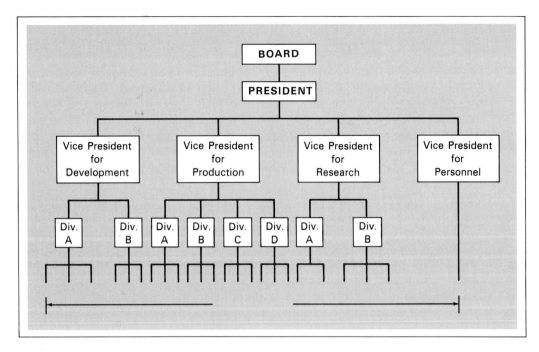

FIGURE 9–1. Organizational chart.

The Formal Organization   The formal organization is a structure for accomplishing organizational goals. That means authority and responsibility relationships form a hierarchy. At the top are those who have ultimate responsibility for managing the organization. From there levels of subordination range to the level where workers have no authority over anyone else and responsibility only for their specific tasks. This formal structure is often shown in an organizational chart like the one in Figure 9–1, and organization policy delineates rules and responsibilies for each level.

Organizations are usually made up of numerous smaller groups that are interrelated and interdependent. Production cannot accomplish a task without the aid of engineering, and both depend on purchasing and sales. The need for coordination among the subsystems creates a special need for effective communication to accomplish organization goals.

The Informal Organization   The informal organization, which frequently overlaps the formal, does not clearly follow the official structure and chain of authority. We define the **informal organization** as *a network of interpersonal relationships within the organization but outside the official structure.* Communication in the informal organization forms the background for many actions and decisions taken by the formal organization.

Social and interpersonal interactions among individuals create the informal organization, which has a great deal of power. Communication in the informal organization frequently contributes to official company actions. A conversation on the tennis court or at a cocktail party may result in important decisions at a later date. The informal organization may also expand a person's power beyond his or her position in the formal organization. For example, suppose a company has two vice-presidents. The president and the vice-presidents have a regular Wednesday afternoon golf game that includes department head Jones. Jones, one of the six department heads, will have more power than other department heads. Jones has access to information and interpersonal relationships that the others do not have.

Anyone trying to rise in the formal organization must understand the informal organization. Violating its rules can cost you your job; using it can mean advancement.

Communication Channels

Organizational communication occurs in both the formal and the informal organization structures. *The formal channels are the legitimate interoffice, interdepartment, intraoffice, intradepartment, level-to-level communication systems.* There are prescribed ways to send and receive messages within formal channels. For instance, rarely can everyone pick up the phone and call the president directly. Instead, assistants and secretaries act as **gatekeepers**.[3] They screen messages that get to and from the top.

Official communication normally flows through the formal channels. Jumping channels or using the wrong channels will frequently cause problems when dealing with official communication. The informal channels are usually more flexible, but they require the interpersonal relationships that facilitate communication outside the formal channels. In many organizations, a few employees appear to have more access than others to informal channels. All of the factors of interpersonal relationships influence the informal communication channels in an organization. To increase your opportunities to participate effectively in informal channels, your skills of developing interpersonal relationships are critical. It is also important to be perceived as having a positive attitude that supports the goals of the organization. Organizations rely on their top performers and frequently open informal channels to them because company officials regard such people as able to contribute to the goals of the organization.

Vertical Channels Vertical communication channels are important in the formal organization structure. Messages move both upward and downward along vertical channels.

Downward communication moves messages that originate higher in the organization to lower levels. Examples are messages from board to president, vice-president to department head, supervisor to laborer, or spanning the structure, from president to workers. Downward communication usually serves specific functions:

---

[3] *Gatekeeper* is the term used to describe a person who has the power to control and regulate the flow of information through a channel of communication.

1. To give instructions or orders
2. To give rationales for jobs or relationships within the organization
3. To give information about procedures and practices
4. To give feedback on job performance
5. To provide explanations of organizational goals

Downward communication is usually not directly from the top to the bottom of an organization unless in writing. Oral messages usually pass down the chain of command before reaching their final destination.

Upward communication moves from lower levels up along the chain of command. In the formal channels, upward communication, whether written or oral, does not usually cross more than one level. Only rarely does a laborer write or speak directly to a president or vice-president. Violation of the one level to another "rule" at work may be taken as "going around" one's supervisor.

Horizontal and Diagonal Channels   *Horizontal communication channels are direct communications among peers* or between members of departments with equal status in the organization. Horizontal channels provide relationships among people necessary for the total system to function. They enable the right hand to know what the left hand is doing. They must be kept open for the organization to reach its goals.

In diagonal channels, communication crosses departments and levels. For example, a clerk in engineering may call the head of purchasing to find out what is holding up a late order, instead of first going to the engineering department head. Diagonal channels that cross more than one level tend to be informal. The official chain of command usually doesn't provide for diagonal communication to cross more than one level. In contrast, the informal structure often has diagonal channels that follow networks from top to bottom.

Informal communication channels function for individuals and for the organization. *The informal channels reflect and create opinion leadership that does not appear on the organizational chart.* In some departments, the most influential person is not the department head; in some work units, the real supervisor is not the one with the title at all, but a worker of special strength, expertise, or influence. The climate of some groups is controlled by a leader who has low formal status, but without whose approval and cooperation the unit cannot be successful.

In some organizations important rituals exist. If you are going to operate effectively in these situations, you need to be aware of these rituals. You may need to participate in some that are very important. You need to learn which can be ignored with no penalty, which with some penalty, and which you cannot ignore if you want to stay or advance in the organization.

Assertive Communication

Another problem for many people in their work is the need for assertive communication. Most of us occasionally (or even frequently) allow someone to take advantage of us. Two popular books illustrate the problem in their titles: *When I Say No, I*

Feel Guilty and *Don't Say Yes When You Want To Say No.*[4] Assertiveness is useful in all aspects of our lives, but it is essential in work situations. This is particularly true where you have unequal status relationships, whether they are unequal in the formal hierarchy or in the informal organization.

To be **assertive** means that regardless of the difference in status levels between you and others, *you are aware of the basic rights that parallel your responsibilities and are willing and able to assert these rights.* You will be listened to, and probably respected, if you assert yourself. People who need help in communicating assertively need to work on two factors: attitudes and behavior. The two interact. If you hold certain attitudes, assertive communication is simple. But if you need to *learn* to communicate assertively, you must first become aware of the need for new attitudes. Previous attitudes have led you to behave nonassertively. So we begin by discussing attitudes; then we introduce communication patterns that can change your behavior.

Rights to Be Assertive[5]   Part of building constructive attitudes is being aware that you have certain rights.

RIGHT 1   *You have the right to judge your own behavior, thoughts, and emotions and to take the responsibility for them and their consequences.* This right is based on a point of view expressed throughout this book: Each of us makes the choices that govern our lives. This includes taking responsibility for the consequences of the choices. Sometimes it is a subconscious or even a conscious effort to avoid the consequences of our behavior that leads us not to communicate assertively. Sometimes we don't want to be responsible for our own behaviors. We find it easier to allow someone else to judge or decide, and thus we avoid responsibility for the consequences of our own behavior.

RIGHT 2   *You have the right to stay out of other people's affairs.* Other people will often attempt to manipulate you into feeling responsible for them or their problems. Because many people prefer not to bear the responsibility for their own behavior, they will attempt to find someone else to solve their problems or tell them what to do. The other person then bears responsibility for the wrong choices. You have the right to let others be responsible for their own behavior, without guilt. You have no responsibility to solve problems or to make choices for other people.

RIGHT 3   *You have a right to offer no excuses to justify your behavior.* You can behave as you wish because you want to, and that is a good enough reason. You do not have to justify your behavior to anybody unless you *choose* to do so. Again, this right emphasizes the element of choice. We are all free to choose how to live our own lives.

[4] Manuel J. Smith, *When I Say No, I Feel Guilty* (New York: Dial Press, 1975); and Herbert Fensterheim and Jean Baer, *Don't Say Yes When You Want To Say No* (New York: Dell, 1975).

[5] The material presented here is drawn from Manuel J. Smith, *When I Say No I Feel Guilty.* Copyright © 1975 by Manuel J. Smith. Reprinted by permission of Doubleday, a Division of Bantam, Doubleday, Dell Publishing Group, Inc. This excellent guide to assertive communication contains many illustrations and examples of how to apply these skills.

RIGHT 4   *You have the right to change your mind.* When you make a choice, you may later decide it was the wrong one. Therefore, you have the right to decide you want to do something different, again with no apologies or guilt. We are all human; we all make mistakes. We don't have to make excuses for being human. You are free to take back what you said or undo what you did before. You have the right to change your mind.

RIGHT 5   *You have the right to say, "I don't know."* You don't need to feel guilty for not knowing something. No one has answers for everything. So you don't have to feel guilty if you have no solutions. You neither have to understand nor be able to explain everything.

Acceptance of Self   All the assertive rights grow from the fundamental conclusion that a person is not responsible *to* other people. We are responsible for ourselves to ourselves. Assertiveness also requires recognizing that feelings, whatever they are, are respectable. This communicates acceptance, both of ourselves and others. To behave assertively, you should never feel guilty about the way you feel. You need to accept yourself and your own behavior as legitimate, just as you need to accept the behavior of others. You need to say, "At the moment, this is the way I feel; I may change; I may not feel this way tomorrow, but right now at this moment, I feel this way and I accept it as legitimate." When we are able to accept ourselves and our feelings as legitimate, then we can relate these feelings to other people without guilt.

Assertive Behaviors   So far we have dealt with attitudes. They are the foundation of assertive communication. But because attitudes are only predispositions to behavior, communicating assertively involves more. If you need to *learn* to be assertive, you don't really feel these attitudes even if you intellectually agree with the rights. By that we mean you may believe the rights but still feel guilty about behaving assertively. What you need to do is to begin communicating assertively. From your behavior you will eventually internalize the attitudes; they will become predispositions and you will feel good about your behavior.

PERSISTENCE   Persistence is the first assertive communication skill. Once you have decided your rights have been violated, you must be persistent in getting your rights back. When you resist attempts to manipulate you, the person trying to control you will not give up easily, particularly if your relationship has any history. In the past you have probably done as the person wanted even though you resented it. Or you did not do it and felt guilty. When you refused, your guilt may have been used against you the next time that person tried to manipulate you. So you must learn to resist the manipulation without feeling guilty. That requires persistence. You need to learn to say "no," to say it quietly, calmly, and to continue saying "no," if necessary, over and over and over again. The repetition must not become angry, irritated, or loud. Dr. Smith describes this as the *Broken Record.* Learn to speak as if you were a broken record. Stick to the point.

When, on the other hand, you are the one requesting something of another, it is a matter of learning to say, "I want so-and-so." You must learn to say, "I must have so-and-so. This situation must be corrected," consistently, calmly, and firmly. Broken Record repetition does not increase emotional intensity. This is a very difficult communication skill. Learn it, and you're on the way to being an assertive communicator.

COMPROMISE   Dr. Smith describes the second skill of assertive communication as the *Workable Compromise.* In a situation in which you have been using the Broken Record skill, you will reach a point when the other person recognizes that you will not be manipulated. And you may learn that achieving your goal totally is not possible or reasonable. Then you and the other person must reach a compromise.

The Workable Compromise is a middle ground that will make the situation acceptable for both of you. When no amount of persistence will achieve your goal, you must work out, calmly and without emotion, a reasonable middle ground.

FEEDBACK   The third skill of communicating assertively involves using feedback. From one point of view, communicating assertively is simply a matter of communicating to another person who you are, what you want, and what you expect. A similar skill is getting that kind of information from the other person. If it is not freely given, use feedback to seek it. Empathic listening can help you understand the other person and what is being said. You need to listen totally, to recognize volunteered verbal and nonverbal messages. Then you use feedback to seek information not volunteered.

APPROPRIATE SELF-DISCLOSURE   When seeking information from others, the best way to get it is to be willing to disclose information about yourself. Thus, assertive communication involves the skill of appropriate self-disclosure (see Chapter 7). It requires telling people how you feel, how you react, what things are happening to you as you communicate with them.

What you really say to someone when you communicate assertively is, "No, you cannot manipulate me. I will not do that, and I will not feel guilty." To do that you must share your feelings about the situation and your perspective. You need the skill of talking about feelings and being able to describe the world as you see it without evaluating others. In seeking information from others, don't judge their behavior. Simply focus descriptively on the external situation and internally on your feelings.

FOGGING   Much nonassertive communication occurs in response to criticism by others. When responding to evaluations by others, whether those judgments are fair or not, we often become defensive or we do what others want us to do. *Fogging* is a more effective response. Simply agree in principle. Don't deny the criticism, just agree with whatever truth there is in the statement. This is fogging. You don't have to agree with the whole criticism, but refusing to deny it can deflect the criticism. Dr. Smith gives as an example a parent criticizing a teenager: "You stayed out late again. I tried to call you until after midnight." The teenager could respond: "Yes, I was out late last night." Thus, the youngster accepted no guilt, nor did she bother to dignify any implication of guilt with a denial. She simply agreed with whatever truth there was in the accusation. If you can find no truth to agree with, you can agree with the principle. For instance, the parent might say to the daughter: "Well if you stay out so late, you'll get sick again." The daughter does not have to deny or agree. She can agree only in principle: "Yes, that could happen—that is possible." Of course, anything is possible. So the criticism is blunted.

Dr. Smith describes this technique as fogging because the response is similar to a fog. A fog bank is very assertive. It is very persistent; you can't get rid of it, and you can't do anything about it. At the same time, it is not defensive or aggressive. It offers no resistance. It gets out of the way but doesn't go away. That's the same as the technique of agreeing with whatever truth is in a statement or with the principle. You don't argue, but you don't give in, either.

This will not always end the criticism. But if you respond without being defensive, without fighting back, at least the situation will not intensify. Eventually the critic will learn that nothing is to be gained by criticism because you refuse to feel guilt or behave defensively. Possibly, the critic might get angry because you do not respond. But if you maintain your calm, persistent refusal to react, that anger need not manipulate you either. You are not creating the argument. *The main value of fogging is that you cope with criticism and respond to it without becoming emotionally involved and anxious.*

NEGATIVE ASSERTION   The skill of negative assertion relates to Right 4, that all of us have the right to make mistakes. Negative assertion is saying, "Yes, I made a mistake" without loading the mistake with great guilt. The skill is to be able to recognize whatever truth exists in the evaluation and to accept your own behavior. If you believe in Right 4, negative assertion is easy. Having recognized that we erred, we can say: "Yes, that was a mistake," "Yes, I did a dumb thing," "Yes, it does appear to have been poor judgment." Without anxiety, without guilt, simply recognize the fact. This is a most effective way to blunt evaluative manipulation. When you say, "Yes, I made an error," it is very difficult for someone to keep criticizing.

NEGATIVE INQUIRY   The skill of negative inquiry requires using feedback. This is the ability to turn the question around when you are criticized. Seek to find out what, from the critic's point of view, is the problem. With this skill of assertive communication you learn to improve your personal relationships. If you care about those criticizing you, you care that they do not like something you have done. Instead of just feeling guilty and being manipulated, find out more about it. Use the skill of inquiry to discover what is *causing* the criticism.

In the case of the parent criticizing the teenage daughter for staying out late, the teenager could respond: "Yes, I was late last night. What is it about my being late that bothers you?" The negative inquiry uses feedback to find out what is bothering the manipulator. Negative inquiry makes evaluators focus on their own feelings. If the parent responds, "Well, I'm afraid you might be doing things you shouldn't be doing," then the teenager can answer: "What things are you afraid I might be doing? And why in being late am I any more likely to do them?"

If questions in negative inquiry are calm, without emotion, this approach can gain information for you that you couldn't get with a defensive response. Negative inquiry has two values. First, you find out more about how the critic feels. Second, by asking questions about the evaluation, you force people to evaluate their own judgments. Perhaps the judgment really is not rational or sensible. In being forced to examine feelings, a critic might decide: "I was wrong," or "That really wasn't important to me."

Be Assertive, Not Aggressive Learning to behave assertively involves both rights and responsibilities. When you begin to communicate assertively, you accept responsibility for your own life and do not feel guilty about refusing to let others manipulate you. Similarly, assertive communicators recognize others have the same rights. We do not have responsibilities for others' lives or the right to control them. If we behave assertively and not manipulatively, we can gain our own rights, allow others theirs, and develop closer personal relationships.

This key attitude is how assertiveness differs from aggressiveness. If you are aggressive, you are not simply trying to protect yourself and your right to make your own decisions about your life. Aggressive behavior is manipulative behavior. It goes beyond asserting what you believe to be right for you. It involves imposing what you want on someone else. When you behave assertively, you are likely to be described by someone else as aggressive—but don't let that threaten you. It is not a simple distinction, but ultimately it is a fairly clear distinction.

When you attempt to control or manipulate somebody else or when you attempt to suggest what choices other people should make, then you are not *communicating assertively.* You are behaving manipulatively, and the strength with which you attempt to control others might mean you are being aggressive. The difference is that the person who behaves assertively says: "I am responsible for me and you are responsible for you. If the two of us choose to be close to each other, we may choose to change our behavior in ways that are acceptable to each other. But we emphasize the choice, and we deemphasize the manipulation." Whenever you are in contact with others, you affect each other. When human beings communicate, they cannot help influencing each other. The difference between being *affected* by people around you and being *controlled* by them is the important difference communicating assertively can make.

EXERCISE 9.3   TYPES OF QUESTIONS

OBJECTIVE   **To practice phrasing closed and open-end questions.**

DIRECTIONS   1. Choose two of the situations in Exercise 9.2.
2. For each situation, phrase three open-end questions and three closed questions.
3. For each question, specify purpose. What do you hope to learn by the question, and why did you choose an open or a closed question?

4. In class, in groups, you will be asked to compare your questions and discuss the following questions:
   a. How could each question be improved?
   b. Considering the purpose for which it was intended, was it appropriately phrased as either open or closed?

REVIEW

1. What are the differences between closed and open-end questions?
2. When is it appropriate to use open-end questions?
3. Explain the most important communication principle you learned or found illustrated by this exercise and why you found it important.

SUMMARY

Communicating at work now means working and establishing appropriate relationships in a new workforce, one that places an increasing value on applying the principles stressed throughout this book. Knowing how to communicate effectively in the new workforce involves knowing how to use feedback to ensure that directions are understood, whether you are giving or receiving those directions. It also requires the skills of knowing (1) when and how to clarify your responsibilities at work; (2) how to appropriately prepare and deliver reports, whether short and informal or long and formal, which in turn requires that you know how to properly phrase questions and listen for answers; and (3) establishing appropriate career goals through self-awareness, study of models, and acquaintance with mentors.

The modern workforce is increasingly multicultural, requiring skill at intercultural communication. Effective intercultural communication requires approaching situations with the expectation that the other communicator uses verbal and nonverbal symbols differently from how you do and has different values, and you accept those differences. Especially for United States workers there is a need to guard against excessive ethnocentricism, which is the sense that our own culture is superior to others.

Another difference in the new workforce is the necessity for men and women to learn how to relate to each other in nonstereotypical ways that are appropriate to work roles.

An important situation at work in which communication must be used effectively is the interview, especially the employment interview. Most people get a job through an interview. Securing an interview can be done by applying for a position in person, calling, or writing. Preparing for the interview is perhaps the most important step. If possible, learn whether it is to be a screening or hiring interview, how long it will last, and the role of the person doing the interviewing. Preparing for the interview also involves learning about the organization, learning what appropriate dress will be, determining what questions you will want to ask during the interview, and giving thought to questions you may expect to be asked.

Examine the setting of the interview both before and during the session. Be sure you know or are prepared to find out the expectations the interviewer has of you, and assess your own expectations of the interview and the job. You can ask questions; influence the physical arrangements; and determine which questions you will answer, which need more clarification before answering, and which you will refuse to answer. During the interview, pay attention to nonverbal and interpersonal communication. Use feedback, eye contact, personal space, body action, and voice to give the best impression. A proper balance between confidence and respectfulness will help you achieve your goals.

An organization is defined as a complex system that intentionally coordinates the behaviors of its members to meet certain goals. Most organizations are systems of groups that interrelate to accomplish the goals. These interrelations result from a division of labor. A hierarchy of authority and responsibility coordinates the various tasks and functions.

The hierarchy reflects the formal organization. The informal organization results from interpersonal relationships among the members of the organization. Sometimes it parallels the formal organization, but often it does not. Communication channels follow both the formal and informal organization structures.

Communication along the formal channels is vertical (often called serial), horizontal, and diagonal. Much distortion occurs in vertical communication, both in upward and downward flow of information. Vertical communication is so important to the organization's survival that all organization employees at all levels need to work for accuracy. The primary burden for effective vertical communication lies with those in the higher levels of each transaction.

A final necessity for effective communication at work is knowing how to communicate assertively. To be assertive means that regardless of the difference in status levels between you and other communicators, you are aware of your own basic rights and responsibilities and are willing and able to assert the rights and accept the responsibilities. Assertive rights include the right to judge your own behavior, to stay out of other people's affairs, to offer no excuses for your behavior, to change your mind and to say, "I don't know." Each assertive right grows from self-acceptance, the knowledge that you are not responsible *to* other people. Growing from the appropriate attitudes are assertive communication behaviors, which include persistence, workable (and appropriate) compromise, effective use of feedback, appropriate self-disclosure, fogging, negative assertion, and negative inquiry. Appropriate assertive communication also requires that you permit other communicators their own assertive rights as well, and avoid aggressive behavior, not attempting to control or restrict the communicative choices of others.

QUESTIONS FOR DISCUSSION

1. What steps can you take to prepare for an interview?
2. What behaviors can aid the interviewee during an interview?
3. What types of interviews are used in organizations besides the employment-entrance interview?
4. What are the communication channels within an organization, and how can you use this knowledge to your advantage?
5. How can you cope with problems of unclear job limits?
6. What are some of the major changes that require attention in the new workforce?
7. What behaviors would help you to communicate more assertively?

SUGGESTIONS FOR FURTHER READING

Adler, Ron. *Talking Straight: Assertion Without Aggression.* New York: Holt, Rinehart and Winston, 1978.

_____. *Confidence in Communication: A Guide to Assertive and Social Skills.* New York: Holt, Rinehart and Winston, 1977.

Babbitt, H. Randolph, et al. *Organizational Behavior: A Multidimensional View,* 2nd ed. Englewood Cliffs, N.J.: Prentice-Hall, 1975.

Barnard, Chester I. *The Functions of the Executive.* Cambridge, Mass.: Harvard University Press, 1968.

Bolles, Richard. *What Color Is Your Parachute? A Practical Manual for Job-Hunters.* Berkeley, Calif.: Ten Speed Press, 1981.

Evans, David R. and Margaret T. Hearn. *Essential Interviewing: A Programmed Approach to Effective Communication,* 2nd ed. Monterey, Calif.: Brooks/Cole Publishing Co., 1983.

Goldhaber, Gerald. *Organizational Communication,* 3rd ed. Dubuque: William C. Brown, 1983.

Haney, William. *Communication and Organizational Behavior: Text and Cases.* Homewood, Ill.: Irwin, 1967.

Huseman, Richard, Cal Logue, and Dwight Freshley. *Readings in Interpersonal Organizational Communication,* 3rd ed. Boston: Holbrook Press, 1977.

Kanter, Rosabeth M. *Men and Women of the Corporation.* New York: Basic Books, Inc., 1977.

Kanter, Rosabeth M., and Barry A. Stein. *A Tale of "O" On Being Different in an Organization.* New York: Harper & Row, 1980.

_____. *Life in Organizations Workplaces as People Experience Them.* New York: Basic Books, Inc., 1979.

Koehler, Jerry, Karl Anatol, and Ronald Applbaum. *Organizational Communication: Behavorial Perspectives,* 2nd ed. New York: Holt, Rinehart and Winston, 1981.

Likert, Rensis. *The Human Organization: Its Management and Value.* New York: McGraw-Hill, 1967.

McGregor, Douglas. *The Human Side of Enterprise.* New York: McGraw-Hill, 1960.

_____. *The Professional Manager,* eds. Caroline McGregor and Warren G. Bennis. New York: McGraw-Hill, 1967.

O'Connell, Sandra. *The Manager as Communicator.* New York: Harper & Row, 1979.

Ouchi, William. *Theory Z: How American Business Can Meet the Japanese Challenge.* Reading, Mass.: Addison-Wesley, 1981.

Peters, Thomas J., and Robert H. Waterman, Jr. *In Search of Excellence: Lessons from America's Best-Run Companies.* New York: Harper & Row, 1982.

Redding, Charles. *The Manager's Guide to Better Communication.* Glenview, Ill.: Scott Foresman, 1984.

Reinsch, Lamar, and Michael Stano. *Communication in Interviews.* Englewood Cliffs, N.J.: Prentice-Hall, 1982.

Sargent, Alice. *The Androgynous Manager.* New York: The American Management Association, 1983.

Scott, William E., and Larry L. Cummings. *Readings in Organizational Behavior and Human Performance.* Homewood, Ill.: Irwin, 1973.

Seiler, William E., Scott Baudhain, and L. David Schuelke. *Communication in Business and Professional Organizations.* Reading, Mass.: Addison-Wesley, 1982.

Stewart, Charles and William Cash. *Interviewing Principles and Practices,* 4th ed. Dubuque: William C. Brown, 1985.

Townsend, Robert. *Up the Organization.* New York: Fawcett, 1971.

10 Communicating in the Family

> "The family, the 'giant shock absorber' of society . . ."
> "a new family system is emerging to supplant the one that characterized the Second Wave past. This new family system will be a core institution . . . part of the act of social creation by which our generation is adapting to and constructing a new civilization."
>
> ALVIN TOFFLER, The Third Wave

GOAL

To be able to improve communication within your family

OBJECTIVES

The material in this chapter should help you to:
1. Give examples that show how unstated expectations can cause communication problems.
2. Identify stresses on family relationships caused by intimate living conditions.
3. Discover any unshared goals that are interfering with communication in your family.
4. Use unrestricted code phrasing to communicate with children to reduce their defensiveness.
5. Explain how the possessiveness we have toward members of our families can affect communication.
6. Use communication principles to help reduce communication barriers in your family.
7. Explain why communicating with the aged presents special problems.
8. Suggest two ways you can improve communication with aged members of your family.

The family is a special social structure. Whether yours is a traditional family or one quite different, it shares many characteristics with all other families. Families greatly differ from each other, but they also differ from other types of groups in significant ways. Family members usually share more common experiences than members of other groups. They share the same home, eat similar food (occasionally at the same time), see each other several times a day, and interact with each other on a fairly continuous basis over a number of years. Members of a family know each other in ways that members of other groups seldom do.

As a result, the family is the most familiar group communication situation for most of us. It is also our primary social group. As children, we learned to function within a social unit from our family. The basic patterns we use to relate to all people came from our family—whatever its composition might have been.

Families usually provide our most intimate and lasting interpersonal relationships. Therefore, effective family communication is important to us. Yet even those of us with good family relationships sometimes communicate in ways that hurt each other. All families occasionally have painful communication problems. In this chapter, we suggest principles useful for coping with such communication problems.

COMMON PROBLEMS IN FAMILY COMMUNICATION

Communication problems in families include many problems common to all interpersonal relationships. The long-term nature of most family relationships creates some special problems.

Unshared Roles and Norms

As in any social group, roles, rituals, status, and norms develop in families and affect communication. But because of the primacy and relative stability of a family compared to other groups, members often forget that these roles, statuses, norms, and rituals must constantly be adjusted as family members change.

Unstated Expectations As with any interpersonal relationship, problems may arise simply from assuming that all agree on unstated role expectations. These differences in expectations can be between adult partners or between parents and children. Sometimes the differences aren't noticed. Often people notice but do not discuss them. When differences exist, however, they will emerge eventually, usually at a time of strong emotion, too late for a calm and rational discussion of who expects whom to do what and why.

Newlyweds often assume agreement on unstated expectations. Partners approaching marriage rarely clarify agreements about role choices they will have to make. It feels unromantic to take time to ask: "What behavior changes will it mean to be married? What behaviors do I expect from my partner?" Men and women

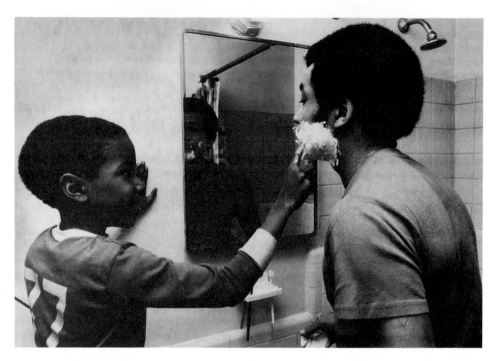

Effective family communication is important since families usually are the source of our most intimate and lasting relationships.

bring different perspectives into the marriage relationship about what their roles are. They have probably gained their perspectives from their parents, and those parents probably have quite different backgrounds. Even families from similar social groups develop the wife and husband roles quite differently. Some people never discuss the gender role expectations they learned as they learned the culture of their social group. To such people gender expectations represent how family life is "supposed" to be. They rarely consider that others might view roles differently. Even for people who hold more flexible views of gender role, family life regularly presents situations in which unstated expectations about sensitive matters create problems.

If newlyweds do not clarify how they expect marriage to affect one another's behavior, the unstated expectations result in hurt feelings when they are not fulfilled. Communication can quickly become burdened with bad feelings. With each succeeding failure to meet unstated expectations, the emotional load piles up and contributes to growing misunderstandings. The following excerpt shows how easily this can happen.

THE TIES THAT BIND:
EIGHT DAYS IN THE MAKING OF THE CLOSED CONTRACT
Nena O'Neill and George O'Neill[1]

John and Sue, very much in love, have been married two weeks. Most of that time was spent on a honeymoon vacation in the Caribbean. Before their marriage, John kept house for himself in the same apartment in which they are now living as husband and wife. He works for an architectural firm, and Sue is going to continue with her secretarial job. Over the threshold they carry not only their vacation suitcases, but also the cumbersome (even though invisible) baggage of their respective pasts, weighted down by their personal experiences, their cultural conditioning and their idealistic expectations. Unconsciously, with only the desire to please one another and to express their love, this young couple begin to bind themselves to a closed marriage contract. They are happy, smiling and in love, for their pleasure in each other is new and fresh, but they are unknowingly painting themselves into corners and guaranteeing themselves future frustration and unhappiness. Let us see how it happens.

DAY 1: It is Sunday morning. Sue wanders sleepily into the kitchen and begins to make breakfast. John follows after bringing in the paper from the hallway. While Sue fries bacon and scrambles eggs, John sits at the kitchen table reading the paper. . . . It is, in one sense, a charming scene. But under the surface, binding assumptions are being made. (CLAUSE: The woman is the cook.) . . .

Later in the day the telephone rings.

"Darling," Sue whispers, "It's my mother. They want to come over and say hello. You know how much they want to hear about the trip. Is it all right?"

"Sure, honey," he answers obligingly. (CLAUSE: When you marry, you marry not only a husband or wife but an entire network of relationships and responsibilities.) John suddenly remembers that they had promised to get together with Linda and Bill, who first introduced them and are their closest friends. . . . Clearly on their first day back it is only to be expected that John will go along with the idea of inviting Sue's parents over. But having agreed this time, he will find it more difficult to say no next time. . . . Sue makes a further assumption, too. "Don't worry," she says, "I'll give Linda a call. We can see them during the week but Mom and Dad can only get free on weekends." (CLAUSE: It is the wife's role to make decisions concerning the couple's social activities. And this presumes the wife's right to decide how the husband's time is going to be spent.) . . .

DAY 2: Sue cooks breakfast, leaving the dishes in the sink, and they both rush off to work. At his office, John is confronted with a new project, as well as some leftover problems from an old one. The old problems involve personality differences and the blueprints for the new project are inaccurate; it's all very depressing. That evening, John arrives home before Sue and makes himself a drink. Sue comes staggering in with two huge bags of groceries. (CLAUSE: Shopping is the wife's job.) He helps her unpack them and then mixes a drink for her while she does the breakfast dishes and prepares dinner. (CLAUSE: Mixing

---

[1] Nena O'Neill and George O'Neill, *Open Marriage, A New Life Style for Couples*, pp. 56–66. Copyright © 1972 by Nena O'Neill and George O'Neill; © 1984 by Nena O'Neill. Reprinted by permission of the publisher, M. Evans & Co., Inc. Quoted with permission of Mary Yost Associates, Inc.

drinks is the husband's job, but the dishes, as well as meal preparation, are the wife's responsibility.) John is preoccupied with his problems at work, but he tries to pretend that everything is just fine. (CLAUSE: The husband must always be strong; if he has problems, he must never communicate them to his wife, because to do so might make him vulnerable.) They eat dinner, making small talk, mostly about Sue's job and when to see Linda and Bill. John, however, continues to be upset about his problem at work. Still, he refrains from saying anything. (CLAUSE: You must always live up to the ideal conception of your role as husband—or wife.) Anyway, he tells himself, Sue probably wouldn't understand what in hell he was talking about—she doesn't know anything about blueprints. (CLAUSE: Women's minds are different from men's—the male's is abstract, the female's intuitive.)

Even if it were true that Sue would not understand the nature of John's problem (although the assumption that she won't understand is a throwback to the Victorian view of women) that is not to say that she couldn't, one way or another, make John feel better. Just to talk about it might relieve some of his tension. By not talking about it, John instead is guaranteeing himself future tension; the underlying, hidden clauses in the psychological contract are binding him to a position of noncommunication with his wife. . . . Misunderstanding between a husband and wife becomes inevitable in this kind of situation. And it is all based upon an attempt to live up to the clauses of an unspoken, crippling psychological contract.

DAY 3: Sue calls John at his office to suggest dinner out with Linda and Bill that night. Although John had hoped for some time alone at home that evening to wrestle with some of his professional problems, he says, "Sure, darling," and they eat dinner out. (CLAUSE: Husband and wife must always see friends as a couple.) . . .

DAY 4: When John arrives home from work, Sue isn't here yet. She can't be shopping since the refrigerator is still stuffed with food from her Monday marketing. John likes to eat around 7:00, but by 6:15 Sue still isn't home. He's tired and hungry and he begins to get irritated. (CLAUSE: Cooking is the wife's job.) In spite of the fact that John made perfectly creditable meals as a bachelor, it never even occurs to him to start preparing the dinner himself. Now that he is married he thinks of the kitchen as Sue's territory and responsibility; he is completely bound by an antiquated concept of proper roles for husband and wife. Not only does he fail to bend with the situation, doing the sensible, practical thing and getting dinner started, he is sufficiently disturbed by Sue not being around to do what he sees as her job that he is unable even to sit down and concentrate on his job now that he finally has a few free minutes to give full attention to his blueprints.(CLAUSE: Husband and wife must surrender their selfhood, or identity, to the couple unit.) John is already so caught up in the myth of couplehood that he is losing his power to act independently.

A few minutes later, Sue breezes in happily. She's late because she ran into an old friend from college just as she left the office. "Harry Bigelow, I've told you about him. Anyway, we had a drink and I told *him* all about my marvelous husband." John smiles and gives Sue a hug, but at the back of his mind he is still a bit piqued (CLAUSE: Each partner in the marriage belongs only to the other and not anybody else.) This kind of possessiveness, since it is based on an unrealistic ideal (CLAUSE: I will be everything to you and you will be everything to me), leads to a basic lack of trust and to a sense of insecurity. Every couple knows, deep down, that they cannot be everything to each other, but since this admission is not made on a conscious level, it finds its way to the surface in terms of mistrust. John, for instance, cannot resist asking, "Did you have to have a *drink* with him?" Sue answers, "Oh, well, the bar was right next door, and he probably won't be in town again for ages."

This is fertile ground for further misunderstanding, though. John, preoccupied with his job problem, is more silent than usual during dinner. His quietness leads Sue to mistakenly assume that he is brooding about her drink with Harry. "You're not mad at me, are you?" she asks. And John, who had been about to ask if she'd mind if he did some work by himself for a while after supper, now feels he has to spend the evening watching television with her. If he said he wanted to be alone, she'd be hurt, and be convinced that he *was* mad at her. (CLAUSE: Togetherness is one of the most important things in marriage. You must always be willing to sacrifice your own needs on the altar of togetherness.)

DAY 5: Morning dawns. John is bleary-eyed from lack of sleep. He lay awake until 3 A.M., too tense to fall asleep. . . . He doesn't mention his insomnia, though, nor does he tell Sue that he really isn't hungry. He manages to get down the hot breakfast she cooks him, but it gives him heartburn all morning long. In fact, if he had only known it, the last thing Sue felt like doing was cooking breakfast. Each, in the name of love and at the expense of self, has done something he didn't want to do, and that it was unnecessary to do, simply because they were both being controlled by the unwritten clauses of the closed marriage contract. Each is responding according to what he *thinks* the other expects of him, instead of trying to find out what is actually expected.

During the day, Lenny, an old friend of John's, calls him to suggest a drink after work some evening, or maybe dinner on Saturday when Sue could join them. Much as he would like a little change of pace, and though he's very fond of Lenny, John refuses the drink for that evening, anyway, and says he'll see what Sue has planned for Saturday. (CLAUSE: The husband's time belongs to the wife, except when he is actually at work.) He has misgivings about Saturday because Sue has always been put off by Lenny's forthrightness and brash sense of humor. And, as he suspected, Sue turns the idea down. "I really don't enjoy Lenny much," and reminds him that the Millers, a couple down the hall, have invited them to drop in at their open house Saturday night. (CLAUSE: All friends of the married couple must be mutual friends.)

DAY 6: Friday, at last. Sue reminds John that she will be late getting home because she is having her hair done. And when John calls Lenny to say they won't be able to make Saturday night, Lenny suggests instead that John join him and his new girl for a drink after work. Since Sue will be late anyway, John agrees, but he feels guilty about it from the start. If Sue really doesn't want to see Lenny, then it's likely to seem kind of pushy of John to have a drink with him the next day—as though he were telling Sue off in a subtle way, which he doesn't want to do at all. If Sue really can't stand Lenny, then he'll just have to give up the friendship.

John has such a good time with Lenny and his girl, though, that it gets to be even later than he realized. He calls Sue to tell her why he's behind schedule. She's just been home a few minutes herself but was beginning to worry about him, she says. He stops at the florist to pick up a dozen roses, beginning the pattern of appeasement that develops inevitably in the closed marriage. It is not, of course, only to appease her that he buys the roses. He is newly married and very much in love. Nevertheless, there is an element of guilt involved—for not being at home when she got there and for seeing Lenny at all. . . .

DAY 7: In the morning, while Sue cleans house, John takes the laundry to the laundromat. Laundry is something he would usually consider one of the wife's jobs, but he is not actually going to sit there and watch it spin around in the machine—he will leave it with the attendant and pick it up later in the day, paying extra for the service of having it done for him. Besides, the laundry bag is heavy and awkward, and Sue would have a hard time carrying it. (CLAUSE: The husband must never do anything out of line with his image of himself as a "man.")

That evening, as they get ready for the Millers' party, Sue asks John what she should wear. "You look good in anything," he says. But when she appears in a slinky, spangled gown, looking very 1920s, he says, "My God, Sue, where are you going, to a costume ball?" (CLAUSE: Husband and wife are reflections of one another; neither is allowed, therefore, to wear clothes that don't suit the other's taste.) Although Sue actually looks terrific, and right in keeping with the tone of the party, John's words are enough—off comes the dress. Both John and Sue are demonstrating their lack of personal identity, or selfhood, here. Sue had the right instinct as to what she should wear, but showed her lack of confidence in herself by asking John's approval in the first place and changing when he disapproved. . . . And John, in making her change, is simply illustrating his lack of confidence in himself: if what his wife is wearing can so easily embarrass him, then his sense of himself as an individual is sadly deficient.

At the Millers' party, John and Sue spend most of the evening moving around as though they were chained to one another. (CLAUSE: Husband and wife exist primarily as a couple, and must always maintain the couple-front. Otherwise someone might think they were not married, or worse still, that they weren't getting along.) Nevertheless, they eventually get separated when Judy Miller asks Sue to give her a hand in the kitchen for a moment. When Sue gets back to the living room, she sees John sitting on the sofa talking intently to a woman she doesn't know, who apparently has only just dropped by. Sue rushes over to join them. (CLAUSE: Neither husband or wife is even allowed to show interest in a member of the opposite sex unless the mate is right there too.) When John introduces her, Sue is perfectly polite. But her physical action in charging over to join them has clearly indicated to the other woman that she is regarded as an intruder. Sue might just as well have said, "He's mine. Get away from him." And, indeed, the woman takes the hint and excuses herself after a moment or two. In fact it turns out that she is also an architect, and had worked before with the client who's been creating John's problems. She was giving John some helpful hints on how to handle the man, but Sue's instant jealousy has brought the conversation to an end. Sue's actions said to the other woman, "He's mine," and to John they say, just as clearly, "I don't trust you." Of course she doesn't trust John—how could she? She has been taught to believe fidelity consists of a rigid, mechanical rule: Never take an interest in any member of the opposite sex. Deep down, Sue knows, as all of us do, that this is a standard impossible for John to live up to. In respect to such a rigid view of fidelity, what mate could trust another? Sue would do better to question the rigidity of the rule.

DAY 8: It is Sunday again. And just as last Sunday, Sue's parents call and suggest coming over. "You don't mind, darling, do you?" Sue asks. John had been hoping they might go to a movie, but if he were to refuse to see her parents, she'd be hurt. "Fine," he says. And the pattern becomes more deeply implanted.

The hidden contract has been accepted by both.

Unstated role expectations often apply to small things (who makes the bed, carries out the trash, gets into the bathroom first, mows the lawn). As a result, differences of opinion about them may at first be ignored. Discussing them isn't worth the hassle. But little things build up when people live together. Ultimately, an explosion over some absurdly small thing will occur, and it won't be over a small thing at all. It will be over a long accumulation of small things.

Expectations of No Change in Conditions of Change   Role expectations that haven't been clarified become especially difficult when combined with an (also unstated) expectation that roles rarely change. In today's increasingly mobile and rapidly changing society, that expectation should be rare but is not. Gender roles, family roles, and work roles have been rapidly adjusting in the United States in recent years. Family relationships, whether new or of long duration, will be affected by these changes. Partners must expect and learn to prepare for adaptations to each other and the new environment.

The arrival of children illustrates this. Working out acceptable husband and wife (or partner) roles in a family, though not simple, presents a minor difficulty compared to what happens when major changes in the family situation occur. Any change requires adjusted roles, but perhaps the most significant ones come with children.

Even when parents plan and want children, partners often fail to prepare for them by clarifying their individual ideas of parental roles and responsibilities in advance. Seldom do people see eye-to-eye on all the issues and decisions that relate to raising children. Parents will generally have many disagreements, ranging from mild to quite serious, about what is the best or the most appropriate course of action in raising children.

Too often in the joy of anticipating a baby, couples spend their time discussing how to decorate the nursery instead of talking about roles. Too rarely do they ask: "What is a mother to do in this family? How is a father to behave?" These are matters of choice. And people can usually discuss these choices rationally and reach agreement when the partners start with love, trust, and the expectation of pleasing each other, *if* that discussion occurs before the choice is made. Once a child is on the way or has arrived, alternatives are severely limited. When differences of opinion occur then, it is more difficult to keep the discussion unemotional and to resolve differences without resentment.

Parents who have built a strong interpersonal relationship before the arrival of children still must work at constructing the new relationships that result from parenthood. The partner who was "wife" now has the role of *mother*; the "husband" now has the role of *father*. The new roles must be integrated into the old ones, as well as each person's self-concept. Their interaction habits must now adapt to the new roles.

The situation takes on different and more complex dimensions now that the families have changed so much. Today, most families include two parents who work outside the home, two people who plan *careers*, not just work to supplement

Parent-child communication needs to balance rights and responsibilities.

the family income. Under these circumstances, adding to home responsibilities burdens both parents. How do the parents' work careers adjust to the added career or parent? These are not easy questions. They are much more difficult if not answered before children are on the way.

Furthermore, the differences in families today make the romantic ideal with which most young people enter marriage far removed from the reality they encounter. In 1984, 26 percent of United States families were single parent households; the number is expected to top 30 percent by 1990. An undetermined but large percentage of two parent households consist of one biological parent and one step-parent, and the children spend varying amounts of time in two different households. These families struggle with three or four parent roles. This latter situation is increasingly common in our society. The term *serial polygamy* has been used to describe it.

Our society today consists of a wide variety of family situations different from the romantic ideal of intact nuclear family. Adjusting expectations from the "ideal" to the real requires regular, open and supportive communication.

Roles of Children Expectations create problems in parent-child relationships also. *Too often children don't know why particular behaviors are expected of them.* Even when they know why, they frequently don't share the expectations. This is especially true of status relationships in the family. Though family membership is largely involuntary for children, roles and status relationships are not. Any parent can testify how quickly children begin to show their individuality in handling the role of child. As children grow from infancy through the teenage years, the roles and relative status of children and parents continually change.

All roles and status relations—especially those of parents and growing children—should be considered as processes and not as unchanging concepts. The role of mother, for example, shifts in responsibilities as children grow. Other changes in the family situation also result. The role responsibilities and expectations of all members, both adults and children, must adapt constantly.

The role of parent might more accurately be described as *parenting*. The term *parenting* suggests that the parental role is *ongoing, developing, and changing*. People who engage in parenting are continually adjusting, or they should be. A continual negotiation process occurs as children mature. They quickly begin to work toward becoming full citizens of the family society. With full citizen status, children see, come rights they don't have. Very young children can quickly recognize their second- and even third- or fourth-class status within the household. One five-year-old put it this way: "I'm five, that's too little; I have to go to bed at eight o'clock; and everyone else gets to boss me." As children mature, they expect to increase their status.

Parents' continued refusal to accept changes in a growing child's status causes difficulties. Adolescents often demand full status in families and are denied it, partly because parents have not accepted changes as children grew toward that critical age. Strong hostilities between adolescents and parents can result from this one factor alone. When parents assume static roles and status, real troubles for the family lie ahead.

This analysis of status relationships also relates to rules established to govern family behavior, especially that of the children. These rules often become rituals: for example, waiting your turn in line, not telling lies, sharing with others, being polite to your elders, not stealing. Children are expected to accept family rituals without challenge even if they did not share in creating them.

Double Standards   Worse than simply expecting children to accept unchanging status, *parents often fail to see that a double standard exists in family rules and roles*. Children quickly notice that many of the rituals they are expected to follow do not always apply to their parents. They find this a hard system to adopt. Parents tell them, in behavior if not in words, "Do what I say, not what I do." Parents say to children, "Don't lie, it's wrong"—then they tell the tax assessor that they donated $300 during the year to a church. The children, listening, know the parents rarely go to church. Parents say to children, "Don't steal," then keep the $10 extra change a salesclerk has returned by mistake. A child may be punished for taking a candy bar off a store shelf by a parent who mails personal letters with company stamps.

Parents are often less aware of the double standard than are children. Children are told, "Don't interrupt adults" by parents who freely interrupt children. In a parent and child conversation, the parent may interrupt the child many times: "Don't talk with your mouth full"; "Say *aren't*, not *ain't*"; "Stand up straight"; "Look at me when you talk to me." But a child who interrupts the conversation of adults is likely to hear, "Don't interrupt when other people are talking." And if a child is talking to one parent, the other frequently feels free to interrupt that conversation. Parents often aren't even aware their behavior expresses a double standard, but this rule clearly says to the child: "Your rights of conversation are different from those of parents and other adults."

The double standard causes special difficulties as children grow and begin asking questions. A thirteen-year-old whose chain-smoking parents forbid her to smoke finds it hard to reconcile the behaviors. Parents who admonish a fifteen-year-old to stay away from drugs while they have martinis before dinner present that youngster with a status relationship difficult to accept without resentment.

Once a child is considered able to recognize verbal commands, parents impose a host of rules to govern behavior. As a second-class citizen, the child usually neither participates in adoption of the rules nor shares agreement regarding how important they are. Still, parents often assume that children have only one choice with respect to those rules: compliance. In reality, even very young children have other alternatives. By early adolescence, compliance for many is no longer an acceptable response. Adolescents, and sometimes much younger children, resort to other choices: They try to argue the parents into acceptance of different norms; or they deviate and deal with the resulting frustrated parents; they may even leave. The fact that thousands of youngsters run away from home monthly is evidence that many make choices other than compliance.

EXERCISE 10.1   FAMILY ROLES

OBJECTIVE	**To become aware of role expectations as they operate in your family.**
DIRECTIONS	1. Circle the roles you play in your family in a typical day: father, mother, son, daughter, sister, brother, husband, wife, aunt, uncle, niece, grandmother, grandfather, granddaughter, grandson, stepson, stepdaughter, stepmother, stepbrother, stepsister, stepfather, other _____. 2. Choose the role in which you spend the most time. 3. List the role positions you interact with when in that "most frequent" role. 4. For each person (role) interacted with, list the expectations that person has for your behavior in your role. List what you expect from him or her. 5. Show the list you compiled to the person. Ask her or him to confirm your perceptions of her or his expectations or to explain why your perceptions are inaccurate.
REVIEW	1. Why are unstated expectations a serious problem in family communication? 2. What are the primary causes of unstated role expectations? 3. What will I plan to do to reduce problems from unstated role expectations in my family? 4. Explain the most important communication principle learned or illustrated by this exercise and why you found it important.

ETIQUETTE LESSON[2]

Erma Bombeck

On TV, a child psychologist said parents should treat their children as they would treat their best friend—with courtesy, dignity and diplomacy. "I have never treated my children any other way," I told myself. But later that night, I thought about it. Suppose our good friends, Fred and Eleanor came to dinner and . . .

"Well, it's about time you two got here! What have you been doing? Dawdling? Shut the door, Fred. Were you born in a barn? So, Eleanor, how have you been? I've been meaning to have you over for ages. Fred! Take it easy on the chip dip or you'll ruin your dinner.

"Heard from any of the gang lately? Got a card from the Martins—they're in Lauderdale again. What's the matter, Fred? You're fidgeting. It's down the hall, first door on the left. And I don't want to see a towel in the middle of the floor when you're finished. So, how're your children? If everybody's hungry, we'll go in to dinner. You all wash up, and I'll dish up the food. Don't tell me your hands are clean, Eleanor. I saw you playing with the dog.

"Fred, you sit there, and Eleanor you sit with the half glass of milk. You know you're all elbows when it comes to milk. Fred, I don't see any cauliflower on your plate. You don't like cauliflower? Have you ever tried it? Well, try a spoonful. If you don't like it, I won't make you finish it, but if you don't try it, you can forget dessert. Now, what were we talking about. Oh, yes, the Grubers. They sold their house, and took a beating, but— Eleanor, don't talk with food in your mouth. And use your napkin . . ."

At that moment in my fantasy, my son walked into the room. "How nice of you to come," I said pleasantly.

"Now what did I do?" he sighed.

The Pressures of Intimacy

Most intimate, long-term relationships, whether in a family or not, satisfy basic human needs. The intimacy inherent in living with others adds richness to lives that might otherwise be lonely. At the same time, *the demands and pressures of living together create tremendous stresses on interpersonal relationships.* The way you handle the stresses in these longterm relationships will determine the satisfaction or frustration that develops over time. It may determine whether the relationships— and their benefits—endure.

Restricted Freedom Even as it prevents loneliness, living with someone restricts your freedom to behave at every moment just as you please. Others may determine the time you eat, bathe, sleep, or dress. Restrictions of dozens of small freedoms become a source of interpersonal stress. For instance, a breadwinner just home from a hard day at work and a nervewracking bout with commuter traffic may want nothing more than to collapse into an easy chair for a few quiet moments. But that may not be possible—responsibilities and demands from others in the household face that person immediately upon opening the door.

---

[2] Erma Bombeck, *At Wit's End.* Courtesy of Field Newspaper Syndicate, © 1974.

To show how restricted freedom can create pressures that cause communication problems, consider the following. Our breadwinner, entering the door, is immediately confronted:

Question: *Do You Know What Jackie Did Today?*

Answer 1: "No what?" (in a resigned, unenthusiastic tone of voice) [Verbally expresses the internal expectation that this is how a good parent/spouse behaves, but nonverbally says, "No . . . and I don't want to know." Communicates lack of concern in spite of verbal expression of interest.]

Answer 2: "I really couldn't care less at the moment." (irritated voice) [An honest response, if not tactful. Fails to report the reason for lack of interest, while nonverbally communicating anger. It's not clear whether anger is with the question, the questioner, Jackie, or the answer.]

Answer 3: "Of course not—I just got here." (sarcastic voice) [Responds to the verbal message, not the real question. Expresses anxiety and emotion—perhaps caused by the hard day and traffic, not the question—but does not make clear the source of the anger.]

Answer 4: "No, but let's talk about it later, O.K.? I'm really bushed." (voice contains traces of irritation) [Is an honest expression of feelings that shows concern for the other person, though still leaving open the possibility for misunderstanding. Receiver can infer many other reasons for not wanting to talk about Jackie's behavior.]

In any of these responses, the speaker may assume the receiver should understand all the messages. As we all know, that doesn't always happen.

Assuming Shared Experiences Equal Understanding Family communication problems arise from assuming that shared experience equals understanding. Family members believe shared memories create shared ideas. This is often true—family members usually do know what others in the family mean better than do strangers. But not always. Intended and perceived messages differ between family members just as they do between other communicators. In talking with strangers, however, people more often use feedback to check understandings. We rarely do this with members of the family. We assume members of our family should *know* what we mean and often become angry if they don't. How often have you heard, "Oh you know what I mean!" and been rewarded with irritation if you say, "Well, no, I really *don't.*" *In families, the assumption of shared meanings leads to much apparent agreement that is not real.*

Intimates in families, particularly married partners, often believe in the romantic fallacy, "If you love me you'll know what I mean." The folklore of romance leads lovers to believe that some sort of intuitive click of sensitivity links all intimates. They don't realize how much work it takes to communicate well even within families.

Intimate communication requires that partners make understandings clear just as in other settings. Yet often information is withheld from a family member in the name of tact or because of role expectations or game playing. One spouse or parent may not want to burden the other with problems, or for other reasons isn't completely open with the other. People often don't share information about sexual preferences, for instance. People assume their partners will know what they think or feel, and then are hurt when the other's behavior shows they don't. Once this information is exposed, as it usually is eventually, the shielded partner may then feel he or she wasn't trusted or that the other didn't care enough to share. Sometimes partners actually cause one another to withhold information without knowing it by a habit of reacting evaluatively. For these and many other reasons, partners often do not know what each other mean or want.

Emotional Baggage Grows   For people in intimate relationships, words, phrases, and communication situations gradually build up emotional loads. The human memory system then attaches this emotional "baggage" to succeeding communication situations. This can cause total misunderstandings and different intended and perceived messages in situations that would be simple between people with less intimate relationships.

For example, consider a question intended as a simple request for information, "What time will dinner be ready?" The emotional load of shared past experiences includes times when dinner was late and the cook felt guilty; other times when dinner was ready on time but the questioner was late and the meal was ruined; times when the questioner grew enraged and yelled at the cook when dinner was late; times when the meal was late because the cook had burned the biscuits or charred the steak beyond recognition. If any of these shared experiences occurred, the question is probably not perceived as a simple request for information. The emotional load affects both intended and perceived messages.

What emotional baggage might be developing between the tired breadwinner and partner previously mentioned? To almost any of the answers, the questioner could infer the following:

"She/he doesn't care about the kids and me."
"He/she is still angry from yesterday."
"She/he is never interested in anything except that job."
"What a grouch!"
"He/she doesn't understand how hard it is to stay here all day and cope with these kids. What an insensitive lout!"

These, of course, do not exhaust the list of possible responses. The problem of intimates is that such emotional loads usually continue to grow.

Differing Goals

Goals Not Shared   In many situations, problems stem not from unstated goals, but because members have different goals. At one time, family members worked together for survival and shared their social lives. Today, members of nuclear families seldom share work goals. Even though work is a major part of their lives, family members do not usually share work tasks. The commercial phrase, "The family that plays together stays together," recognizes this situation. Families no longer work together, so logically they feel they should share their leisure activities. But people do not automatically share interests just because they are a family. Some wives consider themselves widows to their husbands' hobby; husbands may be bored with social activities their wives enjoy. Children develop their own interests at an early age.

Often the only shared goals in nuclear families are establishing effective interpersonal relationships to satisfy personal needs for love and belonging. When a member of any group uses it primarily to satisfy personal needs, monumental stresses on the group result. This is as true in families as in any other group. When parents see children as their reason for living, or when couples believe intimacy will solve personal insecurity, problems follow. Self-centered interpersonal relationships cause major communication difficulties in groups of all kinds, including families.

ON MARRIAGE[3]

Then Almitra spoke again and said, And what of Marriage, master?
And he answered saying:
You were born together, and together you shall be forevermore.
. . . .
But let there be spaces in your togetherness,
And let the winds of the heavens dance between you.

Love one another, but make not a bond of love:
. . . .
Give your hearts, but not into each other's keeping.
For only the hand of Life can contain your hearts.
And stand together yet not too near together.
For the pillars of the temple stand apart,
And the oak tree and the cypress grow not in each other's shadow.

Antagonistic Goals   When family members have antagonistic goals, problems are more serious. As you recall from Chapter 8, when members of a group have *antagonistic goals*, they cannot both achieve what they wish. The circumstances of a family or changes in the environment can lead to conflicts among members' goals. Or, sometimes, the individuals themselves bring the antagonistic goals to the relationship. In either case, problems result.

DOMINANCE   One such serious problem in family communication emerges from struggles about dominance. In many relationships, one or more parties feels a need to be dominant; the other(s) naturally resists. We don't have space here to analyze where such needs originate. Perhaps biology is involved; doubtless cultural roles, especially those related to gender, are also involved.[4] But in any relationship where

---

[3] Reprinted from *The Prophet* (Pocket edition, pp 16, 17) by Kahlil Gibran, by permission of the publisher, Alfred A. Knopf, Inc. Copyright 1923 by Kahlil Gibran; renewal copyright 1951 by Administrators C. T. A. of Kahlil Gibran Estate and Mary G. Gibran.

[4] If you find this topic of particular interest, explore it further in sources cited at the end of this chapter.

one person seeks to dominate and others choose not to submit, the parties' goals conflict.

Dominance problems may stem from unstated expectations and can be solved without too much difficulty by clarifying differences. In other cases, clarification may not bring differing expectations closer together. Problems caused by dominance relationships vigorously resist solution.

POSSESSIVENESS   A related cause of antagonistic goals results from **possessiveness,** a common attitude in family relationships. Possessiveness stems from a belief that members have a right to control or influence the behaviors of each other. Many people interpret family as a situation in which they "own" another person's behavior. Think what it means to say, "That's mine." If something is mine, it belongs to me. Now think how commonly we hear (or say) "my" husband, "my" wife, "my" children. How many parents have said, "No child of *mine* is going to . . ."? These common phrases imply ownership or possession. This attitude of "you are mine," implies covertly, if not openly, an *expectation of control* over the other person.

In communicating with one another, family members often forget their relationships are matters of choice. At the beginning, married partners recognize they are choosing each other. But once the choice is made, they frequently behave as if they have a right to control the other's behavior and to limit the other's freedom. Commonly we think, "My wife shouldn't dress that way"; "My husband shouldn't behave that way"; "My husband/wife shouldn't _____." You can fill in the blank easily with many phrases whether you're married or not. The expression is familiar.

Of course, we state the attitude differently. We say, "If you loved me, you wouldn't behave that way." Parents tell their children "If you cared about us, you would do this." The implication is that what the speaker *expects* from another person will be done because of concern for the feelings of the speaker. To a limited extent, it is. People who love each other usually want to please each other. But such expectations extended to changes of behavior and personality reflect controlling, possessive attitudes.

ON CHILDREN[5]

And a woman who held a babe against her bosom said, Speak to us of Children.

And he said:
Your children are not your children.
They are the sons and daughters of Life's longing for itself.
They come through you but not from you.
And though they are with you yet they belong not to you.

You may give them your love but not your thoughts,
For they have their own thoughts.

[5] Reprinted from *The Prophet* (Pocket edition, pp. 18–19) by Kahlil Gibran, by permission of the publisher, Alfred A. Knopf, Inc. Copyright 1923 by Kahlil Gibran; renewal copyright 1951 by Administrators C. T. A. of Kahlil Gibran Estate and Mary G. Gibran.

You may house their bodies but not their souls,

. . . .

You may strive to be like them, but seek not to make them like you.
For life goes not backward nor tarries with yesterday.

Intimate partners usually, at least at the beginning, want to please each other, as children want to please their parents. They often try to change to please the other. But wanting someone to change is evaluative; it implies the person is now inadequate. Thus, defensive reactions are natural. Even those who respond to evaluation by trying to change may resent the implication that they are inadequate. When any family member feels something must be changed (or hidden) to please another, conditions for trust deteriorate. The absence of acceptance has been recognized, and honesty often begins to diminish as a result.

Possessiveness also causes defensiveness in parent-child relationships. Children cannot choose their parents, but they do have choices regarding how they perform the role of daughter or son. Parents, however, often forget that. Many parents feel, or act as if they feel, that children are *theirs* to be controlled, molded, and developed as the parents desire. Parents set rules, issue ultimatums, and feel they may control the smallest behaviors of their children. Then, seldom parents recognize their possessiveness as the cause of defensiveness in growing children.

Right now, we can hear many of our readers who are parents protesting, "But it's our responsibility to protect our children. We have a duty to raise them to know right from wrong." Of course that parental protest is accurate. Parents have the responsibility to protect their children from an environment with which they are not prepared to cope. Parents also have the responsibility to help children learn how to cope with that environment. Very early, parents can begin to teach children that life consists of a series of choices and that each choice has inevitable consequences. As soon as a child can accept the consequences, that child matures best by learning to make the choices. Children can begin learning to guide their own behavior when quite young.

A basic element of maturity is learning that in any situation you have at least one and usually many alternatives and that the consequences in your life depend on the choices you—not someone else—make. Even not to choose is to choose. It's a choice to let someone else decide. Failure to permit or require children to make choices about their own lives or to understand their behavior has consequences delays the maturing process, sometimes forever. Parents should begin to apply this principle to communicating with their children as soon as possible. Certainly by adolescence the learning process should long since have begun.

We're trying to be clear here. You may believe parents have a "right" to control their children's behavior. Or that husbands and wives have the "right" to expect certain behaviors from each other. To so believe is, of course, *your* right. Your parental or marital philosophy is not an issue. We want only that you recognize the consequences of such attitudes.

In the United States, with its strong value of individual freedom, the belief that some family members should control others' behaviors will inevitably encounter resistance. Family members who attempt to limit one another's freedoms create defensiveness. Even the attitude that one should be able to control others in this manner will eventually surface in words or actions. Growing children in particular will demand these expectations be renegotiated, but the same result can be expected from marital partners. At some point, the person(s) being controlled (or that one is trying, usually unsuccessfully, to control) will demand her or his share of individual autonomy in the relationship. When that occurs, interpersonal role negotiation will be required or the relationship will suffer.

EXERCISE 10.2   POSSESSIVENESS IN MY FAMILY

OBJECTIVE   **To become aware of possessive behaviors in your family, whether by yourself or others.**

DIRECTIONS   1. Keep a journal for one week. Record situations in your family when you observed possessive attitudes and resulting control behaviors, and tell what your perception of the result was.
2. Be sure to watch your own as well as others' behavior.
3. For the situations in which you notice ineffective communication, state behaviors you believe could have improved it.

REVIEW   1. Explain how possessive attitudes affect family communication.
2. What specific steps can be taken to improve communication in my family?
   a. with respect to possessiveness
   b. with respect to the other potential causes of communication problems within the family
3. Explain the most important communication principle illustrated or learned from this exercise and why you found it important.

   Note: Attach your journal

IMPROVING COMMUNICATION WITHIN THE FAMILY

In the first part of this chapter we discussed how the familiarity inherent in family life creates strains on communication. Roles and norms are often not clarified, faulty assumptions exist, family members have trouble accepting changing roles, and children resist double standards. Other pressures result because of the restricted freedom inherent in intimate living and differing goals of family members.

As in all long-term relationships, family members must exert special efforts to maintain good communication. The efforts will almost always be rewarded because we all find family relationships important.

Effective communication can help families grow and develop strong relationships.

Clarify Expectations

Each member of a family needs to work at clarifying expectations about roles and behaviors. Still, one member of the family will often be more sensitive to communication problems and techniques than others. If that person is you, apply your skill and knowledge to help others improve their communication. If the basis of a problem is the failure to clarify expectations, it might be easily solved. Encourage everyone to talk about what they expect of each other, using what you know about communication to be sure you do so at the appropriate time and place. And don't expect to discuss the issues once and be finished with them. Remember, family members' roles and status constantly change, so make this kind of negotiation a regular practice in your family.

Settle Issues as They Arise

Learn to discuss the communication problem when it occurs. This is important. It demands that family members listen, hopefully with empathy, to each other. But if you bottle problems inside, the same events occur over and over again. If emotions are high, a short cooling off period is usually a good idea. It will let intense feelings subside and give you time to think about the problem with some detachment.

Making an appointment to discuss the issue is usually a good idea. Family members shouldn't be blindsided with a talk for which you have prepared but they have had no chance to think about. That is game playing, not an honest effort to improve communication. But don't defer excessively. Deal with the issue while it is reasonably fresh in your mind and feelings. (We recognize that the appointment suggestion will not work in every case. It assumes that both members of the relationship care about it and have reasonable emotional health. In some cases, surprise is the only way to get the idea discussed. In those cases, the value of the talk supercedes the value of forewarning.)

Use The I Message Formula

Remember this suggestion from Chapter 7. Apply it in your family. This way of talking can ease confrontations, clarify issues, and contribute more to solving problems than virtually any other suggestion we can make. Indeed, applying it in families may be easier than in any other situation because the loving relationships involved permit you to teach the formula to all members of the family. Once each member of a relationship has learned to use this formula when discussing problems, solutions become much easier to deal with.

Cope with Power

The family has a structure that tends to define relationships, at least in a limited way: Parents have more freedom and responsibility than children, and older children usually have more freedom and responsibility than younger children. But in the give-and-take of daily life, these differences frequently become blurred. As a result, family members, especially children and spouses, often engage in struggles over dominance.

To deal with the problems that develop from power-based relationships, family members need to be aware of the implications of control. First, recognize that unfair use of power will probably boomerang within a short period of time. Second, show willingness to interact openly and provisionally rather than to dominate; trust and acceptance may well be reciprocated. If you interact with someone who seeks to dominate, apply the techniques of assertive communication introduced in Chapter 9. Implementing these suggestions is neither simple nor easy, but if you are persistent, communication in the family can be improved.

Talk with Unrestricted Codes

A communication pattern established early between parents and children appears to have long-range implications. This pattern involves the use of restricted codes when talking to children. A **restricted code** refers to *the general use of command statements without complete explanations*. "Tom, don't light that match," is such a statement. An **unrestricted code** *provides an explanation*: "Tom, if you light that match, you can easily burn yourself and the furniture. Don't light it." To influence children without controlling their lives, parents can learn to use unrestricted code phrasing. Then a child's compliance will be based on understanding of predicted consequences, not on expected blind obedience to authority.

Children respond well to unrestricted models of interaction. Two four-year-olds arguing over the use of a wagon quickly settled their conflict when one explained, "I just started to play with this. I want my turn, then you can have a turn." A child who had learned this pattern of interaction would be able to see that the explanation was reasonable. Using unrestricted codes gives the reasons for behavior. Very young children are able to use and respond to unrestricted codes. They learn to base behaviors on understanding of the consequences of various acts, not on fear of punishment or desire for reward. They can learn *self*-discipline by learning to rely on themselves, not external forces, to guide their behavior.

Use the Principles of Effective Communication

One suggestion for solving the problems of family communication is to use the principles of communication. That is not an oversimplification. Most of the ideas from the preceding chapters of this book apply to improving family communication. Little value would be served by repeating those ideas here with admonitions that you use them. So we'll just suggest that you review the earlier portions of the book and work at applying the ideas to this set of relationships—probably the most important place you could choose to use the ideas.

EXERCISE 10.3   FAMILY GROUP CHARACTERISTICS

OBJECTIVE	**To become aware of the characteristics of your family group.**

DIRECTIONS	1. Describe your family according to the following group characteristics:
	  a. Purpose
	  b. Goals: agreement between member and group goals; goals shared or not shared
	  c. Communication patterns
	  d. Cohesiveness, satisfaction, attractiveness
	  e. Interdependence and control
	  f. Roles, norms, status: external and internal
	  g. Decision-making processes
	  h. Influence of power and authority
	2. Analyze how the factors described affect communication within your family.

REVIEW	1. Describe family group characteristics that contribute to effective and supportive communication within a family. 2. Why are listening skills important in family communication? 3. Explain the most important communication principle illustrated or learned from this exercise and why you found it important.

COMMUNICATING WITH THE AGED

Any analysis of family communication must include a discussion of communicating with the aged. Most of us now have, have had, or will have members of our family who have reached the so-called golden years. At best, these are people who add richness and experience to our family group. At worst, they are rejected isolates who contribute little but friction. For most families, communicating with elderly members falls somewhere between the two extremes. The experience is not totally unpleasant, but neither is it as pleasant as it could be. In this section we discuss some of the problems of the aged that affect their communication, and suggest some approaches for improving interactions with them.

Aging and Unmet Needs

By 1990, more than 30 million United States citizens will be over sixty-five, and the number increases every year. Watch their faces and the story unfolds—too many feel unneeded and unwanted. They have so many unmet needs, and yet they have so much they can still give. For too many, the years of old age are not golden at all, but instead years of loneliness and boredom.

Forced Retirement   The situation of many aged in our country is not of their own making. Retirement was forced and pensions inadequate. Present social insurance, though very expensive to government, does not meet the income needs of the elderly at a comfortable level. Millions live on social security or welfare, barely at survival level. Others' income is from retirement programs that do not keep up with the continually rising cost of living. Thus, for many who are forced out of their jobs, fixed incomes are inadequate, and survival needs only partly satisfied.

Low income also leaves safety needs unmet. Housing and transportation present problems. Homes that required a lifetime to pay for deteriorate. It becomes impossible to meet rising taxes and maintenance bills. Many houses cannot accommodate walkers or wheelchairs, and getting assistance for physical tasks without becoming entirely dependent is difficult. Adequate, safe, low-cost, and convenient mass transit is absent from most communities.

For most of the elderly, however, the problems of unmet survival and safety needs are less severe than the impact of retirement on the satisfaction of higher-level social and personal needs. Retiring can cause a great loss in satisfaction of the needs for love and belonging, esteem, and self-actualization. Reduced incomes, coupled with an inability to work productively in a work-oriented society, may cause social isolation. The mobility of this society has separated many old people from their families. Work companions no longer exist. Old friends may die. People in the community have no time or interest in "old fogey" neighbors. Yet the need to love and be loved does not diminish with age.

The media celebrate youth and beauty, and our society responds by spending millions on cosmetics and youthful fashions. Aged parents, grandparents, or neighbors are a painful reminder that "this, too, shall pass." In a society in which youth and physical beauty are very important and the prevailing philosophy is to "live for today," the presence of old people is ignored or, worse, resented. When work is no longer a means for the elderly to belong to society, social attitudes isolate them even more.

Above belonging needs in the Maslow hierarchy are esteem and self-actualiza-

Planning for active retirement improves the quality of later life.

tion needs. People need to feel they are of value, that others consider them essential or view them with high regard. For too many of the elderly, these needs for esteem and a sense of self-worth are unmet. People who retire often feel useless. Children are grown up, have moved away, and no longer seek their parents' advice. Many of the aged feel useless, not needed, or unwanted. Without the work that gave them a sense of contributing to society, the absent family connections are even more noticeable and more painful.

Planned Retirement   But what of those who dreamed about retiring, waiting eagerly for the day when they didn't have to get up and go to work? Too few of them have planned for active retirement, and the reality of it is a shock. **Active retirement** is how we describe *the planning and execution of a lifestyle that enables a person to continue to grow after the working years are over*. This preparation is beyond financial considerations. Adequate money is needed, of course. But too many people think of retirement as an escape from the nine-to-five cage—time to fish, hunt, play golf, or just rest and relax. Sadly, they soon become bored and begin to long for the days they had eagerly hoped to leave behind. They wish for the usefulness they had when employed; they miss the job that made weekends worth looking forward to. When all of life is a weekend, it may be less fun.

Melvin Swartz is a lawyer practicing in the retirement community of Sun City, Arizona. In his fifteen years of work there, he says, he has counseled more than 4000 retired persons. Not more than twenty had planned properly for retirement. The time of retirement, he concludes, seems to be a time of misinformation or no information.[6]

[6] *The St. Louis Post-Dispatch*, March 8, 1976.

Planning for active retirement is essential. An avocation, part-time or volunteer work, political campaigning, supervising investments, learning new skills, returning to school—all or any could fulfill needs for esteem and self-actualization. The necessity to fulfill these high-level needs does not end at age sixty-five; indeed, the trauma of a drastically changing lifestyle often intensifies them. Unless they can feel productive and useful, it is difficult for the aged to maintain a sense of self-esteem in a work-oriented society.

Being productive is only part of active retirement. It should include activities that make a person feel needed. Older people feel, often accurately, that their families no longer need them. When they fail to plan for active retirement, they find it difficult to meet new friends, to continue to develop relationships with others. Thus they reduce the chances of fulfilling esteem, belonging, and love needs. When these are unmet, the sense of self-worth is weakened. Active retirement involves continuing activities to which a person feels committed, activities that offer interpersonal relationships and a sense of continued growth.

These factors are related. Everybody requires a sense of worth, which in part comes from being loved and needed and in part comes from self-actualization. When these needs are not met, self-concept may be damaged, and communication increasingly difficult. The lowering of self-esteem begins a vicious cycle that is no less destructive to older people than to youngsters. The self-fulfilling prophecy takes over. Persons often *become* inactive and useless because they believe they must be. The result confirms the lowered self-esteem. The spiral continues—downward. An elderly person who feels unwanted may not call the children or grandchildren—"They're busy and not interested anyway." He or she may not seek to make new friends—"Who wants to know *me*, I'm old and ugly"; may not volunteer for community services—"They don't *want* me." As a result, many elderly isolate themselves from community and family. They become more and more difficult to communicate with.

Improving Communication with the Aged

Communicating with elderly people who have some of these problems may be difficult. Those whose survival and safety needs are unmet are frightened and insecure; those who have increasingly lowered self-esteem perceive interactions as threats. They are closed and guarded and suspicious. Thinking badly of self leads to thinking badly of others—another vicious circle. It is common to evaluate others negatively in order to try to feel one isn't alone in being "not O.K." Communicating with people who desperately need to love and be loved is difficult; they can be totally negative and rejecting, or they can cling and grasp and often stifle others in the relationship. Freedom and empathy are difficult to extend to people whose personal problems cause them to be demanding, suspicious, and self-pitying, or closed, "turned off," and uncommunicative.

Recognize the Problems   You may find the catalog of problems listed here rather depressing. Communicating with elderly persons is often difficult and demanding. Moreover, good communication cannot solve many of the problems. They have societal causes and require societal cures, especially those related to survival and security. But some suggestions can be helpful.

First, *be aware of the range of unmet interpersonal needs that may exist.* Listen to your old relatives actively and empathically. Empathy can enable you to realize the importance of communicating regularly with elderly family members. Many of us live long distances from aging parents and grandparents, and we don't realize how important a visit or phone call can be to them. Others who live close enough to visit often, do so with dread. We expect complaints, evaluations, distrust, and self-pity. But we forget the Pygmalion effect of our expectations. If we keep in mind that we tend to receive the kinds of messages we expect, we'll see how much we may contribute to the very behaviors we dread. Moreover, understanding all the causes of defensiveness in the elderly can help us prepare to deal with it. A basic understanding of the problems of the aged can in itself lead to empathy, acceptance, and other kinds of supportive communication.

Reject the Myths One important problem facing many people as they age is that they and the society share largely inaccurate stereotypes about older people. Books, plays, television, movies, and magazines all reflect these stereotypes. We are frequently confronted with the image of the senile, dirty old man and the crabby, meddlesome old woman. How long has it been since you've seen a *non*comic hero or heroine in a TV show who was over sixty-five? And even though more women grow old than men, aged media stars are very rarely women.

The media are only reflecting popular attitudes. Our interpersonal interactions reflect the same stereotypes. For example, what happens when sex over sixty is mentioned? It's the subject of snickers and jokes. Yet most recent research demonstrates that sex for older people is much the same as sex at any age. Old age does not mean automatic senility, but our expectations of old age might cause behavior that resembles it. If we reject the myths about the aged, we can begin to *communicate* with them—we can listen to them and personally benefit from their experiences. This can be a two-way street, increasing their sense of worth and, indeed, their *real* worth; we can learn from their experience.

One result of prevailing societal myths about aged uselessness has been the gathering of the elderly into retirement communities. Because human beings are endlessly adaptable, the results of these communities are not entirely negative. One analysis found that residents of a "senior citizen" housing project became increasingly involved with one another as a source of friendship, largely because of their segregation from families and places of work.

Provide for Active Retirement If we reject the stereotype of the sexless, useless aged, we can help them develop active retirement. Our communities can become places in which the elderly can participate without withdrawing from the larger society. We can provide the aid, encouragement, and situations that allow older people to satisfy their needs for love, belonging, esteem, and self-actualization. We can assist them in finding ways to meet and develop relationships with others, both of their age and younger. We can assist them in developing interests and activities outside their living rooms. We can help them find transportation to and from volunteer work or political or church activities. We can use their talents, skills, and knowledge in many situations. From all of this, we too can be richer.

SUMMARY

Communicating within families is at once the most rewarding and most difficult communication that many people have. There are many sources of communication problems within families: the absence of agreement on family rules and rituals and on the status and roles of family members; the failure to clarify or state the expectations members have for themselves and others within the family; the failure to remember that roles and status relationships in families require constant adjustment as members grow and develop and as the outside society changes; the imposing of parental double standards on children about adherence to rules and rituals; the absence of shared goals; the existence of different or conflicting goals.

Many problems of family communication arise solely out of the pressures of intimate living conditions. Living with someone else restricts the freedom of each individual. Many problems are caused in family groups when, despite apparent agreement, there is really disagreement because of the assumption that meanings are shared by communicators. Also, because of closely shared experiences and faulty assumptions, there is a buildup of emotional loads on words and situations.

Perhaps the greatest source of communication problems in families, however, is the attitudes members have toward one another. People who behave possessively toward others, or seek to dominate others, must learn to recognize that their behavior causes defensiveness. Parents can teach children right and wrong by using unrestricted code phrasing. Acceptance between partners or parents and children provides more opportunity for the person to change than do evaluation and control.

There are ways to improve family communication. These include seeking to clarify roles, expectations and goals; being supportive in communication; using "I" messages; using feedback to clarify messages; displaying empathy; being accepting and honest; and employing noncontrolling attitudes.

A special problem of family communication is the necessity to deal with aging members. Retired people in the United States are subject to decreased self-esteem because they no longer feel useful and because the society degrades age and worships youth. Too few have planned for active retirement, and they find retirement a negative experience. The resulting decreases in need satisfaction produce people who are lonely, hostile, and defensive, with obvious communication problems. By understanding the problems, family members can more easily respond with supportiveness, acceptance, and empathy. They can also seek means of providing active retirement for the aged in their families.

QUESTIONS FOR DISCUSSION

1. How does contemporary society affect communication in families?
2. Why is communicating within the family one of your most difficult communication situations?

3. How do goals, roles, and expectations affect communication within your family?

4. How does possessiveness affect your family communication?

5. How can supportive communication be used to improve family relationships?

6. How can you cope with the special problem of communication with aged members of your family?

SUGGESTIONS FOR FURTHER READING

Adams, Bert N. *Kinships in an Urban Setting.* Chicago: Markham Press, 1969.

_____. *The Family.* Chicago: Rand McNally, 1980.

Blisten, Dorothy R. *The World of the Family: A Corporate Study of Family Organizations in Their Social and Cultural Settings.* New York: Random House, 1963.

Blood, Robert O., and Donald M. Wolfe. *Husbands and Wives: The Dynamics of Married Living.* New York: Free Press, 1960. (Reprinted in 1978 by Greenwood Press.)

Blumstein, Philip, and Pepper Schwartz. *American Couples: Money, Work, Sex.* New York: William Morrow, 1983.

Elkind, Frederick, and Gerald Handel. *The Child and Society.* New York: Oxford University Press, 1979.

Erikson, Erik H. *Childhood and Society*, 35th Anniv. ed. New York: Norton, 1986.

Galvin, Kathleen, and Bernard Brommel. *Family Communication, Cohesion and Change*, 2nd ed. Glenview, Ill.: Scott, Foresman, 1986.

Ginott, Haim. *Between Parent and Child.* New York: Avon Books, 1969.

_____. *Between Parent and Teenager.* New York: Avon Books, 1971.

_____. *Teacher and Child: A Book for Parents and Teachers.* New York: Avon Books, 1975.

Goode, William. *The Family*, 2nd ed. Englewood Cliffs, N.J.: Prentice-Hall, 1982.

Gordon, Thomas. *P.E.T.: Parent Effectiveness Training.* New York: Wyden, 1970.

Laing, Ronald D. *Politics of the Family.* New York: Random House, 1972.

Lavetelli, Celia A., and Faith Stendler. *Readings in Child Behavior and Development*, 3rd ed. New York: Harcourt Brace Jovanovich, 1972.

Matza, David. *Becoming Deviant.* Englewood Cliffs, N.J.: Prentice-Hall, 1969.

O'Neill, Nena. *The Marriage Premise.* New York: Avon Books, 1978.

O'Neill, Nena, and George O'Neill. *Open Marriage.* New York: Avon Books, 1972.

Pearson, Judy C. *Gender and Communication.* Dubuque: William C. Brown, 1985.

Phillips, Gerald M., and Nancy Metzger. *Intimate Communication.* Boston: Allyn and Bacon, 1976.

Rogers, Carl. *Becoming Partners: Marriage and Its Alternatives.* New York: Delacorte Press, 1973.

Ruddock, Ralph. *Roles and Relationships.* London: Routledge and Kegan Paul, 1969.

Skolnick, Arlene, and Jerome H. Skolnick, eds. *Family in Transition: Rethinking Marriage, Sexuality, Child Rearing and Family Organization*, 5th ed. Boston: Little, Brown, 1986.

_____. *The Intimate Environment: Exploring Marriage and Family,* 4th ed. Boston: Little, Brown, 1987.

Winch, Robert. *The Modern Family.* New York: Holt, Rinehart and Winston, 1971.

Winch, Robert, et al. *Familial Organization.* New York: Free Press, 1978.

11 Preparing Speeches: Organizing Thoughts

> The world is already full of speakers who are too busy to prepare their speeches properly, and the world would be better off if they were also too busy to give them.
>
> WILLIAM NORWOOD BRIGANCE
>
> Trifles make perfection, and perfection is no trifle.
>
> MICHELANGELO

GOAL

To learn the basic steps in preparing to speak effectively

OBJECTIVES

The material in this chapter should help you to:
1. Choose appropriate general purposes for different speech situations.
2. Distinguish among speeches that are made to
   Inform
   Entertain
   Persuade
3. State specific purposes appropriate for speeches in different types of situations.
4. Gather the information needed to analyze an audience, and adapt a speech to that particular audience.
5. Choose thesis statements appropriately limited for speeches of various types.
6. Choose main and subpoints to develop organized speeches.
7. Use the following standard outlines to organize speeches:
   Time pattern
   Space pattern
   Topical pattern
   Cause-effect pattern
   Problem-solution pattern
   Advantages-disadvantages pattern
8. Develop effective introductions and conclusions.

The thought of speaking in public strikes fear into the hearts of people from all walks of life—from executives to students. A national poll in 1976 indicated that four of every ten Americans feared speaking in public more than anything else. Little wonder so many people avoid even thinking about the subject.

Perhaps in response to the fear, many students say they don't need to study public speaking. They claim giving speeches is something they never do. We doubt that is true, for even though making formal "speeches" may be rare, most of us do a lot of informal public speaking. Remember the definition of public communication: communication in situations where many people receive messages largely from one source. These situations occur often at work, at school, in church, and in many other social situations. Thus, even though you may not have thought of them that way, you probably give lots of public speeches. Moreover, public speaking is merely one type of communication. Most of the principles in this book apply when you speak in public. To speak well in public, you must communicate effectively.

Because public speaking is communication, it is a process. Achieving a speaker's goals involves complex interactions. So whenever students ask, "Will this work?" we answer, "It depends." These next three chapters include many suggestions for speech situations. But the suggestions will not always be relevant to your particular case nor will they always work. It depends. It depends on the speaker, on the others involved, and on the situation. But learning these principles can help you analyze your own speaking. The information can prepare you to continue improving your speaking long after you leave this classroom.

One last introductory comment. The key to successful speaking is no secret. It is careful preparation. For that reason, our discussion of public speaking begins with suggestions for preparation. We start there because we agree with Brigance's comment: If people cannot prepare their speeches properly, "the world would be better off if they were also too busy to give them."[1]

ESTABLISHING GOALS

The first step in preparing a speech is to decide on its goals. In the words of a popular poster, if you don't know where you are going, you're likely to wind up somewhere else. In public speaking, that is especially true.

Select a Topic

One of the first questions students have about public speaking is, "What can I talk about?" This may be the main reason students are nervous about their speech courses. What, they ask, can I say that others want to hear? This problem is largely limited to speeches in the somewhat artificial setting of the classroom. In the "outside" world, it is rare to be invited to give a speech without a predetermined purpose. The situation and the invitation themselves carry a topic to talk about.

[1] William Norwood Brigance, *Speech Composition* (New York: Appleton-Century-Crofts, 1953), p. 49.

Speaking effectively in public is important in many ways in modern society.

In the classroom, however, speech topics may be a serious problem. Still, the solutions are not difficult. For many assignments, your instructor will indicate a general subject area. Specific tasks are often assigned to help you learn certain techniques. At other times, you will be on your own in topic selection. In those cases, don't panic—simply do what you'd do outside the classroom: Start with what you know. In most speeches, people are talking because they know something about the topic. Use the same solution in class. Talk about what you know: yourself, your work, your past experiences, your feelings, your beliefs, your hobbies, your family, your goals in life. Your *self* provides more speech topics than you'll ever need in one class.

Some students protest, "My audience isn't interested in that!" Quite the contrary, they are probably very interested. You are the one who will be standing in front of them. At the beginning of the class, you are probably a stranger. They will be curious about you. Most of us find other people endlessly fascinating. We watch them, talk about them, read about them in the newspapers, and go to movies and watch TV to see stories about them. A newspaper reporter seeking a story always tries to answer the question, "What is the human angle? How did or will this event affect people?" People are news. Similarly, *you* are interesting to your classmates. Talk about who you are and what you know. You won't need to worry about their interest in your speech.

This is the first step in topic selection. Ask: "What have I to offer in an exchange between the audience and myself? What have I and they in common?" Answer those questions, and you will have more speech topics than you can use. The next step will be to refine and develop a speech topic.

State a Purpose

We classify general speech purposes into three categories: informing, entertaining, and persuading. These categories name three broad goals you might want to accomplish. Do you want listeners to learn something they do not know? If so, the general purpose is *to inform*. Do you want only to make them laugh or enjoy the time they spend listening to you? Then your general purpose is *to entertain*. Or do you want to change your listeners' behaviors or attitudes in some way? To get some specific action from them? To intensify their feelings about something? If you answer yes to any of these last three questions, your general purpose is *to persuade*.

Knowing the general purpose helps you state a specific purpose. A **specific purpose** states *the specific response wanted from the listeners*. It is the answer to the question, *What, exactly, do I want my audience to do, think, or feel when I finish?* Public speaking is more than a performance. One gives a speech to accomplish something, to get some response from the people who are listening. To prepare effective speeches, start by stating specifically the response you want.[2]

---

[2] As you think about purpose, remember that both specific and general purposes are strongly influenced by situation. In class your teacher usually assigns at least the general purpose. Outside the classroom, the reason for your invitation may determine the general purpose. The audience itself affects what you choose as your specific purpose.

The following examples illustrate both general and specific purposes:

General purpose: To inform.
Specific purpose: Lions Club members will understand how the college awards the scholarship they have endowed.

General purpose: To persuade.
Specific purpose: My classmates will vote for me in the Student Association election.

General purpose: To entertain.
Specific purpose: The Scouts and their parents at the annual awards banquet will enjoy hearing about my humorous experiences as a Scout.

Analyze the Audience

After tentatively choosing a specific purpose, analyze your listeners and the situation. This is called **audience analysis,** and it should be done before you state the specific purpose with certainty.

To analyze an audience, first decide what you need to know about your listeners. Almost any information will help you know listeners as people, but some kinds of information are more useful than others. You need answers to the following questions:

1. What does my audience already know about this topic?
2. What is their specific interest in this topic?
3. What are their beliefs and feelings about my thesis and purpose?
4. What are their beliefs and feelings about me in relation to this purpose and topic?
5. What are their feelings and beliefs about related subjects, issues, and persons?
6. How will the situation affect my efforts?

Audience analysis helps you decide exactly what your purpose will be. It helps you know what organization of ideas will work best; how best to amplify and develop the ideas; how to gain credibility; how to keep listeners' attention, change their minds, or motivate them to act. It helps you know how to cope with any physical barriers or other problems in the setting. Making these decisions is one of the most important steps in preparing a speech. So how do you go about analyzing an audience?

Secure Needed Information

Ask Questions You may have to ask only one or two people to learn what you need to know about your audience. You may know some members of the group who will be your listeners. Even if you don't know them personally, you can still contact them and ask them directly what you need to know.

Sometimes gathering information is more complicated. It may require polling, sending questionnaires, or interviewing several people. Many politicians, for example, spend thousands of dollars on research to answer the important questions of audience analysis. But you probably won't have either the time or the resources to do that kind of audience analysis. Nor is it usually necessary—at least for most of us. We can get most of what we need to know by asking the right questions of a few carefully selected people.

Infer from Demographic Data At times we can't use direct questions to learn what we need to know. Either we can't find people whose judgment we trust, or they aren't sure of the answers. In these cases, we have to draw inferences from **demographic data.** Demographic data are *statistics about groups of people.* We can draw many useful inferences if we know some of the following things about our audience: age; sex; occupation; income level; education level; special areas of education or experience; religious, political, ethnic, or social affiliations; whether they are from rural, urban, or suburban locations; and what part of the country they are from.

This kind of information can help us infer how listeners will decode what we say. It can assist us in knowing what level of language to use, in selecting effective illustrations or comparisons, and in realizing how listeners' attitudes and values will affect their reactions.

Inferring from demographic data is less desirable than having direct answers to questions but is sometimes the only alternative. With accurate demographic data, we can infer quite accurately about listeners.

Use Feedback while Speaking The final step of audience analysis is not done in advance. It is something you prepare for by knowing you need to do it: Use feedback while speaking. Audience analysis should not end after you have prepared the speech. Your conclusions, whether based on answers to direct questions or on demographic data, are still only inferences. They are conclusions about the unknown, the attitudes of a group of people. Since attitudes are internal states, you can never be certain your conclusions are accurate.

Speakers who remember their audience analysis conclusions are tentative will watch and listen for feedback while they talk. They will use feedback to assess the accuracy of their conclusions about an audience. When listeners do not respond as expected, these speakers make adjustments as they speak. Good speakers consider consequences as they plan for the speech. We'll discuss that approach later. A checklist like the following can help you keep in mind the kinds of information you need for audience analysis.[3]

I. Demographic data
   A. Size
   B. Sex
   C. Age
   D. Occupation
   E. Educational level
   F. Other group identifications
II. Knowledge and awareness of subject

[3] Adapted from Alan Monroe and Douglas Ehninger, *Principles and Types of Speech*, 6th ed. (Glenview, Ill.: Scott, Foresman, 1967), p. 166. Copyright © 1967, 1962 by Scott, Foresman and Company. Reprinted by permission.

III. Attitude toward thesis and purpose
    A. What will listener(s) accept?
    B. What must be proved?
IV. Attitude toward speaker
    A. Previous acquaintance
    B. Image (Does audience like and/or trust the speaker? Believe in speaker's expertise?)
    C. Specific disagreements
 V. Occasion
    A. Purpose of meeting or gathering
    B. Rules or customs governing conduct
    C. Events preceding and following speech
    D. Physical conditions
    E. Level of listeners' organization
    F. Degree of listeners' polarization

Reexamine Purpose

After analyzing the audience, look again at your purpose statement. You may have learned some things that show your tentative specific purpose is not appropriate. If so, restate that purpose using the new information. Remember, state specifically what you want your listeners to do, think, or feel when you finish speaking.

ORGANIZING IDEAS: THE THESIS

After establishing goals for the speech, the next step is to specifically state the thesis. The thesis of a speech is not the same as its purpose. The purpose describes the desired audience response. The **thesis** is *the main point of a message* used to achieve the desired response. The thesis is a subject-centered statement which can be thought of as a single-sentence summary of the speech. It is often called a **central idea.** This is a useful term because a thesis should be the one idea central to everything you say in the speech.

A thesis is not the same as the speech subject or topic. One subject (or topic) could lead to many different thesis statements. For example, take the subject (topic) of basketball. Any of the following could be a thesis statement:

1. Basketball is an exciting sport.
2. Basketball "plays" are more complex than most people realize.
3. Club basketball is a good way for adults to stay in shape.
4. The number of scholarships for the college basketball team should be increased.

You could probably list many others. To illustrate, your instructor may ask you to complete Exercise 11–1.

Thesis and Purpose Differ

Sometimes it is difficult to distinguish among the subject, the thesis statement, and the purpose of a speech. The following example may help clarify the differences:

Situation:	Giving a book report in a class.
Subject:	The book, *Huckleberry Finn*.
General purpose:	To inform.
Thesis:	Mark Twain's *Huckleberry Finn* is more than a children's book.
Specific purpose (apparent):	My classmates and teacher will understand why I believe *Huckleberry Finn* is significant adult literature.

Notice something else about this example. The word *apparent* is in parentheses. This emphasizes that speakers may have purposes other than the apparent ones. Hidden general and specific purposes often exist. For most students giving a book report, the following would be the hidden, or underlying, purpose:

General purpose (hidden):	To persuade
Specific purpose (hidden):	My instructor will give me a good grade on this book report.

One idea could be a thesis for different speeches with different purposes. For the thesis *basketball is an exciting sport*, several different purposes could be appropriate. For example:

1. My listeners will understand why I enjoy going to basketball games (to inform).
2. My friend (or wife or husband) will attend a basketball game with me (to gain action).
3. My classmates will support the college team by attending the home games (the speaker might hope to change some listeners' behavior and to intensify other listeners' beliefs).

When you have chosen a topic, analyzed your audience, and stated thesis and specific purpose, you have set the goals for the speech. You are now ready to begin developing its verbal content. Remember, however, this process of setting goals is never really finished. As you gather information, practice, and actually present the speech, you may learn things that require you to reexamine and revise both purpose and thesis. To prepare effectively, remain flexible so you will be able to make changes if they become necessary.

EXERCISE 11.1   DEVELOPING SPEECH THESIS STATEMENTS

OBJECTIVE   **To become aware of the differences between the thesis and subject, or topic, of a speech.**

DIRECTIONS
1. Using basketball as the subject, write five possible thesis statements (different from the examples we suggested) for a speech.
2. Use the following checklist to make sure each statement is a thesis, not a topic (subject).
3. Bring your list to class and share it with others. Compile a total class list of all the different possible theses, eliminating all duplications.
4. Rephrase any topics so that all statements in the list are theses, not topics.

CHECKLIST FOR THESIS STATEMENTS:
——Is written as a complete sentence
——Contains one and only one idea
——Is a declarative sentence

5. Report the total number of thesis statements that were developed from the single subject, basketball.

REVIEW

1. Explain the difference between a thesis and the subject of a speech.
2. What are the basic steps in checking a thesis statement?
3. Explain the most important communication principle illustrated or learned from this exercise and why you found it important.

ORGANIZING IDEAS: THE OUTLINE

Building a speech from a thesis involves two processes: organizing ideas and supporting them. As people develop speeches, they tend to do both processes at the same time. The reason is obvious if you think about it. We cannot organize ideas until we have some idea of what we want to say. On the other hand, we cannot develop ideas without having some structure in mind.

Though the organizing and supporting processes interact, we discuss them separately to clarify the two processes. We cover organizing first because we expect you to follow our advice and choose topics you already know well. If so, you won't need to go to the library or some other source of information to "find something to talk about." You'll have something to talk about. What you'll need to do first is organize your thinking about that topic. If, in the unwise event you give a speech on an unfamiliar topic, you'll need to seek information before you try to organize your thoughts. In that case, read pp. 329–332 before continuing.

Stating a thesis starts organizing the speech. If we compared a speech to a wheel, the thesis would be the hub, the center. And just as a wheel consists of more than a hub, a speech needs a structure so the ideas will make sense to an audience. **Organization** involves *ordering and categorizing the elements of a verbal message*. Speech organization is reflected in an outline.

Value of Outlining

An outline helps speakers for three reasons. First, it gives direction in reaching the goal. Whether a speech is to inform, persuade, or entertain, you need to plan strategy to achieve the purpose. An outline reflects this strategy. It shows how you plan to present ideas to achieve the desired audience response. An **outline** is *a planned sequence for reaching the goals of a speech*. It helps a speaker as a road map does a traveler. A map helps a driver decide what routes to take to reach the destination. Like a road map, the outline guides the speech. But it is not a rigid path from which the speaker never strays. Changes may be made along the way.

A second value of an outline is that advance planning helps in evaluating feedback received during the speech. An outline shows the specific points at which you plan that the audience will accept or understand certain ideas. Listener feedback should match the outline. If audience reactions show that listeners understand when you have developed a point, you may go on to the next idea. However, if feedback indicates listeners are not responding as planned, you will want to repeat, restate, or add more explanation or information. Advance planning for such alternatives can help you know how to adapt. Outlines should include such contingency plans.[4]

A third reason for organizing ideas into an outline is that it helps the audience. An outline helps you make your thought structure clear to others. If listeners are able to perceive structure in ideas, they'll find it easier to listen and remember. But the organization must be clear to the listeners or it won't help them. Use audience analysis when you outline so you will emphasize what is necessary for listeners to understand.

Choose Main Points (Establish Structure)

After stating the thesis and specific purpose, the next step in outlining is to decide on *the main ideas you will use to support the thesis*. These main supporting ideas are called **main points.** What you choose as main points depends on both purpose and audience. The speech should include nothing more (or less) than the ideas necessary to accomplish your specific purpose with a given audience.

Use Standard Patterns   Choosing main ideas for the outline is a task beginning speakers often find difficult. They have trouble distinguishing main ideas from less important ones. One way to solve this problem is to use a standard structure for choosing main points. Of these standard patterns, the following are most helpful: time, space, and topical arrangements of cause-effect, problem-solution, and advantages-disadvantages.

TIME PATTERN   The time pattern organizes ideas according to time. This pattern can be chronological: The speaker discusses what happens first, then what happens second, third, and so on. This arrangement is good for "how to" speeches. When explaining how to do something, it helps to start with what you do first!

The time arrangement for main ideas is not limited to chronological order. A speech structured by time could start by discussing the way things are now, and then go back to examine earlier stages. The following outlines illustrate two different main point structures arranged by time.

---

[4] The concept of contingency planning is discussed in some detail in Linda and Richard Heun, *Developing Skills for Human Interaction*, 2nd ed. (Columbus: Charles E. Merrill, 1978), pp. 164–91.

Main Points Arranged by Time

   Thesis: Mandatory retirement should be eliminated.
   I. In the U.S. mandatory retirement is a common employment practice in business, industry, and government.
   II. In earlier years, it was not common to force people to retire at a set age.
   III. The reasons for the change cannot justify the negative effects that mandatory retirement has brought over the last fifty years.
   IV. Eliminating mandatory retirement now would have several beneficial effects.

Main Points Arranged by Time (Chronological)

   Thesis: Swinging a golf club properly involves four actions.
   I. First, grip the club properly.
   II. Second, take the club back correctly.
   III. Next, shift body weight to start the downswing.
   IV. Finally, use the proper follow-through.

SPACE PATTERN   Some topics lend themselves naturally to a spatial organization. If you were going to discuss the effects of water pollution, for example, you might talk first about what happened to Lake Erie, and then about pollution in other lakes. One common type of speech that uses space arrangement of main points is the travelog. People who travel are often invited to speak to groups about what they saw and learned. Usually the audience isn't interested in what the person did on each day of the trip. People want to know what the traveler saw in Paris, in London, in Rome, and so on.

Main Points Arranged by Space

   Thesis: Water pollution has become a serious problem in the United States.
   I. Lake Erie was so polluted that almost no fish survived.
   II. The Ohio River had such serious pollution that in places it was not unusual to see the river on fire.
   III. Raw sewage had polluted the Mississippi River so badly that it became dangerous to swim in some places.

TOPICAL PATTERNS   Perhaps the most common and useful main point structure is topical. Many subjects divide naturally into topics. Most chapters of this book, for instance, use a topical outline. Some of the examples presented above could be developed in a topical pattern. A speech on water pollution could discuss the topics of pollution in lakes, in rivers, and in the ocean. A speech on mandatory retirement could note the problems in private industry and then discuss government agencies. Several specific topical models can help a speaker choose the main points of a speech.

Choosing main points according to causes and effects is often effective. In a **cause-effect** structure, *main points relate to a cause and its effects*. For example:

Main Points Arranged in Cause-Effect Structure

> *Thesis: Energy is a serious problem in the United States.*

I. U.S. oil and gas consumption exceeds domestic production.

II. Oil and gas are essential to the economy.

III. The United States is dangerously dependent on imports, which it cannot control.

Here the speaker analyzes one cause of the energy crisis, then says why the effects are a problem.

A reverse order of presentation may be used. It may work best to start with effects, then talk about what caused them. In discussing energy problems, a speaker could first discuss the results of relying on oil imports: disrupted supplies, high prices, danger of war in the Mideast, and so forth. Then, as a second main point, the speaker could examine what caused those results:

Main Points Arranged in Cause-Effect Structure

> *Thesis: The energy shortage is a serious problem in the United States*

I. Reliance on foreign oil has caused problems for the United States.

II. This reliance has several causes.

The **problem-solution** structure is especially useful for choosing main points of persuasive speeches. To use problem-solution organization, a speaker first *analyzes what a problem is and then proposes and/or explains a solution or solutions*. The problem-solution pattern can be combined with cause-effect thinking. Analyze cause and effect in points one and two, and then deal with solutions in the third main point. The following example illustrates:

Main Points Arranged in a Problem-Solution Structure

> *Thesis: The United States needs to take action about the energy situation.*

I. Energy shortages have caused many problems.

II. The energy crisis has three primary causes.

III. Solutions to the energy problems are complex.

Another useful pattern is an **advantages-disadvantages** structure. To present a balanced analysis of a controversial subject, *choosing main points according to advantages and disadvantages* works well. This pattern can also be used for persuasive speeches. In comparing the disadvantages and advantages of a proposal, you can emphasize how the pros outweigh the cons, or vice versa.

Main Points Arranged in an Advantages-Disadvantages Structure

> *Thesis: Decontrol of oil prices has been a good way to conserve energy.*

I. Decontrol has had many disadvantages.

II. Decontrol has had more advantages.

Use Brainstorming Another approach to choosing main points involves making a list of all the ideas you can think of that relate to the thesis and might help achieve your specific purpose. Use the brainstorming technique. List as many ideas as you can think of. It's also helpful to work with a friend and make the list on a chalkboard or flipchart. Next, review the list. Identify and combine statements that restate the same idea, and group the statements into clusters that relate to each other. Examine the statements within each cluster to decide which idea is the main idea of that group. You have thus identified the main point for each cluster of ideas and those points that are subordinate or supporting in nature.

The brainstorming will have developed many main points—probably more than you can use. So, now review each of the points in relation to the thesis. Identify those that are essential to support the thesis and accomplish your purpose. Put the others into a file to be used as contingency plans. Arrange the remaining main ideas in a logical relationship and you have your outline—the basic framework for the speech.

This process has involved answering the following questions:

1. What ideas can be used to develop this thesis?
2. Which ideas are essential to achieving the purpose?
3. Which ideas can be used as contingency plans, to be used if feedback shows an audience doesn't understand a point?
4. Which ideas are less important and can be omitted?

Having completed this listing and sorting process, you may find your ideas fit well into one of the standard patterns discussed. But if not, it doesn't matter. You'll have a clear topical structure to guide your planning and speaking.

Limit the Main Points   Earlier we said main points should develop the thesis, and no more. It is important not to have too many main points. You may have noticed that the examples in this chapter include at least two and no more than four main points. That number is a good guideline. Since main points are ideas needed to develop the thesis, they are important for listeners to understand. Using too many main points interferes with understanding by making your thinking difficult to follow.

On rare occasions, a thesis requires more than four main points. If it does, use a visual aid to help the audience follow you. Handing out copies of a key word outline is one way to do that. Listeners can also use the outline to make notes. Better yet, use a flip chart. Show each main point as you talk about it. You can use a chalkboard in the same way.

Arrange Main Points

Speakers have much flexibility in arranging main ideas. Only the chronological pattern makes it easy to decide what to say first.

Use Audience Analysis   A speaker should choose arrangement of main points based on audience analysis. For instance, some ideas may be more interesting than others. If so, don't put all the interesting ideas together and leave all the others until the end. If the speech will end by asking the audience for some action, the strongest point should be last. If you are talking to an audience that opposes your proposal, start with an idea they agree with. If the audience is likely to doubt your credibility, begin with your strongest, most easily accepted idea to win them over early in your speech.

Much research has been done to try to establish the best order or arrangement of main points. The conclusions are not definite, and there are no easy answers.[5] The best arrangement of main points depends on you, your ideas, and the audience.

Consider Overall Speech Structure   One influence on arrangement of main points is overall speech structure. Primarily that means where the speaker places the thesis statement. Two basic types of thesis placement exist, the choice depending largely on the purpose of the speech.

When you use a **deductive structure** you *state your thesis early* in the speech, usually at the end of the introduction. All the main point outlines presented so far in this chapter use deductive structures. Deductive speech structure should be used in two situations: (1) if the purpose is to inform; (2) if the audience must quickly understand what you are talking about for you to accomplish your purpose.

Informative speeches should use the deductive pattern. It will improve clarity and help listeners remember your ideas. By stating the thesis first, you can relate each main point to the thesis as it is introduced. This helps clarify ideas. Moreover, the repetition caused by the deductive structure helps listeners remember ideas.

Persuasive speeches often benefit from inductive speech development. The **inductive structure** *withholds thesis statements until midway through a speech or at the end.* The thesis is allowed to emerge as the ideas that support it are developed. Persuasive speeches usually use an inductive arrangement because they are often made to an audience that disagrees or is hostile or skeptical.

If listeners know in advance that a speaker is trying to sell them something, influence their behavior, or change their beliefs, they will naturally be defensive. In these situations, it's better to let the thesis emerge after developing some credibility with your listeners. Moreover, before you state an idea your listeners may disagree with, it helps to give some reasoning that supports it. You should be able to reduce audience defensiveness by giving evidence or developing awareness of a need before asserting that a particular solution should be adopted. The following main point outline illustrates one way to use the inductive thought structure.

Inductive Speech Structure

   I. Reliance on foreign oil is a serious problem in the United States today.

  II. The primary cause of this shortage is gasoline consumption by private automobiles.

     Thesis: The best solution to the oil import problem is improved mass transit.

 III. Improving mass transit would reduce use of automobiles.

 IV. No other solution would cut down gasoline consumption as much as improving mass transit.

---

[5] Chapter 14 includes a discussion of the most persuasive ways to arrange ideas. If your speech has a persuasive purpose, review the material presented there before developing your outline.

Develop Main Points

Once you have selected main points, the next step is to develop them. To extend the earlier analogy, with a thesis and main points you now have the hub and spokes of a wheel. To complete it, connect and strengthen the spokes by developing and expanding the main points.

Developing main points involves choosing the *supporting* or *subordinate* ideas. That means for each point, giving the reasons that support (amplify, clarify or prove) the statement made. Having supplied these subordinate ideas, you will then turn to the problem of providing the supporting materials—a concept discussed in the next chapter. Here, the task is to complete building the framework of the speech—that is, to add the subpoints.

Selection of subordinate ideas is sometimes a simple task. If, for instance, you used the advantages-disadvantages pattern for choosing main points, the subpoints consist of stating the advantages and the disadvantages. If you used the approach to choosing main points that involves listing all the ideas in the speech and then grouping them into clusters of similar thoughts, you probably have many of the subpoints in these clusters.

In other cases, choosing the appropriate subpoints is more difficult. One good approach is to ask the question: What ideas must be developed for this main point to be understood or believed? Then list the answers. You will have many possible subpoints (subheads) from which to choose the best ideas to accomplish your task. Using one of the main points outlined above, the following shows one possible arrangement of subpoints to develop the outline:

I. Reliance on foreign oil is a serious problem in the United States.
   A. We are vulnerable to other nations who disagree with our policies.
   B. Our balance of payments is negative due largely to billions spent for foreign oil.

II. The primary cause of this problem is gasoline consumption by private automobiles.
   A. Private autos use more gasoline than any other form of transportation.
   B. Gasoline for private autos is less essential than home heating oil or gasoline for trucking.

Thesis: the best solution to the oil import problem is improved mass transit.

III. Improving mass transit would reduce use of automobiles.
   A. Many persons drive to work now because they have no alternative means of getting there.
   B. Recreational use of autos could also be reduced by better train and bus service.

IV. No other solution would cut down gasoline consumption as much as improving mass transit.
   A. Energy conservation in home heating cannot achieve more savings without large costs and risks.
   B. Millions of commuters cannot car pool; they could use mass transit.
   C. Industrial and commercial uses of gas and oil cannot be further reduced without serious environmental side effects.

EXERCISE 11.2   AUDIENCE ADAPTATION

OBJECTIVE	**To practice audience analysis, adaptation, and informative speaking.**
DIRECTIONS	1. Assume a situation in which you will give speeches to two different groups, but with the same basic goal. You will ask for financial support for a project of your club from both the student association and the faculty governing body.
	2. Using the audience analysis outline, note the differences in the two situations.
	3. Describe how you would adapt the same basic appeal to the two different audiences. (Remember to think of both verbal and nonverbal adaptations.)
REVIEW	1. What are the key questions in audience analysis?
	2. How can the information needed for audience analysis be found?
	3. How can nonverbal communication be adapted as a result of audience analysis?
	4. Explain the most important communication principle illustrated or learned from this exercise and why you found it important.

DEVELOPING THE INTRODUCTION AND CONCLUSION

The final step in organizing the speech is to plan the introduction and the conclusion. You should not prepare these parts of the speech until you know what the body of the speech includes. You can make better decisions about the beginning and end when you know what the body consists of. So defer planning both until you have planned all other parts of the speech. Preparing both introduction and conclusion at the same time also makes it easy to relate them to each other, an excellent technique to unify a speech.

Introductions

Introductions may be the most important part of a speech. If listeners decide early that they like you it will positively affect everything else you say. If listeners have negative impressions at the beginning, they may retain a mental set against everything else you say.

Purposes   An introduction should accomplish three things. Listeners should give you favorable attention; gain a favorable first impression of you; and begin thinking about the subject. In planning introductions, seek to accomplish these three goals.

Listeners' attention is essential at the beginning. If you don't have it then, you may never get it. Moreover, their attention should be favorable. You could easily get listeners' attention with insults or outlandish behavior. Neither, however, would help much toward reaching your goal.

The introduction is often your listeners' first chance to know you. A study of how people form impressions indicates that we form long-lasting images of others in the first minute of interaction. Once we have them, these impressions are difficult to change. Whether you want listeners to like you, to believe you are a competent authority, or to think you are interested in them and their concerns, it is important they get that impression in the first few minutes of your speech.

Finally, an introduction should begin to focus listeners' thoughts toward your thesis. Doubtless you have been in situations where a speaker started with two or three jokes and then abruptly shifted to a serious topic that seemed completely unrelated to the humor. The abrupt shift was not only jarring; it wasn't necessary. Humor is a good way to start a speech, and it can relate to the idea content of the speech. Since attention is so fleeting, don't take the chance of losing your listeners. Speakers take that chance if listeners have to refocus their thoughts after the introduction.

How long should an introduction be? That depends on the task. If you are unfamiliar to the audience and need time to secure their good will, you need a longer introduction. It takes a while to feel acquainted with strangers. Some situations demand formalities that must be followed. They take time. On the other hand, if the speech is short, the introduction should not be long. If you are well known, or listeners have a great interest in the topic, long introductions aren't necessary. The goals of an introduction should guide its length.

Techniques Several techniques can be used for introductions, and each is effective in its own way. Some are effective used together. Learn to use each technique, because with various subjects some are more useful than others. A skillful speaker can use whichever type of introduction is best for each speech subject and situation.

HUMOR One of the best ways to begin a speech is with humor. Using humor is good because it can accomplish all three purposes for an introduction. We like people we laugh with. Humor gains attention. And properly chosen humor can relate to the thesis of the speech.

A speaker can use several types of humor. The most obvious and familiar is a humorous story or anecdote. In other words, tell a joke. Telling jokes is a common pastime for many people, and when the point of the joke relates to the speech topic, it is an excellent speech introduction.

Remember, however, that telling a funny story is not the only way to use humor. You can use humor without ever telling a joke. It is possible to find humor in the occasion or the situation. You can join with your audience in laughing at yourself or the situation. Using wit or irony is often as effective as telling a humorous story. In 1975, Daniel Moynihan, a Catholic politician, was speaking to a Catholic audience on the subject of an encyclical issued in 1963 by Pope John. His introductory comments illustrate our point:

We were—if a parochialism may intrude here—between the generation of Catholics such as Al Smith, who once asked Robert Moses what in the hell a papal encyclical was, and the generation now coming along which shows every disposition to wonder why anyone bothers to issue them. . . . I was then an Assistant Secretary of Labor and was at some pains to assure the Harvard graduates in the administration and the press that the Holy Father was indeed in favor of the minimum wage. Being so heavily Catholic, the AFL-CIO was not accustomed to paying much heed to what the papacy thought about working conditions, but the Harvards appeared to be impressed.[6]

ANECDOTES OR ILLUSTRATIONS   Stories without humor may also be good speech introductions. Human interest, attention value, and relevant points can all be found in serious anecdotes. Telling a story that illustrates the idea or problem you're discussing can gain attention and introduce ideas.

Dr. William Stanmeyer, in a speech critical of our methods of trying criminals, provides an excellent example:

On July 2, 1972, four-year-old Joyce Ann Huff, a beautiful little girl, to judge by the newspaper photos, happily went out to play in the yard of her home in Los Angeles County. She played awhile, her mother occasionally glancing out at her from the kitchen a few feet away . . .

Neither Joyce Ann nor her mother noticed a yellow 1966 Chevrolet carrying three men roll up the street and pause while a man in the back seat took aim with a shotgun at the little girl. But they heard a thunderous explosion as the shotgun drove forty-two pellets into Joyce Ann's body and drove her soul forever from the face of this earth. Spattered with blood, Joyce Ann died within five minutes in the arms of her sobbing mother. Witness identification enabled the police to arrest the three. . . .

What, if anything, under our present system of criminal justice, will happen to the murderers?[7]

QUOTATIONS   Another effective way to begin a speech is to use quotations. Quote the words of famous and well-known speakers, leaders, writers, philosophers. Or quote someone known only to the audience if that person is respected by the group. You can quote poetry, music, or philosophy. Take a familiar phrase and twist it in a slightly new way. Because it is usually easy to find a poet or writer who captures your ideas well, quotations are easy to find as well as very good introductions.

Julia Stuart, the national president of the League of Women Voters in 1967, spoke that year to a meeting of the league in Detroit. Her speech illustrates the technique of introduction using quotation:

The title of my talk to you is "What Can I Do That Matters?" It is taken from a poem in the form of a prayer written by Stephen Spender thirty years ago. "Living," he said, "in the shadow of a war, what can I do that matters?" In his day the shadow was the depression and the growing edge of fascism. In our day we wage war against crime and poverty and for a more orderly world, but the cry, "What can I do that matters?" is still relevant.[8]

---

[6] Daniel Moynihan's speech is in *Vital Speeches of the Day*, January 1, 1976, pp. 172–76.

[7] From *Vital Speeches of the Day*, January 1, 1973, pp. 182–86.

[8] The text of Stuart's speech is in Donald Bryant and Karl Wallace, *Fundamentals of Public Speaking*, 5th ed. (Englewood Cliffs, N.J.: Prentice-Hall, 1976), pp. 512–21.

QUESTIONS   Introductions often use either rhetorical or direct questions. **Rhetorical questions** are *those to which speakers do not expect answers.* Listeners answer rhetorical questions to themselves or, sometimes, just think about the answers. A good example of a rhetorical question that implies its own answers can be found in remarks by Mary Cunningham, "To the extent that we continue to accept barriers which prevent certain talented individuals from achieving the most responsible levels of corporate power, to that extent we are wasting our greatest resource, the intelligence, creativity and judgment of our people. Can this country really afford to pay such a price for discrimination? Is American industry really willing to provide the receptacle for such waste?"[9]

A direct question seeks overt audience response. Suppose you need some information from an audience. If you want to talk about a popular movie and need to know how much you can assume your listeners know about it, you might ask, "How many of you have seen the movie *Gone With the Wind?*" Or if your speech is a travelog, you may start by asking, "How many of you have been to the French Quarter in New Orleans?"

Using direct questions has more than one value. Sometimes, it's the only way to get information you need. In addition, it gets at least some overt response from listeners. It helps you begin with a sense of interaction. It helps listeners know that the speech will be a two-way exchange. They'll feel they are participating, not just attending a performance.

Questions are often used in combination with other techniques in introductions. Combining questions with anecdotes, humor, quotations, or reference to occasion or subject is often effective.

STARTLING STATEMENTS OR STATISTICS   For some speeches, citing an impressive statistic or making a startling statement is a good beginning. It can create curiosity and attention. A speaker whose topic relates to the danger of cigarette smoking could start by looking directly at the audience and saying: "At least three people in this audience will someday have lung cancer; five will have heart disease." This statement is direct, immediately involves listeners, and is somewhat alarming. It presents familiar information for most people, but bringing it directly to listeners' lives makes it hard to ignore.

The startling statistic is easily combined with the rhetorical question. Just add, "Did you know that . . ." to your statistic. For instance, in a speech on storm safety, a speaker started with: "Did you know that lightning kills more people every year than tornadoes and hurricanes combined?"

Reference to Audience, Occasion, or Subject   Sometimes it is best to begin with direct reference to occasion, situation, listeners, or the reason you are there. If you are speaking at a meeting called for the purpose of discussing the subject of your speech, a long introduction wastes time and loses interest. Direct reference to the reason you are there may be the best way to begin.

---

[9] Productivity and the Corporate Culture," speech to the Commonwealth Club, San Francisco, February 27, 1981; published in Anita Taylor, *Speaking in Public* (Englewood Cliffs, N.J.: Prentice Hall, 1984).

If the audience is interested in the topic, part of the goal of the introduction is already accomplished. On these occasions, the speaker may benefit by immediately using the strong interest that brought the audience together. A speech by Bella Abzug to a conference for Southern women convened by the Women's Political Caucus illustrates. She began without fanfare: "As co-chairwoman of the National Women's Political Caucus, I welcome you to the women's political power movement. I am not an authority on the South, but I suspect that this is the first time a conference such as this has ever been held here. You are making history today."[10]

At other times, directly relating subject or thesis to audience needs is the best attention-getting device. Can what you plan to talk about directly help your listeners feel more secure, solve problems, gain the esteem of others, make money, and so forth? If so, your topic is your means of gaining attention. Showing how what you plan to talk about can help people satisfy their needs is one of the best ways to begin. Referring to the discussion of the Maslow hierarchy in Chapter 6 might be useful here.

Conclusions

Ending the speech is the most difficult part for many speakers. A conclusion with the appropriate mood and content requires a delicate touch. Also important is to know *when* to end. Haven't you, on many occasions, listened to speakers who passed three or four good conclusions? And each time the speaker ignored the possible ending, you got a little more frustrated with the effort of listening? That often happens because speakers find conclusions so difficult to do right.

Purposes The conclusion may be the last impression the audience has of you. Obviously it needs to be a good one. The goals of a conclusion are to refocus your listeners' thinking on the thesis and/or purpose and leave them in the right mood. For some speeches, this requires an appeal for action. Whatever the type of speech, a conclusion has these two goals. Plan your ending to reach them.

Techniques Conclusions, like introductions, can use many different techniques. *Each technique we discussed as a way to introduce a speech can be used to close one.* You can use a stories, humorous or not; quotations; rhetorical or direct questions; reference to the situation and occasion; a startling statistic or piece of information. Whatever you choose, the final sentence should bring a sense of finishing.

LINKING TO THE INTRODUCTION With good planning, you can often relate the conclusion to the introduction. If you started with an apt quotation, perhaps you can finish by restating it. This will refocus thinking on the ideas it suggests. If you started with a rhetorical question, you can answer it in the conclusion. If you started

---

[10] Speech to Southern Women's Conference on "Education for Delegate Selection," Scarritt College, Nashville, Tennessee, February 12, 1972. Complete speech can be found in Waldo Braden, ed., *Representative American Speeches* 1971–72, Vol. 44 (New York: The H. W. Wilson Co., 1972), pp. 38–48.

with a story, you may not finish it in the introduction. You can provide the end in the conclusion.

One of the best student speeches we ever heard used that technique. This student began by telling the story of a seven-year-old child at a picnic on the last day of school in the spring. The youngster came home that night with tired, aching legs. The next morning she was taken to the hospital. Polio—a dread crippler of children in those days—was the diagnosis. During the speech the student talked about how the March of Dimes helped people like that by paying for iron lungs, hospitalization, years of physical therapy. The speech had a persuasive purpose: seeking contributions to the March of Dimes. In conclusion, the student said: "I started by telling you the story of that youngster taken to the hospital with polio. Thanks to the March of Dimes, its financial and moral support, that child is standing in front of you today, able to live a normal life. Won't you help others like me? Please contribute." And she passed around contribution envelopes.

This example also shows one way to make a direct appeal for action in the conclusion. Though beginners are often reluctant to do so, speakers can—often should—ask for specific responses or specific behaviors. A speech seeking action should end with an effort to secure at least verbal commitment to the behavior. Don't fail to ask because you fear negative responses.

SUMMARIZING   In many, if not most, speeches, a summary is a good technique for conclusion. Summarizing your main ideas helps refocus listeners' thinking on your thesis and main ideas. Indeed, if any fixed rule about public speaking exists, it is that *conclusions to all informative speeches should include a summary.* When ideas are repeated, they are more likely to be remembered. And for listeners to remember what you say is important in most situations. So main ideas and theses should be summarized at the end of most speeches.

Most often, however, a summary should be only part of the conclusion. A summary is not interesting. At least for persuasive speeches, a summary alone is rarely appropriate. It will not put the audience in the right mood. For informative speeches, a summary combined with a direct question—"What questions do you have?" or "What else can I tell you?"—is a good way to conclude. In situations where the audience is expected to have many questions, this may be all the conclusion you need. In other cases, combine summaries with a direct appeal, a story, or a quotation.

Whichever technique of concluding you choose, know when to finish. Don't say, "In conclusion . . .," and then go on for five more minutes. Don't pass the end of the attention span of your listeners. Questions and discussion are better at holding attention than continuation of the same voice. Plan a finish; plan a time for it; and use it.

EXERCISE 11.3   INTRODUCTIONS AND CONCLUSIONS

OBJECTIVE   **To practice using the various techniques for introducing and concluding speeches.**

DIRECTIONS   **1.** Select a recent issue of *Vital Speeches* from your library. Pick out a speech to analyze.
2. Identify the techniques of introduction and conclusion the speaker used.
3. Prepare a possible introduction for the speech using three techniques the speaker did *not* use. (This could require you to prepare three different possible introductions.)
4. Prepare a possible conclusion for ending the speech using three techniques for conclusions the speaker did *not* use.
5. Your instructor may have you present your suggestions in an oral report.

REVIEW   **Provide brief answers to the following that may be used as a writing assignment or basis for class discussion.**
1. What are the main purposes for a speech introduction?
2. What are the major functions speech conclusions should accomplish?
3. Describe the techniques most useful for introductions. For conclusions.
4. Explain the most important communication principle illustrated or learned from this exercise and why you found it important.

A SAMPLE OUTLINE

Here is a complete outline for an informative speech that was prepared by Rosalie Moyer, a student in one of our classes. Based on material in a book by James T. deKay,[11] it provides an illustration of the planning we have discussed in this chapter.

Introduction

Attention step: How many people here are left handed? (wait for answer). Did you know that Casey Stengel swore that left handers have more enthusiasm for life? He said "They sleep on the wrong side of the bed, and their heads become stagnant on that side."

Orientation step: H. G. Wells wrote, "We know Neanderthal men were right handed because the left side of the brain . . . was bigger than the right." He believed—along with many others—that left handedness was insignificant. He was wrong.

Central Idea: People who are left handed live their lives differently from the way right-handed people do.

  I. Left handers are treated differently.
    A. Physical equipment is designed primarily for right handers.
      1. The cockpit of an airplane is designed for right-handed pilots; if the pilot is left handed he still isn't allowed to sit on the other side to work the controls.

---

[11] *Left-Handed Book* (New York: M. Evans, 1966).

      a. Can you picture me as your pilot, saying to you, "Hello, I'm Lefty Moyer, your pilot." You would probably want to bail out if you thought about it for a moment.

  2. Violins, banjos, and guitars have to be restrung before lefties can use them.

  3. School desks have writing areas convenient for right handers, impossible for left handers.

  4. Polaroid cameras are almost impossible for lefties to use.

  5. Scissors, can openers, and watches are for right handers (DEMONSTRATE SCISSORS, CAN OPENER).

  6. If you are a leftie trying to use a typical power saw, you have to cross your arms to use it, and then you can't see where you are going.

B. Our writing and reading are meant for right handers.

  1. Our alphabet was invented by the Romans, militantly right-handed people, who had words to describe left- and right-handed people:

    a. In Latin, the word for right is DEXTER (FLIP CHART).

    b. In Latin, the word for left is SINISTER (FLIP CHART).

  2. The Chinese give lefties a better chance. They write in vertical columns, from right to left, indicating a slight left-handed preference.

  3. Ancient Egyptians wrote in upward or downward vertical columns, or from left to right, or from right to left horizontally, depending on their whim.

  4. But not in American English. We must write from left to right, guaranteeing that lefties smudge, smear, and cannot see what they have written.

  5. Left-handed people, themselves, often write like this (DEMONSTRATE WITH FLIP CHART).

II. Left handers think and act differently.

(transition): James T. deKay says, in *The Left-Handed Book*, "Being left-handed in a right-handed world can be frustrating, which may account for the fact that both Jack the Ripper and the Boston Strangler were left-handed." Well, we don't all act quite that differently.

A. The total effect of right-sided dominance on attitudes is unknown, but there must be some effect.

  1. Left handers tend to make waves, are frequently nonconformists.

    a. When people try to change our handedness, we resist violently and consistently.

  2. When world leaders are left handed, they are frequently perceived as enigmatic and difficult to deal with diplomatically.

    a. Alexander the Great, Ben Franklin, Harry Truman, Charlemagne, King George VI, and Lord Nelson were all left handers.

B. Only 10 percent of the population is left handed, but approximately half of people in remedial reading courses are left handed.

  1. Where is the center for learning to read located in the brain? Is it simply on the wrong side for lefties?

  2. Is learning to read, on the other hand, more difficult for lefties because written language was probably developed by right handers for themselves?

C. Left handers are three times as likely as right handers to become alcoholics.

  1. Does brain dominance affect the body's chemistry so that we react to alcohol differently?

  2. Or is frustration at not being understood a cause of the excessive drinking?

D. Left handers excel in other kinds of activities.

  1. Among actors/performers are: Peter Lawford, Rock Hudson, Paul McCartney, Ringo Starr, Dick VanDyke (who, incidentally, is also alcoholic), Judy Garland.

  2. Among artists are: Picasso, Holbein, Michelangelo, Raphael, and Leonardo.

  3. Among athletes are: Babe Ruth, Casey Stengel, Ty Cobb, and there are many others, but the baseball players are probably the best known because the game singles them out so.

III. We should take some active steps toward coping with our left handedness.
    A. We should support the Bill of Lefts:
        1. BE IT RESOLVED THAT ALL LEFT-THINKING CITIZENS, MINDFUL OF THEIR BIRTHLEFT, SHALL HENCEFORTH STAND UP FOR THEIR LEFTS.
    B. We should buy left:
        1. Use Borden's Cheese Spread—its tear strip opens both left and right.
        2. Buy an English car and get a free left-handed gearshift.
        3. Insist on left-handed checkbooks from the bank.
    C. We should support the arts—that's where the lefties seem to congregate, and where one good hand deserves another.

Conclusion

In conclusion, we should remember that while we must live our lives differently from right handers because they have designed the physical equipment as well as our reading and writing, they haven't taken from us what we do well. We think and act differently from them and often for the better. We're often better athletes, artists, and leaders. So, remember, if you can't get a left-handed tool to do the job at hand, forget it. Let a right hander do it for you.

SUMMARY

Speaking in public is common for many of us, even though we do little that we think of as formal public speaking. Speaking in a public situation is merely one type of communication, so effective public speaking is effective communication. The study of public speaking is guided by one overriding principle: What is effective depends on the speaker, the situation, and the listeners. We have only guidelines, not rules, for speaking in public.

Preparation for speaking in public begins with establishing a goal. Topic choice is usually determined by the reason for giving the speech. Topic should always be related to goals. The first step in goal setting is to determine the general purpose of the speech. General purposes include informing, entertaining, and persuading. Next, a speaker establishes a specific purpose. Establishing a specific purpose involves answering the question, What exactly do I want my audience to do, think, or feel when I am finished speaking? The third step in goal setting is audience analysis. Answers to six specific questions can help determine what information you need about the audience: (1) What do they already know about the topic? (2) What is their specific interest in it? (3) What are their attitudes and feelings about the thesis and purpose? (4) About the speaker? (5) About related subjects and issues? (6) How will the situation affect the speech? Answering the questions sometimes simply involves asking a few people; in other cases it requires inferring from demographic data. Audience analysis is never complete until the speech is over and assessed. A good speaker will continue to use feedback from listeners while talking. After studying the audience, the speaker reexamines the statement of specific purpose. What the speaker learned may require a revision of the purpose.

Next the speaker states the thesis, which is a subject-centered statement; it is a single sentence summary of the speech. A thesis is the main point or central idea of the speech. Developing a thesis requires organizing. Organizing thoughts involves outlining the speech, choosing two, three, or four main points that will be used to develop or support the theses. Several standard plans for choosing main ideas are the time pattern, the space pattern, and three specific topical patterns. After selecting main points, the speaker arranges them, using audience analysis. With a deductive structure, the thesis is stated early in the speech. With an inductive structure, the thesis is withheld until midway through or at the end of the speech.

Finally, main points are developed with subpoints and supporting materials and the speaker prepares the introduction and the conclusion. An introduction needs to get the listeners' favorable attention and to begin pointing their thoughts toward the subject of the speech. Introductions may use several techniques: humor, serious illustrations, quotations, questions, a startling statement or statistic, or in some situations direct reference to audience, occasion, or subject. A conclusion should refocus listeners' thinking on the thesis and leave them in an appropriate mood. Techniques for conclusions are the same as those for introductions, with the addition of a summary. Combining one of the techniques with a summary is recommended, especially for informative speeches. Relating conclusion to introduction can also give a speech unity.

QUESTIONS FOR DISCUSSION

1. What are the three general purposes of public speaking?
2. What distinguishes specific from general purposes?
3. What is audience analysis, and how do you analyze and adapt to an audience?
4. Why is the use of thesis statement important to the speaker? to the audience?
5. What are the differences among subject, thesis, and purpose in speech organization?
6. What are some useful organizational plans for speeches?
7. Where can you go to find information to develop the speech thesis?
8. What should introductions and conclusions accomplish, and what techniques can be used to reach these goals?

SUGGESTIONS FOR FURTHER READING

Amato, Phillip, and Donald Ecroyd. *Organizational Patterns and Strategies in Speech Communication*. Skokie Ill.: National Textbook Company, 1975.

Bradley, Bert. *Fundamentals of Speech Communication*, 5th ed. Dubuque: William C. Brown, 1987.

Bryant, Donald C., and Karl R. Wallace. *Fundamentals of Public Speaking*, 5th ed. Englewood Cliffs, N.J.: Prentice-Hall, 1976.

Ehninger, Douglas, Bruce Gronbeck, Ray McKerrow, and Alan Monroe. *Principles and Types of Speech Communication*, 9th ed. Glenview, Ill.: Scott, Foresman, 1982.

Gibson, James. *Speech Organization: A Programmed Approach*. San Francisco: Rinehart Press, 1971.

Gibson, James, and Michael Hanna. *Audience Analysis: A Programmed Approach to Receiver Behavior*. Englewood Cliffs, N.J.: Prentice-Hall, 1975.

Markle, Marsha, and Thomas R. King. *A Program on Speech Preparation*. Columbus, Ohio: Charles E. Merrill, 1972.

Mudd, Charles, S., and Malcolm Sillars. *Speech: Content and Communication*, 5th ed. New York: Harper and Row, 1985.

Phillips, Gerald M., and J. Jerome Zolten. *Structuring Speech*. Indianapolis, Ind.: Bobbs-Merrill, 1976.

12 Preparing Speeches: Developing Ideas

Remember every time you open your mouth to talk, your mind walks out and parades up and down the words.

EDWIN H. STUART

GOAL

To be able to make effective use of supporting materials

OBJECTIVES

The material in this chapter should help you to:
1. Distinguish between giving information as a purpose and as a technique.
2. Explain the functions of supporting materials in speeches.
3. Cite and use examples of the factors of attention:
    Importance
    Concreteness
    Movement and/or variety
    Humor
    Familiarity
    Curiosity
    Conflict
4. Use each of the following types of supporting materials to develop speech ideas:
    Examples
    Statements of observation
    Statistics
    Quotations
    Comparison and contrast
    Repetition and restatement
5. Use visual techniques of giving information effectively.
6. State the cautions to be followed in using visual aids.
7. Use library and other resources to find supporting materials.

We can compare developing a speech to constructing a high-rise building. First the framework goes up—steel girders and beams. This is like the outline of speech ideas. Then the rest of the building is put into place—brick or steel outside wall, inside partitions. This "finishing" transforms a framework into a building. Similarly, a speech changes from framework (outline) to finished product with *supporting materials*. In this chapter we review types and uses of supporting materials and discuss how to find and select them.

USES OF SUPPORTING MATERIALS

Supporting materials include facts, statements of observation and opinion, narrative, examples, explanation, quotations, restatement and repetition, and comparison and contrast. All may be used to develop ideas in the outline.

Developing Ideas

Supporting materials perform many functions in a speech. In this section, we discuss the most important uses: to give or clarify information, to amplify, to give a new perspective, to prove, to motivate, and to maintain attention.

Sharing or Clarifying Information   Perhaps the most obvious use of supporting materials is to give listeners information they don't have. A related use is to clarify ideas or information. Often, listeners will have heard an item of information but will not understand it or realize its importance. Appropriate use of supporting materials can help them achieve this new understanding.

We want to be clear here: using supporting materials to give information differs from the speech purpose, speaking to inform. The distinction lies in how the speaker uses the information. If the speaker's purpose is only to share information, to have listeners understand information or ideas presented, the use of supporting materials to inform and the speech purpose are the same. Often, however, we give information for the purpose of persuading or influencing people. In these cases, the supporting materials perform the function of giving or clarifying information, but the speech purpose is not to inform.

When people need to understand an idea or have new information before they will do what a persuader wants them to, giving information is a technique, not a goal. In both situations (speaking to inform or persuade), speakers usually need to use supporting materials to give or clarify information.

Offering Proof   Supporting materials are also used to prove points. The persuasive situation involves a speaker making claims listeners may not believe. For instance, if a speaker claims most rivers are too polluted to swim in, many listeners won't believe it. This situation requires evidence to change their minds. Facts, statistics, opinions of authority, examples, and explanations are supporting materials most commonly used to prove, but any of the techniques discussed later may be helpful.

Motivation   In both persuasive and informative situations, supporting materials help motivate listeners. When the goal is to inform, supporting materials can help people want to learn what the speaker is telling them. In some persuasive situations, the speaker does not need to change any minds but does need to arouse feelings so listeners will be motivated to act. For example, most smokers agree that they should stop. They know it's harmful for their health, but they continue to smoke. If a speaker's goal is for them to quit, supporting materials are needed to motivate, to make them feel strongly enough about the hazards of smoking and the benefits of quitting that they will do something.

Amplification   Another purpose for using supporting materials is to amplify. Again, whether your purpose is to inform or persuade, people must remember at least your important ideas. The "bigger" an idea is to people, the more likely they are to remember it. Just as amplified music makes a larger impression than music without amplification, so too with ideas. The bigger they seem, the more likely listeners will pay attention and remember. Supporting materials can help by amplifying your important ideas.

Giving a New Perspective   Supporting materials can create a new perspective, to get people to look at something they already know in a new way. You may want listeners to have new insights or deeper understanding.

In a speech to the national convention of the Speech Communication Association in 1974, the Reverend Jesse Jackson used analogy, explanation, and humor as techniques to give his listeners a new perspective on the role of ethnic groups in America. Jackson noted that the popular analogy of the melting pot was inappropriate. He felt the image of metals being heated and synthesized into a new product didn't fit the American experience. He contended:

. . . a better example is that we're more like a bowl of vegetable soup [laughter] than a melting pot. [applause] First of all, vegetable soup is more digestible than steel. [laughter] . . . The second point is that in the vegetable soup you may have a tomato base and this is the homogenous dimension of American culture. There are many things that we have in common. We have common geographical soil, common air, common water, common tax system, common military system, common government. There is an American base that's more American than it is European, African or anything else . . .

But beyond . . . that American base, . . . corn and beans, peas and chunks of meat are floating up on the top of that soup. And those things appeal to us. Our Irishness, our Italianness, our Catholicism, our Protestantism, our Jewishness, our Blackness, our Arabness appeal to us, and it's up on the top of the soup. And when it gets hot, those elements do not lose their identity, but each one of them has extracted from it some of its vital juices. And that's what makes the soup tasty. Because there are some Blacks and some whites, some males, some females, some young and some old, but no one loses his essential identity, just gives up some of this essence for the common wealth.[1]

[1] This speech, which was given in Chicago in December 1974, can be heard on cassettes sold by the Speech Communication Association, 5105 Backlick Rd., Annandale, Va. 22003.

Jesse Jackson.

Maintaining Attention

One of the most important functions of materials within the speech is to maintain the attention of listeners. Without listeners' attention, you have little chance of reaching your goals.

Recall from Chapter 1 that attention is quite variable. Paying attention requires people to constantly refocus their receiving senses. In the case of listening to a speaker, members of the audience must watch, focus to hear, and direct their minds toward what the speaker is saying. Constant attention is hard work. It uses much physical energy. For these reasons, the speaker should be aware of the necessity to help listeners reduce the effort required.

Types of Attention   Remember that we classified attention into two categories: focal and marginal. Speakers want to take advantage of both, (1) to keep the ideas of the speech in the focus of listeners' attention; and (2) to use all aspects of verbal and nonverbal communication so what is received marginally supports the ideas.

Another way to classify attention is as voluntary or involuntary. **Involuntary attention** *means the listener can't help paying attention*. If a loud explosion occurs in the next room while you're reading this, it will take your attention from the book. A flash of light or someone walking by is likely to do the same thing. These are examples of involuntary attention. You don't intend to pay attention to them, but you do. **Voluntary attention** *means you must make yourself pay attention*. This is conscious, willed attention.

A speaker's goal is for listeners to give involuntary attention. Listeners shouldn't have to work at listening. To avoid that, speakers use content to attract involuntary attention. This is described as using the **attention factors.**

Factors of Attention

RELEVANCE, PROXIMITY, OR IMPORTANCE   People listen to things they care about. If something is relevant or important to listeners, they are likely to pay attention. Things that people are proud of, are close to them, or are important to them will capture their attention. If you can show how ideas have relevance, will benefit, or will affect your listeners in some important way, they will pay atttention.

Eric Sevareid used this approach in his speech before the Washington Journalism Center when he said, "Until rather recently, those in the printed press who became disturbed by direct government assault on broadcasting were saying to us, 'Look out, your end of the boat is sinking.' This has greatly changed, thank heaven. We all know now that we occupy a common vessel."[2]

CONCRETENESS   Concrete images are more attention-getting than abstract ones. People respond to things they can see, things they recognize, things that recall actual images or events. Abstractions are hard to visualize and pay attention to. You can get vividness by providing concrete pictures of things or by visualizing ideas. For example, philosophy as an abstract concept is not likely to hold most listeners' attention. But if you talk about how philosophy affects your listeners' lives, it can hold their attention. Concreteness is one reason visual aids hold attention. They provide something concrete for listeners to see.

VARIETY, MOVEMENT, ACTIVITY   A kind of "Newton's law" might be applied here: A moving stimulus is always more attention-getting than one at rest. If you're looking at two things and one of them moves, you'll notice the one that moves. Variety, activity, and movement are among the best attention factors for speakers.

This principle applies to the nonverbal as well as the verbal content of speeches. A lively, animated, varied speaking style helps hold attention. A speaker who uses body movements purposefully will hold attention better than one who stands still and never moves. A speech that consists of only one kind of supporting material will not hold attention well. A single or a few good statistics can catch attention. A long series of numbers or explanatory statements will turn most people off. And though quotations and explanations are necessary in most speeches, if not combined with examples, visual aids, and analogies, the speech may become boring. To hold attention in a speech, use a variety of supporting materials and lively, varied presentation.

HUMOR   Humor is an important attention factor. Though what is funny to one person may not be to someone else, if people in an audience find something funny, they will pay attention. Hasn't this happened to you? Listening to a speaker, kind of daydreaming, you hear: "That reminds me of a story. . . ." All of a sudden

---

[2] The text of Sevareid's speech is in *Vital Speeches of the Day*, July 1, 1967, pp. 562–67.

you popped back to attention and heard the story, though you had no idea why the speaker told it. Speakers must be careful to use humor that is appropriate to the situation, the subject, and to themselves. But if appropriate, humor is a superior attention factor.

FAMILIARITY COMBINED WITH NOVELTY   People pay attention to familiar things as long as the diet doesn't become monotonous. If you are presenting something your audience is familiar with, combine it with a new point of view, a new perspective. Present old ideas with a new twist. Give information with a novel approach, a new phrasing. Martin Luther King's well-known "I Have a Dream" speech contains several examples of this. One of the best is Dr. King's comparison of the promises of the U.S. Constitution and Declaration of Independence to a check. He said, "America has given the Negro people a bad check—a check that has come back marked, 'insufficient funds.' We refuse to believe that the bank of justice is bankrupt."[3]

CURIOSITY   When people are curious they pay attention. If you suggest that an idea might be beneficial or relevant or important to them, listeners will be curious. Most of us are filled with natural curiosity, especially about things that might affect us. We enjoy learning about new things if we can see a use for them. Arouse your listeners' interest in the unknown, show them how they can gain from knowing what they don't now know, and curiosity will keep them listening.

COMPETITION AND CONFLICT   A vital attention factor is conflict. People love to watch conflict and to hear about it. They go to football games by the thousands, but they don't attend the practices. Conflict is what attracts. The lure is competition. Well-executed plays thrill fans, but they seldom attend an event unless it involves competition. Knowing this can help you devise ways to hold an audience's attention.

If you can use conflict to side with the audience against a cause or an opponent, it will help hold attention. Be careful, however, not to arouse conflict between yourself and the audience. That might well hold attention but will destroy the chances of accomplishing most goals. People pay attention to someone they are arguing with, but they are usually neither informed nor persuaded.

It should be clear that *being able to hold attention depends heavily on the materials you use to develop the ideas of the speech.* The speech outline will be attention-getting only if the ideas are significant to the audience. Materials used to develop the outline will keep attention if they have one or more of other qualities we've noted: concreteness, humor, curiosity, importance, variety. As you select supporting materials, keep these attention factors in mind.

[3] Speech to participants in August 1963 People's March on Washington.

EXERCISE 12.1   AUDIENCE ATTENTION

OBJECTIVE   **To practice identifying attention devices and related audience analysis.**

DIRECTIONS   1. Select an advertisement that catches your attention in a popular magazine.
2. Identify the audience to which the ad is directed.
3. Identify the factors of attention used in the advertisement, showing how these would catch the intended audience's attention.
4. Your instructor may ask you to report in a speech your conclusions about the advertiser's audience analysis and use of attention factors.

REVIEW   **Provide brief answers that may be a writing assignment or the basis for class discussion.**
1. What major factors are used to gain and hold attention?
2. What can you do if you notice listeners losing attention while you talk?
3. Explain the most important communication principle illustrated or learned from this exercise and why you found it important.

TYPES OF SUPPORTING MATERIALS

Verbal Techniques

Verbal supporting materials include explanation, narration, example, observations and statistics, quotations, comparison and contrast, repetition and restatement.

Explanation   Explanation—*telling how something works*—is a good technique to clarify ideas. If you wanted listeners to know how to file their tax returns, for example, you would use explanation.

Betty Ford, speaking in 1975 to the American Cancer Society, used explanation to clarify how she overcame the problems resulting from her cancer operation:

It isn't vanity to worry about disfigurement. It is an honest concern. I started wearing low-cut dresses as soon as the scar healed, and my worries about my appearance are now just the normal ones of staying slim and keeping my hair and make-up in order. When I asked myself whether I would rather lose a right arm or a breast, I decided I would rather have lost a breast. The most important thing in life is *good health*. And that I have![4]

Narration   Narration, *which tells a story or relates an event*, is useful. Telling how something happened helps people understand it. Narration holds attention as well as improving clarity. Narration can also amplify ideas, prove, and motivate. An example of narration was in the student's conclusion to the March of Dimes speech cited on p. 311.

[4] Betty Ford's speech was made November 7, 1975. Complete text is in Taylor, *Speaking in Public*, pp. 279–280.

Example Perhaps the most valuable of all supporting materials is example. An **example** is a *case of something*. If you look back through earlier chapters in this book, you will see dozens of examples, cases used to illustrate a point. In this chapter, for example, you read how Betty Ford used explanation and Jesse Jackson an analogy.

There are several types of examples—long or short, real or hypothetical. We call long examples, cases given with great detail, *illustrations*.[5] We describe short examples as *instances*. Often illustrations and instances are used in combination, as was done by a student in one of our classes. She spoke about air pollution and its remedies. She talked at length about what was done to clean up the air in London, a city that not many years ago had the most polluted air in the world. She related much detail, using both explanation and narration in the illustration of how London cleaned up its air. Then to amplify, she said: "Similar techniques were followed in Dublin, Newcastle, and Edinburgh. Each city has experienced the same dramatic changes."

Examples can also be real or hypothetical. A *real* example has the great value of showing that what you're talking about actually happened somewhere. But sometimes you're in a situation where you ask the audience to suppose that something happened, and you give them a *hypothetical* example. Suppose you want to explain survival techniques in case of fire. You might involve listeners best with a hypothetical case: "Imagine yourself at midnight in a hotel room hearing an alarm that indicates the building is on fire. What would you do?" Then take your listeners through the steps you recommend. Have them "see" themselves taking the steps. This is a vivid and memorable way to give an example.

Observations and Statistics Another useful means of supporting ideas is using statements of observation (what people often call facts) and figures. Names, dates, dimensions, descriptions, and so on are especially helpful in giving people new information. Statistics are equally useful. **Statistics** *consist of many observations, added up, with the relationships among them analyzed*. To report that the American Medical Association said 200 deaths in Los Angeles in 1978 were due to air pollution would be using figures but not statistics. To report an AMA conclusion that 55 percent of deaths from respiratory illnesses were from emphysema caused by air pollution would be using statistics. Statistics count things and use inferences to show relationship among data.

Statistics are especially useful in persuading, but they are also informative. Statistics can help explain how or why things happen. Statistics can support conclusions about large groups of people, describe trends, help forecast events.

PRECAUTIONS IN USING DATA Speakers should remember some cautions about the use of observations and statistics. The first: Don't overdo it. Many listeners do not find data interesting. So speakers who rely heavily on data may have an uninformed

---

[5] This name for a long example suggests its function. We think of "illustrating" as showing a picture. The detailed example—an illustration—gives a verbal picture. Thus, a long example can be thought of as a word picture.

Corazon Acquino.

audience that gets bored and loses attention. It's also easy to give too many figures. Since many people are not good at processing numbers mentally, too many figures can quickly confuse. Most listeners understand and remember stories and examples better than figures. If listeners cannot keep up with you, they often quit trying to understand.

The second caution: *Be sure data are clear.* Because clarity is so essential, it is almost always helpful to present data visually as well as orally. Charts and diagrams aid attention, understanding, and remembering. Use them whenever possible when presenting statistics. We give some guidelines for using visual aids to present figures and statistics in the next section.

Quotations The use of **quotations**—*repeating someone else's exact words*—was discussed in Chapter 10 as a means of introducing or concluding a speech. It is equally useful as a means of supporting ideas. You can quote experts, nonexperts, poets, singers, someone you know, people you don't know but have talked to, something you heard, or something you read.

Quotations add attention value. They also emphasize points and give credibility to ideas or information. Unless you are an expert in a subject area, people will more readily accept what you say if you cite a recognized expert to verify your ideas. At other times you use a quotation because it makes the point so well. It may be a beautiful choice of words. To use the words and be honest about the source, you quote. For example, when talking about good citizenship, you might say, "John Kennedy expressed this idea better than I could when he said in his inaugural address, 'Ask not what your country can do for you, ask what you can do for your country." The most widely used quotation in this country may be Abraham Lincoln's government "of the people, by the people, and for the people."

Its use not only gains a speaker credibility through association with Lincoln, but the rhythmic beauty of the phrase is unmatched in making the idea vivid.

Neither should you overlook the potential of quoting from "average" people who have experienced the situations you're discussing. Whether you use expert or nonexpert quotations partly depends on the reason for using the quotation. Both have value. Relating what other people, like your listeners, have to say about your subject can be both informative and persuasive. That we see this technique often in advertisements shows how persuasive it is.

One of the most useful kinds of quotation is described as reluctant testimony. **Reluctant testimony** occurs *when a person expected to believe one way speaks against that position.* Ronald Reagan won many votes by claiming: "I used to be a liberal Democrat. I now see I was wrong." When a person admits what he or she wishes were not true, this is also reluctant testimony. When a conservative barber concedes that long hair looks good on men, it's impressive. Reluctant testimony is especially helpful in establishing credibility.

Comparison and Contrast   Another type of supporting material is use of comparison and contrast. To use **comparison** in a speech, you *point out similarities between your idea and something the audience is familiar with.* **Contrast** shows how *the idea differs from the known.* The two processes are often used together.

In using comparison and contrast, you may note similarities or differences not apparent on the surface. We could say that a speech is like a meal—the introduction is the appetizer, the body is the main course, and the conclusion is the dessert. This kind of comparison is called *analogy.* **Analogy** *shows similarities in things that on the surface are not similar.* It is an imaginative comparison. Jesse Jackson's vegetable soup comparison was an analogy.

To be most useful, comparisons require you to analyze receivers carefully. Choose comparisons meaningful to listeners, not just to you. Be sure the items chosen for comparison are familiar. Comparing the effect of psychosis to the state of mind of a person lost in a blizzard would have little effect if your audience had never been north of Florida. They wouldn't have experienced the terror and confusion that would make the comparison vivid and memorable to someone who has been outside in a snowstorm with a 30 mph wind.

Repetition and Restatement   Repetition and restatement can also be used to support ideas. **Repetition** is *repeating something in the exact words used before;* **restatement** is *repeating the same idea but using different words.* Both help listeners understand or remember what you say.

Sometimes listeners do not hear what you say or aren't able to understand the whole idea. Then you need only repeat the exact words for them to hear and understand. At other times people may understand the words but not the idea. They may not decode words the way you intend. In these cases, restatement is helpful. Using different words to express your intended meaning can help them decode as you want.

Simple repetition is often used for emphasis. By repeating words or phrases, you highlight ideas and help listeners remember them. An idea stated only once or twice is not half as likely to be remembered as one repeated three or more times. Repetition can be used to make ideas memorable. Good examples of this are found in Martin Luther King's famous "I Have a Dream" speech. In the conclusion, he repeated "Let freedom ring" nine times. The phrase, "I have a dream," repeated seven times during the speech, became a watchword for the civil rights movement.

Visual Techniques

Many techniques of giving information are visual. It would be difficult to overemphasize the value of using visual aids. Using many senses to support ideas can increase clarity, amplify and emphasize ideas, and improve recall. We noted that this is especially true with data and statistics, but it is not limited to use of figures.

Whenever you want listeners to remember something, use as many senses as possible for them to receive it. If you both say and show something, it is nearly six times more likely to be understood and remembered than if you only say it. According to Robert Craig, chief of the United States Public Health Service Audio Visual Facility, when people are taught with both visual and oral tools, they have better recall (both immediate and delayed) than when oral tools alone are used. In his research, when people were merely told, immediate recall was 70 percent; recall three days later was 10 percent. When people were taught with both visual and oral means, immediate recall was 85 percent; three days later it was still 65 percent.[6]

Guidelines for Visual Aids   Visual aids include diagrams that explain, graphs or charts that repeat data, cartoons or models, pictures that clarify or emphasize, flip charts or demonstrations that reveal outlines or processes. Films, slides, overhead projectors, and chalkboards can present materials visually. All can reinforce what you say verbally. Or you may actually bring in objects. One of the most vivid speeches we ever heard was made by a young woman who brought her pet alligator to class.

People, including the speaker, can also be visual aids. Speakers' actions clarify ideas, amplify them, or prove points. In criminal trials, a reenactment often shows a jury how a crime was committed. Talking about poverty-striken children is much more effective if pictures of them are also shown. As noted in Chapter 4, visual reinforcement of verbal messages is important to all communicators, including public speakers.

Visual aids are helpful, but if not used effectively, can detract from what you say. The following guidelines can help.

VISUALS ARE ONLY AIDS   Remember the visual is an *aid*; it should not be the entire speech. Even when you have been invited to the local PTA to talk about your trip to South America, the slides you bring are aids. They help you tell about

---

[6] Speech by Craig quoted in the *Kansas City Times*, April 19, 1967.

Visual aids used well improve understanding and retention and may help persuade.

the people you met and places you learned about. *Visuals should complement, supplement, clarify.* They make your words easier to understand, believe, or remember. Don't let them substitute for or replace the speaking part of the speech.

VISUAL AIDS SHOULD BE APPROPRIATE   Anything you use should be relevant and fitting. Gimmicks not related to the ideas you're talking about can detract. Make sure your models, displays, or demonstrations don't take listeners' attention away from what you want them to hear or think about. Be sure the visuals fit the situation, the speech, and the audience.

A highway patrol officer who comes to a school to talk about driving safety might use pictures of accidents and accident victims. But full-color pictures taken at the scene of an accident might be so grotesque that many (if not most) listeners won't even look at them. How much will the visual add? Better to show the wrecked car after victims are removed, along with shots of hospitalized and bandaged victims— or coffins. These pictures will be looked at and probably remembered.

VISUAL AIDS SHOULD BE CLEAR   Simplicity is usually required. Visuals should clarify, not confuse. Leave out anything that is not absolutely necessary. Take out all irrelevant details. Avoid clutter: Design charts, diagrams, and graphs to emphasize the important points. Use contrast in color, size, or arrangement of figures to highlight major ideas.

Visual aids should be visible! Make them large enough to be seen. Put them where the whole audience can see them. If you are using objects or pictures so small the audience cannot see them from where you are, move closer to the listeners or magnify them.

VISUAL AIDS SHOULD NOT INTERFERE   When you use visuals, be sure they do not interfere with the speech. *Visual aids should focus on the message and not on the visual or the speaker.* For example, suppose you want your audience to see some pictures or objects that are too small to display for all to see at once. Don't pass them around while you talk; wait until the speech is over. Passing things around is distracting in itself. Even worse, audience members will not be listeners while they are looking at the objects or pictures.

How you use visuals is also important. When a visual is displayed, the speaker should talk to the audience, not to the visual. How often have you seen a speaker talking to the chalkboard instead of the audience? Too often, probably. Similarly, don't place yourself between your audience and the visual. If some members of the audience can't see the visual, it has little value for them. Usually flip charts are superior to chalkboards in this respect. You can easily stand beside a chart but almost always must stand in front of a chalkboard. Having material on the chalkboard before listeners arrive does help. Still, you will often turn your back on at least some members of the audience as you discuss what is on the board. For this time, you lose eye contact. Overhead projectors are superior to a chalkboard for the same reasons.

Charts or diagrams should not be put up until you use them. Then cover them up or put them down when you're through. If you leave them in front of listeners during the speech, especially if you have used statistics, figures, or a complex diagram, listeners' attention may drift back to the visual when you are talking about something else. In contrast, if your visual consists of a key word listing of main points, it will probably reinforce your ideas to keep it in front of listeners. Using a flip chart, chalkboard, or overhead projector is good in this situation. They let you add one point at a time to help audience members focus on the ideas as you talk about them.

VISUALS SHOULD BE PREPARED AHEAD OF TIME   If you plan to use a chalkboard rather than a prepared graph or chart, be aware of how long it will take to write or draw what you want on the board. Will it take so long that your audience will get bored while you write? Remember, you can talk more rapidly than you can write, and they can listen more rapidly than you can talk. So writing on a chalkboard has value only in limited cases. Single words or line drawings can be put on a board while you talk. A chalkboard can be used to show how words are spelled or to help reinforce important words. You can use simple drawings to show ideas as they emerge. But prepare more complicated visuals in advance. They will be neater, more likely to accomplish your purpose, and avoid the pitfalls discussed before.

Use a flip chart or overhead projector when possible. When you use a flip chart, you have all the advantages of chalkboards and none of the disadvantages. You can show development of ideas by having them prewritten on various pages of a flip chart. By turning pages as each new element is added, you let the idea emerge just as it would on a chalkboard. Moreover, you have the advantages of saving time, words written neatly instead of hastily, and easier eye contact with listeners.

In addition, when your visual is prepared in advance, you can pretest its clarity. You can show it to friends (or strangers) and have them give you feedback. You can find out if it communicates the ideas and effects you want.

The overhead projector is especially valuable. It allows you to use printed visuals and to face your audience while you talk about the visual. The overhead projector has many other advantages. You can be assured the visual can be large enough for all listeners to see. The same transparency, small enough to carry in a brief case, can be used in a ballroom with audiences of hundreds or a conference room with only five or six listeners. If you are fortunate in your class situation, you'll have access to both transparency and opaque projectors. Ask your instructor for assistance in learning how to operate these two kinds of equipment. They can be useful.

SOURCES OF SUPPORTING MATERIALS

Now that you understand the nature and uses of supporting materials, a reasonable question is, Where do I find them? This chapter concludes with some answers to that question.

Personal Experiences

Use What You Know Remember, we urged you to speak about things you know. This means the best source of supporting materials is what has happened to you. Think about the thesis and main points in relation to your own experiences. What have you done, seen, or read that proves, amplifies, or clarifies the points you want to make? Start with what you know.

Ask Questions and Listen For some—perhaps most—speeches you will need more information than you already have. In these cases, you'll have to do some searching. Since this happens often, students of public speaking learn several tested techniques for finding information. One of the best is the simplest and most obvious. Talk to people. Ask questions. Listen to people who have information you can use to develop your ideas. Seek out experts who may be available to you.

Politicians use this technique. They talk about spending time with their constituents. Their speeches are filled with statements like, "This is what the people in my district want. I know because they tell me."

Observe A related technique is observation. Watch what happens and report it. A speech by a student in one of our classes used this technique. His thesis was that Chevrolet cars are better than Fords. To get evidence, he spent a day at two independent car repair places—places where cars are repaired, not sold. (We think he worked at one!) He counted how many cars of each type were brought in for repair during that day. He concluded that since he saw more Fords needing repair, they were not as reliable as Chevrolets.

Library Research

Sometimes you won't be able to talk to or observe the people who have the information you need. Then, most likely, you will turn to a library. You probably know the basics of library use, but some specific guidelines for finding information for speeches may be helpful.

Catalogs and Indexes   You know, of course, how to use a subject catalog to find books on a topic. When doing research for speeches, the subject catalog is an excellent resource. But sometimes you need more recent information than can be found in books. Then you need relevant magazine and journal articles. Several indexes can be used to find magazine articles on your subject. About 100 popular magazines are indexed in the *Readers' Guide to Periodical Literature*. Looking under the subject, you will find articles on any given topic in many different magazines. Speakers should know how to use the *Readers' Guide*.

Many other indexes are available. Each relates to a specific area and includes publications not in the *Readers' Guide*. Most of them include fairly technical periodicals, and some include publications other than periodicals. These other indexes are sources you should become familiar with. You'll find many occasions to use the following:

> *Applied Science and Technology Index*
> *Art Index*
> *Business Periodicals Index*
> *Cumulative Index to Nursing Literature*
> *Education Index*
> *Essay and General Literature Index*
> *Humanities Index*
> *Public Affairs Information Service Bulletin*
> *Popular Periodical Index* (similar to *Readers' Guide*, covering more "offbeat" kinds of publications)
> *Social Sciences Index*

In addition to these, most scholarly publications publish cumulative indexes. If one of the listed indexes does not include the source you are seeking you may need to look at the index of that particular publication.

Newspapers are also good sources of information. Most libraries keep a file of recent papers and a microfilm historical file of major newspapers, which includes at least *The New York Times*. Many libraries have files of newspapers extending as far back as colonial times. University libraries will also have major foreign newspapers in their microfilm files.

Sometimes you are looking for a single item of information, like a date or a statistic. Obvious sources for that kind of information are encyclopedias, but many other sources also exist. One of the most useful is the *Statistical Abstract of the U.S.* Another is a publication called "Facts on File."

A wide variety of information is available to those who know how to use the library.

Many government publications contain statistical and demographic data. Each library catalogs these reference materials somewhat differently. If you are looking for specific data, you may need to ask a reference librarian to show you how to use the government publication catalog and other indexes in your library.

SPECIAL MATERIALS AND FILES   Pamphlets and materials not published on a regular basis are called *fugitive materials*. Because they are not published regularly, these materials are seldom indexed in the publications we have listed. Yet they often contain information not available in other places. To find fugitive materials, consult the *vertical file*.

Each library has many different things in its vertical file, and not all libraries file them the same way. But each library will have a subject guide to its vertical file. The librarian at your college can show you where it is and how materials are filed and indexed. Because it is a source of valuable information often not available anywhere else, you'll want to know your library's vertical file.

One particularly useful source for public speakers is Bartlett's *Familiar Quotations*. This book contains thousands of quotations on many different topics. Whether you're seeking a quotation for an introduction or conclusion, or something to use in supporting ideas in the body of the speech, Bartlett's is an invaluable resource.

Whichever index you use, you will find many books, articles, and pamphlets on your chosen subject. In fact, you will probably find more information than you could ever use in one speech. That is the goal. Having more information than you can use has several benefits. First, it allows you to pick and choose. Having looked at many sources, you know you have the best material available.

Perhaps more important is the self-confidence it gives you. When you know you have more information than you've used in the speech, you'll have fewer fears that someone might ask a question you can't answer. Your additional data are like an insurance fund to be used when someone questions you.

Having more information than can be put into the speech also helps you adapt to the audience. Using your audience analysis, you'll be able to select the most impressive or persuasive information. You can choose materials most likely to hold attention. Perhaps most important, having many possible supporting materials gives you something to add or use for restatement when feedback shows that the audience doesn't understand or agree with something you say.

EXERCISE 12.2   SPEAKING TO INFORM

OBJECTIVE   **To practice the techniques of informative speaking.**

DIRECTIONS
1. Prepare and present a four- to six-minute speech in which your general purpose is to inform your listeners.
2. Your instructor will schedule the time for your speech.
3. The speech should be prepared with the purpose of informing your class-mates unless the instructor specifies some other audience.
4. As a measure of the degree to which you accomplished the purpose of informing your listeners, do the following:
   a. Prepare five multiple-choice questions that test the information content of your speech.
   b. Have listeners answer the questions before and after your speech.
   c. After the speech, ask listeners to write down what they understood your thesis to be.
   d. By comparing the follow-up test to pretest scores on the five multiple-choice questions and the listeners' understanding of your thesis to the one you stated in your outline, you can assess how well they understood what you said.

REVIEW   **Provide brief answers that may be a writing assignment or the basis for class discussion.**
1. Summarize and report your listeners' responses to your thesis and questions, assessing how nearly you accomplished your goal of informing them.
2. What techniques for informing listeners did you make an effort to use?
3. What sources of supporting materials did you consult?
4. After the speech, assess what techniques and sources you did not use that might have been helpful in accomplishing your goal.
5. Explain the most important communication principle illustrated or learned from this exercise and why you found it important.

SUMMARY

To develop a speech, a speaker learns to use supporting materials, which serve many functions. Information in a speech can be used to inform or to persuade. Whether a technique or goal, information may be given to clarify, amplify, prove, create a new perspective or ideas or information people already know, or hold attention.

Maintaining attention is important to a speaker. The speaker wants the ideas to be involuntarily in the focus of listener attention rather than for listeners to have to work at paying attention. The factors that can be used to help accomplish this goal are relevance, proximity, importance, familiar ideas presented with novelty, variety of content and movement, curiosity, conflict, humor, and concreteness.

Many things may be used as supporting materials. Verbal supporting materials may be explanation, narration, use of examples—which vary from real to hypothetical and from long (illustrations) to short (instances)—statistics, testimony, comparisons, and repetition and restatement.

Statistics are valuable when used to persuade, but remember some cautions about their use. Don't overuse. Many people do not mentally process numbers well. Secondly, statistics must be made clear, and the use of visual presentation is helpful. Analogies are imaginative comparisons that show similarities in items that on the surface are not similar. Visual techniques of supporting ideas may vary from charts, graphs, diagrams, pictures, cartoons, and models all the way to objects and demonstration. Types of media may be movies, slides, overhead projectors, chalkboards, or people and objects.

Remember that the visuals are aids—they should complement, supplement, or clarify verbal presentations, not substitute for them. Visuals should be appropriate to the information and the situation. Visuals should be clear; they should not interfere; and they should focus on the message and not on themselves or the speaker. Visuals should be prepared in advance when possible, both to save time and to be able to give neat presentations.

QUESTIONS FOR DISCUSSION

1. What are the uses of supporting materials?
2. What guidelines should a speaker use to choose supporting materials?
3. Can you give examples of each type of supporting material a speaker can use?
4. What pitfalls should a speaker avoid when using visual aids as supporting material?
5. Why is understanding the processes of attention important to a speaker?
6. What techniques can a speaker use to gain and hold attention?

SUGGESTIONS FOR FURTHER READING

Bradley, Bert. *Fundamentals of Speech Communication*, 4th ed. Dubuque: William C. Brown, 1984.

Brigance, William N. *Speech Composition*, 2nd ed. New York: Appleton-Century-Crofts, 1953.

Bryant, Donald C., and Karl R. Wallace. *Fundamentals of Public Speaking*, 5th ed. Englewood Cliffs, N.J.: Prentice-Hall, 1976.

Ecroyd, Donald, and Dwight Freshley. *The Analysis of Speech Content*. Skokie, Ill.: The National Textbook Company, 1976.

Ehninger, Douglas, Bruce Gronbeck, Ray McKerrow, and Alan Monroe. *Principles and Types of Speech Communication*, 9th ed. Dubuque: William C. Brown, 1982.

Hart, Roderick P., et al. *Public Communication*, 2nd ed. New York: Harper & Row, 1983.

Jeffrey, Robert, and Owen Peterson. *Speech: A Text with Adapted Readings*, 3rd ed. New York: Harper & Row, 1980.

Olbright, Thomas H. *Informative Speaking*. Glenview, Ill.: Scott, Foresman, 1968.

Rogge, Edward, and James Ching. *Advanced Public Speaking*. New York: Holt, Rinehart and Winston, 1966.

Taylor, Anita. *Speaking in Public*, 2nd ed. Englewood Cliffs, N.J.: Prentice-Hall, 1984.

13 Public Speaking: Using Voice and Body

> . . . it is not enough to know what to say—
> one must also know how to say it.
>
> ARISTOTLE

> Delivery, then, is not a separate act, but one aspect of the whole speech act.
>
> JANE BLANKENSHIP

> Reading a speech is like kissing through a veil.
>
> ANONYMOUS

GOAL

To learn how to use voice and body to communicate effectively in public speaking situations

OBJECTIVES

The material in this chapter should help you to:
1. State and explain the guiding principle for speaking effectively.
2. Explain why most good public speaking is conversational.
3. State the reasons beginning speakers should speak extemporaneously.
4. Use environment to improve your speaking.
5. Use five specific nonverbal and nonvocal types of message carriers to speak more effectively.
6. Identify the parts of the vocal mechanism and indicate the role each plays in producing speech.
7. Know how to use rate, volume, pitch, and voice quality to improve vocal message sending.
8. Distinguish between good articulation and good pronunciation.
9. Make effective use of several techniques to cope with speech anxiety.

After you have planned what to say, it's time to think about presenting it. Giving a speech is often described as delivery, but we don't use that term. To us, delivery denotes what the postal service does with the mail (and with many speakers, the analogy may be valid, but we aren't recommending that as an ideal). Speeches aren't "delivered." They aren't ideas in neat packages to be placed in listeners' heads. A **speech** is a particular type of communication—a *situation in which a single person tries to communicate ideas she or he wants a group of others to understand or be amused or influenced by.* In this chapter we discuss how to use voice and body to increase the chances of reaching that goal.

THE GUIDING PRINCIPLE

The basic public speaking "rule" relates to purpose. *Any* behavior that helps to achieve the purpose is recommended. That is the only generalization about speech presentation we believe makes sense. Everything else, as noted in Chapter 11, "depends"—on speaker, listener, and situation. What works in one time, place, and situation for one speaker may not work in that same time and place for a different speaker—or for the same speaker at another time and place.

One guiding principle, however, does apply to all situations: *A speaker should sincerely want to communicate, should be prepared, and should be natural.* If a speaker really wants to share ideas or information with a group of listeners, and the listeners sense that desire to communicate, they will overlook many distracting speaker behaviors. A speaker who is well prepared will usually appear knowledgeable, and the audience will tend to see that person as credible. And, finally, perhaps the best aid to credibility is sincerity. Speakers should not pretend to be what they are not.

With those thoughts as a preface, we will give some prescriptions about speech presentation. Remember, however, all are only suggestions. These ideas may— depending on the situation—be helpful as you seek to become a more effective speaker. But you will have to adapt them to your own style, and to various situations. That means you will need to try them out. Public speaking is like any other skill— it improves with appropriate practice. You learn to speak well only by doing it. Listen to the comments of your classmates and instructor; analyze your successes and failures; then try again. That is the only way to learn to communicate more effectively in public speaking situations.[1]

---

[1] Indeed, it's unlikely you can get enough practice in the class in which you are now enrolled. At best, you are likely to have the opportunity for only five or six speeches. We strongly urge you to consider this speech course (and text) only the beginning of your public speaking practice. Find opportunities to do more. Most colleges offer speech activities in forensic events of all kinds. If that kind of speech activity takes too much time, toastmaster/mistress opportunities offer constant speaking practice. Opportunities to practice also exist in church or political activities. What situation you find is not important; the fact of continued practice is.

Michael Dukakis campaigning for the presidency.

USE CONVERSATIONAL STYLE

Public speaking is an expanded conversation. Instead of conversing with one or a few persons, a speaker talks with many people at once. Therefore, the best speaking—in most situations—captures the natural animation and spontaneity of conversation. Your goal should be to capture that quality in your public speaking situation.

Speak Extemporaneously

Speaking extemporaneously is generally the best approach to achieving conversational style. Extemporaneous speaking does not mean speaking off the cuff (what we call impromptu) or without preparation. A person who speaks extemporaneously should spend as much time preparing as one who speaks in any other mode. **Extemporaneous speaking** does not mean speaking without notes. It does mean *speaking from notes rather than manuscript*, most likely using a key word outline written on cards. These notes may also include complete quotations you plan to use and statistics or data to be presented. Most critically, speaking extemporaneously means *choosing the words to say at the moment of the speech*. Except for important ideas, phrases, and quotations, an extemporaneous speaker does not worry about every word in advance. Speaking this way has several advantages.

Directness   Extemporaneous speaking allows direct contact with the audience. Maintaining eye contact assures two-way communication. An extemporaneous speaker can see listeners' responses and use feedback from them. This style of speaking allows corrections as necessary during the speech, and use of contingency plans when appropriate. Such use of feedback may be the most important difference between good and poor public speakers. In addition, good eye contact helps convey impressions of poise, confidence, and competence, all assets in accomplishing goals.

Naturalness   Speakers are most natural when speaking extemporaneously. Yes, that includes some hesitations, some "ums" and "uhs," some awkward pauses, and repetitions. The presence of some of these *disfluencies*, as such hesitancies are called, does not prevent effective speaking. Unless too many exist, listeners won't even notice, because natural conversation includes such disfluencies. Practice in speaking can help reduce hesitations, but no speaker ever totally eliminates them.

A natural personality is a more important part of total speaker impression than a few disfluencies. Thus, extemporaneous speaking is better than either reading or memorizing, as we discuss shortly. A few hesitancies will do far less damage than lack of eye contact, failure to respond to the audience, or an artificial sound.

Conversational Quality   Extemporaneous speaking helps speakers sound natural and animated. It enables them to use spoken style, which varies greatly from written style. Written style is more formal, less direct, less repetitive than spoken style. It uses a different vocabulary. Most listening that people do is to conversations, not to essays that are read aloud. The natural phrasing and rhythm of conversation is more easily understood than an essay read aloud.

People who become speech writers must learn to write in a spoken style, but most of you reading this book are not learning to become speech writers. You are learning to speak. Thus, when speaking in class, use what you already do well—conversation. A conversation is, at least most of the time, an animated two-way interaction. Extemporaneous speaking allows you to bring that quality into your speeches.

Use Appropriate Language Style

We have emphasized the benefits from conversational style gained primarily through speaking extemporaneously. Now we should remind you that this doesn't negate comments made earlier, primarily in Chapter 3, about appropriate use of language. The extemporaneous speaker seeks to use the animation and variety of conversation but must remember that the speech situation is ordinarily more formal than a conversation. Therefore, the language style will usually be more formal.

Concreteness   Also from earlier chapters, notably 3 and 12, you'll recall the benefits of concrete, specific language. Not only will concreteness help you maintain a listener's attention better, it will also improve clarity, reduce ambiguity, and increase the accuracy with which you speak. Use of supporting materials to develop ideas and attention factors will require you to use specific, concrete language.

Transitions As we also noted in Chapter 12, repetition and restatement greatly assist listeners to understand and remember what you say. Using appropriate transitional language as you move from point to point of the outline can achieve those goals. Especially useful is verbal "pointing" to your outline structure, introduced with what we describe as a presummary. Following is an example, using the outline presented on p. 305, that shows how to use the presummary and appropriate transitions to clarify and emphasize the ideas. To conclude the introduction and provide a transition into the body of the speech, a speaker might say the following:

. . . so what I want to spend a few minutes talking with you about today are the problems caused by our excessive reliance on imported oil and what we might do to reduce the problem.

After this quick presummary, a good transition into the main points should follow:

I'll begin by describing how serious the problem is and analyzing what has caused it. It's important that we all understand that reliance on foreign oil is a serious problem in the United States. It's especially serious for two reasons: We are vulnerable to other nations who disagree with our policies; and we have a large negative balance of payments largely due to the billions spent for foreign oil. Let's examine the evidence supporting these two claims. First, why is it serious to be vulnerable to other nations? Well, here is why . . .

Note that the speaker "pointed" out that the first main point had two subheadings (serious for two reasons). After presenting evidence in support of the first subpoint, the transition to the next subpoint follows:

Now, having seen how vulnerable we are to other nations because we rely on them for so much of our oil, let's look at that second reason it's a problem for the United States to rely on foreign oil: our negative balance of payments. Did you realize that . . .

Then, after giving evidence in support of the second subpoint, a transition to the second main point will follow, and inform the listener two subheads will follow.

In short, what all this has shown is that reliance on foreign oil is a serious problem in the United States. Now let's discuss that second main point: The primary cause of our huge consumption of foreign oil is gasoline used in private automobiles. What evidence is there for that? It revolves around two issues: First, private automobiles use more gasoline than any other form of transportation in the United States, and second, gasoline for cars is less essential than fuel used for trucking or the oil used to make home heating oil. Again, let's examine the evidence for these two points one at a time. Is it accurate that private autos use more gasoline than any other form of transportation? Indeed it is. Statistics from . . .

After presenting the evidence developing the first two main points of the outline, the speaker's next transitional words are those which provide what is called an *internal summary*. This summarizes the two points previously developed, states the thesis, then forecasts the next two main points used to support the thesis.

Well, now that we've seen why relying on foreign oil is a problem for the United States and that the primary cause of this problem is gasoline use by private autos, it's reasonable to ask, what is the solution? To me it's clear that the best solution to the oil import problem in the United States is improved mass transit. This is true for two reasons: First, improving mass transit would reduce the use of automobiles, and second, no other solution would reduce gasoline consumption as much. Let's look at the evidence for these two points one at a time. How will improving mass transit reduce use of automobiles? It would provide an alternative for people who drive to work, and it would reduce recreational use of autos. First let's examine the evidence for that first subpoint, that many people driving to work today have no alternative. According to . . .

After citing the evidence to support the first subpoint, a quick "pointing" will again highlight the main point:

So you can see, much gasoline is used by commuters to get to work either because they have no quick, reliable mass transit, or they have none at all. Now, not only will less gas be used by commuters, improved mass transit through better train and bus service could also reduce recreational use of autos. My support for this claim is . . .

Then, after giving the evidence demonstrating the second subhead of the third main point, another internal summary points to the fourth main point:

Now that we have seen how improved mass transit would reduce the use of automobiles, it's reasonable to ask, 'Are there other solutions which would reduce gasoline consumption as much as improving mass transit?' The answer is an unequivocal no. It's 'no' for three reasons: Energy conservation in homes cannot achieve much more savings without enormous costs and risks; millions of commuters cannot carpool but could and would use better mass transit; and third, industrial and commercial uses of gas and oil cannot be further reduced without serious environmental side effects. Let's look at the evidence for these three subpoints one at a time. Remember, the first subpoint was that energy conservation in home heating cannot achieve much more savings without huge costs and risks. What is the evidence? Well, to start with, data from . . .

We have taken space here to give you these many examples of transitional phrasing for several reasons. First, it often isn't clear to students what it means when we say to use transitions to "point" to your speech structure. Reading through the possible words for a speech as cited above makes it easier to see. Verbal pointing highlights each main point and subpoint. The introduction clearly identifies the first half of the speech structure. The second half is made equally clear after the thesis is stated.

The second advantage of the extensive quoting from the speech is to show how evidence and speech structure relate. The argument of this speech is clear from the outline. But it will take evidence to convince a listener who doesn't agree with the thesis. Each main point will need supporting materials to make the argument persuasive. The citations also show how good transitions between points will help your listeners remember what you say. If a speaker needs to repeat a point three times for it to be remembered, you accomplish that goal simply with a presummary, good transitions from one point to another, and the recommended final summary.

Finally, these citations illustrate the use of extemporaneous language style. The language is somewhat more formal than a conversation but less formal than if it were an essay. Moreover, the language is more repetitious than would be appropriate for an essay. Also illustrated is variety in phrasing while retaining repetition of the key words from the outline.

Many other transitional devices could be used. Many more stylistic elements could be introduced here but weren't due to limitations of space. If you study public speaking in more depth—either through an additional course while in school, or on your own with practice in forensic activities, Toastmasters or Toastmistresses, or some other setting—you'll want to study much more about language style, as well as about supporting and developing ideas and persuasion. The readings suggested at the end of each chapter can be helpful in that study.

NONVERBAL, NONVOCAL COMMUNICATION

When we stated the most important principle for effective public speaking, we said that speakers should have a sincere desire to communicate. We want to emphasize that point. If you don't want to talk with your audience about your topic, few "tricks" of presentation can cover up that feeling. No suggestions about speaking are any more important than this: You should *want* to talk with your listeners about your topic. Beyond that, there are some steps you can take to ensure that your nonverbal, nonvocal communication is effective.

Speakers usually feel a strong need to communicate their ideas to an audience.

Improve the Environment

When you can affect the environment in which you speak, make sure it supports you. Several aspects of environment are worth noting. Audience arrangement is one. How is your audience going to be seated? Can you seat listeners in a way that improves communication? If your purpose is to create interaction among your listeners, arrange the chairs in a circle or semicircle or around a table. If you want to display authority and to discourage interaction among the listeners, use a typical classroom or theater-type setting. If the auditorium or room is only half full and everyone is seated at the back, get them to move; ask them to come up where you can talk to them. Or perhaps you will need to move closer to them.

The point is, improve the setting in any way that supports your purpose. Remove distracting objects; choose a room of suitable size and seating and that has suitable surroundings. Be sure you have a microphone and easel or table for visuals if you need them. Plan in advance for all aspects of the setting you can control. When you cannot change the environment in which you speak, you may need to compensate for it. Be prepared to do so.

Use Action and Appearance

Dress Appropriately   Recall how important personal appearance is in interpersonal perception. In your daily life it might not matter too much how you dress, but in public speaking, appearance makes a big difference. If you are speaking to people who care how you look, dress and groom yourself accordingly. You don't necessarily have to conform to the dress of your audience, but you should not offend them. If you are speaking, for instance, to a group known to be conservative and your hair is long, comb it neatly. You don't have to dress as the Lions do if you are speaking to a local Lions Club, but ragged blue jeans or cut-offs aren't likely to be appropriate.

The way you dress and look is important to credibility. Appearance tells listeners things about you, how you feel about them and the occasion. You show respect or disrespect for them by your appearance. Listeners draw conclusions about your personality and authority from the way you look. Review the information in Chapter 4, and plan your appearance with care.

Have Good Posture   One of the biggest problems for most public speakers, both beginning and experienced, is posture. This is because most of us have bad personal habits, and the speaking situation requires us to stand in front of an audience. This focuses on those bad habits at a time when we are likely to be more nervous than usual. It seems terribly trite here to give a prescription about improving posture, but a speaker must hear that advice. You may need to work on changing your habits. Work on how you stand at all times, not just when speaking. Certainly the solution is not to hide behind a large podium. Too many speaking situations will not provide that crutch. Solve the problem; don't try to hide it.

Speakers should stand straight, with weight on both feet. Most of us have legs of slightly different lengths, so standing with feet side by side is uncomfortable. If we do that without adopting the soldier's "parade rest" posture, we look and feel uncomfortable. The solution is to place one foot slightly in front of the other and balance the weight on the balls rather than the heels of the feet.

Few things give a total impression that is more negative than poor posture, including constantly shifting weight from one hip to another in a slouch. Since a speaker's goal is to appear poised, confident, and in control, poor posture is a serious nonverbal contradiction.

Use Your Hands Effectively A sizable problem for beginning speakers is what to do with their hands. Our response goes back to that guiding principle: Do what is natural for you in animated conversation. Think back to Chapter 4 and the functions of nonverbal communication. Then, watch people in any conversation. You will notice that when they are comfortable and involved in a conversation, they gesture in ways that reinforce their ideas and occasionally substitute gestures for words and to regulate interactions. The effective public speaker does the same.

Of course, again the problem is transferring the comfort and animation of conversation into the public speaking situation. As a result, most of the prescriptions given about effective use of hands in public speaking wind up being "don'ts." They are notations of mannerisms to avoid because they are distracting. They are things you don't do in conversation or things you *do* do when nervous about or bored with that conversation. Since speakers seldom want to convey either impression to an audience, these are mannerisms a speaker wants to avoid.

As we list these things, you won't find any surprises; you've seen them all many times. The key is to remember them and work to avoid them while you speak. It will take practice and the suggestions of your teacher and classmates to indicate which are the biggest problems for you and therefore to point out which you need to work on most.

1. Don't grasp the podium as if it were about to run away.
2. Don't shove both hands in trouser/skirt pockets so they can't possibly get out to gesture. One hand in a pocket will often free the other one to gesture normally, but don't keep the hand in the pocket all the time while you speak. Remember what we pointed out in the last chapter: Variety of action as well as content is a key to maintaining listeners' attention.
3. Don't put even one hand in a pocket if that pocket contains keys and coins. To put this another way, take coins and keys out of the pocket in which you expect to put your hand during the speech.
4. Don't clasp hands behind you or in front of you. Generally it's wise to keep the hands separated while you speak, though occasionally the "steepling" gesture *might* be appropriate.
5. Do hold note cards in one hand so you can comfortably move away from the podium but don't fidget with or fold the cards. In short, keep your hands apart.

As we noted at the beginning of this chapter, if you are sincere, well-prepared, and natural, you can probably speak effectively even with the bad habits just outlined or any of a number of others we haven't mentioned. But as long as your goal is to do the best speaking you can, these are important "do's" and "don'ts."

Use the Podium Effectively   Earlier we said, don't try to hide poor posture behind a podium and don't clasp it with your hands as if it were about to escape. Indeed, in many speaking situations, you are more effective if you leave the podium. That may allow you to move closer to a small audience seated in the back of a large auditorium or help in a situation where the podium elevates you above and far away from listeners. Ignoring the podium is often the very best way to use it effectively.

Sometimes you must use a podium because you have a microphone. At other times you use it for other good reasons. For example, if you are using a flip chart to present information visually, you may not have an easel for the chart. Then the podium can serve as the easel and provide a way for the pages to be turned one at a time. In these situations, you must learn to use the podium well.

Probably the worst habit speakers have in using a podium is similar to the "gripping it for support" problem referred to before. Many speakers don't grip the podium, but they do let their hands hold on to it, and as a result their hand gestures are restricted. Haven't you occasionally seen a person whose hands were resting on the podium and the resulting gesture of emphasis was to wave a finger or two? The easiest solution to this problem is to get away from the podium. Don't use it at all; don't let it become a crutch as you practice speaking. But if you are going to speak a lot where a microphone will be used, you need to practice using the podium. As you practice, don't allow yourself to hold on to the podium. Learn to keep your hands off it, or at best rest lightly on it; then when your body wants to gesture, your hands will be free to follow the impulse.

Use Your Face and Eyes

Maintain Eye Contact   Perhaps the single most important behavior for a speaker is to maintain good eye contact with listeners. That means to make eye contact with individual members of the audience, not just to look out in the direction of the audience. We won't repeat the discussion of eyes as nonverbal communicators from Chapter 4, but a review now might be helpful.

You know from experience the many negative impressions formed if a person does not look at you while talking to you. Similarly, you know the positive impressions received when you are in a classroom, for example, and the teacher looks directly at you a number of times during the class. You feel involved, personally important; you can sense the confidence of the person speaking; you can recognize the speaker's feelings about the subject of the discussion. We have mentioned the other direct benefit of eye contact before: Without audience feedback, you won't know if any of your contingency plans are necessary to accomplish your goal.

Smile   In most situations, you want to establish a friendly sense of interaction with the listeners. A smile will help you do that. Even when discussing the most serious of topics, you usually want to have the audience like you, and perceive you as a sociable person. Keeping a "friendly face," best done by talking directly to listeners and smiling, is an important nonverbal cue that helps you achieve that goal.

At times, smiling is inappropriate, especially if it isn't sincere. At other times, even a sincere smile may convey the wrong impression about the speaker. Smiling can be a submissive, approval-seeking behavior displayed by a person of low power. Rarely does a speaker want to make such an impression. Smiles, like all behaviors, should be appropriate to the situation and to the speaker's goals.

VOCAL MESSAGE CARRIERS

The public speaker takes for granted the act of adding voice to words. How a speaker uses voice, however, will influence whether or not the speech accomplishes its goal. Recall from Chapter 4 some of the messages people infer from a speaker's voice. Now let's discuss some specific factors of voice useful to public speakers.

Rate and Volume

Rate refers to *the speed at which a person talks*; **volume** to *the loudness with which sounds are spoken.* In public speaking, *appropriateness of rate and volume varies according to the situation.* Speakers with a large audience or a microphone can't talk as rapidly as can speakers in a more casual setting. A large audience without a microphone requires a considerable volume. One problem many speakers have when they have a large audience and a microphone is that they cannot adapt to both. They speak too loudly for the mike. Speaking on a complex or difficult subject will probably require a slower rate than speaking on less difficult subject matter. Speaking too loudly when the room is small or when the subject calls for a calm discussion is ineffective. In conversations, volume and rate tend to increase with excitement or anger. Therefore, if the voice is loud in a situation when neither excitement nor anger is appropriate, the effect will not help the speaker.

Appropriateness of rate and volume also depends on the speaker. How rapidly you speak in any situation depends partly on your normal rate of speaking. An unnatural speaking voice will amost always interfere with your effectiveness. Moreover, often when people are told they speak too rapidly, the problem is not rate but poor articulation. If a speaker cannot be understood, the cause is not always— or even usually—rate. If a person's articulation is poor, slowing down may not improve audience understanding.

As a general principle, you should speak at a rate that is natural for you. Although varying rate is one good way to hold audience attention, natural conversation usually has enough variety. And trying to change a natural rate of speech usually causes far more problems than it solves, at least for the beginning speaker.

In contrast, volume cannot always be what you would naturally use. Our natural volume is often too low for groups of more than four to six. And ideas obviously will not be effective if listeners can't hear them. More than that, if the audience has to strain to hear, attention will tend to wander. A weak voice can also give the impression that you lack confidence or that you don't feel strongly about the ideas. Soft voices sometimes indicate a lack of concern. For most of us, none of these impressions is desirable.

Pitch

Pitch is a term describing *how high or low a voice tone is*. Pitch, like rate and volume, *should be appropriate to both speaker and situation*, but it is less easily changed than either. To a large degree the vocal mechanism itself controls the pitch of a voice. We all know, of course, that male physiology results in lower pitched voices than female. Speaking pitch can and does change, however. Understanding how the body produces voice can help you learn to control the pitch at which you speak.

The vocal mechanism involves four sections of the body: (1) diaphragm, lungs, and windpipe; (2) larynx (pronounced lair-inks) and vocal folds; (3) resonators; and (4) articulators. These are shown in Figures 13–1, 13–2, and 13–3.

Speech is formed from sounds created by vibrating vocal folds as air passes through the larynx. You know that all the air you breathe passes through the windpipe, but not all of it produces sound. Indeed, it is doubtful that the human larynx and vocal folds evolved for the purpose of creating speech at all. The primary function of this part of our body is to close the windpipe when we swallow food or water to prevent us from choking.

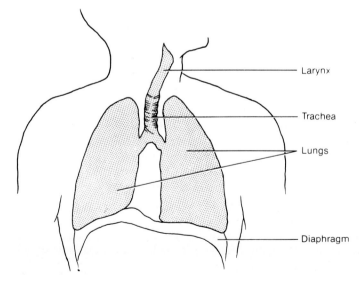

Larynx

Trachea

Lungs

Diaphragm

FIGURE 13–1. Vocal mechanisms of the body.

FIGURE 13-2. The vocal folds: closed, as when speaking; open, as in free breathing.

Fortunately, the muscles of the larynx perform double duty. They usually manage to keep food and water out of the windpipe, and they also enable us to talk. They do this because we have learned to use the larynx to tighten the vocal folds so they can vibrate.

Try this: exhale. Feel the air passing through your larynx. It makes no sound, except the slight disturbance of air as it passes through the mouth. You have heard the air but no vocalized sound. Now, try saying "aaaaah," as if a doctor were about to look down your throat. You passed air through your larynx as before, but by tightening the vocal folds, you created vocal tone. If you want to feel the difference in another way, put your fingers on the outside of your larynx—on both sides of your windpipe—and do it again. You can feel a vibration when you exhale with sound but not when you breathe out. The vibration you feel is the vocal folds creating sound.

The more rapidly vocal folds vibrate, the higher the pitch. Some other factors are involved in differences of pitch, but those other factors influence pitch mostly because they affect the frequency of vibrations. The length, size, tightness, and elasticity of the vocal folds and the pressure with which the air is exhaled determine how fast the folds will vibrate.

Though each of us has a normal or natural pitch level, we all vary the pitch with which we talk. We do that by changing the tightness of the vocal folds, the pressure with which we exhale air, and, to a limited extent, the elasticity of our vocal folds. Can you recall how you sound when you are afraid? Fear and anger always change our pitch.

Tension usually tightens the vocal folds, raising the pitch and causing problems for public speakers. Tension that raises pitch to an unnatural level can lead audiences to sense a lack of poise and confidence. Women speakers, particularly, need to be cautious about pitch, since tension can increase their pitch to unpleasant levels, thus reducing their effectiveness as speakers. Another problem for some speakers is a habitual and repeated pitch pattern. A regular rising and falling pitch pattern is often described as speaking in a "sing-song" manner. Not only is this pattern unnatural in English as spoken in the United States, but it quickly becomes boring.

To increase your awareness of pitch in communication, sit in some public place. Try listening to the tones of conversation. Notice how pitch varies. Since variety contributes to attention, the natural variety of pitch in conversational speech is desirable in public speaking situations.

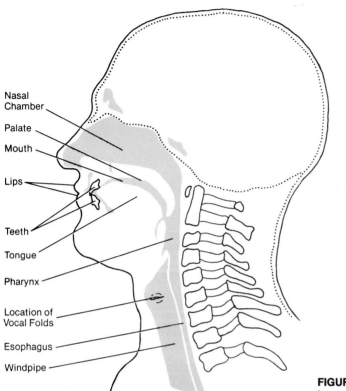

Nasal
Chamber

Palate

Mouth

Lips

Teeth

Tongue

Pharynx

Location of
Vocal Folds

Esophagus

Windpipe

FIGURE 13–3. Resonators and articulators.

Quality

The sound people hear when you talk differs greatly from the simple tone vibrating vocal folds produce. The resonators of the upper body and head are the primary sources of the *distinctive sound of each human voice described as* **voice quality.** Voice quality is what allows you to identify a caller on the telephone just by hearing "Hello."

Resonators create voice quality. The walls and cavities of the body change the tone created by vibrating vocal folds. Your bones and the walls of the sinuses, throat, nose, and mouth cavities are all resonators. All affect the sound (see Figure 13–3). Resonation increases the complexity of the voice tone. We'll skip the details about how this happens. All that most speakers need to know is that by affecting these resonators (as you do when you're tense, for instance, or when you have a head cold and don't use them), you change the quality of your voice.

Different vocal qualities are described as strident, thin, resonant, breathy, husky, harsh, nasal, or denasal. Many of these terms have negative connotations.

Good voice quality may be the biggest factor in the effectiveness of some speeches. The voices you hear regularly on nationwide television news are chosen, at least in part, because people respond positively to their quality. As you know, Walter Cronkite's deep, full voice is much more impressive than a weak, thin voice. Quality is the biggest difference among these voices.

Physiology largely controls vocal quality, but not entirely. No speaker is "stuck" with poor voice quality. We can improve voice quality by using the vocal mechanism properly. Especially, we can change most negative qualities. We can eliminate nasality or lack of it, excessive breathiness, harshness not associated with illness, and stridency.

Being able to change voice quality, however, goes beyond just knowing how voice is produced. It requires practice and study far beyond the scope of this book. If voice quality is a problem for you, consult with your instructor for sources of help. None of us should tamper with our voices without professional assistance. We could permanently damage the vocal mechanism.

Articulation

Articulation refers to *the movements of lips, tongue, jaw, and soft palate to form speech sounds*. Articulation is what changes vocal sound into recognizable speech. Good articulation means producing sounds that are clear and distinct, without being overly precise or affected.

Articulation should not be confused with pronunciation. **Pronunciation** is *combining speech sounds into recognizable words*. Both factors are important to speakers. Good articulation is possible with pronunciation that is not acceptable to an audience. For example, suppose a person says, "I ĕt (with an *e* as in *bet*) dinner," or "I called the pō'-lice" (with a long *o* and the emphasis on the first syllable). Some people consider "ĕt" and "pō'-lice" "incorrect" pronunciation. But as long as the sounds are clear and distinct, the articulation is fine, regardless of which *e* and *o* sounds are produced. In contrast, "Ja ēt?" may have the word eat "correctly" pronounced, but it demonstrates poor articulation. The sounds of "did you" are not clear and distinct. Poor articulation leaves out sounds, distorts them (most often by running them together), substitutes one sound for another, and occasionally adds sounds.

As with other aspects of voice, articulation should be appropriate to both speaker and situation. In public speaking, however, you can't vary articulation as much as you can other aspects of voice. You must be understood. If articulation makes you difficult to understand in a conversation, the person you are talking with can stop you and say: "What did you say? I didn't understand that." But when speaking in public, that isn't usually possible. If you aren't understood, that idea is lost. Public speakers must be *instantly intelligible* because audiences cannot get instant replays.

Moreover, most people closely associate poor articulation with casual situations and uneducated speakers. "Watcha got?" and "Nuthin. Wanit?" may communicate quite well in some situations, but this kind of articulation will interfere with your effectiveness in most speech situations. Think back to the discussion of language use in Chapter 3. Articulation and pronunciation are important components of dialect and style. Appropriate use of both can improve the impression you make as a speaker.

We should add one note of caution here. Do not think you must always form every sound very precisely. Overpreciseness is also poor articulation. Good speech doesn't call attention to itself. If you said, "I went to the movie last night" and tried to clearly articulate every *t* in the sentence, your speech would call attention to itself. In addition, the word *the* in that sentence should be the sound "thu." To say *thē* with a long *e* would overstress the word and would not be natural. It is this overstressing of sounds that causes some people to read aloud so badly. They are not using the natural rhythms of speech.

EXERCISE 13.1   USE OF VOICE

OBJECTIVE   **To practice using vocal variety.**

DIRECTIONS
1. The class will be divided into pairs.
2. Each pair should write each of the following words on a separate piece of paper, fold each so the word is inside, and mix them all together: *anger, love, happiness, joy, excitement, fear, sadness, anxiety, disgust, serenity.*
3. Each person should alternate drawing one of the folded slips.
4. That person then will use variation of voice (changes in pitch, rate, volume, and quality) and one or more nonsense syllables to communicate the feeling he or she drew. The syllables could be put together, repeated, and so on. Use one or more of: *oom, la, fe, zi, su.*
5. After each person's attempt to communicate the emotion, the other will indicate what she or he thinks it is. If the receiver did not perceive the message the source intended, the two should decide why not, and the source should practice using variations of voice until the partner is satisfied that he or she would have understood it.
6. The two should take turns being source and receiver until each has tried communicating four different emotions.

REVIEW   **Provide brief answers that may be a writing assignment or the basis for class discussion.**
1. Why are the nonverbal qualities of voice important to a speaker?
2. Describe the vocal message carriers that have the greatest influence on whether or not a speaker's goals are accomplished.
3. What specific qualities of voice are your strongest?
4. What voice qualities are areas of weakness for you? Cite specific steps you could take to minimize this problem while speaking.
5. Explain the most important communication principle illustrated or learned from this exercise and why you found it important.

COPING WITH SPEECH ANXIETY

The final thing about speaking that most of us have to deal with is nervousness. This nervousness is called **speech anxiety,** though it is often mislabeled stage fright. Since speech anxiety is a very common feeling, let's examine how a speaker can deal with it.

Sources of Anxiety

If you know why you get nervous before speaking, it is easier to deal with the anxiety. Knowing its cause is the first step in coping. Recall the discussion of self-confidence in Chapter 2. It will help you understand the phenomenon of speech anxiety.

Anxiety is a natural response to any risk situation, and for most of us, a speech is a risk situation. When we give a speech, we risk not doing as well as we want. If people aren't anxious before a speech, most likely they don't care about the outcome or they don't understand the situation. Public speakers, of course, should care about the outcome. So being anxious before a speech is natural and normal. Indeed, *not* to be nervous might be a problem!

But it is important not to be scared to death. Nervousness, properly used, can help speakers do a better job. They can use the anxiety to get "up" for the situation. The following ideas can help you use speech anxiety to your advantage.

Preparation

Being thoroughly prepared is the best way to cope with speech anxiety. Preparing well can develop self-confidence, which in turn reduces anxiety. You won't approach the speech afraid of not being ready. Remember, self-confidence is neither the absence of fear nor the elimination of anxiety. *Self-confidence is being sure you can cope with whatever situation is causing the fear or anxiety.* Knowing that you are ready, you can say to yourself, "I'm sure I can cope." Good preparation is the best way to control speech anxiety. To build self-confidence, follow the steps discussed in Chapter 11.

Practice Part of preparation is practice. Practicing will help you know you are prepared. Of course, some ways to practice may actually reduce your effectiveness. The following ideas can make your practice useful.

DO NOT WRITE THE SPEECH   Reading a written speech is called giving a manuscript speech. This is probably the most difficult type of public speaking. To speak well from a manuscript requires great skill. So beginning students shouldn't try it. Perhaps a president must read a written speech—a wrong word can cause an international crisis. Fortunately, students needn't worry that their words might cause the dollar to weaken. Thus, they have no need to tackle the toughest kind of public speaking.

Practicing a speech helps build confidence.

DON'T MEMORIZE   If you haven't written a speech, you probably can't memorize it—and you shouldn't do either. Memorization creates barriers between speaker and audience. It causes speakers to worry more about words than about listeners and ideas. It creates more anxiety than extemporaneous speaking. Fear of forgetting is stronger for most of us than fear of speaking.

DO PRACTICE VARIOUS PHRASINGS   As you practice, try to express your thoughts in different ways. No one way to express an idea is greatly superior to any other. So practice saying your ideas in several different ways. Then, when you give the speech, you'll be able to choose from several different expressions. Having these options can itself help give you confidence. You won't worry so about forgetting if you have several choices. During the speech, if feedback shows someone doesn't understand what you're saying, you may need to restate. If you said the same ideas several different ways in practice, you'll be prepared to restate when it's necessary.

Using Nervous Energy

One way to control speech anxiety is to use up the energy it creates. Nervousness is actually a physical reaction, and it causes several others. Whenever we face a challenge, our body generates the energy to help cope with it. This energy needs to be used. Although most of us can't run around the block before we give a speech, we can do some other things!

Isometrics   One alternative is to do some simple isometric exercises just before speaking. Clench the fists, hold them tight a few seconds, and then relax. Repeat this two or three times. Or push down on the arms of a chair for several seconds, then relax. Repeat this or other simple isometrics two or three times right before it's time to speak. The principle is that when we tighten and hold muscles tense a little while, we use energy. The tighten and relax cycle also helps relax other muscles in the body.

Actions during Introduction   Doing something during the introduction that requires you to move around also will use up excess energy. Use a visual aid; show some chart. Carry out some specific actions; perhaps demonstrate something. Physical movement uses energy.

Perhaps the most important behavior comes when you reach the speaker's stand. Pause, look directly at the listeners, take a deep breath, and smile. Do that before saying a word. Remember good public speaking is an enlarged conversation. It needs a friendly relationship between you and your listeners. The best way to get that is to smile at them. The number of people who will smile back will probably surprise you. A friendly smile is the best way to relax and start your speech off right.

In cases of extreme nervousness, it may be helpful to acknowledge the tension. Just mentioning it helps establish rapport with listeners. After all, most listeners have shared your feelings. They can empathize with you, and that empathy will show in their reactions. Furthermore, in acknowledging your reactions, you perform a kind of catharsis. You get them out of your system.

We recall a speaker who used this technique. After being introduced, he said: "I don't know what I'm doing here. I agreed to be a part of this program because I believed I had several ideas that should be shared. Now that I'm here, I'll be darned if I can remember what they were." We laughed with him; we all empathized; and he relaxed and gave a fine speech.

EXERCISE 13.2   SPEAKER USE OF VOICE AND BODY

OBJECTIVE   To analyze effective use of voice and body in public speaking.

DIRECTIONS
1. Select the best and worst speakers that you have listened to in the past year.
2. Describe both speakers' use of voice and action.
3. Compare and contrast the two speakers, indicating how much of your rating of them as best and worst was based on how they used their voice and body while speaking.
4. Your instructor may ask you to report your conclusions in a paper or in a four- to six-minute informative speech.

SUMMARY

Presentation of speeches is often referred to as delivery, but this book does not use that term. Delivery connotes giving something. Speaking in public is an effort by one person to communicate a message that he or she wants a group of others to understand or be influenced or amused by. Effective speaking in public is communicating, not delivering ideas.

The most important thing for public speakers to remember is that everything about the speech relates to purpose. We recommend any behavior that helps to achieve the purpose. In general, one rule guides all speech situations: A speaker should sincerely want to communicate, should be prepared, and should be natural. Adaptations of this rule depend on the audience, the speaker, and the situation.

Using the body to communicate in public speaking is similar to using the body in all communication. Public speakers should use a conversational style. Conversational style lets a speaker talk directly to listeners and use feedback from them. Conversational style also lets a speaker be natural, which involves a lively, varied voice and body. Appearance is important to the public speaker. Appropriate dress is valuable: A speaker should not offend an audience.

Voices are important to public speakers, and most can use their voices more effectively. They can change rate and volume. Rate is the speed at which a person talks, volume the loudness with which the sounds are spoken. Appropriateness of rate and volume depends on the situation. Another important characteristic of voice which a speaker can control is pitch, how high or low a voice tone is. Like volume, pitch should be appropriate to speaker and situation, but it is less easily changed. Pitch is determined to a large extent by the physiology of the vocal mechanism: the lungs and diaphragm, which produce an airstream; the larynx and vocal folds, which create sound; the resonators; and the articulators. All people have a normal or natural pitch level, which largely depends on size of body and vocal folds. But all people can and do vary the pitch at which they talk.

Quality, the distinctive sound of each human voice, is determined primarily by how the resonators of the head and body change the sound after it has been created. Voice quality is not easily changed, although speakers should try to avoid some of the more unpleasant voice qualities, such as nasality, harshness, and weakness. These result in strident, hoarse, nasal, or denasal voices.

Articulation refers to changing the sound created by the vocal folds into recognizable speech sounds. Good articulation involves producing speech sounds that are clear and distinct without being overly precise. Pronunciation is combining speech sounds into recognizable words. It is possible to have good articulation and poor pronunciation and vice versa.

A speaker also needs to cope with speech anxiety. This is done partially by simply knowing the sources of anxiety and recognizing that nervousness is a natural reaction to a situation in which a person is concerned about doing as well as possible. Being prepared is probably the most important way to overcome speech anxiety. Part of good preparation is to practice in effective ways. A speaker also should learn to use up the excess energy caused by nervousness. Do isometrics, or move around prior to the speech or during the introduction of the speech. Using a visual aid, smiling at listeners, and in extreme cases acknowledging the tension can also help to cope with speech anxiety in the public speaking situation.

QUESTIONS FOR DISCUSSION

1. What "rule" applies to all public speaking situations?
2. What are the factors you should consider to use your voice effectively?

3. How do voices differ in quality? Why? Is there anything a speaker should do about voice quality?

4. Can you distinguish between articulation and pronunciation? Why are these aspects of voice important?

5. Why is it helpful for a speaker to use a conversational style?

6. What is good extemporaneous speaking?

7. What is important about personal appearance for a speaker to understand?

8. What techniques help overcome speaker anxiety?

SUGGESTIONS FOR FURTHER READING

Adler, Ronald. *Confidence in Communication.* New York: Holt, Rinehart and Winston, 1977.

Blankenship, Jane. *Public Speaking: A Rhetorical Perspective,* 2nd ed. Englewood Cliffs, N.J.: Prentice-Hall, 1972.

Carlson, Karen, and Alan Meyers. *Speaking with Confidence.* Glenview, Ill.: Scott, Foresman, 1977.

Eisenson, Jon. *Voice and Diction: A Program for Improvement,* 5th ed. New York: Macmillan, 1985.

Fisher, Hilda. *Improving Voice and Articulation,* 2nd ed. Boston: Houghton Mifflin, 1975.

Hanley, Theodore, and Wayne Thurman. *Developing Vocal Skills,* 2nd ed. New York: Holt, Rinehart and Winston, 1970.

Hicks, Helen. *Voice and Speech.* Dubuque: William C. Brown, 1963.

Jones, Merritt, and Mary Pettas. *Speech Improvement.* Belmont, Calif.: Wadsworth, 1969.

King, Robert G., and Eleanor M. DiMichael. *Articulation and Voice: Improving Oral Communication.* New York: Macmillan, 1978.

Mayer, Lyle V. *Fundamentals of Voice and Diction,* 7th ed. Dubuque: William C. Brown, 1985.

Nelson, Paul, and Judy Pearson. *Confidence in Public Speaking,* 2nd ed. Dubuque: William C. Brown, 1984.

Rizzo, Raymond. *The Voice as an Instrument,* 2nd ed. Indianapolis: Bobbs-Merrill, 1977.

Zimbardo, Philip. *Shyness.* Boston: Addison-Wesley, 1979.

14 Persuasion: Theory and Practice

"In a real sense, we do not persuade others at all; we only provide the stimuli with which they can persuade themselves."

HERBERT SIMONS[1]

"There is only one way under high Heaven to get anybody to do anything and that is by making the other person want to do it."

DALE CARNEGIE[2]

"Rhetoric is the art of ruling the minds of men."

PLATO

GOAL

To be able to plan and use verbal and nonverbal messages to achieve persuasive goals

OBJECTIVES

The material in this chapter should help you to:
1. Explain how reinforcement leads to development of or changes in attitudes.
2. Explain the major theories of attitude change and indicate how they can be used to achieve persuasive goals.
3. Make effective use of balance theory in persuasive communication.
4. Establish specific persuasive goals that are appropriate to various situations.
5. Apply cognitive response theories when planning persuasive efforts.
6. Assess your credibility as a persuader in various situations, indicating ways to increase it when necessary.
7. Use appropriate organization, evidence, and argument to achieve specific persuasive goals.
8. Make effective use of motive appeals in persuading.

---

[1] "Persuasion and Attitude Change," *Speech Communication Behavior: Perspectives and Principles*, eds. Larry Barker and Robert J. Kibler (Englewood Cliffs, N.J.: Prentice-Hall, 1971), p. 232.

[2] *How to Win Friends and Influence People* (New York: Simon & Schuster, Inc., 1936), p. 29. Copyright © 1936 by Dale Carnegie; renewed © 1964 by Donna Dale Carnegie and Dorothy Carnegie. Reprinted by permission of Simon & Schuster, Inc.

In a classic volume written over two thousand years ago, Aristotle, then a student of Plato, examined *persuasion*—a topic as relevant today as it was then. In doing so, he provided a definition of rhetoric that is still useful. **Rhetoric,** said Aristotle, is *the art of finding, in any situation, the available means of persuasion.* And while today we use quite different technology from anything Plato or Aristotle could have imagined, we will still benefit from approaching persuasive tasks as did these ancient philosophers. A thorough study of receivers, subject and situation provides the strongest foundation for successful persuasion.

Trying to persuade others is doubtless one of the most common communicative goals for all of us. At the same time, we're all subjected daily to others' efforts to persuade us. Little that you study about communication will be more useful than an understanding of persuasion.

Yet the very familiarity of persuasion interferes with our using the process effectively. Perhaps most troublesome is the word itself. We all use the term *persuasion* to mean a number of different things. We recognize it as a process; we see it as a result; we think of it as a goal. "Being persuaded" can involve a change of mind, of behavior, of feelings—or of all three. Learning to use persuasion to achieve communicative goals benefits from remembering that it is all of those things.

THE NATURE OF PERSUASION

First, persuasion is communication, with all that that involves. Thus, in earlier chapters we discussed much that you need to know in order to persuade effectively. The effective persuader knows what it means to describe communication as process, and will remember the influences of perception, self-concept, language, culture, motivation, and attention. These concepts from earlier chapters form the base for the discussion of persuasive strategies.

As most communication is intended to induce some kind of response, some writers argue that all communication is persuasive. We believe such a broad definition not useful. We prefer a more precise definition. That definition focuses on process, describing **persuasion** as *communication initiated with the intent that a receiver or receivers will internalize new or changed attitudes, beliefs or values, or behave in a specific way.*

The behavioral goals of persuaders are easily recognized. Persuaders may try to get receivers to buy products, quit smoking, vote for a particular candidate, go to church, drive more safely, be "good," make contributions, or do many other things. One useful analysis describes persuasion as a process that creates, shapes, or changes responses.[3] These could be any responses, though overt behaviors are the most easily observable.

We less easily recognize other types of persuasion because the goals (of changing beliefs or attitudes) do not deal with observable behaviors. A persuader may seek to:

[3] Michael Roloff and Gerald Miller, *Persuasion: New Directions in Theory and Research* (Beverly Hills, Calif.: Sage Publications, 1980) pp. 16–22.

Persuasive speakers try to change attitudes.

1. Reinforce or intensify existing beliefs or attitudes (make you feel more strongly about helping the needy, which you already support)
2. Add something new to existing attitude systems (convince you that you need vitamin G, a product you never heard of before)
3. Create a disbelief in an existing idea (convince you that Senator Blue, whom you like, is really a very bad senator)
4. Modify existing attitudes by weakening their stability or importance (change your attitude about getting a new car from, "I absolutely must have a sports car" to "It would be nice to have a sports car if I could")

The observable and not observable goals interact. When seeking an overt behavorial response, for instance, you may first need to change existing beliefs. Selling a new product may require convincing people it is better than the one they already have.

It's important to keep in mind that the persuasive process involves at least three things: the intent of the source (what the persuader wants to accomplish); the actual messages or message carriers, verbal and nonverbal, and the effects in receivers (the changes that actually occur). An understanding of the persuasive process involves a consideration of all three aspects.

In this chapter, we look first at some theories about how persuasion occurs. We present several points of view because each provides a useful perspective from which to analyze persuasive situations. No one theory explains all persuasion, but each gives valuable insights to apply to our efforts to use the process or to analyze others' efforts to influence our behaviors. Finally, we discuss specific persuasive strategies useful for creating, shaping or changing others' responses.

Persuasion from Attitude Change Perspective

We defined *attitude* in Chapter 2, as a predisposition to respond in a particular way when confronted with a relevant stimulus. But remember, you'll never see an attitude. Attitude is a mental construct, a concept used to help explain behavior. Thus, although *attitude* is an abstract term, it has been used in much study of persuasion. So we first review some attitude theories and discuss some relationships between attitudes and behavior.

Learning Theories   As children learn to deal with their environments, they develop attitudes, beliefs and values. As you recall, people learn to perceive what things "mean" by experience with and naming those things. Attitudes are a kind of meaning, so attitudes develop as we learn language. When we learn language, we learn that words and other symbols stand for objects, events or concepts. And we develop positive or negative reactions to most words. Indeed, children often have these positive or negative feelings (and, hence, have a sort of attitude) about things before they associate the thing with a word. Similarly, there are often attitudes toward words before there are clear denotations for them.

REINFORCEMENT   As children, we learn that some things and behaviors bring us pleasure and others do not. In fact, some behaviors result in pain rather than reward. Thus, we develop some attitudes through direct association with pain or pleasure. For instance, we gain positive attitudes toward food because it satisfies hunger, and some of it tastes and smells good.

The process of learning behaviors (and attitudes) through receiving rewards is called **reinforcement.** We discussed this process as it affects self-concept (attitudes toward self) in Chapter 2. Now we emphasize the role of reinforcement in developing all attitudes. For infants, food may be directly rewarding, but learning to eat with

(*Funky Winkerbean* by Tom Batiuk. Reprinted with special permission of NAS, Inc.)

silverware is not. This learning process requires rewards from parents. As we grow, we are rewarded for using spoons and later for using knives and forks. We may be punished if we continue ot use our fingers. So we develop attitudes about eating. For instance, about using our fingers: it's okay for some food in some places, but not in others. Or about certain types of food: Spinach is awful; candy is good.

Through reinforcement, we learn to behave in approved ways and to avoid disapproved behaviors and beliefs. As we are rewarded, we learn what is "good." Eventually we develop a complex, interlocking attitude structure. But learning values and attitudes is not a rubber-stamping process. As children we don't just soak up the values and attitudes around us as a sponge does water. We individually interpret our experiences. We develop personal attitudes that may not directly reflect the attitudes of the significant people around us. That's because each of us interprets our own experiences. *What one person will interpret as a reward, another will not.*

The process of learning what is "good" and what is "bad" from rewards, no rewards (lack of reinforcement), or punishment will not result in identical attitudes, even for people who grow up in what appear to be identical circumstances. People with similar childhoods will usually have attitudes and values more alike than people who grow up in different environments. But no two attitude structures will be identical, because no two people will interpret their experiences exactly alike.

Still, the reinforcement process does cause us to learn socially approved behaviors and values, so it is useful to look more closely at it. Reinforcement occurs in at least two ways.

CLASSICAL CONDITIONING **Conditioning** is *a process in which some behavior caused by a primary stimulus becomes associated with a secondary stimulus.* The classic example of conditioning is the experiment the Russian scientist Pavlov conducted with dogs. By ringing a bell every time dogs were given food, he conditioned them to respond to the bell as if it were food. The food was the primary stimulus, the bell the secondary. Conditioning resulted in association of the secondary and primary stimuli. As a result, either caused the same behavior. The dogs salivated at the sound of the bell because they associated the reward of food with the bell. A human example of this kind of conditioning is association of time with eating. We all know someone who gets hungry at noon no matter how late breakfast may have been. For these people, the stimulus (noon) is associated with hunger. For them hunger (mentally at least) exists whenever the stimulus—midday—occurs.

Association in classical conditioning represents a direct stimulus-response model of behavior. To describe human behavior in these terms is, in most cases, oversimplification. People usually do more than just associate stimuli; they more often evaluate whether rewards are worth changing behavior for. This involves secondary reinforcement.

SECONDARY REINFORCEMENT In secondary reinforcement, the reward is more significant in the conditioning process. Rewards reinforce behavior by fulfilling some perceived need. For example, a dog may be taught to retrieve for a hunter if the trainer gives the dog rewards. The dog learns to associate the act of bringing back birds with receiving affection, which is the reward. Thus, the reward becomes a reinforcer for the behavior. Eventually, with sufficient repetitions, a hand signal or verbal command becomes the stimulus for retrieving.

In using reinforcement to develop attitudes or change behavior, rewards are probably required every time the desired actions first occur. Teaching a child to be a sharing person may at first require parental approval every time the child shares something. Repeated rewards can build an association so the behavior itself can become rewarding.

In humans, reinforcement can create such strong rewards from attitudes themselves that the primary stimulus may never have to be reintroduced. A person who believes sharing is "good" will be rewarded by the act. An internal reward system reinforces many people who donate to charities, helping people they never see. The act of giving itself is rewarding; we see ourselves as "good," generous, or prosperous people. We don't need responses from the grateful receivers.

Social approval by a valued group is an important form of reinforcement. If we perceive that a group we identify with holds certain attitudes and values, sharing their attitudes rewards us. If you can show listeners that a group they identify with approves a certain behavior, it often influences them. Being able to identify with the admired group is your listeners' reward. This reinforcement can occur even if no one in the reference group ever knows of the listeners' behavior: The identification itself is the reward. In other words, it is secondary reinforcement. The positive consequences of the behavior (perceived group identification) are associated with the behavior. Therefore, the behavior itself is rewarding. The example of contributing to charities illustrates this association. The giver can identify with "good" or "religious" persons, even through anonymous contributions.

NEGATIVE CONDITIONING   So far we've discussed only positive conditioning. Negative conditioning can also occur. Negative consequences can become associated with a secondary stimulus. A child can find playing with matches fun and, therefore, directly rewarding. But if the child starts a fire accidentally and is burned, she or he may associate pain with playing with matches. If the pain or fear is strong enough, the result can be changed behavior. The child no longer plays with fire.

Punishment is often used as a negative conditioning device. As a means of securing attitude changes, however, punishment is generally less effective than reinforcement. Punishment often results in unexpected and undesired effects. Let's take a familiar situation. Good grades are supposed to reward students, and the reinforcement should cause students to work for good grades. Poor grades are supposed to punish and create a negative association with not studying. So, the theory goes, children will study to avoid punishment and gain rewards. This use of the theory fails to consider that grades don't necessarily reinforce. If family or friends do not reward a child for good grades, grades probably won't reinforce study habits.

Moreover, the negative conditioning of receiving poor grades can eliminate any reinforcement of good grades. Failing or poor grades can reinforce a poor self-image. Getting an *F* can reinforce the belief, "I knew I wasn't smart enough to do that." Or negative responses can be associated with the source of the punishment.

Students who get poor grades often conclude they don't like school or don't like teachers.

To understand reinforcement, you must remember that *punishment differs from nonreinforcement.* Not reinforcing means absence of rewards. But the absence of rewards is not necessarily punishment. Each of us interprets what is rewarding for us and what isn't. Thus, the person who gives punishment (the punisher) may find that the "punishee" finds it rewarding. Some students find it rewarding to get bad grades or cause trouble for the teacher. Either can confirm a previous belief or increase identification with peers; either can be rewarding. Moreover, if good grades were never a reward for a child, poor grades will not punish.

This phenomenon (the difference between nonreinforcement and punishment) may explain the confusion and lack of consistency in results found when researchers have studied the effects of threats or fear appeals in persuasion. From the discussion of motivation in Chapter 6, you know that people are motivated to seek pleasure and avoid pain. But what one person intends as punishment another will not always perceive as painful. Therefore, the threat of punishment will not always persuade.[4]

Consider some of the uses of fear appeals that do seem to be effective. Advertisers have successfully sold the need to use deodorants, mouthwashes, perfumes, and after-shave lotions. It seems important to people in the United States to "smell good." Many ads promoting these products imply punishments for not doing so. The ads suggest that people who don't use a deodorant or mouthwash will offend others. We might conclude, therefore, that the ad is an effective use of fear appeal— it threatens punishment. But these ads also promise rewards. They suggest that people who use a deodorant or mouthwash will be liked. That powerful reward may provide the effect wanted.

Much advertising reflects this combination of reward and threat. Note ads selling smoke detector devices (fear of fire), radial tires (fear of blowouts causing accidents), and life insurance (fear of family having no income). Each offers a reward, not just a threat: safety, security, a family cared for. The reward may be the real motivator. Its results are both predictable and reinforcing; the threat may be only the attention-getter.

Consistency Theories Consistency theories best explain some attitude changes. Several such theories have been developed. Each has a slightly different point of view, and for our purposes here, a summary is sufficient. If you find these theories of interest, you may explore the ideas in more depth in the sources cited.

---

[4] Literally dozens of studies have been conducted in the attempt to settle which appeals are most effective. A good summary and critique of the research is found in Gerald Miller, "Studies on the Use of Fear Appeals: A Summary and Analysis," *A Reader in Speech Communication*, ed. James Gibson (New York: McGraw-Hill, 1971), pp. 307–15. Students who want to pursue this topic can find thorough bibliographies on the subject in Gary Cronkhite, *Persuasion Speech and Behavioral Change* (Indianapolis: Bobbs-Merrill, 1969) and Kenneth Higbee, "Fifteen Years of Fear Arousal: Research on Threat Appeals," *Psychological Bulletin*, December, 1969, pp. 426–44. More recent though less thorough summary is in Michael Burgoon and Erwin Bettinghaus, "Persuasive Message Strategies," in Michael Roloff and Gerald Miller, eds. *Persuasion: New Directions in Theory and Research* (Beverly Hills, Calif.: Sage Publications, 1980), pp. 141–169.

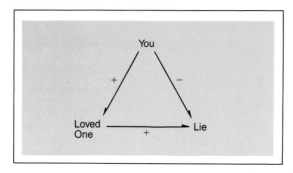

FIGURE 14–1. Imbalance in Attitudes.

BALANCE THEORIES **Balance theories** *hypothesize that people need to feel consistency or balance among beliefs perceived as related to each other.*[5] A perceived inconsistency (a lack of balance) among related beliefs and values results in an uneasy state described as imbalance. For example, suppose you love someone and also believe honesty is important. Then suppose you learn the person you love has lied to you about an event that happened last week. Because what you have just learned causes you to perceive an inconsistency between these related attitudes, you have imbalance. The perceived dishonesty of the person you love causes you much unhappiness. Figure 14–1 reflects a balance theory description of such an imbalance.

Balance theory suggests that *if people perceive related attitudes as inconsistent (unbalanced), they change in some way that helps them restore balance.* Several alternative changes could restore balance. Using the same example, let's illustrate. One possibility would be to change your attitude toward the person you love (see Figure 14–2). Another possible change would be to hold a new attitude toward lying. You might decide lying is okay if that person thinks it is (see Figure 14–3).

Usually, of course, shifts in attitudes are not this dramatic. Several smaller shifts are likely to occur: reducing the intensity of beliefs; adding intermediate link explanations. You could decide the lie wasn't a real dishonesty or that the behavior wasn't a lie but a misunderstanding. You could decide that the circumstances leading to what you had thought was a lie made it permissible or that the event was an isolated case, a freak event that would never happen again.

In some situations where one might expect imbalance, a person can dissociate the two attitudes. If two ideas aren't seen as related, they will not be seen as inconsistent. For example, a person might argue that strong criminal penalties for using heroin should be enforced because it is a harmful drug. A listener might respond: "Shouldn't use of alcohol also be treated as a criminal offense because it too is a harmful drug?" The question shows an inconsistency between the speaker's attitudes toward heroin and alcohol. Rather than recognizing the inconsistency,

[5] Fritz Heider, "Attitudes and Cognitive Organization," *Journal of Psychology*, 21 (1946), pp. 107–12 is the first writer in balance theory. Many theorists have published research in the area since then. A later development of the theory is in Heider's *The Psychology of Interpersonal Relations* (New York: Wiley, 1958).

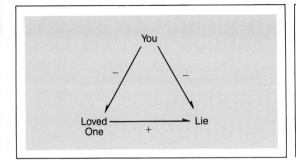

FIGURE 14–2. A Way to Restore Balance.

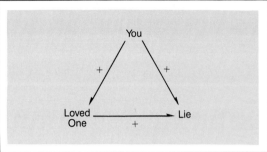

FIGURE 14–3. Another Way to Restore Balance.

the speaker could dissociate the two and answer: "Alcohol isn't a drug; it's quite different from heroin."

COGNITIVE DISSONANCE   If you perceive two beliefs as inconsistent, and if you see the two ideas as related, dissonance exists. The cognitive dissonance theory (a form of balance theory) argues that in such situations people actively seek to restore balance.[6] It also explains one process by which we eliminate the dissonance.

The basis of cognitive dissonance theory is similar to other balance theories: People cannot tolerate inconsistencies in relevant values or beliefs. The **cognitive dissonance theory** *suggests that when perceived inconsistencies cause dissonance, people engage in an active mental process to reduce the dissonance.* For example, suppose a person wants an expensive car but finds the purchase inconsistent with an attitude that people should not spend money foolishly. The person could rationalize: "Well, the expensive car will last longer; it will run longer without maintenance; and besides, it's necessary for my business." The rationalization doesn't reduce the perceived inconsistency—it only explains or justifies it.

Dissonance theory differs from other balance theories in that it suggests dissonance causes an active process to reduce the state of unease. The person with dissonance actively searches for reasons to justify behavior that has already occurred. A common example will illustrate the process. After making a purchase—whether a car, furniture, or clothes—don't you notice many more people using that particular brand than before? Aren't you aware of more advertisements for it? And now you actually pay attention to them.

Part of the reason you now notice what you didn't before is that you are reducing any dissonance you have from the purchase. You are making an active effort to confirm your reasons that the purchase was justifiable. If others—many others—have made the purchase, it helps you reduce dissonance. If you now learn from ads the good reasons for making the purchase, it helps reduce dissonance.

These attitude development and change theories can be helpful to you in persuasive efforts. They can help you decide how to secure the desired responses.

[6] Leon Festinger's *A Theory of Cognitive Dissonance* (Stanford, Calif.: Stanford University Press, 1957) is the original publication of this theory.

Use these ideas when you plan specific strategies. Creating dissonance and providing arguments for your listeners to restore balance are among the best ways to achieve persuasive goals.

Persuasion from Cognitive Response Perspective

We have mentioned an important concept, that of mental processing by the person toward whom efforts at influence are directed. We noted, for instance, that one person can interpret an event as rewarding while another person will not be influenced, and yet a third might think of that event as negative. This concept of mental processing has been developed into a theory of persuasion, the **cognitive response theory.**[7]

Cognitive response theories concentrate on what receivers of persuasive communication think about. If on hearing a message intended to persuade, the receiver thinks about the ideas involved, that's a form of response. It's a cognitive response. This thinking mediates the receivers' overt behavioral responses. In short, *cognitive response theories of persuasion draw the* (perhaps obvious) *conclusion that our thinking about what persuaders say and do is what persuades, not just the persuaders' words and deeds.* The important contribution of this theory is to remind us that receivers may think many things the persuader doesn't say. Receivers attempt to relate elements of the messages received to what they already know or believe.

Cognitive response theories are especially useful in explaining the persistence of persuasion. We all know that sometimes we have a positive response to a persuader's arguments immediately after listening to them, but in the long run we change beliefs, feelings or behavior little. The issue of persistence deals with the question: When receivers respond to messages differently at different times, what accounts for the changed responses? Cognitive response theories suggest that the persistence depends on the amount and type of mental processing that occurs during and after receiving the messages.

At least three general types of cognitive responses are possible: *message rehearsal, pro-argument*, and *counter-argument*. Message rehearsal occurs when receivers simply think about (mentally repeat) the points made by the persuader. Mentally summarizing what a persuader says is engaging in message rehearsal. Pro-argument occurs when receivers develop their own reasons doing as the persuader suggests. In counter-arguing, receivers develop their own reasons for *not* doing as the persuader suggests.

The evidence developed in support of the cognitive response theories of persuasion tends to support the following conclusions about the various types of mental message processing by receivers.

---

[7] A good summary of the material supporting these theories is in Lee Roloff, ". . . 'And Thinking Makes it So': Cognitive Responses to Persuasion," in Roloff and Miller, *Persuasion*, pp. 67–99. This chapter relies heavily on that summary. For someone interested in this theory, two thorough examinations of it are Richard E. Petty and John T. Cacioppo, *Communication and Persuasion: Central and Peripheral Routes to Attitude Change*, (New York: Springer-Verlag, Inc., 1986), and Richard E. Petty, Thomas Ostrom, and Timothy Brock, *Cognitive Responses in Persuasion* (Hillsdale, N.J.: Lawrence Erlbaum Associates, 1981).

1. Pro-argumentation is more persuasive than message rehearsal.
2. When dealing with an opposed audience, high-credibility persuaders are more persuasive than low because high-credibility reduces counter-arguing by receivers.
3. If receivers are predisposed toward the persuader's goals, lower-credibility sources may be more persuasive because higher-credibility sources also inhibit pro-argumentation by receivers.
4. Persuasion by low-credibility sources tends to persist due to more pro-argument by receivers (the sources may be forgotten, but the arguments persist).
5. High receiver involvement results in high levels of message processing; therefore, effects of persuasive messages interact with levels of receiver involvement.
   a. for messages easy to counter-argue, high receiver involvement increases resistance to persuasion.
   b. for messages difficult to counter-argue, high receiver involvement may increase persuasibility.
6. Moderate repetition of persuasive arguments tends to increase persuasion, but high levels lead to resistance, probably due to related levels of counter-arguing. (Excessive repetition creates boredom or irritation, and increases counter-arguing.)
7. Presentation of higher numbers of reasons to do as the persuader suggests, whether in message rehearsal or pro-argumentation, tend to increase agreement.
8. Distracting receivers from attending carefully to persuaders' messages increases persuasion, probably due to reducing counter-argumentation.
9. Forewarning reduces susceptibility to subsequent persuasion by creating anticipatory counter-arguing and increasing levels of counter-argument during message reception.

The distinctions among types of mental responses to messages may be the most useful contribution cognitive processing theories make. In learning how to persuade, we benefit by knowing we are likely to be most effective when we induce our receivers to pro-argue, or when we create circumstances that reduce counter-argument by receivers. Since most of us, at least early in our careers, do not have high credibility, we'll have the highest probability of success if we can get listeners to think about what we say and draw their own positive conclusions. Similarly, we'll have better results if we can skillfully use the persuasive situation to distract receivers from thinking about why our persuasive arguments are wrong.

This concept of distraction is one reason the study of advertising can be helpful to students of persuasion. We'll also note, as we examine successful advertising in the next chapter, why effective consumers of mass communication are alert to efforts by persuaders to distract their attention from the persuasive arguments in the ads themselves.

Credibility and Persuasion

A final concept we want to introduce is credibility. This term became popular at the time of the Vietnam War, as a "credibility gap" separated official sources of information and the public. While the press had adopted a new term, the concept was familiar to students of communication. For over 2,000 years we have known that a person's character—what Aristotle called *ethos*—plays a major role in the persuasion process. If receivers do not believe that a persuader is credible (believable),

Credibility is a perception.

evidence may be of little value. In contrast, if listeners respect and trust the persuader, they may believe what appears to someone else as utter nonsense.

What, then, is this important quality of credibility? The question makes us uneasy because no definitive answers exist. Like attitudes and motivation, credibility exists only within a receivers' mind. Credibility cannot be seen, and is hard to measure. Yet the concept is useful, so let's examine what is known about persuaders' credibility.[8]

Most important, remember that *credibility is a perception.* As with any perception, it may not be consistent with reality. If a receiver does not perceive a persuader as honest or competent, the "fact" of that person's honesty or authority is irrelevant. **Credibility** is not an attribute of the persuader; it is *the receiver's perception that the persuader is believable.* As such it depends on the source (the persuader), the receiver, the messages, and the situation. Credibility is high or low, present or absent, depending on how believable a receiver thinks a source may be. In most cases, chances of achieving persuasive goals increase when the source is perceived as credible.

Sources of Credibility Many students want to know how to increase their credibility when they try to persuade others. This information will be useful, however, only if they keep in mind that no single factor guarantees their credibility, nor will being perceived as credible guarantee the desired persuasive outcome.

CHARACTER AND COMPETENCE Among the several elements that lead to perceptions of credibility, character and competence appear to be most important. Perceiving a person as honest, friendly, and pleasant increases credibility based on character.

---

[8] Controversy has surrounded the concept of credibility as researchers have found experimental results inconsistent. One of the best summaries of the findings is in Robert Bostrom's *Persuasion* (Englewood Cliffs, N.J.: Prentice-Hall, Inc., 1983) pp. 63–87.

Persons seen as dishonest, unfriendly, and/or unpleasant are usually low in credibility. To be perceived as having high character also seems to involve being seen as having good intentions toward the listeners. This involves being seen as sincere, as caring about what happens to the people you're talking to.

Being perceived as competent means the person is judged reliable, informed, qualified, and intelligent. Persons seen as unreliable, uninformed, unintelligent, or inexpert will lack credibility based on competence. Moreover, while these two factors affect each other, their interaction is not predictable. Being seen as honest won't cause you to be seen as an expert. Or they may think you're an expert, but a dishonest one.

Perceptions of competence and character will themselves vary, primarily because credibility isn't global. One receiver or group may consider a person competent, while another receiver or group may see the same person as incompetent. Credibility is related both to the topic and the situation. People considered as authorities in their work may not be seen as informed or expert on other matters. One's reputation may have some "halo" or spill-over effects in other areas, but the effects vary. O. J. Simpson is an authority on football who is known for his running. So he was credible as an advertiser for Hertz. The effects of his views on who should be governor of California are less predictable. For some listeners, the halo would make him credible as a political persuader. For others, it would not.

INTERPERSONAL ATTRACTION   Whether receivers like a person seems also to be related to credibility, but this depends very much on the situation. You may like a friend, but your friend may have no credibility at all regarding how to repair your car. On the other hand, you may know an auto mechanic whose personality leaves much to be desired, but in whose honesty and mechanical ability you have complete confidence. On the question of how to repair your car, the disliked mechanic will have higher credibility than your friend. Yet, given two equally skilled mechanics, one you like will probably have higher credibility than one you don't like.

Likability probably influences credibility in interpersonal situations more than in public speaking, but as President Reagan's record has shown, the effects of interpersonal attraction can powerfully aid public persuasion as well. Certainly receivers will be attracted to people they perceive as honest or friendly, but liking involves more than that. To use this factor in persuading, you may want to review the discussion of interpersonal attraction in Chapter 7.

POISE AND DYNAMISM   Two other factors seem to affect credibility, especially in public situations. The first of these is poise. To be seen as poised is to be perceived as in control of your emotions. Speakers and persons in group leadership situations benefit from being seen as poised, relaxed, and confident. Being perceived as nervous, tense, or uptight can reduce credibility.

Recognize, of course, the fine line between being poised and cold. A cold or unemotional person in a situation where strong feelings are expected won't benefit from high credibility. Being emotional can add to perceived honesty and concern. The key, as with all factors of credibility, seems to be appropriateness to the situation and to the individual. A display of emotion that seems unfitting to the source or

Even in an emotional situation, a speaker needs to maintain control.

the situation can be damaging. Emotion that seems insincere or dishonest will not increase credibility.

Generally, even emotional speakers need to be perceived as under control or at least capable of regaining control quickly. Any political campaign provides examples. It's okay for candidates to choke up and show emotion at certain times—in victory or defeat, or when returning home after a long absence. But when a candidate breaks down and can't finish speaking, the effect is quite negative.

Another factor influencing credibility may be dynamism. Extremes—aggressive-passive, bold-meek, or introverted-extroverted—best describe this factor. Persuaders seen at either extreme receive negative reactions in most situations. Usually you should seek to achieve a position near center on the active end of a dynamic-static continuum.

A popular term to describe the desired evaluation is *assertive*. An aggressive person seems to interfere with the rights of others. A passive person seems trampled on by others. The person perceived as assertive is seen as pursuing her or his rights without destroying the feelings or rights of others. Recall the discussion of this concept in Chapter 9. Again, remember both situation and speaker personality affect this factor. Only in some situations will a speaker benefit greatly from perceived boldness. Similarly, some people will be positively evaluated for being bold; others will not.

HOMOPHILY   *The degree to which communicators are similar in attributes* also affects listener perceptions of speaker credibility. This factor, called **homophily,** was described in Chapter 7 as one of the elements involved in interpersonal attraction, though we didn't use that term. Some of the attributes that contribute to homophily are attitudes, values, socioeconomic status, appearance, family background, age, sex, and ethnic origin. Two dimensions of homophily exist: actual and perceived.

The two need not be the same and often are quite different. You can, for instance, perceive someone who may actually have the same education as you as being very different.

For the persuader, perceived homophily is probably more important than actual. Receiver perceptions will be based on appearance, language, behavior, and previous knowledge. Some of the things you can do to use each element to improve credibility are discussed later. At this point we stress only that when a receiver perceives you as homophilous in those attributes important to the situation, it increases the chances of successful persuasion.

Homophily is most helpful when perceived similarities are situation or topic relevant. However, resembling your receivers in every way is not always desirable. If you have been invited to speak on a topic because you are an expert in the area, you will not benefit if listeners perceive you as just another member of the "rank-and-file."

Communication between people who perceive themselves as homophilous will be more frequent and more effective. More frequent contact leads to more opportunities for influence. More effective communication, obviously, is more likely to accomplish stated goals.

Homophily may explain the powerful role of opinion leaders in gaining attitude change in group situations. An opinion leader is a kind of "superrepresentative" of a group—similar to members in group identification or background but superior in several ways. He or she is usually better informed and has wider contacts, is "more" of everything group members are or would like to be. Gang leaders as well as many politicians may be thought of as opinion leaders. They share a common background with the people they represent or lead but are different. They're "better" or they would not have become leaders. The type of homophily such group leaders have contributes strongly to their credibility.

EXERCISE 14.1 ASSESSING AUDIENCE ATTITUDES, IMBALANCE, AND DISSONANCE REDUCTION

OBJECTIVE To practice assessing audience attitudes and use of imbalance in persuasion.

DIRECTIONS
1. Assume you have to give a persuasive speech. To achieve you goal, your audience members will have to change their existing attitudes. (The situation could be inside or outside the classroom.)
2. Identify your specific purpose for the situation.
3. Analyze the assumed audience to determine their attitudes toward your goal (purpose).
4. Identify attitude changes that would create imbalance in your listeners.
5. Identify attitude shifts that would restore balance or rationalizations that would reduce the dissonance created.
6. Your instructor may have you report in a speech your analysis of imbalance and the dissonance-reducing rationalizations the audience would need for you to achieve your goal.

> **REVIEW** **Provide brief answers that may be used as the basis for a writing assignment or class discussion.**
> 1. Explain the various meanings attached to the term, *persuasion*.
> 2. Briefly state the major theories of attitude change.
> 3. State the concepts from cognitive response theories of persuasion that seem most useful to you.
> 4. What was the most important communication principles illustrated by or learned from this exercise?

PERSUASIVE GOAL SETTING

The first step in preparing for a persuasive effort should be to answer the question, What do I want to accomplish? The answer should be stated specifically, and phrased in terms of desired receiver response. *A goal statement should specify what you want done, who should do it, and when.* For example:

Situation:	Talking to an instructor about the grade received on a term paper.
Specific goal:	The instructor (*who*) will change his opinion about the paper and give it a grade of C instead of D (*what*) before awarding final grades (*when*).

The importance of goal setting is difficult to overemphasize. Poorly clarified goals cause many persuasive efforts to fail. For that reason, we urge persuaders to give detailed attention to goal-setting. As we stressed in earlier chapters, it's important to state goals in terms of desired receiver response. Doing so will help you keep in mind that *you accomplish what you want only when the receiver does it.* Persuasive success is not measured by what the persuader says. It is measured by the match between what the persuader wants and what the receiver says, does, thinks or feels.

Receiver Analysis Influences Goals

In planning for a persuasive effort, receiver analysis involves two parts: gathering information and drawing conclusions. The steps for gathering information for persuasion differ little from those outlined for audience analysis in Chapter 11. Many of the inferences to be drawn from the information are also similar, but the analysis differs somewhat.

Receiver analysis in planning for persuasion is used to refine the persuasive goal. It *involves analyzing your receivers to decide whether the goal can be accomplished and what will be required to do so.*[9]

---

[9] Keep in mind that persuasion may be directed toward one person or to a group of people. In order to simplify the references, we often use receivers as a plural term, but remember that much of the persuasion you do involves just one receiver. Most of the discussion in this chapter applies to either situation.

Receivers' Position before Persuasion First, decide where your receivers stand with reference to your goal. This will help you know the dimensions of the persuasive task. You want to know what your receivers believe about your goal, how they feel about it, and what is their behavioral predisposition toward it. These questions examine the affective, cognitive and behavioral tendency components of attitudes. They help you use the concept of receivers' attitudes toward your goal to assess their pre-persuasion position.

What are often called "attitude scales" can be used to depict these attitude components. We illustrate these (Fig. 14–4), with a goal of persuading an instructor to change the grade on a term paper. The scales provide a way to "see" your assessment of what the receivers think about your goal, how they feel about it, and on the basis of this and other factors, how likely the desired behavioral response is.

Keep in mind that although these are described as attitude scales, they only *represent* an attitude. Even if, before a persuasive effort, you could give scales like these to your potential receivers and ask them to mark the number that best reflects what they feel and think, the results would not show your receivers' attitudes. The results would report a belief or opinion, a feeling, and a projection of a likely future response.

An attitude is neither opinion nor behavior, but a mental construct representing a *predisposition to respond.* It oversimplifies receiver analysis, therefore, if all you ask is what a receiver thinks about your goal. Certainly, you need to know, Do my receivers agree with me? If you are seeking action, a yes answer is helpful. But this is only part of what you want to know. Many smokers, for instance, agree with the statement, "I should quit smoking." So if your persuasive goal were for them to quit, knowing their belief would be helpful, but it wouldn't give you many clues about reaching your goal.

You need to think about other factors, especially as you consider the behavior tendency element of attitudes. Those factors are the *strength, importance and stability*

Disagree			No opinion			Agree
−3	−2	−1	0	1	2	3

Feeling:						
Intensely Negative		Negative	Don't Care/ Ambivalent	Positive		Strongly Positive
−3	−2	−1	0	1	2	3

Desired Behavior Is:						
Very Unlikely		Unlikely	Neutral	Likely		Very Likely
−3	−2	−1	0	1	2	3

FIGURE 14–4. Attitude Scales and Behavior Prediction.

of the attitudes in question, and other, related attitudes as well. The issue of strength may be partly addressed by a combination of the belief and feeling components. If one agrees with a statement and also feels intensely about it, it is likely that one's attitude is strong. But it is possible to agree with something and not feel intensely about it. Under those conditions, the attitude is not strong.

To illustrate these four factors, examine some possible persuasive goals involving people who do not smoke. Most of them probably agree that it is more pleasant for nonsmokers if smoking in public places is prohibited. Some nonsmokers feel strongly about this issue; they're allergic to smoke or they want to avoid the hazards to their own health from someone else's behavior. Some of these nonsmokers also believe in asserting their own rights vigorously. Such people might easily be persuaded to join efforts to pass laws or regulations banning smoking in public places. Other nonsmokers, who feel equally strongly about avoiding smoke, may also believe that in regulating smoking, government improperly invades personal freedom. It would be hard to persuade this last group to support regulation of smoking in public places. Indeed, they might be more easily persuaded to oppose such efforts.

The process of receiver analysis should not stop with attempting to determine what receivers might think or feel about your particular goal. You also want to consider these other related issues:

1. How strong is the attitude? With what intensity are the beliefs held?
2. How important is the attitude? Do the receivers believe the issue makes a difference to them or to people they care about?
3. How stable is the attitude? Is this a belief that they have held for a long time? Is it one they have acted upon and been reinforced for?
4. How does this attitude relate to other beliefs and attitudes of the receivers?

GROUP OR INDIVIDUAL PERSUASION   When your goal involves more than a single receiver, you need to consider these questions somewhat differently. If the situation involves only a few people, the questions should be answered for each individual receiver. Often, however, you will deal with groups of people. That situation will involve making inferences about the group as a whole, or about various subgroups, or sometimes just about the opinion leaders of the group.

Obviously, receiver analysis must take into consideration all the important people toward whom the persuasive effort is directed. When persuasion can be effectively aimed at only a few persons, it simplifies the task of planning. Therefore, in dealing with a group, you will sometimes work only with its leaders. At other times you may generalize a composite person who symbolizes the group. At still other times your receiver analysis may be directed at two, three or more subgroup composites, the number depending on the complexity of the situation and the receivers.

Amount of Shift Required   After assessing receivers' positions with reference to your goal, compare where you must begin with what you wish to accomplish. The scales depicted on p. 371 can help in visualizing the task. First, identify where your receivers will be on each scale *when you accomplish your goal*. Then compare that to your assessment of where the receivers are before you begin. You have then answered the question, How much change in receivers' attitudes will be required for me to accomplish my goal?

Minor changes are usually easy to achieve. Securing action from people who already agree with you may require motivation, but usually less effort than changing established beliefs. Similarly, moving a person from a neutral or no-opinion status, if their lack of opinion is based on absence of information, can also be relatively simple. But if you seek to change someone's mind and get action all in one effort, that is quite different and not at all simple.

If the change required of a receiver is great, it may suggest that your goal cannot be accomplished, or that repeated efforts will be required to accomplish it. You may decide the shift required is so great that the probability of success is low, and that you have an unrealistic goal. You may choose to try it anyway; but do so fully aware of the magnitude of your task.

If you are facing a homogeneous group (whether of neutrals, opponents or those who agree with you) the task differs greatly from that of facing a mixed or polarized group of receivers. With a group of mixed receivers, you want to avoid alienating anyone, if that is possible. At the same time, you will probably best use your time if you concentrate on the people who are most persuadable. A one-time effort can make some gains with people only mildly opposed to your goal; long-range efforts will probably be required with strong opponents.

This analysis will help you determine the best ways to accomplish your goal— or to decide that the goal should be modified before you make further plans.

Set Realistic Goals (Usually)

Our discussion so far has assumed that persuaders are seeking immediate or short-range success in accomplishing their persuasive goals. If so, they will use audience analysis to set achievable goals. If your audience analysis shows your receivers strongly oppose the speech thesis, you will usually change the goal to seek a smaller shift. Suppose you are a campaign worker trying to convince voters they should reelect Senator Bristow. If audience analysis tells you that your listeners passively agree Bristow has done a good job or that they know nothing about Bristow, getting them to vote for the senator's reelection is a realistic goal.

Suppose, however, that you discover a sizable number opposed the senator when she was first a candidate, and that the record since election has merely reinforced their opinion. To conclude that one persuasive appeal will influence them to vote for reelection is unrealistic. Indeed, if you don't write this audience off altogether, you'll probably conclude that getting them to vote for Bristow is a long-range goal. You'll adjust your immediate, or short-range, goal to something more realistic, more achievable. You might first simply try to get them to come and meet the senator, to have the opportunity to express their views. Even better, you might seek an opportunity for the senator to come meet them.

Another possibility is to decide that, with a particular group of listeners, you

Although the women's movement goals seemed unrealistic to some, activists like Gloria Steinem worked to achieve them.

can't reach the goal. The attitudes may be so stable and so intense that no amount of time or effort will change them. In these cases, being realistic might mean not bothering with a hostile or opposed audience. This is not to suggest you avoid all efforts to persuade strong opponents, but that you be realistic about the results. When one effort—or even a whole series—won't achieve some persuasive goals, changing goals may be the best response.

In other cases, persuaders may decide deliberately to seek goals they know cannot be reached. In these cases, the persuader may be seeking to prepare the way for a long-range goal. Or the persuader may promote an unrealistic goal for the purpose of accomplishing some unstated goal. Leaders of the major social movements of the Sixties and early Seventies—militant civil rights activists, radical feminists, and student radicals—illustrate the point.[10] These people wanted sweeping changes and were serious about it, even though getting them was not realistic at that time.

The demands for radical changes served another purpose, though. They made more moderate goals achievable. Most people wouldn't have considered these more limited goals moderate without the radical demands for comparison. For example,

---

[10] We want to emphasize that our intended meanings for the word *radical* do not imply negative connotations. We use the term to refer to sweeping changes, indicating no approval or disapproval. To us, radical means only that the changes sought were major changes.

an original spokesperson for the women's movement, Ti-Grace Atkinson, repeatedly demanded radical changes of behavior from the women to whom she spoke. Those radical demands made the more limited aims of equal pay for equal work seem moderate.

Without the calls for extreme changes, the moderate goals would themselves have seemed radical and unreasonable. Whether Ti-Grace Atkinson was aware of performing this function, or whether she really expected to achieve radical goals isn't clear. Nor does it really matter, because the principle is our point here: Sometimes a persuader knows that stated goals are unrealistic, but pursues them anyway to make less radical demands seem moderate.

Long-range versus Short-range Goals

You may decide a goal that is unrealistic in the short run can be achieved over a period of time. You may then seek a series of realistic smaller shifts in attitude. Several steps in a campaign might be planned, each to accomplish a specific, limited goal. The campaign plan would be that the complete series will accomplish the long-range goal.

Movements seeking civil rights for minorities in the United States have produced many leaders whose efforts over the years illustrate this approach. Martin Luther King's initial attempts to desegregate lunch counters were only the first steps toward achieving the long-range goal of equality for blacks. At the time Dr. King began his efforts, that goal was far removed—nor has it been achieved to date. Yet to reach that long-range goal he and many others have planned and presented countless messages to achieve short-range goals as steps along the way.

Goal Reassessment

An effective persuader will plan much as we have suggested public speakers should. First, state tentative goals in the early stages of planning. Second, analyze receivers to decide the chances of successful persuasion. Then you may need to revise the statement of goals. Study of the potential receivers may show that your tentative goal is unrealistic. At this point, you may decide

1. To go ahead knowing success isn't likely
2. To divide goals into long- and short-range efforts
3. To change goals

Whatever the choice, persuaders should remember that receiver analysis is never complete. All the time you're planning and presenting persuasive messages, continue to study the people you want to persuade. Receiver adaptation in persuasion, like audience analysis in public speaking, is not finished until the effort is finished and you have assessed how close you came to reaching your goal.

Receiver Analysis Techniques

The questions outlined below provide a summary of the discussion about receiver analysis for persuasion. Like the public speaker, the persuader uses direct questions, observation, and demographic data to decide how best to accomplish his or her goals. The following list of questions should help guide the receiver analysis for most persuasive situations.

1. What is the persuasive goal? (State specifically: What will my receivers say, do, think, or feel if I am successful?)
2. What specific things do I *know* about my receivers that will help me to assess their "attitudes" toward my goal?
   a. relevant knowledge?
   b. relevant experiences?
   c. relevant reference groups?
   d. relevant values, beliefs, and feelings?
3. What receiver beliefs, values, or feelings can I *infer*?
   a. toward the subject?
   b. toward related issues?
   c. toward me as a persuader?
   d. toward the goal?
4. What will be the impact of situation?
   a. will anything about time, place, climate, environment, relationships among receivers, or other aspects of the situation affect the effort (positively or negatively)?
5. What other factors might affect the persuasive effort?
   a. receiver expectations: of me? of relevant others?
   b. receiver commitments?
   c. specific physical or psychological barriers?

EXERCISE 14.2   **SETTING PERSUASIVE GOALS**

OBJECTIVE   **To practice setting goals for persuasive situations.**

DIRECTIONS   1. Choose three real-life situations in which you might try to persuade someone.
   2. For each potential persuasive effort:
      a. State the situation.
      b. Name the persons you are going to try to persuade.
      c. State specifically the effect you desire as a result of your persuasive effort (what the receiver will do or say if you are successful).
   3. Now, check your responses in item 2. Have you, for each goal statement, specified
      a. Who?
      b. Is to do what?
      c. Under what circumstances?
      d. When?
         If not, rephrase the goal statements until you have.
   4. Your instructor may ask you to share your goal statements in class.

DEVELOPING THE PERSUASIVE ARGUMENT

Once your goals are clear, planning for persuasion proceeds much as planning for a speech. The steps outlined in Chapters 11, 12 and 13 will be useful. In addition, persuaders should attend to some other factors.

Create Imbalance and Reduce Dissonance

In much persuasion, you deal primarily with beliefs—the cognitive component of attitudes. You will need to weaken existing beliefs and/or create a need for new ones. You want to create imbalance in your listeners. You want them to experience dissatisfaction with their existing attitudes and then to accept the means you suggest as a means of restoring balance.

Several techniques can be used to create the desired dissonance and restore balance with the beliefs you want audiences to have. Among the most important are evidence and argumentation and the use of motive appeals.

Evidence   The subject of evidence was introduced in Chapter 12 in the discussion of supporting materials. Now we focus specifically on the use of evidence in persuasion.

In persuasion, **evidence** means *statements, believed by receivers, that form the basis for believing other statements.* From this point of view, the receiver determines what is evidence. It's both more and less than facts, statements of observation, statistics, or conclusions by authorities. *Any* statements accepted by receivers as reasons for believing other statements function as evidence.

This use of the term *evidence* is based on a basic principle of communication that a persuader needs to understand. Something that you think is evidence may not function as evidence for someone else. To persuade, view evidence from your listeners' perspectives. No matter how logical your reasoning, how obvious your facts, or how high your authority, if your audience does not accept what you offer as evidence, it isn't evidence—not for that audience. For example, the biblical injunction that Jesus Christ is the Son of God is sufficient for most Christians. "The Bible says so" is sufficient evidence for them to believe the conclusion. But this is not evidence to millions who believe in other religions and consider Jesus' status similar to that of other prophets or great teachers.

Chapter 12 presented many materials that can be used as evidence. Persuasive speeches might use any of them: facts or other nonverbals, statements of observation, explanations, comparisons and contrasts, short narratives, statistics, quotations, examples, repetition and restatement. Some persuasion uses primarily facts, statements of observation, explanation, and statistics. At other times, quotations from authorities will be the major evidence. But to decide what evidence you need, consider what materials will be persuasive to your particular listeners. What will *they* believe? That is the persuader's critical question in choosing evidence.

Argumentation Evidence becomes effective when placed in persuasive arguments. For many people, the word *argument* brings to mind images of heated debate. And such images accurately reflect what happens in some efforts at persuasion. But more effective persuaders use **argumentation** differently. For them, *argumentation* is a process of reasoning.

The discussion of reasoning processes in Chapters 4 & 5 will help as you consider appropriate persuasive arguments. In any persuasion, the basic unit of reasoning is the **argument.** We use that term to refer to *a unit of thought that contains a conclusion, evidence, and the connection between the two.*

The connection is as important as the evidence itself. For example, look at the following argument: "Nine out of ten heroin addicts first smoked marijuana (evidence); there, marijuana use should be illegal because it leads to heroin addiction (conclusion)." Many people reject the conclusion for reasons that have nothing to do with the evidence. They reject the causal reasoning that links marijuana to heroin use. They observe that heroin addicts also drank milk before they used heroin and conclude, "That one event precedes another, doesn't mean one causes the other."

Other people might accept the causal link, agreeing that marijuana causes heroin addiction, but still reject the conclusion that it should be illegal. They might say, "Accuracy of the conclusion that marijuana causes heroin use is not relevant to legality. Heroin addiction is an illness, not a crime. If addiction isn't criminal, then what causes it shouldn't be criminal either."

A Model for Argument Persuasive efforts usually involve several connected arguments. Developing messages that persuade is helped by looking carefully at the connections. Stephen Toulmin offers a useful model for analyzing arguments.[11] You can use this model to examine the quality of your reasoning (see Figure 14–5).

In the Toulmin model, all sound arguments contain three basic elements. These are evidence, conclusion, and a warrant. *The warrant is the link between evidence and conclusion: It's the reason for believing the evidence is relevant.* Many weak arguments do not state the warrant. Persuaders can't assume receivers will follow mental processes that seem obvious to the speaker.

The following argument shows these three essential elements: Interstate Com-

---

[11] The model is developed in *The Uses of Argument* (London: Cambridge University Press, 1958), pp. 94–145. Reprinted with the permission of Cambridge University Press.

FIGURE 14–5. Toulmin's Model of Argument: The Essentials

merce Commission regulation of trucking discourages competition (evidence); therefore, deregulation would reduce freight costs, and, ultimately, consumer prices (conclusion). The conclusion is based on an unstated warrant, that competition in trucking would lower prices.

Three other elements may be involved in arguments (Fig. 14–6). These are the *reservation*, which is an "unless" clause; the *qualifier*, which is a clause that limits or restricts the conclusion; and the backing, or *support for the warrant*. These three are needed when the receiver won't accept a conclusion on the basis of the evidence and warrant alone.

A qualifier comes between the claim and the other elements. It limits or specifies the conclusion to make it acceptable. Inserting words like *usually* or *probably* often makes a conclusion more believable. Suppose the above example had a conclusion, "therefore, deregulation would reduce most prices." *Most* would be a qualifier.

Backing or support for a warrant is often needed. Just as the connection between evidence and conclusion isn't always obvious, the warrant is not always acceptable. It may need evidence itself. The other element sometimes needed is the reservation. A reservation cites possible exceptions. It's usually introduced by words like *unless, except, other than.*

Adding to the example will illustrate the qualifier, support for warrant, and reservation. ICC regulation of trucking discourages competition; therefore, deregulation would reduce most (qualifier) prices, unless firms now protected by regulation cannot stay in business (reservation). Support for the warrant: deregulation of commercial airlines lowered prices in that industry.

The Toulmin model of argument is useful because it exposes the essentials in an argument. You can use it to examine a reasoning process and decide where the weaknesses are. You can see if further evidence is needed or if a warrant to link it to the conclusion should be stated. If neither the evidence nor the reason for connecting it to the conclusion are believed by the receivers, the argument will not be persuasive.

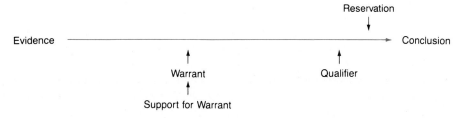

FIGURE 14–6. Toulmin's Model of Argument: All Elements.

In a persuasive argument, the conclusion of one argument often becomes evidence for another. In the example we have been using, for instance, some listeners would not accept as evidence the statement that ICC regulation discourages competition. Another argument, supporting that claim, would be needed to make the statement acceptable as evidence for those listeners. Some (or most) listeners would also want data to demonstrate that deregulation of airlines reduced prices in that industry.

Use Motive Appeals

Probably the most important task for persuaders is to relate their arguments to receivers' relevant motivations. This is described as using motive appeals. The following argument is a motive appeal: "Buy Roger's Automatic Sentry; it will protect your house from burglary and break-ins." The claim is that if listeners do as the persuader suggests, their need for safety will be met. Any need can be the basis for a motive appeal as long as it is relevant to your thesis.

The warrant in a motive appeal is the causal reasoning that connects the behavior and the need satisfaction. Let's take an example to illustrate.

> *Conclusion*: You should use Brand X deodorant.
> *Evidence*: Using Brand X will prevent you from offending people around you.
> *Warrant*: Brand X will keep you from smelling bad.

To make the entire argument clear would require several intermediate links, as well as reservations and qualifiers. But a motive appeal usually doesn't try to make the entire argument clear. It often intentionally shortcuts the reasoning required for a structurally sound argument.

Because human behavior is motivated to satisfy perceived needs, a persuader who ignores motive appeals runs a great risk. A fundamental argument in all persuasive messages should show how the proposed action or belief will satisfy listeners' important needs. Evidence, arguments, organization, and language should all lead receivers to think, "If I believe or behave as suggested, my need for _____ will be satisfied."

Motive appeals will be most effective when directed at *unsatisfied* needs. Recall Maslow's hierarchy of needs, and you understand why McDonald's and Burger King's television commercials are so often aired just before dinnertime. Any unsatisfied need, if related to the behavior you're urging, can increase the likelihood of the desired response. For best results, choose unsatisfied needs that your receiver analysis has shown to be strong motivators for your listeners.

Persuaders must be familiar with the information about motivation introduced in Chapter 6. In planning for persuasive efforts, they need to consider all theories of motivation and decide which needs are most important to receivers and most related to the persuasive goal. Then the persuader plans arguments that show how those needs will be met by doing or believing as suggested.

ORGANIZING PERSUASION

Whether your persuasive efforts involve formal speeches, thirty-second advertisements, or conversations involving give-and-take, careful advance organization of your arguments will improve your chances of success. Indeed, many of the suggestions for speech organization easily adapt to persuasion. Three are especially valuable.

Standard Outlines

Problem-Solution Approach Much persuasion involves explaining a problem and showing how a particular approach will solve it. For this situation, you can develop a problem-solution outline much as you would with a speech:

INTRODUCTION
    A. Gain attention and good will
    B. Develop credibility, if necessary
    C. Orient receiver to subject
BODY
    I. Explain problem
       A. Symptoms or results (problem description)
       B. Size and/or significance
       C. Cause
   II. Present solution
       A. Explain solution
       B. Show how solution eliminates problem
CONCLUSION
   Appeal for action or desired belief

You can use the problem identification step to create imbalance in listeners. The solution step reduces dissonance and restores balance by showing how to eliminate the problem.

The following outline is an example of an argument developed with a problem-solution outline:

    I. Pregnancies among unwed teenagers are a serious problem.
       A. The problem can result in many legal and illegal abortions, unwanted children, and lifelong poverty.
       B. The number of pregnancies among unwed teenagers rises every year.
       C. Several factors combine to cause the problem.
   II. Sex education and contraceptives provided without parental consent would reduce the number of pregnancies.
       A. Here's how the solution would work: . . .
       B. This proposal would reduce teenager pregnancies because . . .

A variation of the problem-solution outline occurs when the persuader aims only to convince listeners that a problem exists. Receiver analysis may have shown that listeners do not believe a problem exists. In these cases, it might be unrealistic to expect them to agree to a particular solution. First, achieving a short-range goal might be necessary. This could call for an argument seeking listener agreement on the problem. In these cases, a topical outline organized around need issues would be appropriate. The following outline would be appropriate for convincing receivers that it's serious to waste energy.

Thesis: The overconsumption of energy in the U.S. is a serious problem.

    I. Natural resources are being used up.

    II. Reliance on imported energy endangers the nation's defense.

    III. Shortages of supply and excessive demands damage the economy, causing both inflation and unemployment.

    IV. Poor and lower income people are hardest hit by shortages and high prices.

These examples follow outlines appropriate for speeches. That is intentional. Sometimes you will use speeches as part of a persuasive effort. At other times, you will use quite different formats. But all efforts at persuasion involve the same essential elements: gaining attention and good will; establishing credibility; developing the persuasive arguments; and ending appropriately. Pay attention to the next advertisement you see on television. Effective ads use these same four elements, usually developed and presented with great sophistication. Indeed, noticing advertising will show you many of the elements of persuasion we have discussed.

Motivated Sequence   One standard approach to persuasion has been called Monroe's motivated sequence.[12] The suggested main points of this outline follow a motivational sequence, and are generally based on the problem-solution form. In the motivated sequence outline illustrated below, the material in parentheses shows the similarities. In any given situation, you may find one approach more useful than the other. Knowing these similarities will help you decide which will work best for you.

    I. *Attention Step* (introduction): Call attention to the problem.

    II. *Need Step* (develop problem): Demonstrate that a need exists and how serious it is.

    III. *Satisfaction Step* (explain solution): Indicate how the need can be met and the problem solved.

    IV. *Visualization Step* (show how solution meets need): Show the need being met somewhere else or on a smaller scale.

    V. *Action Step* (conclusion): Appeal for action.

Advantages-Disadvantages Outline   Another good persuasive approach uses an advantages-disadvantages outline. The following shows how this might be used:

[12] This outline was first presented by Alan Monroe in 1939 in *Principles and Types of Speech*, 2nd ed. (Glenview, Ill.: Scott, Foresman and Company).

INTRODUCTION
  I. Get attention and orient audience
BODY
  I. Disadvantages of present situation
  II. Advantages of new idea (proposal, policy, situation, or whatever)
  III. Compare advantages to disadvantages
  IV. Show advantages can't be obtained without proposed changes
CONCLUSION
  Appeal for action

This approach, like the problem-solution outline, enables the speaker to first create imbalance by showing "what's wrong," then to restore balance by explaining a "better" way.

Issues of Overall Organization

During the planning process, several issues of overall organization confront the persuader. Among these are, How many messages should I use? How clearly should I present the goal? Should I mention opposing points of view?

Number of Messages We briefly noted the issue of number of messages in the earlier discussion of long- and short-range goals. Now let's return to the question. Dividing arguments can positively affect goal accomplishment. Some research has demonstrated that a receiver who complies with a first small request will agree more readily to a larger request at a later time. The research has shown, indeed, that the tendency to agree to later requests exists even when the second request is made by a different person or when the first request was refused.

Many examples from experience reinforce our acceptance of this principle. We all know that when we seek donations for a charity we'll get better results by returning to last year's donors. If you're trying to sell magazine subscriptions, it's best to start with people who used to take the magazine or who subscribe to other magazines. These are better prospects than people who subscribe to no magazines.

Almost every sales training course includes a "yes response" technique based on the concept of gaining small agreements before seeking larger ones. The courses teach a carefully planned sales pitch so potential customers will answer "yes" to an opening series of questions. Then, when the request to buy is made, the "yes response" has been predisposed. Receivers find it difficult to reverse direction and say "no."

Think back to your last visits with salespeople. The one selling insurance starts with, "You love your family, don't you? You do want to save money, of course? How would you like to have your money working for you?" The computer salesperson uses a similar series: "You love your children, don't you? Of course you want them to do well in school? Haven't you often wanted to improve your recordkeeping? Wouldn't you like to have a yearly calendar that didn't cost you a single cent?"

You can recall a similar pitch from people selling books, records, cosmetics, cleaning supplies, vacuum cleaners, and so on.

A different situation often calls for almost the opposite approach. This involves making a large initial request that you expect to be refused. You then follow up with a smaller request, which is accepted. Almost ritualized uses of large initial demands followed by smaller requests appear in negotiations of all kinds. You see it not only in collective bargaining and the purchasing of many products, but in many daily life situations. The youngster who asks the parent for $25 to go to the beach for a weekend spree, when refused, counters with, "Well, how about $5 for a movie?" And usually gets it. This youngster demonstrates an intuitive understanding that refusing a large initial request often predisposes a person to agree to a smaller request.

The persuasive effect may result from a number of factors. It may be that saying no to a first request generates some guilt feelings that encourage a favorable response to a later, smaller request. This may be especially true since the speaker's move from large to small request appears to initiate a reasonable compromise. An appearance of willingness to compromise sometimes motivates the other person to respond in kind.

For this strategy to succeed, the first request must be within the bounds of reason. If the initial request is so large it appears absurd, the "bargaining" process may be stopped before it really begins.

The persuader decides whether and when to use either of these approaches by considering all the possible alternative outcomes. If either strategy is to be well used, receiver analysis and contingency planning are essential. Decisions about whether to use either method depend in large part on the relationships between the persuader and listeners, and on the appropriateness of the strategy to a particular goal. Other situational factors must also be considered.

Clarity of Goal Presentation   The persuader also needs to decide how clear to make the desired outcome to the listeners. In Chapter 11, we stressed the value of stating the thesis clearly at the outset of an informative speech and noted that the thesis of a persuasive speech is often not stated until later in the speech. In many situations you should make your goal clear. At other times, it is better if the goal is not made clear.

When the shift of opinion sought is not large, or does not involve changes in basic values, persuaders benefit when receivers understand exactly what is asked of them. When you seek to intensify feelings or induce action based on existing beliefs, making both arguments and desired behavioral outcome clear is advantageous. Indeed, failing to make clear exactly what is wanted causes many persuasive efforts to fail. The novice persuader, particularly, often fears asking for money or hesitates to ask listeners to "sign up right now," and needs to learn to ask. "Closing" sales of all kinds often requires specific appeals.

In contrast, the desired outcome sometimes becomes more likely when the persuader does not make the goal totally clear, but presents information in such a way that listeners convince themselves. Think back to the information about the cognitive response theory of persuasion. Most of us believe most strongly what we decide for ourselves. Also, the relationship between persuader and receivers might create a situation in which defensiveness is reduced and positive responses enhanced when receivers decide issues for themselves. This approach has other benefits. We are all more satisfied with decisions we participate in making; our beliefs persist longer.

No easy answers to this question exist. Defensiveness can be caused when listeners feel a persuader may be tricking them or being less than honest. Such defensiveness can cause rejection of the speaker's ideas. In other cases, defensiveness may distract listeners from counterarguing, leaving them more susceptible to your persuasive arguments.

In short, a persuader who wishes to use the strategy of not stating clearly what he or she really wants from the listeners must do so with caution. But, when you can honestly achieve your purpose by leaving listeners free to decide for themselves, it's an effective persuasive strategy.

Presentation of Both Sides   Closely related to the issues of honesty and clarity is the question of whether to use one- or two-sided messages. A *one-sided message presents only the arguments that support your goal; two-sided messages give both pros and cons.* Several receiver analysis questions help you decide which general approach to use.

A one-sided message is more appropriate when receivers basically agree with you, or when they are uninformed or undecided. By presenting only one side, you won't raise issues receivers may not know about or haven't thought of. Some well-informed receivers, however, will consider the one-sided approach biased or unfair. In these cases, the best alternative is to give both sides.

Two-sided messages are generally more effective when the receivers are well-informed or initially opposed to your ideas. Some evidence suggests that well-educated receivers prefer to hear both sides of issues. It's also a good idea to present both sides if listeners will later hear the other point of view. This forewarning provides a kind of "inoculation" against counterarguments. And, obviously, if you follow someone whose argument differs from yours, you need to respond.

When you use two-sided messages, you need to decide which argument you should develop first. The order in which ideas are presented may make a difference in their effect. When you give both points of view, it's probably better to present your argument second, although research is not conclusive on this matter. Basically, as long as receivers are aware of your point of view, and you present a stronger argument for it than do those who oppose it, the order of arguments isn't too important. You might gain some advantages by "slipping in" undesirable information about the opposite point of view after stating your position. Or you might name a "few" problems and then show how the advantages of your proposal outweigh these difficulties.

The following summary may be helpful in deciding whether or when to present opposing arguments in persuasive efforts. In organizing for persuasion:

1. Include both sides of the argument if receivers
   a. have previously been exposed to both sides
   b. are well-educated
   c. generally oppose your side.
2. Present one side if receivers basically agree with you or are relatively uneducated or uninformed.

If receivers will later hear opposing persuasion, you can:

1. Present both sides.
2. Use attack methods to present the other side.
3. Answer, without overemphasizing, counterarguments the opposition could use against you.
4. Try to anticipate the opposition's arguments, and bring them up on your own ground first.

IMPROVING CREDIBILITY

Persuaders benefit from establishing and using credibility relative to their goal. Credibility, a receiver perception influenced by what you say and do, is largely a composite. Thus, plan to do and say specific things to encourage receivers to perceive you as competent, of good character, likable, poised, dynamic, and appropriately similar to them.

Advance Knowledge

Knowledge receivers have about you before they hear your arguments strongly affects perceptions of your credibility. So, an important part of receiver analysis is to learn what impressions of you the listeners have. If the impressions are favorable, you can use this advance knowledge to advantage. If not, you will have to plan ways to change the impressions.

If the receivers don't know you, you benefit from providing in advance information that will positively affect their perceptions. First, of course, you need to decide, *What impressions do I want to make?* Do I want these people to perceive me as an expert? Or should I be seen as a competent peer? Should we appear to approach this situation as equals, thinking through a problem that confronts us both? In answering these questions, keep in mind where you are (receivers' knowledge) and where you want to go (the final impression you want to achieve).

Creating the desired impression can involve advance work. In some situations, you can suggest what should be included in any advance publicity. Advance planning can help you develop arguments that will help create the appropriate first impression.

What is the situation? Will you be introduced? By whom? Can you influence what that person plans to say? When you can benefit from an introduction, arrange one and influence what it consists of. You may also benefit from a "halo" effect if associated with people your receivers know, like or respect. Many such factors, considered early, can positively affect your credibility.

In contrast, you may approach situations where advance knowledge helps little. If you come with background or experience receivers will not find impressive, you may prefer to approach them "cold," and let your presentation, your arguments and your evidence develop credibility as you talk.

The Environment—Setting

The first thing receivers see in most situations is the setting. The total environment can either add to or detract from the impression you want to make. If you are planning carefully, you'll be aware of the total setting, and take steps to influence it. Signs, flags, and emblems can proclaim relationships. In public speaking situations, speakers' stands, microphones, tables, and audience seating arrangement, all affect how you speak. All can either help you establish the impression you want, or interfere.

A well-prepared persuader knows what the environment will be and uses it to advantage whenever possible. If changes are needed and you can't make them in advance, plan ways to change or cope with them.

Appearance and Behavior   Appearance and behavior affect credibility. Pay attention to them. Will listeners get the impression you seek if you dress as they do or if you dress differently? Should you dress formally or casually? How should you look and behave? Sometimes you must be just as the audience expects; other times you benefit by emphasizing differences. Permissible appearance and behavior vary from situation to situation. Use the information from Chapters 4 and 13 to find ways to increase your credibility. All these factors are part of adapting to the situation.

Verbal Messages   Words themselves can help increase credibility, as pointed out in Chapter 3. The first words are especially important. An introduction requires careful thought whether your persuasive effort is a speech or an interpersonal interaction. You can quote people your receiver(s) respect; tell of associations with people they respect; relate experience that gives you expertise. You can cite figures and statistics that demonstrate you know what you're talking about, and use language to create the degree of warmth or competence you're seeking.

You can say many things to establish your credibility, but caution is in order. Remember, one of the most important aspects of credibility is perceived honesty. Anything you say or do that appears to be insincere or out of character will be damaging. Above all, persuaders must be perceived as sincere. If receivers sense you are being in any way less than truthful with them, you can't expect them to believe you.

Listeners must perceive efforts to establish credibility as appropriate. If receivers sense you are spending a lot of time telling them how good you are because you fear they won't think so, they'll doubt your competence. If you're good, need you tell them? Name dropping can have negative effects, too, especially if it's done too much or tactlessly. A persuader must try to establish credibility, but unless it's done well, it can backfire.

Identification One way to increase credibility is to *help receivers identify with you in ways that are important in the situation.* This use of homophily is described as **identification.** Identification can result from role-oriented characteristics (such as occupation or status) or from personality traits (such as honesty or nervousness).

Role identification can be important if a persuader wants changes that will affect receivers in their occupations. Farm workers will pay more attention to a fellow farm worker when it comes to joining a union than they will to a steelworker. A dry alcoholic is more persuasive to active drinkers than someone who's never suffered from alcoholism. An ex-drug addict can have more impact telling teenagers to stay "off the stuff" than someone who has never used drugs. The perception of common experiences and goals aids in identification. Belonging to a group from which you're seeking action can make you seem more believable and trustworthy.

Role identification is not always possible or valuable, however. To be perceived as expert, you don't want your receivers to think you're just like them. In these situations, *personality identification* may be more useful. To identify with your personality, receivers must perceive some personality trait in common with you. To identify with an expert, receivers generally must perceive that the expert has empathy and understanding and its trustworthy. Many of these qualities are partially inferred from roles. Many are based on appearance and other nonverbals.

At other times, persuaders use verbal means to point out shared characteristics. Persuaders can express preferences for similar things or beliefs in similar ideas. They can tell about like experiences or show in other ways that they have the same attitudes and personalities as receivers.

Using this method, a persuader tries to develop perceived **common ground.** Common ground refers to *attitudes, beliefs, and experiences that source and receiver share.* The best common ground is shared concern about the ideas of the speech. You can, early in the persuasive effort, identify points that you and your receivers agree upon. You can also show receivers you share other interests. Salespeople often use this technique. They will tell customers about similar experiences they've had. To establish common ground with prospective buyers, encyclopedia salespersons have been taught to "invent" children of their own.

Karlyn Campbell, a professor at Kansas University, talked to a gathering of women's groups in a small upstate New York town on the topic of contemporary feminism. Aware that her audience would perceive her as quite different from them, she also knew that most of them had negative connotations for the concept of feminism. The following excerpt from her introduction illustrates her use of the principles of homophily, identification, and common ground to alleviate those two problems.

When I listened to Mrs. P's introduction, I thought to myself that if I were sitting out there where you are, I'd be feeling a bit wary about this Dr. Campbell who's about to speak. After all, she's got a Ph.D., she teaches in a university, and she lives in a city. Why, she's not like us.

Well, I want to let you in on a secret. I grew up on a 138-acre farm in central Minnesota where I spent the first seventeen years of my life. My first memories include using a child-sized hand to push down the cabbage in the two-quart jars my mother used to make sauerkraut. I may be a city slicker now, but I started out as a "sod." It's true that my life is different now, but I hope I can combine some of what I learned growing up on a farm with some of what I've learned in school and in my career to talk to you about something that concerns all women—farm women and town women and city women, young and old, housewives and professionals, mothers and grandmothers, married and single.

I want to begin by telling you a story of a woman very like my mother who lived down the road from us. She worked on the farm, as my mother did, all of her life. Like most farm women, that didn't mean just working in the house, cleaning and cooking and sewing and canning. It also meant work outside—feeding the animals, gathering eggs, working in the fields. This woman had never heard of joint tenancy nor had she ever read the marriage laws in Minnesota. She had two sons. One was killed in World War II on one of those Pacific Islands with strange names. The other died in a tractor accident. When her husband died at age 61, she was all alone, but she hoped to stay on the farm, rent out the land, keep her garden, and raise chickens. But the law wouldn't allow that. It said that, since there was no will and everything was in her husband's name, only one-third was hers. The rest of his estate went to his nearest relative, a cousin she'd never met and who wanted his share now. The farm had to be sold, and there she was without a home and cheated out of most of what she had worked so hard to create.

When people hear the phrase "women's liberation," they don't think of women like that. They think of Betty Friedan or Gloria Steinem. But women's liberation is about laws that cheat wives, laws that assume that women's work isn't real work. It's true that the women who write and speak are often educated and from the city, but that's true of most people who write and speak and are covered by the news. But the problems of women aren't urban and educated, they are legal and economic, and they affect all women. What I want to talk about tonight are these major concerns of the contemporary feminists.[13]

Checklist for Planning the Persuasive Effort

I. State persuasive goal. What specifically will my listeners do, think, believe, or feel when I am finished?

II. Analyze receivers
   A. Identify feeling, belief, or behavioral change required for goal accomplishment.
      1. What is receivers' present position with reference to goal? (Where do they fit on an agree-disagree continuum?)
      2. What is the intensity and importance of listeners' beliefs? Strength of their feelings?
      3. How much change will be required to achieve the goal?
   B. Identify factors related to goal achievement.
      1. What are receivers' motivational and belief structures regarding my goal and related issues?
      2. Have they publicly stated their positions?
      3. What is the level of their knowledge about topic and related issues?

[13] From *The Rhetorical Act* by Karlyn Kohrs Campbell, pp. 238–39. © 1982 by Wadsworth, Inc. Reprinted by permission of Wadsworth Publishing Company, Belmont, California 94002.

4. To what are receivers most likely to give favorable attention?

5. What is my credibility related to this thesis and goal?

III. Analyze situation

    A. Are there specific problems in the situation that will create barriers to my goal accomplishments?

        1. Can the barriers be eliminated or overcome? How?

        2. If barriers cannot be removed, what compensating action will I need to take?

    B. Will receivers encounter other (opposing or supportive) messages before, during, or after my persuasive effort?

    C. Are there specific factors in the situation that can be used to my advantage?

IV. Assess likelihood of goal achievement

    A. Is the desired goal realistic, considering receivers' present positions?

    B. Should goal be revised to improve chances of achievement?

        1. Will more than one effort be required?

        2. Should a larger or smaller request be made first?

    C. Should goal be retained to enhance chances of long-range achievement?

V. Plan the persuasive "message(s)"

    A. Identify all possible arguments

    B. Use receiver analysis to choose strongest arguments

        1. Arguments close to current beliefs

        2. Arguments related to strong motivations

        3. Arguments most likely to create imbalance among related beliefs

        4. Arguments for which evidence is strongest

        5. Arguments most likely to hold attention

    C. Organize ideas

        1. Decide on overall structure

        2. Decide on structure of arguments and evidence

    D. Develop arguments

        1. Identify all possible evidence

        2. Choose evidence most persuasive to receivers

    E. Develop contingency plans

    F. Plan introduction and conclusion

EXERCISE 14.3   PERSUASION

OBJECTIVE   **To increase ability to use persuasion techniques to achieve a stated goal with a group of listeners.**

DIRECTIONS

1. Identify a realistic persuasive goal you believe you can achieve with other members of your class. Confer with your instructor to ensure that you have not selected an impossible goal.

2. Identify the major obstacles you will have to overcome to achieve your goal.

3. Assess your receivers to determine their persuadability and what strategies will be most effective with them.

4. Plan a communication strategy to achieve your goal.

5. The instructor will specify a time limit for your effort and schedule your time to present it.

6. To assess your effectiveness, survey the class both before and after talking to them.

     a. Prepare index cards for each listener. Write your central idea statement on these cards.

     b. Pass these out to students at least one class period before the day your persuasion is scheduled, and ask them to record how they feel about that statement by writing a number on the card according to the scale suggested (see p. 371)

     c. Compile an average of the score you got before your presentation.

     d. After sending your persuasive message, hand out blank index cards. Ask receivers to write what they perceive as the central idea of what you said. Ask them to use the same scale as before to report how they feel about that central idea now that they have heard your message.

     e. Compile an average of the score you got after sending your message. Assess the amount of improvement.

7. Compare your statement of central idea with the statements written by your receivers. How much similarity is there?

8. If time permits, pass out another set of cards with the central idea written on it about two weeks following the presentation of your message. Was there a loss from the time immediately following your presentation?

9. The instructor may choose to conduct a class discussion or to have you discuss this project in class after all have made their presentations. The discussion will cover the following questions:

     a. Which messages caused the greatest shift of opinion? Why?

     b. Which messages caused the least shift of opinion? Why?

Note: Attach your persuasive speech outline.

REVIEW

Write brief answers to each of the following:

1. What factors did you take into consideration as you planned your persuasive speech?

2. Explain the communication principle illustrated by this exercise that you found most important and why you found it important.

3. What aspects of this study of persuasion will be most useful to you in the future?

SUMMARY

Persuasion is a term describing any communication process during which a source attempts to change beliefs or attitudes or to induce overt behaviors in one or more receivers. Persuasion is not limited to public speaking. It occurs in all aspects of life. Persuasion is confusing because the word is often used to mean three different things: what the persuader wants to accomplish; what the speaker says and does to accomplish the goal; and the effects in receivers. Study of persuasion requires understanding all three.

Students of persuasion need to understand the relationships between persuasion and attitudes. Attitudes are learned. Therefore, the persuader may need to use a relearning process to change attitudes. One way attitudes are learned is through reinforcement, which is receiving rewards for doing and believing in certain things. Types of reinforcement are classical conditioning and secondary reinforcement, which is a more accurate description of most human learning. Rewards in secondary reinforcement are more significant. The person perceives the reward as being sufficient to justify the changed behavior.

Approval from peers, from significant people, and from groups with which a person identifies are all rewards. Negative conditioning (associating negative consequences with an event) can also occur. Punishment is often used as a negative conditioning device, but it is not always effective in either persuasion or learning because unforeseen consequences can occur. Punishment is not the same as lack of reinforcement. Not reinforcing means the absence of rewards, which is not necessarily punishment.

Other theories of attitude change may be useful to persuaders. One of these is consistency theory, which hypothesizes that people need to perceive consistency among related attitudes. Any perceived inconsistency causes a lack of balance. This is an uneasy state which people want to reduce. They do so by re-creating consistency. Balance theory suggests that we can and do change attitudes to regain consistency. Sometimes people dissociate the attitudes; that is, they see no relevance between the attitudes. Therefore, there is no imbalance. The cognitive dissonance theory suggests that when people perceive two beliefs to be related and inconsistent, they will actively seek to reduce the dissonance. Cognitive response theories also suggest important conclusions that should be considered as persuaders plan strategies.

Persuaders need to establish goals and then determine whether they are attainable. To decide if goals are attainable, persuaders must analyze existing receiver attitudes. This involves determining the likelihood that listeners can be persuaded, based on amount of prior knowledge, existing attitudes, and expectations. Persuaders must also be aware of receivers' total attitudes and recognize that stable attitudes and those related to self-concept will be much more difficult to change than more specific, less stable, or newer attitudes. Persuaders often need to divide their goals into long- and short-range goals, and if necessary, after receiver analysis, a persuader should restate the specific goal.

One strategy to increase the probability of successful persuasion is to establish credibility or believability. Inferences of credibility depend largely on receivers' perception of a persuader's character, competency, likability, dynamism, poise, and similarity to the receivers. A speaker can improve credibility by advance knowledge, associations with persons receivers respect, appearance, behavior, and verbal messages.

Persuasive messages should create imbalance in listeners and provide information to give listeners a way to restore balance and reduce dissonance. One technique is the use of evidence. Evidence becomes persuasive through argument, a unit of thought that contains a conclusion and the evidence leading to the conclusion. The Toulmin method for analyzing arguments is a way to understand how conclusions are drawn and how people might be persuaded to believe these conclusions.

Organizing the persuasion is important. We recommend two types of organization: problem-solution and advantages-disadvantages. Strategies for overall organization depend primarily on how well-informed listeners are and whether the persuader is followed by an opponent. Finally, persuaders should use motive appeals. Persuaders' arguments should be related to the receivers' relevant needs, showing how doing or believing as the persuader suggests will enable a listener to satisfy important needs.

QUESTIONS FOR DISCUSSION

1. How can a persuader use the process of reinforcement?
2. What is reinforcement? Can you distinguish negative conditioning and punishment from nonreinforcement?

3. What useful knowledge do the balance theories provide?

4. Describe how you could use the theory of cognitive dissonance in a persuasive effort.

5. Discuss five ways you can use cognitive response theories as you try to persuade.

6. How do you set persuasive goals, and why?

7. Under what circumstances might a persuader establish both long-term and short-term goals?

8. How can you assess the likelihood of persuading your receivers?

9. What is evidence, and how can a persuader use it to advantage?

10. Define argument and construct an argument, including the elements of the Toulmin model.

11. How can motive appeals be used in persuasion?

SUGGESTIONS FOR FURTHER READING

Andersen, Kenneth E. *Persuasion: Theory and Practice*, 2nd ed. Boston: Allyn and Bacon, 1978.

Bettinghaus, Erwin P. *Persuasive Communication*, 4th ed. New York: Holt, Rinehart and Winston, 1987.

Bostrom, Robert N. *Persuasion*. Englewood Cliffs, N.J.: Prentice-Hall, 1983.

Brembeck, Winston, and William S. Howell. *Persuasion: A Means of Social Influence*, 2nd ed. Englewood Cliffs, N.J.: Prentice-Hall, 1976.

Cronkhite, Gary. *Persuasion: Speech and Behavioral Change*. Indianapolis: Bobbs-Merrill, 1969.

Heider, Fritz. *The Psychology of Interpersonal Relations*. New York: Wiley, 1958.

Hovland, Carl, et al. *The Order of Presentation in Persuasion*. New Haven, Conn.: Yale University Press, 1957.

Larson, Charles. *Persuasion: Reception and Responsibility*, 3rd ed. Belmont, Calif.: Wadsworth, 1983.

O'Donnell, Victoria, and June Kable. *Persuasion: An Interactive Dependency Approach*. New York: Random House, 1982.

Petty, Richard E., and John T. Cacioppo. *Communication and Persuasion: Central and Peripheral Routes to Attitude Change*. New York: Springer-Verlag, 1966.

Reardon, Kathleen. *Persuasion Theory and Context*. Beverly Hills, Calif.: Sage Publications, 1981.

Roloff, Michael, and Gerald Miller, eds. *Persuasion: New Directions in Theory and Research*. Beverly Hills, Calif.: Sage Publications, 1980.

Ross, Raymond. *Understanding Persuasion*, 2nd ed. Englewood Cliffs, N.J.: Prentice-Hall, 1985.

Shea, Gordon. *Managing a Difficult or Hostile Audience*. Englewood Cliffs, N.J.: Prentice-Hall, 1984.

Simons, Herbert. *Persuasion, Understanding, Practice and Analysis*, 2nd ed. New York: Random House, 1986.

Smith, Mary J. *Persuasion and Human Action: A Review and Critique of Social Influence Theories*. Belmont, Calif.: Wadsworth, 1982.

Toulmin, Stephen. *The Uses of Argument*. London: Cambridge University Press, 1969.

Zimbardo, Philip, Ebbe Ebbeson, and Christina Maslach. *Influencing Attitudes and Changing Behavior*, 2nd ed. Reading, Mass.: Addison-Wesley, 1977.

15 Responding to the Mass Media

> For most of modern civilization, three institutions—government, the church, and business—have been the dominant forces in our lives. Today, . . . there is a fourth major force: the mass media . . . Many consider these media collectively as more powerful and influential than the government or the church, especially when allied with all of the other businesses with which they are closely associated.
>
> SAMUEL BECKER[1]

GOAL

To be able to respond appropriately to media persuasion

OBJECTIVES

The material in this chapter should help you to:
1. Explain the influence of gatekeepers in mass communication.
2. Describe how feedback operates in mass communication.
3. Explain the major theories of media effects and show how they differ.
4. Identify the major purposes of advertisements.
5. Describe how images, attention devices, motive appeals, and identification are used to persuade in advertising.
6. Recognize how packaging and credit are used as sales techniques.
7. Explain how distraction is used to persuade using media.
8. Apply techniques of effective listening to mass communication.

[1] Samuel L. Becker, *Discovering Mass Communication*, 2nd ed. (Glenview, Ill.: Scott, Foresman and Company, 1987), p. xviii.

Did you realize that some radio stations broadcast commercials at the rate of twenty minutes each hour? That thirty-minute television programs often include eight minutes of advertising? That more homes in the United States have television than indoor plumbing? That in 1987 the average television set stayed on more than seven *hours* daily? Since some people rarely turn on their television set, that means well over two hours of advertising is beamed into millions of United States homes.

Literally dozens of times daily you receive messages from the media urging you to buy something, contribute to some cause, vote for some person, or advise your representatives to vote in some way. In 1986, United States advertisers spent 94 *billion* dollars on mediated persuasion. How appropriately do you respond to these efforts at changing your behavior? That you gain the information helpful to respond appropriately is the goal of this chapter.

Many people, when they hear figures describing media advertising, respond, "Oh, that doesn't really affect me. I never pay any attention to advertising." Perhaps they don't. But someone thinks they do. Consider this: In 1987, businesses paid $600,000 to purchase *thirty seconds* of advertising time on the Superbowl football telecast. In addition, they paid $200,000 or more to produce the commercials aired.

The "hard-nosed" executives in successful corporations who approve such advertising costs rarely waste their company's money. Marketing executives buy television or other media advertising only after careful research into how such advertising affects consumers. *Someone* knows the media affect receivers, at least to some extent.

RESPONDING TO MASS COMMUNICATION

To exercise more control over your responses to persuasion received through the mass media, employ all that you know about communication. Processing information received from any source involves thinking clearly and using the techniques of effective listening. The information in Chapters 5 and 6 applies as well to analysis of messages received through the media as to messages received from face-to-face communication. All the principles of critical listening should be used when responding to mediated persuasion.

Because few persuasive effects have a single cause, all types of communication situations call for effective listening. Persuading you to buy a car, for instance, takes more than a few advertisements. You also base such decisions on what parents, friends, and other people you admire think about the car, the company, the style. Deciding to buy a particular car involves advertisers, salespeople, and interpersonal influence, as well as your own opinions and needs.

Responding to persuasive communication is never as simple as reacting to a single stimulus. Therefore, although this chapter focuses on persuasion received through mass media, it is not limited to that. Most of the information can be used to respond effectively whenever anyone tries to persuade you to do something, believe something, or feel a particular way. In most cases, however, dealing effectively with persuasion today involves understanding mass media as well as principles of communication and persuasion.

MASS MEDIA

The mass media form a major part of the modern environment. In the United States, there are almost 100 million more radios than there are people, an average of 5.4 sets per household. In 1985 it was estimated that the average person watches seventeen hours of television a week. Few of us could conceive of a world without television, musical recordings, radios, magazines, newspapers, and films. Yet far too few of us really understand the media that so permeate our lives.

In Chapter 1, we defined *mass communication* as electronic or mechanical transmission of message carriers. Usually, the receivers are widely scattered. Thus, mass communication really began with the invention of the printing press. But the communication explosion that followed the development of electronic media has no precedent, and these media remain only vaguely understood influences in our lives.

We'll present some recent scholars' thoughts on the impact of media shortly, but first we want to be sure you understand the basics of the United States media system.

Gatekeepers Control Media Content

The first important fact about media is that access to the channels of transmission is limited. Those who control the access to media channels are called *gatekeepers*. Certainly gatekeepers exist in other types of communication as well, but they influence mass communication more strongly.

The electronic media pervade modern life.

Media gatekeepers decide what we see and how much we see.

Gatekeepers control both the information content of media and the format of delivery of that information. Station executives determine how much time is devoted to news or public affairs, how much to entertainment programming, and how much to advertising. Such executives also determine when each type of programming will be aired. Newspaper and magazine editors and publishers make similar decisions. By deciding how much of what kind of content will appear, when, and in what format, these gatekeepers determine what receivers may read, hear and see.

At another level, gatekeepers influence the content of each show. Editors and news directors determine what stories will be covered as news in any given day; reporters determine what details about those stories will be reported. Managers at every level determine what films will be shot, what songs recorded and by whom, what music will be played on particular stations at what times, and so on.

Recent developments in technology and marketing have widened the options available to media receivers. Consumers of mass communication have more variety in choices about what they read, watch, and listen to. Still, no medium of information is free from the influence of gatekeepers, no source untouched by the filters gatekeepers apply in making their choices.

Commercial Gatekeepers   Some gatekeepers are individuals; some are institutions. Because most United States radio and television stations are privately owned, most gatekeepers are commercial. Companies, for instance, choose to sponsor or advertise on a particular show or to drop it. A television station or network may decide not to air a show if there is no advertising for it, or if a small audience leads the station or network to fear that advertising will be reduced in amount or value. These commercial sponsors and advertisers influence, in varying degrees, the content of television and radio entertainment shows, the choice and placement of stories in newspapers, what and how information is presented in magazines.

As commercial enterprises, networks, stations, and publications need to show a profit (or come close). Profitability depends largely on advertising revenue. Thus, the media in the United States rely on advertisers to buy time or space. Usually the advertiser-content connection isn't direct. Sponsors may drop a television show, but the network or station may continue it because other advertisers buy time. Cases have occurred, however, when individual stations have refused to run a network show, or when networks or stations dropped shows due to lack of advertising revenue.

Commercial sponsors usually influence media content more indirectly. Advertising rates depend on the size of audience a network or station can promise for the time at which they will air the ads. So the *ratings system* plays a significant role in determining which shows survive. The ratings system doesn't apply only to television entertainment programming. Ratings that fit the particular medium strongly affect the content of that medium. Television and radio ratings influence who the newscasters are, what stories are identified as news, and how the stories are presented. Advertising provides the main source of revenue for most magazines and newspapers as well. Since circulation rates determine advertising rates and amounts, and changes in content affect circulation, content depends in a real—if indirect—way on advertising.

In the United States, public broadcasting presents the major exception to what has just been discussed. To avoid complete commercial control of mass communication, some radio and television channels are set aside for use by educational or public, nonprofit institutions. In recent years, national public networks have developed. Government, business, and institutional funding, along with listener contributions, support these alternatives to commercial programming. Similarly, some noncommercial print media exist.

Among the electronic media, however, noncommercial broadcasting will have little influence until audience habits change dramatically. Relatively few in the United States watch public television or listen to public radio, and most of those are occasional users. For example, how much do *you* watch public television or listen to public radio? How about your friends?

Children's shows, such as "Sesame Street" and "Electric Company," are the most watched shows on public television. They seldom reach more than 11 percent of homes with TV sets. Compare that to "Dallas," "The Cosby Show," or NFL football. In a typical rating week in April 1978, 37.5 percent of United States television households watched an average of four hours of public television.[2] That's four hours in the entire week for just over *one-third* of homes with television sets! Contrast that with the seven hours plus viewing time of *all* homes with TV. Clearly, most of the information we receive from mass media is subject to commercial gatekeepers.

[2] Dale Rhodes and Ken Wirt, "April 1978 PTV System Carriage and National Audience Estimates," Memorandum of the Public Broadcasting Service to General Managers, Program Managers, Development Directors, and Public Information Directors, August 7, 1978.

Government Regulation   In addition to advertisers and media executives, other gatekeepers of mass media communication also exist. Because the media are so powerful and access to them so limited, government provides some regulation. Print media receive less attention from government than the electronic media do.

The argument for more regulation of radio and television than of print media rests primarily on two premises. First, because everyone has easier access to print media, a free press is supposed to guarantee all ideas a hearing. Second, the consumer must purchase a particular print item (a book, magazine, or newspaper), but radio and television broadcasts are "free." Consequently, children's exposure to media content cannot be controlled in the same way as with print.

The only overt government control of the content of newspapers and magazines is libel law and laws regulating commerce. Some indirect influence may result from the 1978 Supreme Court ruling that allows police searches of news-gathering organizations such as newspapers, or from other rulings that affect how reporters may protect their news sources. The long-range effects of these rulings in terms of news content remain unclear.

At first, no laws controlled the electronic media. But early broadcasters abused their access to the airwaves, and stations with massive power drowned out others as their signals wandered across the dial. These and other abuses of unregulated broadcasting led to the establishment of the Federal Communications Commission (FCC).

Television and radio are now "regulated" by the FCC. This agency, established by the Federal Communications Act in 1934, does not openly dictate what shall or shall not be broadcast. FCC regulates media content more indirectly. It awards and renews broadcast licenses. It monitors stations to see that they transmit on the channels to which they are assigned and with the power they are permitted.

Massive changes in electronic media and how we use them are now occurring. VCRs, video discs, and combined telephone and computer connections may revolutionize media use by millions of people. Multiband cable broadcasting and satellite transmission make access to broadcasting much wider than it used to be. The enormous costs of radio and television, however, still mean that few people have access to these media for expression of their ideas.

At the moment, electronic media remain more controlled than print, though control mechanisms are changing. For several years, Congress has considered revisions in the Federal Communications Act. Major changes are proposed; deregulation is widely supported, though exactly what that means or what changes will result is not at all clear. In addition, cable and satellite distribution is changing patterns of both commercial and government control of the media. Although at this writing local communities still maintain the authority to issue cable franchises, and satellite broadcasters can still foil video pirates, such authority is under challenge.[3]

The amount and kinds of advertising are also subject to limited controls. The industry does some self-regulation; government imposes other regulations through the FCC and Federal Trade Commission. Enforcement of these controls is a compli-

[3] If this topic interests you, see recent issues of *Broadcasting* and other media periodicals for updates on current developments.

cated, lengthy, and, many argue, not very effective process. Moreover, deregulation of commerce is also currently underway. Since the trend is toward less control of advertising and sales persuasion in general, your critical evaluation of mass communication will become even more important in the future.

Delayed Feedback

In mass communication, sources and receivers do not face each other directly. As a result, sources receive only delayed and indirect feedback. Thus, many receivers feel they have no influence on the sources of mass communication. That, however, is a popular misconception. Receivers do strongly influence media content. Producers, owners, advertisers, stations, and networks all work hard at discovering what information readers and listeners retain from what they receive, and how they react to it.

Efforts to get feedback are sometimes simple and sometimes complex, but feedback is both sought and used. In the case of radio, stations often ask listeners to write or call the station. Both radio and television stations engage in listener polling. They seek to learn the size and composition of their audiences as well as the effects of shows and advertising. Interviews are conducted in person and by telephone.

In broadcasting, the ratings system is especially powerful. Executives study viewing habits of selected samples representing the total population. Nielsen ratings can determine the life and death of television programs. Arbitron ratings have the same effect on radio programming formats, announcer and disc jockey firings and hirings, and various forms of promotional broadcasting.

Networks and advertisers use information about listening and viewing habits to assess the effects of shows and advertisements. Ratings affect the amount charged for advertising at various times and on different stations. As a result, ratings affect what is broadcast and how.

Critics of the ratings system charge that audiences aren't really measured. They attack the sample size and measurement error. More important, they ask, "Why do many people not watch television or listen to radio at all?" At any given time, nearly as many sets are turned off as are on. Why? Broadcasters and marketers work hard to answer that question.

Raters and advertisers conduct many follow-up studies to learn who watches what shows. When the ratings are published, statistical assessments of the accuracy of the results are also available. Sometimes researchers conduct studies to identify who isn't listening. And although the critics are partly right—the ratings system is far from perfect—the ratings fairly well describe the behavior of the media-consuming public. Media content that few people attend to seldom lasts.

EXERCISE 15.1   EFFECTS OF GATEKEEPERS

OBJECTIVE   **To assess the results of gatekeepers in reporting a news event.**

DIRECTIONS   1. The class will be divided into groups of five or six.
2. Each group will choose a current national event on which to compare news coverage.
3. Members of the group will develop a schedule of news listening so that someone in each group hears the news reported on each local television channel and also on the different local radio stations. If the area is a large metropolitan area, the group should not try to hear every radio station report the news, but should divide up so that someone listens to two or three leading stations of each type (rock, classical, general middle-of-the-road, easy listening, educational, country, and an all-news channel, if there is one in the area).
4. Groups should also collect all newspaper and national newsmagazine coverage of the event.
5. After following the news coverage for a week (groups may decide the event needs to be followed for a longer time), group members should compare reports. They should attempt to answer at least the following and as much more as is necessary to cover the comparisons:
   a. Were there details reported by some stations that were not by others?
   b. What were the differences between print and electronic media reporting?
   c. Were the differences in reporting due to selection of what observations to report? or in the observations themselves?
   d. Were any of the differences contradictory?
6. The instructor may ask the groups to report their findings to each other in class.

REVIEW   1. Describe five types of gatekeepers and their roles in mass communication.
2. What is known about effects of mass media, especially television?
3. Explain the principle of communication illustrated by the exercise that you found most important and why.

MEDIA EFFECTS

The pervasiveness of mass communication naturally generates questions. How do these changes in environment affect our lives and society? Clearly, media influence our lives, if only through the economic effects of the large numbers of people employed in the media and advertising businesses. Moreover, mass communication influences the habits of most people in the United States. Most of us cannot imagine a life without television, radio, newspapers, magazines, films, or musical recordings.

The commercial media system of the United States is the most technologically advanced in the world, one that provides a wide variety of programming remarkably sensitive to audience interests. Content that audiences do not read or watch, or content that offends significant numbers of media consumers, does not survive in commercial media.

Beyond the economic and entertainment impact, however, little about media effects on our beliefs and behaviors is known or understood with certainty. The limited state of our knowledge seriously concerns communication scholars. The advertising industry devotes large sums to research, but it is largely marketing research, supported by the advertisers or the commercial stations and networks, carried out to discover what programs attract viewers and what advertisements persuade. Not only is the research unconcerned with social effects, but the findings remain private. The knowledge is available to the marketers, but not to the consumers they seek to influence. Other research, funded by government and private sources alike, aims at gaining a broad understanding of media effects, but their work is limited and poorly funded in comparison to marketing research.

Still, what communication scholars have learned provides at least a base for understanding the social effects of mass communication. Thus, in seeking to understand how the mass media and mass communication affect our lives and society, looking at the findings of early media-effects research can be useful. What that research demonstrates mostly is that at different times and for different people, media have different effects. If you examine your own life, you'll see this.

Direct Effects

The Hypodermic Effect   On some occasions, mass communication is directly and immediately responsible for behavior. If you watched CBS Evening News on January 25, 1988 and saw a network anchorman engage in a heated exchange with Vice-President George Bush, you may have become angry and called the local station to complain, or you may have been one of many who called and volunteered to work in the presidential campaign. If so, you reflected what media scholars refer to as the **Hypodermic Effect,** or the "bullet" effect.

When mass communication achieves a direct, strong, and immediate influence on a large audience, the hypodermic effect is at work. The symbol of a hypodermic needle suggests that media inject information into an audience (see Figure 15–1). In a hypodermic effect, masses of receivers get information at one time and are affected equally and directly.

The vast amounts spent for advertising on prime-time television or in Sunday newspapers show the power of the hypodermic effect. When advertisers spend $600,000 for thirty seconds of advertising, they expect some direct, immediate responses. The hundreds who streamed into the streets in panic after Orson Welles's broadcast of the invasion from Mars in 1938 illustrated the hypodermic effect of mass media.

The One-step Flow   Mass communication does not affect everyone equally. In many cases, people don't react immediately. Though thousands may have heard and responded immediately to the Dan Rather-George Bush interview of January 26, 1988, hundreds of thousands more heard the interview and were angry about

George Bush.

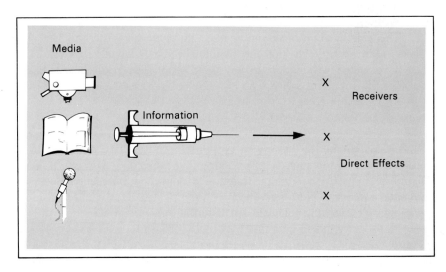

FIGURE 15–1.   The Hypodermic Effect.

it but did nothing for several days. Or they reacted less intensely and largely ignored the interview and the discussions that followed. Or they believed the journalist appropriately asked the questions and were irritated at not hearing the answers. If these people are affected by the media-transmitted information, it occurs in a **one-step flow** effect.

Like the hypodermic effect, a one-step effect shows a direct influence of information on receivers, but the impact does not occur simultaneously or uniformly. Some receivers react to and adopt ideas more slowly than others. Figure 15–2 illustrates the one-step flow.

Rates of Adoption   Information does not reach or affect viewers equally. Therefore, the speed with which people adopt ideas varies. The *rate of adoption* refers to the length of time it takes a person to adopt an idea. Usually this rate is measured in relative terms. Persons can be classified according to whether their rates of adoption are fast, slow, or somewhere in between. The categories can be described as *innovators, early adopters, early majority, late majority,* and *laggards.*[4]

To illustrate the categories of adopters, consider how the practice of using water fluoridation to reduce tooth decay spread across the country. Word was first spread by the mass media; print, television, and radio passed on the information as it was reported by scientists and doctors. A few cities and towns began the practice immediately. These were the innovators. Others had to hear the worth of the idea discussed further, and required more interpersonal influence, but still responded relatively quickly. These were the early adopters.

Then, as the media sent more messages and the people in towns and cities that used the practice shared their experiences, many other towns and cities adopted the process. These were the early majority group. Following wider and wider application throughout the society, a remaining large percentage, the late majority, began to fluoridate water. Decades after the practice was introduced, some towns do not yet fluoridate their water and probably never will. These are the laggards.

This classification of adoption rates illustrate an important fact about media effects. Many people do not act on information received from media until after they have talked with other people about what they read, heard, or saw. Thus, much media impact is indirect.

Indirect Effects

An examination of the variety of responses—even when media transmit widely received information such as a live summit meeting between world leaders or the Olympics competition—demonstrates why mass communication does not directly influence everyone. Not everyone receives the messages when transmitted. Some people aren't watching television or listening to radio at the time; they don't read

---

[4] Everett Rogers and F. Shoemaker, *Communication of Innovations* (New York: Free Press, 1971) coined these terms. We emphasize that no positive or negative connotations are intended by the descriptive terms. No value is ascribed to being either an "early adopter" or a "laggard." Most people are probably in each of the categories at one time or another, depending on the particular innovation.

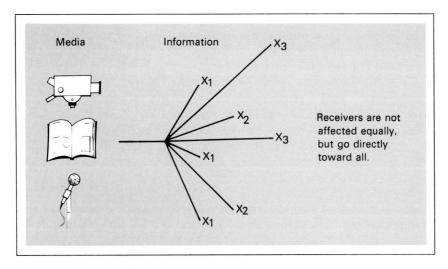

Media   Information X_3

X_1

X_2

X_3

X_1

Receivers are not
affected equally,
but go directly
toward all.

X_2

X_1

FIGURE 15–2. The One-step Flow Effect.

the newspaper when a story is first reported; they never see a popular movie or hear a top charted song. That such people do not receive the mass communication, however, does not mean they remain unaffected by it. The **indirect effects** of mediated messages may impact their lives.

Indirect effects involve the *nonmedia* elements in the communication system of a society or social group. Generally, these are interpersonal interactions. We want to introduce two such personal influences.

Opinion Leaders and Change Agents   Gatekeepers other than those who control access to or content of the media affect the impact of mass communication. One of these is the opinion leader. An **opinion leader** is a person, generally well-informed, who serves as an influence in the decision processes of others. Some people look to opinion leaders to *interpret and evaluate information received*, whether from the media or from other sources. Note that all kinds of people may be opinion leaders. The influence of a person on the opinions, beliefs, or feelings of others depends on many factors and varies from issue to issue. Who you listen to when deciding which basketball team is better, for example, may be quite different from who you ask about a new car purchase, who may differ from your opinion leader regarding political choices. For other people, one person is the opinion leader on all issues.

Generally, the more similar (homophilous) communicators are, the more perceived credibility there will be.[5] A receiver is more likely to accept messages received from someone who is credible. Heterophily (dissimilarity) seems to be one reason media messages do not affect some receivers. These receivers apparently do not

---

[5] Recall the discussion of credibility and homophily in Chapter 14.

perceive sufficient similarity between themselves and the source for the information to be credible. They won't accept information until people they perceive as like themselves interpret and evaluate it. These opinion leaders are important gatekeepers in processes of spreading ideas in a social system.

Another person who influences acceptance of new information or attitudes in a social group is the **change agent.** We use the term *change agent* to refer to an external source of persuasion. The change agent may be the originator of an idea, as happens when the U.S. government supports adoption of a particular technology in a Third World nation. But change agents aren't only institutions. A salesperson who convinces the purchasing agent at city hall to add chloride to the salt the city uses on icy streets is a change agent for that city. In one sense, media themselves (or the advertisers, performers, and newcasters) are change agents. Change agents may be missionaries of their own ideas, or they can be persons hired or appointed to represent people or groups who want changes. The distinguishing element about a change agent is that *such a person or institution is a promoter from outside the system or group he or she (or it) wants to change.*

An effective change agent needs to do more than present new information clearly. The agent needs good relationships with opinion leaders and media gatekeepers in the social system. The principle of homophily (similarity) may explain why change agents have less influence than opinion leaders. Change agents often don't seem to have as much in common with people inside a system. Their messages are usually less credible than those of opinion leaders, with whom receivers can identify.

Change agents are usually most effective when they influence a system through opinion leaders. This contact may be through the mass media or through interpersonal influence or both. Opinion leaders in a social system are likely to be early adopters of ideas from outside. They often hold leadership positions, which expose them to new ideas from outside. As leaders, they are often actively interested in changes they believe will improve the social system.

The Two-step Flow Effect A **two-step effect** results when people turn to opinion leaders for assurance about an idea before accepting it. The two-step influence shows another reason the effects of mass communication vary from person to person. Some people consider themselves sufficiently knowledgeable on a particular issue to decide what they think about it immediately upon hearing about it for the first time. For them, new information via mass media will have a direct effect. Others, lacking information or confidence, will want to hear the thoughts of others and to talk about their own reactions before deciding what they think (see Figure 15–3).

This two-step effect leads modern political campaigners to seek to create their own "spin" on an idea or event. After a political speech or debate, the candidates' supporters will talk vigorously about how well their candidate did (whether or not the candidate did in fact do well). They'll claim a "victory"—on air if they get the chance—or talk enthusiastically to reporters who later will be on the air or in print. They'll talk to friends and colleagues about how well their candidate performed, hoping to influence the conclusions of those who may (or may not) have seen the

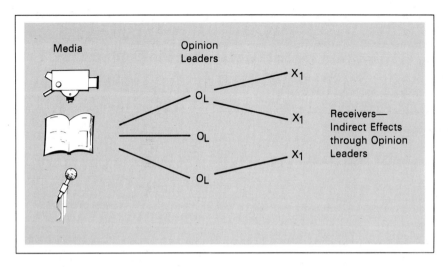

FIGURE 15–3.   The Two-step Flow Effect.

candidate perform or who haven't decided for sure what they thought about the performance.

Similarly, when you hear a campaign manager complain because a newscaster said something negative about a speech by the candidate, it is the two-step effect the manager is worried about. Attacks on the media by politicians often deliberately seek to destroy the credibility of a newscaster, network, or newspaper, if those media sources do not report positively about the politician. Careful consumers of mass communication will notice that candidates or people receiving positive press rarely attack the media.

The two-step effect demonstrates that receivers have choices about how much mass communication affects them. It shows why on some issues a person might immediately adopt or reject an idea received from the media, but on other issues that same person might turn to someone—friend, acquaintance, or media personality—who serves as an opinion leader.

The Multi-step Flow Effect   In most cases, when examining the effects of media within an entire social group or system, all the preceding descriptions oversimplify. Rarely, if ever, does any mediated message affect all parts of a social system, whether directly or indirectly. In these situations, **multi-step flow effect** better describes the effects of mass communication. The multi-step flow shows that in a total system all three effects we have described exist in a number of stages (see Figure 15–4). Some receivers are immediately and directly affected (X): the hypodermic effect. Others are directly affected but respond more slowly (X_1): the one-step flow effect. Other people (X_2) respond only after the information has been received and approved by opinion leaders (O_L): the two-step flow. These individuals (X_2) may then pass information to and serve as influences for still others (X_3 and X_4).

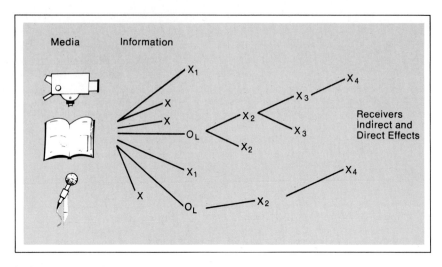

FIGURE 15–4.   The Multi-step Flow Effect.

The multi-step effect shows the broad range of possible responses to mass communication. Information of great importance often has a hypodermic or a one-step effect. If television stations in Los Angeles or New York City announced that a tidal wave would arrive in one hour, the effect would be immediate for most viewers. But some skeptics wouldn't respond until it was repeated several times or until they received confirmation on radio, illustrating the one-step effect. Many people wouldn't hear the media announcements and would respond only after being informed by a person they respected, an opinion leader, showing the two-step effect.

The best description of how information diffuses through an entire social system is the multi-step flow (see Figure 15–4). Opinion leaders, media, and the perceived impact are all factors in influencing how rapidly a person will adopt an idea.

Media Effects Theories

The explanation of media effects presented above describes some, but not all, impacts of mass communication. Most problematic is that the explanation concentrates too heavily on the message or the source. From your previous reading in this book, you know that understanding the impact of any communication message—whether interpersonal, public, or mediated—must include recognition of how the receiver of the message carriers perceives, interprets, and values what she or he receives. In short, as with all communication, it is receivers who ultimately give meaning to mass communication. Thus, understanding the effects of mass communication involves an understanding of receiver use and interpretation.

Much of what we have already discussed applies here, but what you've learned from previous chapters about perception and interpretation, listening and thinking,

The media sometimes aid in public agenda setting.

and motivations and belief can be aided by applying them to some theoretical analyses by mass communication scholars. Specifically, we'll look at the work of three sets of theorists.

Agenda Setting[6]   One analysis suggests that, for "public" issues at least, the media play an agenda-setting role. That is, the media do not cause people to hold any particular belief, but through exposure, they set the agenda for what a society or social group will focus on. During a political campaign, for example, the events covered by newspapers and television may dominate attention while other events are ignored. Reformers and activists stage "media events" in order to secure media coverage, hoping to encourage the public to see the issue as important. People who engage in hunger strikes to advance their cause, terrorists who take hostages, and local police who take a wrecked car from shopping center to shopping center to draw attention to the danger of driving while intoxicated, are all attempting to use the media to set the agenda of their "public."

[6] This theory was probably first articulated by Walter Lippmann in his classic book *Public Opinion* (New York: MacMillan, 1921), and it has been the subject of a great deal of research in subsequent years. Perhaps the most thorough statement of it can be found in Donald L. Shaw and Maxwell E. McCombs, *The Emergence of American Political Issues* (St. Paul, Minn.: West, 1977). A good analysis and criticism of the theory, as well as others discussed in this chapter, can be found in Werner J. Severin with James W. Tankard, Jr., *Communication Theories: Origins, Methods, Uses*, 2nd ed. (New York: Longman, 1988).

Uses and Gratifications   Another analysis concentrates on the uses receivers make of mediated information. This point of view suggests that mass communication affects people only to the extent that receivers can *use* what they receive. If a receiver does not find the information communicated through mass media useful, it will have little or no impact. In contrast, if information received through mass media satisfies some need for receivers, its impact will be significant.

This approach to understanding mass communication fits well into the understanding of the communication process used throughout this book. To be useful, however, the theory requires that we not oversimplify the issues of motivation. As noted in our discussion of both interpersonal communication and persuasion, motivation is a complex process. Sources of individual needs (and therefore motivators) vary from physiological needs to a wide range of social, cultural, and psychological factors. To say that mass communication affects individuals to the extent they find it useful in satisfying needs may generally explain some media effects, but the statement raises as many questions as it answers.

Cultivation[7]   Another way of examining media effects is to see how, by becoming part of the environment, mass communication cultivates a particular view of the world. A long-running and careful program of research conducted by George Gerbner and associates at the Annenberg School of Communication has shown a high correlation between television viewing habits and one's perception of the world.

Gerbner and associates analyzed the picture of society presented by prime time television. They found, for example, that television programs depict the United States population as more white, younger, more male and more subject to violence than statistics show it actually is. They then constructed questionnaires and sampled a wide variety of citizens, asking how they viewed such situations as how likely one is to be involved in a violent act (crime, abuse, fighting, etc.). They also asked respondents about their television viewing habits. The results showed that people who are heavy viewers of television view the world as more like it is depicted on television than as it actually is.

Gerbner argues that television has become the primary storyteller in modern society, the primary source of information about what the world is like. In this view, television provides the myths, rules, and principles by which the social system educates its young and creates community.

THINKING ABOUT MASS COMMUNICATION

After reading all this, you might agree with communication researcher Joseph Klapper, who said in 1960 that research into effects of television has "not only failed to

[7] This research program is, of course, more complex than a quick summary can adequately report. Those who find this argument of interest can read further in some of Gerbner's writing, especially George Gerbner and L. P. Gross, "Living with Television: The Violence Profile," *Journal of Communication*, 26 (1976), 172–199. See also George Gerbner, L. P. Gross, M. Morgan, and N. Signoielli, "The Mainstreaming of America: Violence Profile No. 11, *Journal of Communication*, 30 (1980), 10–29, or other sources cited in the readings list at the end of the chapter.

provide definitive answers . . . [but has] provided evidence in partial support of every hue of every view."[8]

Clearly, the media are powerful, and the effects of mass communication pervade our lives. To know that you need only view the behavior of people on Superbowl Sunday, count the political ads on television during an election year, or look at the people who emulate the dress and behavior of whoever is the current rock star. But it is equally clear that mass media do not have the massive social effects that many people claim. Can evidence really be found to demonstrate that rock music lyrics cause drug use? Or that television has changed (lowered, many argue) moral values in modern society? A critical analysis of the evidence demonstrates that receivers influence the media even as they are influenced by mass communication.

If, indeed, mass communication has the causal effects that many people argue, many recent changes in the United States social system would not have occurred. Gerbner's research and that of many who examine images in advertising have demonstrated, for example, that changes occurred in society before media depicted them. Prime-time television and both television and print advertisements rarely showed Black people in other than subservient or stereotypical roles until well after the civil rights movement of the 1960s had begun to open opportunities for Blacks in the United States. Similarly, women rarely appeared in nonstereotypical roles on television until well after they became a major part of the workforce outside the "pink collar" ghetto. For example, ABC aired "L.A. Law" only after women constituted 50 percent of the law school population and 30 percent of the law graduates. Until women entered politics and business in significant numbers, women's events and activities appeared only in society or food sections of newspapers. Creation of *Ms.*, *Savvy*, *Working Woman*, and similar magazines followed the second wave feminist movement of the 1970s.

Recent changes in prime-time television programming provide excellent examples of how media react to receivers' responses. It is unlikely that shows with less stereotyped Black roles resulted from a social awareness brought on by the popularity of "The Cosby Show." More likely, marketing research convinced media and advertising executives that the Black population is an increasingly important segment of the television audience and its product-consuming market. Similarly, shows such as "L.A. Law," "Cagney and Lacy," and "Kate and Allie" responded to an increasing number of working women with disposable income. Changes in how advertising depicts both men and women reflect media response to growing viewer expectations of realistic depiction of people's lives.

Joshua Myerowitz, in an analysis that applies the theories of Marshall McLuhan and Erving Goffman, persuasively explains why the cultural changes of recent decades occurred even as modern mass communication images consistently reinforced an older social order.[9] Myerowitz argues that television has broken down barriers of space and access to information, eliminating viewers' sense of both physical and

[8] Joseph Klapper, *The Effects of Mass Communication* (New York: The Free Press, 1960), p. 2.

[9] Joshua Myerowitz, *No Sense of Place* (New York: Oxford University Press, 1985).

Television has opened up opportunities for women and minorities in recent years.

social distance. Even while being shown televised images that reinforced traditional authority, he says, people of all ages and classes entered the "backstage" and formerly unknown information spaces of authority and came to feel they (viewers) could (or did) inhabit the same spaces. In this sense, McLuhan's "global village" is created by television. Not only is physical distance obliterated, but social distance is also reduced. Viewers watch scenes from around the globe—or from the moon—even as they happen. Viewers gain a similarly close sense of social space to those far removed in authority levels of the traditional social and political hierarchy. Myerowitz's analysis shows that new roles are inevitable in a social system permeated by modern electronic media. This argument should be examined carefully by anyone seeking to understand the impact of television on modern society.

Above all, we should remember that United States media are primarily commercial enterprises. They transmit content that sells. As such, the messages of mass communication both lead and follow cultural trends. Social changes have occurred throughout recorded history. Modern mass media may do little more than accelerate the pace of change.

All students of communication should clearly understand that even seemingly "entertainment" or "information" media content has a persuasive base, if only by reinforcing a particular world view, or by attempting to reduce awareness of, and increase exposure to, surrounding advertising. Effective receivers of mass communication will remember that the principles of effective and critical listening apply to films, sports, television "entertainment," and rock music, as well as to a speech by a political candidate. Effective receivers will not forget that advertising and other mediated messages result from sophisticated research and production, all aimed toward influencing how the receivers spend their money or time.

The commercial media system in the United States has created superb news and entertainment. It reflects and reinforces important ideas of individual liberty and free expression of ideas—ideas fundamental to our political and economic system. The values of free speech and press that underlie our system have resulted in a system that benefits us all. To avoid being mindlessly trapped in changes of which we do not approve or in supporting values we do not share, each of us needs to critically assess and intelligently monitor our media use. Otherwise, we might unwittingly support or even promote world views unhealthy for us and for our social system.

ADVERTISING

Earlier in this chapter, we discussed the impact of the aspects of mass media that are not overtly persuasive. We stressed how even messages that appear to be entertaining or informative involve varying degrees of receiver impact, or persuasion. In this section, we look at mediated messages that are directly persuasive, that is, advertising.

As you are well aware, advertisements aim to increase sales. Indeed, some advertising attempts to achieve an immediate result—for example, the late night record special that urges you to send $8.98 "right now, tonight, to 'Record Hits' in care of this station." AND if you call the toll-free telephone number, you'll receive a "free gift" along with your record purchase—which, of course, won't be available tomorrow. Similarly, the insert cards in magazines that promise a half-price subscription if you simply return the postage-paid card intend to elicit a direct, immediate response.

Most advertising, however, does not expect such a direct or immediate response. Most advertising has other goals, more long-range in nature and part of a comprehensive sales plan. This kind of advertising seeks: (1) to create (or maintain) consumer awareness of the product or service; (2) to "educate" receivers to see this product or service as different from other products that are essentially the same (a marketer would describe this as product differentiation); or (3) to create good will either for the product or the company.

A quick review of the ads you regularly see will show how a single company often places ads seeking all of these results. For example, on Wednesdays newspapers often carry coupons that allow consumers buy a well-known softdrink for "$1.00 off" the regular price between Thursday and Saturday. That same company will buy expensive television time during Saturday and Sunday sports events to keep viewers aware of the brand and to reinforce their habits of associating the drink with relaxation and good times, to convince viewers of the differences between the advertised brand and other brands, and to develop a wholesome, healthy image for the product. The same company will make major contributions to special college events and support—in a very public way—charities and causes known to be considered worthy: the Olympics, the Special Olympics, benefit rock concerts, the college radio station or newspaper.

Strategies

In pursuit of these goals, advertisers use a number of persuasion techniques you now can analyze.

Motive Appeals   Many advertisements seek to create a relationship between the product or service and the basic motivations of the potential consumer. The effort is to identify the product as a means of providing something the listener needs or wants, to arouse a feeling that we "need" the product or service. Vance Packard's popular book, *The Hidden Persuaders*, proposed the idea that media may actually create motivations. He argued that programs and advertising cause people to believe they need items they wouldn't have otherwise wanted.[10] This idea is worth considering. Do people buy new cars every three or four years because they need them or because advertising makes the ones they have look old? Do we really "need" swimming pools, hot tubs, or jacuzzis? Electric can-openers? Designer jeans? The latest video game or compact disc? $200–$300 skateboards? Or do the ads simply identify ways to meet consumers' existing needs or wants? Without the ads, would we find other things that would perform for us what these products do?

Creating Product Images   Whatever the accuracy of Packard's thesis, one thing is clear: We should carefully assess the motivations advertising appeals to. Most ads sell images, not products. Look at a few car advertisements. Durability and economy are important to car owners. But what do the ads emphasize? Comfort and luxury, the fun people have driving the car, the status and recognition of having it. To be specific what do Cadillac, Mercedes, or BMW really sell? Quality, or the impression you'll make by driving the car? Even ads that mention quality emphasize the car's image. Only with the rise in gasoline prices and competition from (then) lower-priced imported automobiles did automobile advertising include any information about fuel economy. With only a few exceptions, today ads for all but the lowest-priced cars still make a stronger pitch for style and class than for economy and durability.

Suggestion   At the base of most advertising is an unstated thesis: Using this product (or service) will satisfy a basic human need or desire. The point, however, is seldom stated openly. The ad (or the image it creates) *suggests* that the product

---

[10] Vance Packard, *The Hidden Persuaders* (New York: David McKay, 1957). This book has been reprinted in paperback, so it's easily available if you're interested in exploring Packard's thesis.

will satisfy certain needs. Think about television car ads again. A narrator may say something about the economy or quality of the car. But the picture emphasizes fun, status, or luxury. Beer and soft drink advertising illustrates the same principle. A narrator may talk about good quality and good taste. But the picture and music show friends having a good time. The real point of the ad isn't, "Buy this drink because it tastes good." It is, "Buy this drink and you will have fun with many beautiful friends."

The thesis of many ads is only "suggested" because the motivators they use are not what people like to admit motivates them. The surface argument of the ads will be "rational" and socially acceptable motivations: quality, durability, economy. The stronger appeal—respect and/or admiration by friends and neighbors—is suggested through the images created. For example, people want to believe they buy a very expensive car because of its high quality, so that's the surface appeal in advertising for the car. But the image created is that elegant people in beautiful surroundings doing exciting things own cars like this. The ad "suggests" that people who drive this car display high status.

Identification   Identification is one way images are used in advertising. The person selling the product, or the one using it, is someone the potential buyer can identify with. The housewife with laundry problems, the hard-working man having a beer with friends, the young parent who worries about children getting an education if she or he dies, the teenager who fears offending a date with bad breath—all are people a listener can look at and say, "Hey, that's me!"

Another identification technique uses people the buyer would like to be like—beautiful people driving big cars or having friends in for a party; an attractive woman getting attention from a man because she wears a certain perfume; the rugged individualist who smokes a particular cigarette; and so forth. Perhaps the ultimate use of this type of identification is having popular heroes push a product. Michael Jackson, Cher, Bob Hope, or well-known sports figures are associated with a product. They tell us how good it is, or we see them using it. We identify them with the product. We experience fame, success, excitement, and adventure through such people. Identifying a product or service with them creates a favorable image for the product. We like the product because we like them or because we want to be like them.

Packaging   Packaging is part of the process of image building. Good examples are clothing sales. Clothes purchased a year or two ago may still be of good quality. But now styles have changed, and if you wear the item, you're out of date. If women wear short skirts for a few years, designers create and manufacturers sell longer skirts as the "in" style, or vice versa! If men wear button-down shirts, long collars become fashionable. Narrow ties are replaced by wide ones, which give way to scarves, which are replaced by turtlenecks. The "preppie" look is "in," then "out." Western-style clothes are fashionable; two years later jeans must have designer labels. Clothes, cars, and dozens of other products show changes in packaging every few years so people will buy new things just to stay up-to-date.

Implications of quality through packaging may also be given by the store where products are sold. The total atmosphere is intended to add to the image of the product. Compare, for instance, a Mercedes-Benz agency to a used-car lot. In a "punk" boutique, the total decorating effect includes flashing lights, music, and clothes hung at crazy angles all around. In contrast, a store that sells only very expensive clothing will be plushly decorated with ornate furnishings. Clothes won't be out where you can handle them. A salesperson will look you over and bring out "appropriate" items for you. The surroundings create images of elegance, which we then associate with the products.

Often packaging suggests things that are only partly true. Boxes may be designed to appear larger than they really are—or sometimes, in fact, will be larger than they need to be. Cereal boxes, for instance, are tall and wide and placed on the shelf so you won't notice how narrow they are. Labeling is also used to make packages appear large. For some products, notably soap, "giant size" is the smallest box. The name itself, as discussed in Chapter 3, influences how receivers perceive the product.

Attention   Advertisers and products must capture attention. Packaging, labels, images, and many other devices are used to attract attention. Color, music, changes in sound, and humor are all devices for gaining attention. Attention is the only purpose of some advertisements. It creates name recognition, helping us differentiate one product from another. Name recognition alone contributes to a likelihood that we'll buy products, especially those that are very much alike. Celebrity sponsorship also catches attention effectively in many ads. We look at or listen to some ads just because we see or hear a sports hero, film, music or media personality.

Humor is also used effectively by advertisers. Humorous ads help create a favorable image for a product or company while at the same time calling attention to the product name—a technique especially useful in markets crowded with similar products. You can surely think of products you use that are regularly brought to your attention through humorous ads. Classic examples of successful humorous advertising were the "beetle" campaign of Volkswagen and the "I-can't-believe-I-ate-the-whole-thing" campaign of Alka-Seltzer. More recently, Federal Express and Strohs beer have used humor in ads you probably remember whether you use the product or not. Lite beer, in fact, revolutionized the beer industry, in large part through a hugely successful humorous ad campaign. Marketing Lite is a classic case of successful persuasion that began by selecting a basic human motivation, and that used most of the persuasive techniques mentioned in this book. We have included an exercise for this chapter based on such campaigns.

Credit   An effective receiver of commercial communication also recognizes that credit is a persuasive strategy. "Buy now, pay later" is a familiar line. First your wants or needs are activated, then you find yourself without the means to satisfy them. Most of us can't walk into a store and pay cash for a new frost-free refrigerator, microwave oven, fur coat, outboard motor, or new car. If we had to save the money for the purchases, fewer of us would buy them. For many of us, the clincher to buy is credit.

Banks and large firms such as oil companies and department stores are very aware of this aspect of persuasion. Banks freely issue credit cards and heavily advertise the benefits of using them. With every sale, department store clerks are instructed to urge customers to apply for the store's charge card. Thousands of businesses accept MasterCard, Visa, or other shoppers' cards. Major oil companies *ask* to send credit cards to large groups of consumers. They know you'll buy their gas more often if you carry their credit card. You may even drive more if you use credit cards. All these sellers know it's easier to get people to hand a credit card across a counter and sign a slip of paper than to write a check or hand over the cash. Credit is, indeed, a seller's strategy.

Distraction   We need to remember another function of these various attention devices. In many cases, such devices direct our attention toward the product name, function, or distinguishing characteristics. In many of the same cases, the devices distract us from paying careful attention to the "real" argument of the advertisement. When we laugh at Spuds MacKenzie or the celebrity arguments in beer commercials, we feel good about the product, are reminded of its name, and don't ask questions about whether the product will really make friends for us or contribute to our health. The humor may distract us from asking, "How much lower in calories is this beer, really?" When women smile at Virginia Slim's "You've come a long way, Baby" now and then comparisons, they may not critically analyze the argument that smoking cigarettes can make them slim, sexy and sophisticated; they may not attend to the Surgeon General's warning in the corner of the ad; and they may forget the statistics pointing out that lung cancer is now the leading cancer-causing death among women.

EXERCISE 15.2   COMPARING ADVERTISEMENTS IN DIFFERENT MEDIA

OBJECTIVE   To increase understanding of different methods of persuasion influenced by differences in media.

DIRECTIONS
1. Select three advertisements from three different media.
2. Attempt to find advertisements for the same product. If that is not possible, at least select ads for similar kinds of products.
3. For each advertisement, identify the overall purpose of the advertisement and the appeals and strategies used to achieve the purpose of the ad.
4. Compare the ads and see if you can determine whether any of the differences in the ads were due to the different medium used or the different audience each might have.
5. Your instructor may ask you to present your comparison orally to the class.

REVIEW	**Provide brief answers that may be used as the basis for a writing assignment or class discussion.**
	1. What are the major differences in the advertisements?
	2. What are other selling strategies?
	3. Explain the most important communication principle you learned or found illustrated in this exercise and why you found it important.

EXERCISE 15.3   ADVERTISING AS PERSUASION

OBJECTIVE	**To analyze the persuasive processes in an advertising campaign.**
DIRECTIONS	**1.** This exercise may be assigned to be done individually or in small groups.
	2. Select a recent advertising campaign used to introduce a new product or service into a market.
	a. Introduction of Lite beer, the first reduced-calorie beer to be marketed as such, is a current classic example.
	b. Other examples might be IBM's introduction of the Personal Computer; Apple's computer with a "mouse" instead of traditional keyboard; Federal Express's overnight package delivery; or MCI, alternative long-distance telephone service.
	3. Find examples or descriptions of examples (obtained by interviews or research in business and marketing periodicals) of all the means used to introduce the product:
	a. magazine and newspaper advertising
	b. direct mail brochures
	c. radio or television advertising
	d. marketing plans
	e. sales strategies by the companies, dealers, salespeople
	4. Analyze the plans for their use of various persuasion strategies described in Chapters 14 & 15 of this text.
	5. Your instructor may ask for individual or group reports; the reports may be written or oral.
REVIEW	**Write brief answers that may be used as a writing assignment or basis for class discussion.**
	1. Summarize the advertising campaign analyzed.
	2. State the primary motive appeals and imagery developed for the product/service.
	3. Report your analysis of the receiver adaptation and effectiveness of the campaign.
	4. Explain the most important communication principle learned from or illustrated by this exercise and why you found it important.

SUMMARY

Responding to persuasive communication, especially as we receive it through mass media, is most effective if we understand the purposes of advertising and how the media influence communication and diffusion processes. Mass communication is defined as the use of electronic or mechanical means to send the same message carriers to people who are widely scattered. Mass communication began with printing, but the electronic media are most pervasive in modern society.

In the media, gatekeepers control the messages. They choose what information will be sent via the media and how it will be treated. Gatekeepers are primarily commercial. Television and radio stations and networks are commercial enterprises and must be supported by advertising revenue. These commercial sponsors not only place ads, they also influence the content of television entertainment and the approach to television and radio news. An exception is public broadcasting, although gatekeepers still choose the content of what is shown.

In public as well as commercial broadcasting, government regulation also influences the content of media messages. The Federal Communications Commission is the primary regulator, though the FTC affects advertising. The FCC's strongest influence is the awarding of licenses and the control of license renewals. It also monitors stations to see that they broadcast on the channels to which they are assigned, use the kind of programming specified in their license application, and do not violate FCC regulations about content of programming.

Many receivers think they have no influence on mass communication. This is not accurate. Feedback does reach the advertisers, the stations, and the networks, though it is delayed. Feedback comes primarily through the ratings system, which is often criticized as an inadequate measure of audience response even though it accurately reports what programs and stations are listened to.

An effective receiver of mass communication will examine scholars' explanations of media effects because laypeople often exaggerate such effects. Early theorists believed in a hypodermic or immediate effect of mass communication. Some people may be so affected, but other people respond more slowly (the one-step flow effect). Even more respond to messages received from media only after talking with other people (friends, coworkers, opinion leaders of all kinds) about what they read, heard, or saw (the two-step flow effect). Perhaps the most accurate description of how information is spread by media is the multi-step flow that combines all three effects.

Other important explanations of media effects are the agenda-setting theory (which posits that media do not significantly affect what people think, but set the agenda for what people focus on, talk, and think about); the uses and gratifications theory (which suggests information received through media affects people only when they can make use of that information or to the extent the information satisfies their needs and motivations); and the cultivation theory, which says that media (television especially) influence how people perceive the world; that is, media create a worldview. Students of communication should think carefully about media and their impact, taking care not to exaggerate or underestimate the power of persuasion received through media, whether it comes from advertising, entertainment, or news and public affairs programming.

An effective receiver of mass communication also needs to understand advertising. People or companies advertise to create consumer awareness, differentiate products, create consumer good will, reinforce existing behaviors, or sometimes to actually sell something. Advertisers primarily try to make us feel we need the product or service. By creating an image, advertisers make us want certain services or products. Advertisers create images in many ways: suggestion, identification, packaging, and the use of credit.

QUESTIONS FOR DISCUSSION

1. How does a receiver become an effective responder?
2. How does gatekeeping affect information received through the mass media?
3. How can understanding gatekeeping make us more effective responders?
4. How does delayed feedback affect mass communication?
5. What purposes does advertising try to accomplish?
6. How can receivers of public and mass communication use understanding of advertising strategies to employ the principle, "let the buyer beware"?
7. Can you identify the roles that images, suggestion, credit, and packaging play in your own personal responses to advertising?
8. What are the theories of media effects, and how do they differ?

SUGGESTIONS FOR FURTHER READING

Becker, Samuel L. *Discovering Mass Communication*, 2nd ed. Glenview, Ill.: Scott, Foresman and Company, 1987.

Cirino, Robert. *Power to Persuade: Mass Media and the News*. New York: Bantam, 1974.

DeFleur, Melvin, and Sandra Ball-Rokeach. *Theories of Mass Communication*, 4th ed. New York: David McKay, 1981.

Emery, Michael, and Ted Smythe. *Readings in Mass Communication*, 6th ed. Dubuque: William C. Brown, 1986.

Heighton, Elizabeth and Don Cunningham. *Advertising in the Broadcasting and Cable Media*, 2nd ed. Belmont, Calif.: Wadsworth, 1984.

Hentoff, Nat. *The First Freedom: The Tumultuous History of Free Speech in America*. New York: Dell Press, 1981.

Key, Wilson Bryon. *Subliminal Seduction*. New York: New American Library, 1974.

_____. *The Clam-Plate Orgy: And Other Subliminals the Media Use to Manipulate Your Behavior*. Englewood Cliffs, N.J.: Prentice-Hall, 1980.

Lowery, Shearon, and Melvin DeFleur. *Milestones in Mass Communication Research*. New York: Longman, 1983.

McLuhan, Marshall. *The Gutenberg Galaxy*. Toronto: University of Toronto Press, 1969.

_____. *Understanding Media: The Extensions of Man*. New York: McGraw-Hill, 1964.

Myerowitz, Joshua. *No Sense of Place*. New York: Oxford University Press, 1985.

National Institute of Mental Health, *Television and Behavior: Ten Years of Scientific Progress and Implications for the 80s, Summary Report*, Volume 1. Washington, D.C.: U.S. Department of Health and Human Services, 1982.

Parenti, Michael. *Inventing Reality: The Politics of the Mass Media*. New York: St. Martin's Press, 1986.

Pember, Don. *Mass Media in America*, 4th ed. Palo Alto, Calif.: Science Research Associates, Inc., 1984.

_____. *Privacy and the Press*. Seattle: University of Washington Press, 1973.

Rivers, William, Wilbur Schramm, and Clifford Christians. *Responsibility in Mass Communication*, 3rd ed. New York: Harper and Row, 1981.

Rodman, George. *Mass Media Issues: Analysis and Debate*, 2nd ed. Palo Alto, Calif.: Science Research Associates, 1984.

Rogers, Everett, and F. Floyd Shoemaker. *Communication of Innovations*, 2nd ed. London: Free Press, 1971.

Roshco, Bernard. *Newsmaking*. Chicago: University of Chicago Press, 1975.

Schiller, Dan. *Objectivity and the News: The Public and the Rise of Commercial Journal-*

ism. Philadelphia: University of Pennsylvania Press, 1981.

Schmidt, Benno C. *Freedom of the Press vs. Public Access*. New York: Praeger, 1976.

Severin, Werner, with James Tankard, Jr. *Communication Theories: Origins, Methods, Uses*, 2nd ed. New York: Longman, 1988.

Skornia, Harry. *Television and Society*. New York: McGraw-Hill, 1965.

_____. *Television and the News: A Critical Appraisal*. Palo Alto, Calif.: Pacific Books, 1974.

Tannenbaum, Percy, ed. *The Entertainment Functions of Television*. Hillsdale, N.J.: Lawrence Erlbaum Associates, 1980.

Tuchman, Gaye. *Hearth and Home: Images of Women in the Mass Media*. New York: Oxford University Press, 1978.

_____. *Making News: A Study in the Construction of Reality*. New York: Free Press, 1978.

John W. Wright. *The Commercial Connection: Advertising and the American Mass Media*. New York: Dell Publishing Co., 1979.

Glossary

abstracting: The process of selecting certain elements of a thing to distinguish it from other things.

abstract words: Words that refer to things or features of things that cannot be seen, that are high on the ladder of abstraction.

acceptance: The ability to relate to another person without judging or trying to control that person.

active retirement: The planning and execution of a lifestyle that enables a person to continue to grow after the working years are over.

advantages-disadvantages outline: Choosing the main points according to advantages and disadvantages of goal or thesis.

agenda: A plan or procedure a group agrees to follow.

analogy: A form of comparison that shows similarities between things that on the surface are not similar.

argument: A unit of thought containing a conclusion and the evidence leading to the conclusion.

articulation: A term that refers to the movements of lips, tongue, jaw, and soft palate to form speech sounds; that which changes vocal sound into recognizable speech.

assertive: Regardless of different status levels, you are aware of the basic rights that parallel your responsibilities and are willing and able to talk about (assert) these rights.

attention: An adjustment of the receiving senses.

attention, focal: All senses focused on the same source.

attention, involuntary: The listener can't help paying attention.

attention, marginal: Receiving sensations indirectly, without focusing on them.

attention, voluntary: You must make yourself pay attention.

attention factors: Elements in communication that create involuntary attention: relevance, proximity, importance, concreteness, variety, movement and activity, humor, combination of the familiar with the novel, curiosity, and conflict.

attitude: A predisposition to respond to stimuli in a particular way.

audience adaptation: Preparing and sending messages in ways that receivers will decode as you intend.

audience analysis: A study of the receivers or potential receivers to determine what their initial attitudes toward source and subject are and to determine how the purpose can best be achieved.

balance theory: The hypothesis that people need to perceive consistency or balance among attitudes seen as related to each other.

behavior: Observable action; this includes talking.

brainstorming: Setting aside some time during which

group members give their ideas without criticism or evaluation of them; seeking to be creative and to think of as many ideas as possible.

cause-effect outline: Choosing main points according to the causes and effects of a problem or situation.

cause-effect thinking: Inferring that one event occurs because of something else.

central idea: Subject-centered statement, the main point of the message; also called thesis statement.

certainty: The attitude that the speaker has all the answers.

change agent: An external source of persuasion.

coding: Choosing words and sentence structures to express intended messages.

cognitive dissonance theory: Suggests that people engage in an active mental process such as rationalization to reduce the dissonance caused by perceived inconsistencies in attitudes.

cognitive response theory: Suggests that people are persuaded by what they think about in response to persuaders' messages, not by the messages themselves.

cohesiveness: The forces that influence members to choose to remain in the group.

common ground: Attitudes, beliefs, and experiences that source and receiver share.

communication: The process of receiving stimuli and interpreting them (assigning meanings to them).

comparison and contrast: Drawing inferences of similarity or difference.

conceptualizing: Synthesizing or combining mental images about experiences into ideas (concepts).

concrete words: Words that refer to objects that can be seen, have tangible referents.

conditioning: A process in which some behavior caused by a primary stimulus becomes associated with a secondary stimulus.

connotations: The attitudes or feelings a user has about a symbol (word) or the object or concept it symbolizes.

consensus: All members of a group agree on a decision.

control: To try to get others to change themselves or to change their attitudes, opinions, or behavior; to try to restrict the choices available to others or to influence their behavior in making choices.

correlation: A relationship between two elements.

creative thinking: Adding, subtracting, and combining experiences to create new ideas; imagination.

credibility: A receiver's evaluation of the believability of a source in a particular situation. Credibility is high or low according to how believable a person is considered by the perceiver.

criteria: Standards; in group decision making criteria are standards that any solution must meet.

decoding: Interpreting stimuli received; giving meaning to sensations.

deduction: Applying a generalization to a specific case.

deductive speech structure: Stating thesis early in speech.

defensiveness: Behavior that results when a person perceives a threat in a situation; generally people who are defensive are not accepting, not empathic, less honest, and intentionally self-disclose very little.

demographic data: Statistics about groups of people; used in audience analysis.

denotations: The objects or concepts referred to, the actual "things" a word symbolizes.

description: The opposite of evaluation; to be descriptive is to be perceived as nonjudgmental.

dialect: A language variant used by a group of speakers that is different from the language of the general community. Dialects involve differences in the use of words, sounds, and syntax.

diffusion: The spread of ideas or information through a social system.

emotion: An aroused physiological and psychological response to a stimulus.

empathy: A sense of experiencing the feelings of another; is the opposite of neutrality.

equality: The climate that counters superiority, a willingness to interact with mutual trust and respect and to attach little importance to differences.

ethnocentrism: An attitude that one's own culture is superior to others.

evaluation: Passing judgment on others, assessing blame or praise.

evidence: Any statement believed by a receiver that forms the basis for believing another statement.

example: A case used to explain or prove a point; can be long (illustration) or short (instance), real or hypothetical.

explanation: Telling how something works.

extemporaneous speaking: The speaker has prepared carefully, decided specifically on goals and main ideas, has written out a key word outline as well as any statistics or special quotes, but chooses exact words at the moment of the speech.

face making: Behaving strategically to influence how others perceive us; constructing images we present to others.

fact: A direct, observable reality.

false alternatives: Applying "either-or" thinking to situations in which the alternatives are not truly contradictory.

fear: A biological process through which a person develops adequate energy to do important tasks.

feedback: A receiver's response interpreted by the source; a sender's interpretation of a response (or nonresponse) to a message.

feedback, directive: Communicating an evaluation of either the source or the message.

feedback, nondirective: Response perceived as non-evaluative.

gatekeeper: A person or agent who has the power to control and regulate the flow of information through communication channels.

generalization: Drawing general conclusions from specific events.

generalization, hasty: Drawing a generalization on the basis of too few instances.

generalized other: The composite view you have of others' views of you.

gender role: Expectations for a person's behavior based on the person's sex.

goals, antagonistic: A situation within a group when one member can reach his or her goals only when others do not reach theirs.

goals, complementary: When each member of a group can achieve her or his individual goals only if other members achieve theirs.

grammar: The formal features of a language; the "rules" for fashioning "correct" sentences; the structure that enables words to be combined into meaningful combinations.

group: A communication system of two or more people in which a series of interactions among members determines a structure and an identity.

hasty generalization: Drawing a generalization on the basis of too few instances.

hearing: Being in the range of and receiving sound.

hidden agenda: Unstated personal goals in group situations.

homophily: The degree to which communicators are similar in attributes. Two dimensions of homophily exist: actual and perceived.

identification: Receivers perceive a source as similar to them in ways that are important in the situation, either role-oriented characteristics (such as occupation or status) or personality traits (such as honesty or nervousness).

inductive speech structure: Withholding thesis statements until midway through a speech or at the end.

inductive thinking: Drawing general conclusions from specific events.

infer: To draw conclusions about the unknown based on the known. The conclusion is described as a statement of inference.

informal organization: A network of interpersonal relationships within the organization but outside the formal structure.

interdependence: The extent to which members need each other to achieve group and individual goals.

interpersonal attraction: Describes the positive regard people have for other people.

interpersonal communication: When you communicate directly with other people in a one-to-one situation or in small groups.

interpersonal perception: Attributing characteristics to people as you interact with them.

interpretation: The mental process of organizing incoming stimuli (sensations received) into a meaningful whole.

intrapersonal communication: Communication with yourself; hearing yourself speak, feeling yourself move, thinking.

judgment: See statement of judgment.

leader: One who performs more leadership functions than others in the group.

leader, opinion: A person to whom members of groups listen with respect and from whom they accept ideas uncritically.

leadership: Any behavior that aids a group in accomplishing its goals.

leadership, climate: Functions relating to maintaining the group.

leadership, shared: Group in which several people perform significant amounts of leadership functions.

leadership, task: Functions relating to accomplishing the tasks that must be done.

listening: A process, occurring on different levels, of receiving and interpreting communication.

listening, active: Seeking to decode all messages received, both verbal and nonverbal, in order to understand a verbal message as accurately as possible.

listening, empathic: Using both verbal and nonverbal cues to understand the speaker; to understand verbal messages so we can determine how the speaker feels.

main points: Main supporting ideas used to support the thesis.

masking: See face making.

mass communication: Electronic or mechanical transmission of message carriers; the use of technical media to send the same message carriers to people who are widely scattered.

meaning: The entire set of reactions that people assign to a symbol.

memory: The ability of the brain to store information based on the sensory input it receives. People have both a short- and long-term memory in which interpretations of experiences are stored.

message carriers: The things a person actually says and does while communicating, as well as cues from context; any stimuli from any source that a source can interpret as meaningful.

messages, intended: The ideas or feelings a source wants a receiver to understand or know; what a source wants to communicate.

messages, perceived: What a receiver hears, sees, touches, smells or tastes and decodes; the meanings a receiver attaches to sensations received.

modeling: Observing the environment and imitating the behaviors seen.

motive appeal: Relating persuasive arguments to receivers' relevant motivations.

narration: Telling a story or relating an event.

neutrality: Communicating an attitude of impersonality.

noise: Something in the situation that causes intended and perceived messages to differ widely.

nonverbal symbols: Nonword symbols.

norm: A standard of expected behavior for the violation of which people must pay a social penalty.

observation: See statement of observation.

opinion leaders: People whose ideas are listened to with respect and often accepted without much examination.

organization: A complex system that intentionally coordinates the actions of its members to accomplish specific purposes.

organization (of a speech): Ordering or categorizing the elements of a verbal message; is reflected in an outline.

organization, informal: The structure of interpersonal relationships within the organization but outside the formal structure.

outline: A planned sequence for reaching the goals of a speech.

perception: The mental process of recognizing the stimuli received.

persuasion: Describes any communication process in which a source attempts either to bring about changes in others' beliefs or attitudes or to induce overt behavior in one or more receivers.

pitch: A term describing how high or low a voice tone is.

possessiveness: An attitude that a person has a "right" to control or influence the behavior of another person; an implication of ownership.

post hoc fallacy: To conclude that one event causes another because it regularly precedes it.

power: The ability to influence someone else's behavior.

problem orientation: The opposite of control; involves communicating a desire to work together to define problems and seek solutions.

problem-solution outline: Choosing main points for a speech based on analysis of a problem and its solution.

process: A series of interactions among elements that results in something different from the original elements.

pronunciation: Combining speech sounds into recognizable words.

provisionalism: The opposite of certainty; to be provisional is to be willing to reconsider behavior, to consider the possibility of being in error.

proxemics: The study of personal space, the distances among people as they communicate.

public communication: When many people receive messages largely from one source.

purposes for communication: Both conscious and unconscious reasons for speaking and listening; usually multiple, related to self, others, and the subject.

pygmalion effect: A tendency to communicate and behave as we think others expect us to.

quotation: Someone else's exact words.

rate: The speed at which a person talks.

receiver: The person or organism that receives communication stimuli; also a source in speech communication.

receiver analysis: Study of receivers by the persuader to assess whether the goal is achievable and how it can be reached.

reference group: A group that a person uses to guide behavior and belief, one with which a person identifies; members use reference groups to evaluate their own behavior.

referent: The object, event, or concept to which a word refers.

reinforcement: The process of learning behaviors (and attitudes) through receiving rewards.

repetition: Repeating something in the exact words used before.

reluctant testimony: When a person expected to believe one way speaks against that position.

response: Any reaction to sensations received; may include awareness, understanding, changed attitudes, and/or behavior.

restatement: Repeating the same idea but using different words.

restricted code: The general use of command statements without complete explanations.

rhetorical question: A question to which a speaker doesn't expect an answer; listeners answer to themselves or think about the question.

role: A word used in many different ways; used here to refer to the behaviors expected of persons perceived to occupy particular social positions; sometimes this is referred to as role expectations.

role performance: How a person actually behaves in a social position.

role playing: Acting out the behavior related to a role.

role taking: The internalizing of role-related behaviors and motivations; involves a self-identification with the behaviors.

selectivity of attention, exposure, perception, and retention: Choosing, consciously and unconsciously, what stimuli we will expose ourselves to, attend to, perceive, and recall from storage.

self-concept: The total complex of ideas, feelings, and attitudes people hold about themselves.

self-confidence: The ability of individuals to predict, with fair accuracy, that they can do what needs to be done to eliminate any potentially harmful results of a situation.

self-fulfilling prophecy: Tendency to behave as we expect ourselves to behave.

sensory receptors: The eyes, ears, nose, skin, and other locations of nerve ends that receive communicative stimuli.

serial communication: Describes communication that must follow a chain; a channel in which messages pass from one person to another to reach their final destination.

setting: See Situation.

significant others: People with whom an individual of any age has an important relationship; people whose attitudes strongly influence our thoughts and feelings about ourselves.

situation: The total context within which the source and the receiver interact; involves physical setting, temperature, background, noise, light or the lack of it, the reasons people are there, the perceived roles of the people involved, the relationships among them, and so on.

source: The person, object, event, or concept from which come stimuli leading to communication. In speech communication, each participant is both source and receiver.

specific purpose: The specific response wanted from listeners; the answer to the question: What, exactly, do I want my audience to do, think, or feel when I finish?

speech anxiety: Nervousness before speaking, whether in an interpersonal or public communication situation.

speeches: Situations in which one person tries to communicate a message that she or he wants a group of others to understand or be amused or influenced by.

speech organization: Ordering and categorizing the elements of a message. Speech organization is reflected in an outline.

speech structure, deductive: When you use a deductive structure, you state your thesis early in the speech.

speech structure, inductive: The inductive pattern withholds thesis statements until midway through a speech or at the end. The thesis is allowed to emerge as the ideas that support it are developed.

spontaneity: The opposite of strategy; to be perceived as straightforward and free from deception.

statement of inference: Stating a conclusion about the unknown or unseen, based on what is known or believed to be known.

statement of judgment: A statement that reports the reaction of the observer and that assesses value.

statement of observation: Statements about facts, descriptions that do not report inferences.

statistics: Consist of many observations, added up, with the relationships among them analyzed numerically.

strategy: Using tricks or manipulation to influence others' behavior; people who use strategy have hidden purposes or private, unrevealed motives, or they use communication for unstated personal benefits.

style: Primarily differences of language related to the degree of formality in a situation, though nonverbals also vary.

superiority: Communicating an attitude of being better than others in some way, or of believing inequalities are important.

supporting materials: Content used to develop ideas in the speech outline; include facts, statements of observation and opinion, narratives, examples, quotations, restatement and repetition, comparison and contrast.

symbol: A thing that represents, or stands for, something else. Speech communication symbols include words, spoken or heard.

symbolizing: The process of using one thing or word to stand for or refer to something else.

territoriality: Staking out a space or a territory that you believe is your own.

thesis (central idea) statement: Subject-centered statement; the main point of the message.

transaction: A statement and the response to it.

trust: Having a confident belief that others' behavior will be positive for you in situations where the outcome could be either positive or negative and they, not you, control that outcome.

unrestricted code: Providing explanations for command statements.

verbal symbols: Words.

vocal symbols: Symbols that use voice; may be words or nonword sounds.

vocalizations: Elements of voice other than words, that convey information.

voice quality: The distinctive sound of each person's voice.

volume: The loudness with which sounds are spoken.

warrant: In the Toulmin model of argument, links evidence and conclusion; is the reason for believing the evidence is relevant.

Photo Credits

Chapter 1: 3 Ken Karp. 7 Rhoda Sidney 12 Ken Karp. 18 Courtesy *American Way*, magazine of American Airlines. 23 (top) Marc P. Anderson; (bottom) AP/Wide World.

Chapter 2: 41 Addison Gallery of American Art. 43 Laimute E. Druskis. 44 RSVP, Action. 45 Ken Karp. 47 Irene Springer. 48 Courtesy Atari.

Chapter 3: 64 UPI/Bettmann Newsphotos.

Chapter 4: 94 Laimute E. Druskis. 95 Eugene Gordon. 99 AFL/CIO News. 103 Rhoda Sidney. 110 Ken Karp. 112 Irene Springer.

Chapter 5: 124 Mount Sinai Hospital. 128 Rhoda Sidney. 130 AT&T.

Chapter 6: 146 Sybil Shelton. 150 Laimute E. Druskis. 153 Mark Mangold/U.S. Census Bureau. 158 Rapho/Photo Researchers. 161 AP/Wide World. 166 Laimute E. Druskis. 170 Ken Karp. 172 Laimute E. Druskis.

Chapter 7: 184 Ken Karp. 188 (top) AT&T Company Photo Center; (bottom) Wagner International Photos, Inc.; (right) Mimi Forsyth, Monkmeyer. 194 Sybil Shelton. 204 American Cancer Society/Hugh Bell.

Chapter 8: 213 United Nations. 214 Stan Wakefield. 228 AT&T Phone Center.

Chapter 9: 237 American Airlines. 240 Shell Oil Company. 246 Massachusetts Division of Employment Security.

Chapter 10: 266 Ken Karp. 272 Laimute E. Druskis. 282 United Nations/Bruno J. Zehnder. 286 Ken Karp.

Chapter 11: p. 293 (top) Catholics for a Free Choice; (bottom) AT&T Phone Center; (right) Ken Karp.

Chapter 12: 319 AP/Wide World. 324 AP/Wide World. 327 Sybil Shelton. 331 French Institute/Alliance Française.

Chapter 13: 336 Office of the Governor, Massachusetts. 340 Boeing. 351 Laimute E. Druskis.

Chapter 14: 357 Laimute E. Druskis. 366 Irene Springer. 368 Catholics for a Free Choice. 374 Donna Ruscavage.

Chapter 15: 396 Ken Karp. 397 Stan Wakefield. 403 Stan Wakefield. 409 Marc Anderson. 412 Stan Wakefield.

Index